Computer Modelling for Sustainable Urban Design

Physical Principles, Methods and Applications

Edited by Darren Robinson

publishing for a sustainable future

London • Washington, DC

First published in 2011 by Earthscan

Earthscan Ltd, Dunstan House, 14a St Cross Street, London EC1N 8XA, UK
Earthscan LLC, 1616 P Street, NW, Washington, DC 20036, USA

Earthscan publishes in association with the International Institute for Environment and Development

For more information on Earthscan publications, see www.earthscan.co.uk or write to earthinfo@earthscan.co.uk

ISBN 978-1-84407-679-6

Typeset by Domex e-Data Pvt. Ltd., India
Cover design by Rob Watts

1006950374

A catalogue record for this book is available from the British Library

Library of Congress Cataloging-in-Publication Data

Computer modelling for sustainable urban design : physical principles, methods and applications / edited by Darren Robinson.
    p. cm.
 Includes bibliographical references and index.
 ISBN 978-1-84407-679-6 (hbk.)
 1. City planning–Computer simulation. 2. Sustainable urban development–Computer simulation. I. Robinson, Darren.
 HT166.C62112 2010
 307.1'21601'13–dc22

2010036346

At Earthscan we strive to minimize our environmental impacts and carbon footprint through reducing waste, recycling and offsetting our CO_2 emissions, including those created through publication of this book. For more details of our environmental policy, see www.earthscan.co.uk.

Printed and bound in the UK by MPG Books, an ISO 14001 accredited company. The paper used is FSC certified.

Contents

Part IV — An Eye to the Future

Figures, Tables and Plates

Figures

Tables

Plates

Foreword

Agricultural mechanization is sweeping to the ends of the Earth to feed its burgeoning population. As it does so, displaced workers and their families migrate to urban settlements and industrial and service employment. It is a process of urbanization that has been occurring in some parts of the world since the beginning of the industrial revolution. Thus, urban settlement is already the social norm in the developed world. As world economies converge, urbanization is also becoming the expected norm in the developing world. But today, the urbanization catch-up story is playing out much faster and on an unprecedented scale. Large settlements in countries like China – often of 100,000 or more – spring up within months. This explosion of urban society in the 21st century presents many challenges, but also new opportunities to better the outcomes of the past. One opportunity is to plan and organize without the millstone of legacy infrastructure. A second, which forms the subject of this book, is to use new and powerful techniques to optimize what was once a heuristic and haphazard planning process.

'Sustainability' is a clear objective. However, for urban settlements it has often been elusive in the past. The undoubted excitement of cutting the tape on brand new housing, roads, schools and hospitals sometimes hides the risk that the future may not find the infrastructure easy to maintain or adapt, or relevant. As this book shows, we can at least now anticipate the physical environmental consequences within the urban environment of what we do. But once the urban planner embarks on this process, trade-offs become evident that temptingly offer the prospect of finding optima. The same settlement density can be delivered by different height and voids. But different trial solutions strike different balances between solar gain, shading and air movement, transport and access. The process of optimization is fiendishly difficult and much of this book reviews some of the latest computational approaches. Given that much new construction is far removed from the received wisdom of vernacular urban architecture, these calculations are essential. And the very complexity of these calculations tells us that it is implausible for property markets on their own to find these optima.

Urban settlements may be initially created through decisions about built infrastructure, but the settlement thrives from movement of people, goods and services. Here a new simulation technique, first introduced into urban studies by transport modellers, comes into its own. 'Multi-agent' models view the opportunities for citizens to make choices in the optimizing context from the individual citizen's perspective. In transport, this may be pedestrian movement or vehicle routes, and here it avoids the pitfall of assuming that just because a road or building is in the plan it will be used in reality. At the micro-level, transport planners are already quite used to applying these techniques to re-engineer road schemes. This book describes the much wider application of this new modelling technology. It is an approach especially appropriate to the urban planning context, and at the moment it is hard to discern its bounds.

This important book shows the power of techniques that have become available. If there is a political will for 'sustainability' then there are new techniques that can make a plausible stab at designing to achieve it. But all models rely on data. If the cost of good modelling is not to become prohibitive, then existing datasets need to be kept both relevant and in good order. This is a dialogue between professionals that has only just begun. As geographic information systems become globally embracing, it is a dialogue that will be essential for good decision-making. This book shows the promise of what could then be achieved.

Professor David Fisk
BP Urban Energy Systems Project
Imperial College London

About the Authors

Dr Kay W. Axhausen is Professor of Transport Planning at the Eidgenössische Technische Hochschule (ETH) Zürich. He holds his post in the Institute for Transport Planning and Systems of the Department of Civil, Environmental and Geomatic Engineering. Before his appointment at ETH he worked at the Leopold-Franzens Universität, Innsbruck, Imperial College London and the University of Oxford. He holds a PhD in Civil Engineering from the Universität Karlsruhe and an MSc from the University of Wisconsin – Madison.

Dr Axhausen has been involved in the measurement and modelling of travel behaviour for the last 25 years, contributing especially to the literature on stated preferences, micro-simulation of travel behaviour, valuation of travel time and its components, parking behaviour, activity scheduling and travel diary data collection. His current work focuses on the micro-simulation of daily travel behaviour and long-term mobility choices and the response of the land-use system to those choices. This work is supported by analyses of human activity spaces and their dependence on the traveller's personal social network.

He was the chair of the International Association of Travel Behaviour Research (IATBR) until December 2005 and is editor of Transportation and DISp. A full CV with a list of recent publications can be found at www.ivt.ethz.ch/people/axhausen/cv_kwa.pdf.

Dr Michael Batty is Bartlett Professor of Planning at University College London where he directs the Centre for Advanced Spatial Analysis (CASA). Previously (1990–1995) he was Director of the NSF National Center for Geographic Information and Analysis (NCGIA) in the State University of New York at Buffalo and from 1979 to 1990, he was Professor of City and Regional Planning in the University of Cardiff. His research work involves the development of computer models of cities and regions, and he has published many books and articles in this area, the most recent being *Cities and Complexity* (MIT Press, Cambridge, MA, 2005) and the edited volume *Virtual Geographic Environments* (with Hui Lin, Science Press, Beijing, China, 2009). His current work focuses on new methods of social physics involving scaling applied to city systems. He is editor of the journal *Environment and Planning B: Planning and Design*. The work of his group can be seen on the website www. casa.ucl.ac.uk/. He was made a Fellow of the British Academy in 2001, and awarded a CBE in the Queen's Birthday Honours in June 2004 for 'services to geography'. In 2009, he was elected as a Fellow of the Royal Society.

Professor Dr Michael Bruse is Full Professor at the Department of Geography leading the Geoinformatics Section and the Environmental Modelling Group at the University of Mainz in Germany. His research focuses on small-scale urban climate modelling and the impact of urban planning and architecture on the environment, building energy performance and inhabitants' wellbeing.

He is also Partner of WSGreenTechnologies Stuttgart (part of the Werner Sobek Group) and has been doing freelance work in environmental meteorology software since 1995 (ENVI-met.com).

Born in Essen, Germany, he graduated in geography with a major in climatology at the University of Bochum in 1995. Also at Bochum he obtained a PhD in physical geography/climatology in 1999. After a three-year scientific assistantship at the University of Cologne he worked as a researcher at the University of Bochum until he was appointed full professor at Mainz in 2007. In 2004 he was visiting professor at the University of Strasbourg in France. He is the author of several publications on urban microclimates.

Dr Flourentzos Flourentzou is co-founder and Director of Estia SA, a spin off company of the École Polytechnique Fédérale de Lausanne (EPFL). For the last 12 years he has been particularly active in decision aid for sustainable development: bioclimatic architecture, low-energy buildings and sustainable refurbishment investment strategies.

Prior to establishing Estia SA, he undertook research in bioclimatic architecture at the Solar Energy and Building Physics Laboratory (LESO-PB) at EPFL; in particular working on natural ventilation and the dynamic thermal behaviour of passively cooled buildings. The software LESOCOOL, which simulates buildings' dynamic thermal behaviour and natural ventilation performance, is one result of his work.

After several years' activity in bioclimatics, he oriented his activity towards decision aid theory. Interested in the link between decision process and Jean Piaget's constructivist theory, he studied the theory of multi-criteria analysis during his doctoral studies. The theoretical results of his work are at the origin of the European project INVESTIMMO (sustainable investment management in building refurbishment) as well as the Albatros decision support system adopted by the county of Vaud in Switzerland to orient initial choices concerning public infrastructure with respect to their sustainability. In this he has contributed towards the decision making of several major public projects in Switzerland.

Dr Frédéric Haldi graduated from the University of Geneva with a masters in Physics in 2003 having written his masters' thesis on a subject related to fluid mechanics. Frédéric Haldi later moved to Ireland and worked on the development and promotion of renewable energies with Sustainable Energy Ireland. He then completed a PhD thesis at EPFL under the supervision of Darren Robinson. This thesis develops new innovative models for the simulation of occupants' behaviour in buildings and the implications of occupants' adaptive actions on their thermal comfort. He is author of nine scholarly archived journal articles and 15 conference papers and co-recipient of the Building and Environment Journal Best Paper Award for the last two years.

Dr Jérôme Kämpf started his undergraduate studies in physics at the University of Lausanne and undertook a part of these studies at the University of Kent at Canterbury as an Erasmus exchange student, where he obtained a Diploma in Physics with Merit and the Isenberg Prize. He concluded his physics studies at the University of Lausanne with a thesis in medical imaging, which was carried out at the Hammersmith Hospital (Imperial College, London) using a Positron Emission Tomography camera. After obtaining a higher degree in computer science at the University of Lausanne and a Post-Graduate Certificate in Education, he completed his PhD at the Solar Energy and Building Physics Laboratory in the Sustainable Urban Development group, where he is now a post-doctoral researcher. His research in this group continues to focus on the modelling and optimization of urban resource flows.

Diane Perez graduated from the École Polytechnique Fédérale de Lausanne (EPFL) with a Masters degree in physics in 2008, having written her masters' thesis in the subject of quantum optics. She is currently studying for a PhD in the Sustainable Urban Development group of the LESO-PB at EPFL, working on an integrated data framework for urban energy modelling and optimization.

Dr Adil Rasheed is a research scientist at the Applied Mathematics Department of SINTEF Information and Communication Technology in Norway. He is currently involved in research and development work in the area of wind engineering with an emphasis on terrain induced turbulence prediction for air traffic management, optimization and safety. In 2009 Adil received his PhD in the field of urban climatology from LESO-PB at EPFL, Switzerland. Prior to that, he completed his master's degree in Thermal and Fluids Engineering and bachelor's degree in Mechanical Engineering from the Indian Institute of Technology, Bombay, India. In his free time he is an avid painter and an amateur photographer.

Dr Darren Robinson is Professor of Building and Urban Physics at the University of Nottingham in the UK. He was until recently (2004 – 2011) group leader of sustainable urban development with the Solar Energy and Building Physics Laboratory (LESO) at the Ecole Polytechnique Fédérale de Lausanne (EPFL) in Switzerland. Prior to this he worked as an Associate within engineering consultancy BDSP Partnership (2000 – 2004) and as a Senior Research Associate at Cambridge University (1998 – 2000).

Darren has been working for over ten years now in urban energy and environmental modelling; this work culminating in the development of the urban energy modelling software *CitySim*. He has published over 50 scientific papers on the subject of urban modelling and was awarded the CIBSE Napier-Shaw Medal for one of these. He is also a Visiting Professor at the Technical Research Centre of Finland (VTT).

Acknowledgements

First, I owe a great debt of gratitude to all of the authors that have contributed to this book, many of whom have taken time out from very demanding schedules to do so. It has been an honour to collaborate with them. Should this book prove to be a success, it will be substantially due to their contributions.

I am personally greatly indebted to Barbara Smith, who assisted me enormously and with great humour and enthusiasm during the latter stages of the editing of this book. Many thanks also to Marja Edelman for her help with preparing the graphics for this book. Warm thanks also to all of my colleagues at LESO-PB of EPFL, for contributing to a familial and intellectually stimulating environment these past years! I would like to particularly thank the director of the LESO-PB, Professor Jean-Louis Scartezzini, for his kind support.

I have been particularly fortunate to work closely with some extremely talented people, both in the UK and in Switzerland, for which I continue to feel very privileged; in particular Frédéric Haldi, Jérôme Kämpf, Jessen Page, Adil Rasheed, Andy Stone and more recently Diane Perez and Urs Wilke.

I would also like to warmly thank all of the staff at Earthscan that have been involved in the preparation of this book. In particular, the generous support and advice from Mike Fell, Hamish Ironside and Claire Lamont is very much appreciated.

Finally, I would like to thank my wife Eva for her selfless encouragement and support over these past years and during the preparation of this book in particular: you're amazing!

Darren Robinson
Lausanne, February 2011

Acronyms and Abbreviations

ASV	actual sensation vote
BEM	building energy model
BPR	Bureau of Public Roads
BREDEM	Building Research Establishment Domestic Energy Model
BREHOMES	Building Research Establishment Housing Model for Energy Studies
BRS	Building Research Station
CAD	computer-aided design
CASA	Centre for Advanced Spatial Analysis
CBD	central business district
CDF	cumulative distribution function
CFD	computational fluid dynamics
CHP	combined heat and power
CIBSE	Chartered Institution of Building Services Engineers
CIE	Commission Internationale d'Eclairage
CMA-ES	covariance matrix adaptation evolution strategy
CNL	cross-nested logit
COP	coefficient of performance
CSA-ES	cumulative step path adaptation evolution strategy
DE	differential evolution
DEM	digital elevation model
DNS	direct numerical simulation
(D)UE	(deterministic) user equilibrium
EA	evolutionary algorithm
ECL	error-component logit
ECS	energy conversion system
EEP	energy and environmental prediction
EP	evolutionary programming
EPFL	École Polytechnique Fédérale de Lausanne
ES	evolution strategy
ETH	Eidgenössische Technische Hochschule
FVM	finite volume model
GA	genetic algorithms
GDP	gross domestic product
GEV	generalized extreme value
GIS	geographical information system
GMRES	Generalized Minimal Residual Method
GP	genetic programming
GSHP	ground source heat pump
GTS	GNU's Not Unix Triangulated Surface
HDE	hybrid differential evolution
HOLISTIC	HOListic Integration of Sustainable Technologies In Cities
HVAC	heating, ventilation and air conditioning
IATBR	International Association of Travel Behaviour Research
IIA	independence of irrelevant alternative

IID	independently and identically distributed
IPF	iterative proportional fitting
IST	Immersed Surface Technique
IVT	Institut für Verkehrsplanung und Transportsysteme
KPI	key performance indicator
LCA	lifecycle assessment
LES	large eddy simulation
LESO-PB	Solar Energy and Building Physics Laboratory
LIDAR	Light Detection And Ranging
MATSim	Multi-Agent Transport Simulation
ML	mixed logit
MNL	multinomial logit model
NCEP	National Center for Environmental Predictions
NCGIA	National Center for Geographic Information and Analysis
NL	nested logit
OD	origin and destination
OGC	Open Geospatial Consortium
PCL	pairwise-cross-nested logit model
PMV	predicted mean vote
PPD	percentage of people dissatisfied
ppm	parts per million
PSO/HJ	Particle Swarm Optimization and Hooke-Jeeves
RANS	Reynolds-Averaged Navier-Stokes
RMS	root mean squared
RPL	random parameter logit
SAP	standard assessment procedure
SEB	surface energy balance
SEP	solar energy planning
SO	system optimum
SRA	simplified radiosity algorithm
ST	thermal state
STL	stereolithography
SUE	stochastic user equilibrium
SUNtool	Sustainable Urban Neighbourhood modelling tool
TEB	town energy balance
TGV	train à grande vitesse
TKE	turbulent kinetic energy
TS	thermal satisfaction
UBP	umweltbelastungspunkte
UCM	urban canopy model
UHI	urban heat island
UML	unified modelling language
URANS	unsteady Reynolds-Averaged Navier-Stokes
μm	micron

1

Introduction

Darren Robinson

This introductory chapter begins with a historical perspective, charting the growth in global population and the urban fraction of this population and discussing what facilitated this growth. We then consider the environmental and societal impacts of mass urbanization and outline some of the challenges that await us in light of future forecasts of the global population, the urban fraction of this population and the resource intensity with which these urban inhabitants maintain and improve upon their standard of living with greater equality.

To help us to address these challenges we need models with which we can test hypotheses for improving urban sustainability. To help understand the attributes that such models need to possess, we then ask and attempt to respond to the seemingly trivial question: how do cities function? In this we consider both environmental and socio-economic factors.

We close this introductory chapter by describing the structure of this book that has been prepared to help us to understand how we might model cities in all of their complexity and optimize their sustainability.

1.1 Urbanization and the environment

As Sachs describes in his excellent book *Common Wealth* (Sachs, 2008), human development can be broadly grouped into four epochs:

1   <10,000BC: hunter-gatherer.
2   8000BC to AD1000: primitive agricultural.
3   AD1000 to 1830: pre-industrial.
4   >1830: industrial.

For the first 90,000 years or so of human existence, the human population was fairly stable, being limited by the ability of small groups to hunt and gather their foodstuffs within complex and competitive ecological systems. Then, around 10,000 years ago, human society learnt to tame its environment; appropriating natural, often forested, ecosystems to convert solar energy into foodstuffs that could be consumed either directly or indirectly through domesticated animals. It was during this period that the first substantial urban settlements started to form, as the carrying capacity of fertile land was increased. With increased trade came also the transfer of knowledge regarding the more efficient exploitation of land: better crop choices, irrigation techniques, soil management etc. Surplus food could thus be used to sustain urban dwellers engaged in manufacturing and services. And so both rural and urban settlement sizes grew, but within the limits imposed by the agricultural techniques being employed. Infectious diseases, which were more easily propagated in denser settlements, also curbed population growth. Nevertheless, there was a steady increase in population size up to the dawn of the industrial revolution (Figure 1.1.1) at which around 10 per cent of the global population was urbanized.

The industrial revolution marked the transition from settlements that were limited by the largely manual exploitation of renewable resources, in a relatively sustainable way, to the use of solar energy embedded in fossil fuels (coal, oil and natural gas). Machines were used to increase the area of land that could be exploited by farmers; chemical processing, in particular the conversion of atmospheric nitrogen into nitrogen-based fertilizers, increased the productivity of land as soil nutrient levels could be artificially increased; railroads, barges and ocean freight enabled products to be transported over large distances.

This industrialization has had two consequences. First, the dramatic increase in both the area and the carrying capacity of land being exploited for agricultural purposes has facilitated a dramatic increase in the global population. Second, it has enabled a far greater proportion of this population to reside in urban settlements, such that the urban fraction of the global

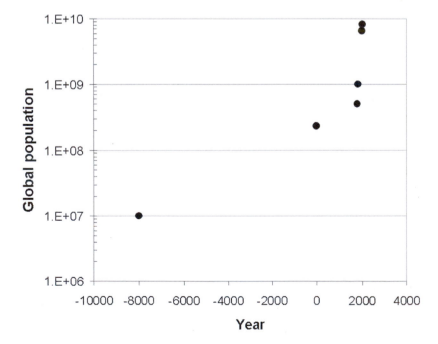

Figure 1.1.1 Approximate global human population: 8000BC to AD2030

Source: After Sachs (2008)

population has increased more or less linearly from around 13 per cent in 1900 until parity was achieved in 2007: the point at which half of the global population was urbanized (Figure 1.1.2).

Equally startling is the increased size of urban settlements, to the extent that there are now some 23 mega-cities accommodating in excess of ten million inhabitants (Figure 1.1.3)!

But what are the consequences of this dramatic urbanization and the intensive exploitation of arable land to support it? Well, these are both global and local. From a global perspective, of most concern are the environmental consequences arising from the intense exploitation of natural resources. Most topical is the increase in atmospheric carbon dioxide concentration from its pre-industrial level of 280 parts per million (ppm) to its current level of around 380ppm; which is almost undoubtedly changing our climate. But also of importance is the irreversible destruction of virgin natural habitats and ecosystems, the depletion of natural mineral resources, the over-exploitation of food (particularly marine) stocks leading to species extinction, soil and water pollution due to excess nitrogen fixation, and so on.

From a local perspective, the high density of modern urban settlements also leads to a harmful concentration of pollutants into the air, soil and water compartments of the geosphere. Other concerns are socio-economic. Both the size of cities and the distribution of wealth within them are thought to follow a Pareto (power law) distribution, so that the majority of wealth is owned by a small number of people and the majority of people are poor. This inequality in the distribution of wealth can lead to social tensions, even violence, and ill

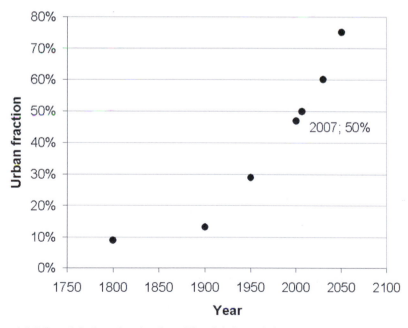

Figure 1.1.2 Growth in the urban fraction of the global population

Source: After Sachs (2008)

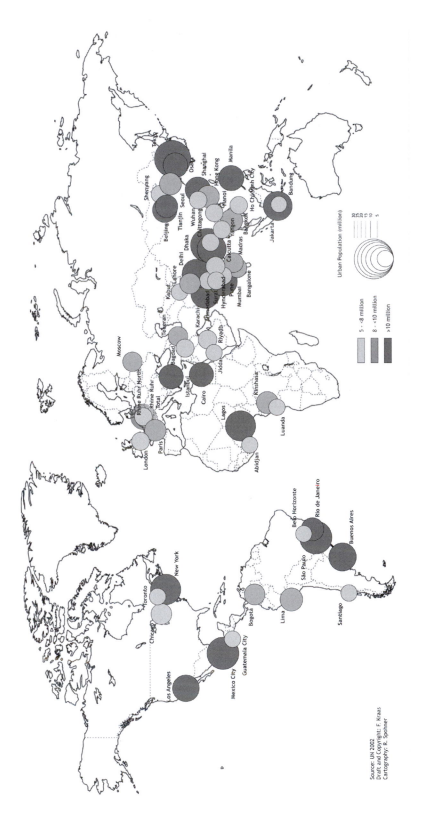

Figure 1.1.3 Global distribution of mega-cities

Source: After Kraas and Sterly, 2008[1]

health linked to poverty. Diseases are also more easily spread, due to the close proximity of urban dwellers. But cities also provide great opportunities for wealth creation and corresponding improvements in lifestyle, for rich social exchanges, for education etc. Indeed, these are the very sources of attraction.

It is for this reason that almost all of the projected increase in the global population (by a further 1.7 billion to 8.2 billion) up until 2030 is expected to be accommodated within urban settlements, at which point some 60 per cent of the global population is expected to be urbanized (UN, 2004). But the population of so-called 'developed' countries, which is relatively stable, is already around three-quarters urbanized. Further growth in this urban fraction is thus expected to be modest, so that the majority of the forecasted population growth is expected to be accommodated within the cities of 'developing' countries, within which considerable economic growth is also forecast.

Somewhat disconcertingly, population (P) and economic activity (A) as well as the technology used to support economic activity (T) – environmental impact per unit of income – are thought to be proportional to environmental impact (I): $I \propto P.A.T$. Thus, with no radical technological changes the environmental impacts of our future population are set to increase considerably. In corroboration of this relationship, Figure 1.1.4a presents the relationship between per capita economic growth and per capita energy consumption for a range of countries and how this has changed with time. The per capita gross domestic product (GDP) of countries such as China, India and Brazil, which are developing at an astonishing rate, is expected to increase significantly with a corresponding impact on per capita energy use and emissions. This is of particular concern because India and China alone accommodate some 38 per cent of the global population.

It is crucial then that the environmental impact per unit of income T of our future urban dwellers, in both developed and developing countries, is considerably reduced (as for example in Figure 1.1.4b). To understand how this might be achieved we should first better understand how current cities make use of the resources they consume.

1.2 How do cities function?

In this section we propose a conceptual framework for understanding how cities function as well as how they may evolve with time. This is intended to set the scene for understanding how we may approach the modelling of cities, define their sustainability and test strategies for improving on this sustainability.

1.2.1 Environmental factors

In order to understand how cities behave physically, it is helpful to consider the thermodynamic concept of entropy S. Entropy is a measure of the dissipation of order. Entropy increases as the thermal disorder of a substance (the thermal motion of its atoms) becomes more vigorous and as the positional disorder of this substance (the range of available positions of its atoms) increases. Thus if we heat the air in a room, the entropy of this air (the thermal motion of its

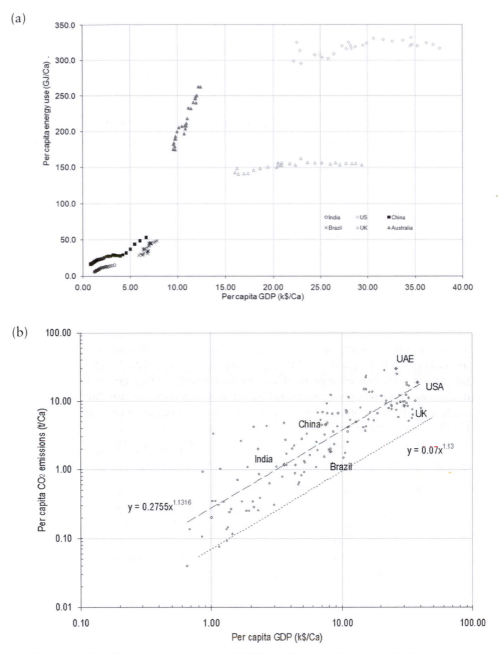

Figure 1.1.4 (a) Per capita energy use and GDP and (b) per capita carbon dioxide emissions and GDP

Note: Note that for (a) developing countries such as China and India have recently experienced rapid growth, which is also reflected in increased energy consumption; the UK and US however reduced their energy dependency following from the 1973 oil crash. For (b) in fact per capita CO_2 emissions and GDP appear to follow a power law relationship ($y = ax^b$ or log $y = b$ log x + log a), but with an exponent close to unity. Assuming that the nature of the energy consuming processes that accompany a given economic activity remain similar, so that the scaling exponent is unchanged, then a transition to more sustainable technologies would imply an offset in emissions (a change in a): a factor of four improvement in technology sustainability would reduce a from 0.28 to 0.7, so that we have an offset from the dashed fit to our data to the dotted line.

Source: Data in (a) from www.eia.doe.gov/emeu/international/energyconsumption.html and www.iea.org/co2highlights/. Data in (b) from www.iea.org/co2highlights/

molecules) will increase. If we now open the door to an adjacent room, these air molecules will be distributed over a wider volume (positional disorder increases) so that once again entropy is increased. Over time this energy will eventually be dissipated to the environment surrounding these two rooms, so that entropy is further increased. This is known as the arrow of time: in any isolated physicochemical system, entropy always increases (order is always dissipated) until equilibrium is reached.

But on observing the mysteries of life, Erwin Schrödinger (1944) noticed that we human beings, in fact all living organisms, do not obey this law. During the early stages of our life, as our cells divide and we grow, our internal order is preserved or increased (dS < 0); we defeat the arrow of time. We achieve this by exchanging entropy across our system boundaries: we take in food and oxygen and export waste and carbon dioxide: dSe(in) < dSe(out) so that overall dSe < 0. In other words, and as coined by Schrödinger, we consume negative entropy, *negentropy*. Thus, although entropy is produced internally due to irreversible internal processes dSi > 0, our body may be maintained in a more-or-less stable state (dS = dSi + dSe ≈ 0), or indeed we may increase in structural order (dS < 0). We are thus an open system. This openness, and the presence of flows, also implies that we are a non-equilibrium system: although the entropy of isolated physicochemical systems tends to evolve irreversibly to equilibrium (dSi > 0, which in our case would imply death), open systems may be maintained in non-equilibrium states. Indeed, Schneider and Kay (1994) suggest that the more energy that is *pumped* through a system, the greater the degree of organization that can emerge to dissipate this energy. They go on to suggest that the two processes are inseparable, so if a structure is not 'progressive' enough it will be replaced by a better adapted structure that will use the available energy more effectively. Thus, we humans have evolved into highly progressive open non-equilibrium thermodynamic systems; we maintain organized non-equilibrium states due to dissipative processes (Nicolis and Prigogine, 1977).

Analogously, our cities may increase in structural order with time, so that their entropy may be reduced. Once again, this is achieved by the exchange of energy and matter across their boundaries (Figure 1.2.1). Entropy is produced within our cities due to irreversible internal processes, such as the combustion of fuel to heat buildings. In principle this internal production may be reduced by coupling processes, but we will come back to this later. Solar energy, fossil fuels, electricity, constructional materials etc. may be imported into our system, while waste products (pollutants) are exported. In common with the metabolism of human beings, we may call the processing of these resources to sustain city life **urban metabolism**, after Baccini and Brunner (1991).

But this urban metabolism is highly inefficient. Indeed Erkman (1998) has likened the metabolism of cities to that of the first primitive ecosystems to exist on earth. The organisms in such ecosystems lived independently from one another, consuming resources from and expelling waste products into their immediate environment in an entirely linear fashion. But such behaviour tends to hysteresis in the abundance of organisms within a given ecosystem, as local pollution initially leads to a population decline, followed by a dissipation of pollution and a subsequent resurgence in population. To resolve these negative

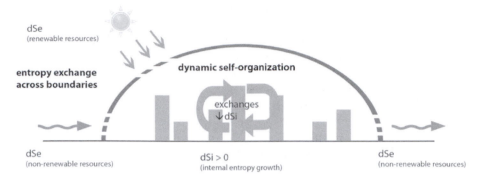

Figure 1.2.1 The city as a conceptual open thermodynamic system

Source: Author

relationships rich synergetic exchanges between complementary organisms in a given ecosystem have evolved, through the millennia, so that some organisms' waste products are useful resources for others. See for example the essentially closed nitrogen cycle in a natural soil–plant system in Plate 1.

If we now return to our anthropogenic ecosystem, the city, represented schematically in Figure 1.2.1, we can see that there is in principle considerable scope for reducing our net internal entropy production through the promotion of synergetic exchanges between complementary elements of this system, by taking inspiration from natural ecology.

This is not a new concept. Ecologists such as Eugene Odum pointed out as early as 1953 (Odum, 1953) the parallels between natural ecosystems and the resource flows due to human activities, suggesting further that industrial systems could be considered a subsystem of the biosphere. An inspirational example of this *industrial ecology* is the symbiosis project at Kalundborg in Denmark. With its beginnings in the 1960s, the industrial ecology employed at Kalundborg came about spontaneously, not for environmental reasons, but due to the clear economic advantages that could be realized from using the waste products of industrial partners to displace the relatively expensive import of energy and materials from external suppliers. From its humble beginnings in the 1960s and 1970s to supply the town's fresh water needs and the power station's cooling water needs, a rich set of synergetic exchanges has emerged (Plate 2). To give a few further examples, waste heat from the power station is used to service the muncipality's district heating needs, to heat the pools of a local fish farm and to provide the steam required for the processing of enzymes by a local biotechnology partner as well as for the refinement of oil by a local refinery. Waste gas from this refinery is also combusted by the power station, which in turn supplies gypsum from its flue gas desulphurization equipment to a local plasterboard manufacturer.

But thus far, there are very few examples of the applications of ecological principles to the design and operation of urban settlements. Perhaps the most successful and comprehensive example is the district of 'Hammarby Sjöstad' in Stockholm, Sweden (Plate 3).

Here organic waste is composted and used as fertilizer to produce biomass that, in addition to combustible non-hazardous refuse, is then combusted in local district heating, cooling and power plants. These plants satisfy the development's space heating and cooling as well as part of its power demands. Most of the remaining power demands are supplied by local or remote renewable energy technologies (solar cells, wind turbines and hydropower plants). Biogas produced from a wastewater treatment plant is used as a fuel for cooking, neatly closing the circle, as well as for transportation using biogas combusting buses. The plant's bio-solids are also used as fertilizer for the production of biomass, in supplement to the organic refuse. Heat is also recovered from the purified water from this plant using a heat pump, so that the district heating return water is preheated. Heat is then transferred to the now cooled treated water from the district cooling return water via a heat exchanger, prior to its discharge to the sea. Finally, solar thermal collectors are used to satisfy part of the development's domestic hot water needs.

The development's water demands have been reduced by installing low water consuming appliances (air-mixer taps, A-rated appliances and low flush toilets). There is no harvesting of rainwater, but storm water is infiltrated either to the ground or to the local canal network. There are also some green roofs to retard this discharge.

Waste is handled in a sophisticated way at Hammarby Sjöstad. Bulky waste products (organic, paper-based and combustible) are separated at source and deposited into the relevant local vacuum suction chute, through which the refuse is transported to centralized collection centres. Other waste products including furniture, glasses and plastics, electrical and electronic devices, and textiles are deposited into recycling rooms located within each apartment block. These are then handled for reuse, recycling, combustion or landfill; though the last of these is effectively minimized. Hazardous wastes, containing aggressive toxins or heavy metals, are deposited at a dedicated centralized collection plant, from which they are removed for recycling or incineration.

But Hammarby and other exemplary urban districts are far from optimal. Indeed, they are not environmentally sustainable. We suggest that one reason for this was that at the time at which these developments were conceived there was no modelling capability with which hypotheses could be tested for minimizing net internal entropy production and the exchange of non-renewable resources across the system boundaries (Robinson and Quiroga, 2009). Fortunately, much progress has since been made in the development of models for the simulation and optimization of urban resource flows and describing these advances occupies much of the remainder of this book.

Returning to natural ecosystems, the fact that their nutrient cycles tend to be closed does not imply that either nutrient flows or species populations are in equilibrium. They are in fact far from equilibrium, owing to complex interactions between species and with the adjacent transient environment. Indeed, and as noted earlier, equilibrium would imply the absence of change: death.

Cities are also in a far from equilibrium state, owing to a complex set of non-linear interactions between the various actors (firms and individuals) accommodated within them and with the outside world (the exchanges across the boundaries of the city). The city is a complex system. It exhibits emergent macroscopic behaviour based on the bottom-up actions of the firms and individuals from which it is comprised.

So how can we model this complexity to enable us to simulate the ways in which cities may evolve with time in response to the key social, fiscal and institutional stimuli?[2] Well, Wegener (1994) suggests that we consider the city as being comprised of eight timescale dependent subsystems:

1 Slow: **land-use distribution** and **networks** (utility, transport and communication) to support these uses.
2 Medium: **workplaces** (which may accommodate several changes in type of employment during their lifetimes) and **housing** (which may accommodate several changes in household during their lifetime).
3 Fast: **population** (changing household composition) and **employment** (changing firm composition).
4 Immediate: transportation of **goods** and **people**.

We also of course need to model the flows of energy and matter within and between these subsystems, and the exchanges across the system boundaries, if we are to simulate the city's metabolism and how this changes with time.

We seem to be suggesting then that there is a need to develop a detailed land use and transport interaction model, in which city land and building (both home and workplace) use change in response to fiscal flows, the changing composition and internal displacement of the city population (composed of residents and commuters to/from the city) and institutional policies. And that this model be coupled with a model of energy and matter flows due to the servicing of buildings and the processes accommodated within them as well as the transportation of goods and people between buildings. This is a bewilderingly complicated task. Part of the purpose of this book is to outline a modelling approach by which this might be achieved.

1.2.2 Socio-economic factors

Much of the complexity in developing the kind of integrated (land use, infrastructure, building use, transport and resource flow interaction) model mentioned above resides in simulating the responses to stimuli that drive change. These stimuli are both tangible: fiscal, regulatory and planning policy; and intangible: social interactions among individuals and human perception of the environment. In this modern era of globalization, cities are also interconnected for the flows of goods and services as well as with rural sources of food production, whether these are local or distant.

Let us first consider the smallest unit of interest: the individual. We human beings tend to interact socially with one another. We enter into relationships, become united in marriage, produce offspring and sadly we eventually die. During this time we consume foodstuffs, clothing and cleaning products to sustain ourselves. We inhabit a home that we furnish, heat and light and that accommodates our personal leisure purchases. We also engage in education and leisure activities outside of the home and possibly in some form of productive activity: work; and we travel between the locations at which these diverse activities are accommodated. These choices are either made for or by us, depending upon our age, culture, economic status and possibly also our gender. Certain choices may also be made in collaboration with friends and family members. Most importantly we are each unique so that our choices, whether taken individually or in concert, depend upon our personal preferences and circumstances at the time, which we cannot know *a priori*. This precludes some simple deterministic model of our choices.

Firms[3] supply a diverse range of goods and/or services according to demand, which may be both internal and external to the city, so that they are sensitive to internal and external market fluctuations. If supplying goods, firms also import raw materials and components that have been produced by other firms. All firms employ individuals, some of whom are empowered to make decisions concerning not only the day-to-day running of the firm, including employment decisions, but also the size and citing of its premises. These decisions may be influenced by proximity to complementary firms as well as by import/export transport infrastructure. But since the decisions are ultimately made by individuals, there is once again a stochastic element.

So the choices of firms and individuals are influenced then by external socio-economic factors. But they may also be influenced by regulatory controls, planning decisions and fiscal incentives; all of which derive from some form of governance, whether based on individuals or a collective, and is therefore stochastic in nature.

The actions of individuals and firms, both of whom require premises, infrastructure and other resources to support their daily activities, are based on stochastic decisions depending upon social, economic and environmental stimuli as well as on stochastic governance decisions; the objective of these decisions being to maximize welfare, whether of the individual, of the firm or of the state. Since we do not (cannot) have access to a cognitive model of each individual within a city, we need some form of abstract model of these decision-making processes if we are to model city dynamics. A useful question then is what is the appropriate degree of abstraction to enable us to simulate the mechanisms of most interest to us? We attempt to address this deceptively tricky question later in this book. One thing is clear however: the answer will depend very much on what we wish to learn from our model.

1.3 Book structure

As noted at the beginning of this chapter, the main aim of this book is to describe advances in computer modelling techniques that can be deployed by urban designers to test hypotheses for improving the sustainability of their design proposals; whether in conjunction with new or existing developments. In this book we place a particular emphasis on environmental sustainability; partly because this concept is easier to grasp, and therefore to predict, than either social or economic sustainability but also because of the urgency with which we must minimize the profligate use of our planet's mineral reserves – especially of fossil fuels and the increasingly evident consequences for climate change arising from their combustion.

From the preceding text, we can identify two types of model: those which consider the structure of urban settlements to be stationary and those which attempt to simulate urban structural dynamics; in particular of building-use and land-use dynamics and the infrastructure that support these uses. The majority of this book is dedicated to the former type of model. This is because these models are now approaching maturity, and so it is timely to disseminate this knowledge to encourage their more widespread use and further development. There is as yet no model that simulates both urban structural dynamics and the metabolism of resources by buildings and transportation systems. But good progress is being made. In the remainder of this book we describe this progress and the considerable challenges that await us as we strive to develop these models so that we can simulate how cities may develop with time with a view to testing scenarios for improving their future sustainability.

Following from this rationale the remainder of this book is contained in four parts.

Part I: Urban climate and comfort

To enable us to simulate the metabolism of urban resources in a satisfactory way, it is important that we account for the urban climate. In this endeavour, we begin Chapter 2 by describing alternative models for simulating the shortwave and longwave irradiance incident on the surfaces from which the urban built environment is composed. This is important for two reasons. First, these radiation exchanges are a key driving force for the thermal energy exchanges across building envelopes as well as for determining the temperature of adjacent outside air. Second, this shortwave irradiance may be used as a direct input to models of solar energy conversion systems (solar cells and solar thermal collectors) or simply to determine the availability of this resource for energy conversion.

In Chapter 3 we present a comprehensive new multi-scale approach for simulating air temperature, velocity and pressure throughout the urban environment; the former of which is a key variable driving the thermal energy exchanges across building envelopes.

The variables predicted by the models in Chapters 2 and 3 also influence pedestrians' comfort, which in turn influences our overall perception of the urban built environment and as such our social sustainability. In Chapter 4 then we present models for predicting the comfort of pedestrians.

Part II: Urban metabolism

The focus of this section is upon models for simulating urban metabolism. By this we mean that we explicitly consider the geometry of buildings and transport systems.

In Chapter 5 we begin with a brief review of models for simulating buildings' energy use in the urban context. We then present in detail new software for simulating urban resource flows (albeit with a focus on energy demand from and supply to buildings). Called CitySim, this includes models of: occupants' presence and behaviour; urban radiation exchange; heating, ventilation and air conditioning (HVAC) and energy conversion systems; the last of these being either building embedded or accommodated within district energy centres.

Chapter 6 is concerned with transport modelling. In this we begin by setting out the nature of the transport modelling problem and in so doing by also introducing different approaches for solving this problem. We go on to describe a general Multi-Agent Transport Simulation (MATSim) framework and how MATSim may be coupled with CitySim to support simulation of building- and transport-related resource flows within an urban development; assuming this to be structurally stationary. We close this part by describing an application of MATSim to a major infrastructure investment in Switzerland: the western bypass around Zürich, the country's business centre.

Part III: Evaluation and optimization

Part III is dedicated to optimizing the sustainability of urban developments. For this we first need to understand what we mean by sustainability and whether sustainability is possible in the urban context; indeed we may even question whether the phrase *sustainable development* is an oxymoron! In Chapter 7 then we attempt to define what we mean by sustainability, considering environmental and socio-economic factors and identify means by which the diverse indicators of these factors may be handled in a meaningful way.

In Chapter 8 we briefly review alternative algorithms with which some objective function, in our case an indicator of sustainability, may be optimized. We then select a candidate algorithm and test applications of this algorithm to optimizing the sustainability of an urban development. In this we start with the relatively simple problem of identifying urban geometric forms that optimize the annual solar irradiation incident on building envelopes and progress in complexity until we optimize the net energy use of a city housing block. We close this chapter by discussing the potential for larger-scale applications.

Part IV: An eye to the future

In Part IV we speculate as to how we might approach the considerable complexity of modelling urban structural dynamics and resource flows in an integrated way as well as ways in which the two might be manipulated to optimize city sustainability. But this is a long-term vision, hence the title 'an eye to the future'.

We begin this challenge with Chapter 9 in which we illustrate a typical model of residential location that offers a generic template for many kinds of interactions that involve flows of people and uses of energy in their transport. We develop this model for four different modes of transport in the Greater London region and illustrate its operation with respect to the impact of a doubling of the cost of travel. This enables us to focus on population and mode shifts that occur as energy costs change. We then show how this model is nested within a wider framework of integrated assessment that contains models that change in scale from the regional to the site specific. We finally postulate as to how the forces driving land-use transport dynamics may be simulated in a more generic way and how this may be coupled with simulations of resource flows, to test means for optimizing environmental sustainability.

We close this book with Chapter 10 by outlining some short- and medium-term trends and research needs in each of the key themes covered by this book: comfort and climate, urban metabolism and measurement and optimization. We then outline some of the challenges that lie ahead of us as we strive towards the development and application of properly comprehensive models for simulating and optimizing urban sustainability, in all its complexity. Key in this will be the need for more interdisciplinary research.

Notes

1   www.reedmidem.com/mipimhorizons/blog/index.php/2008/11/05/10-frauke-kraas-and-harald-sterly-megacities-as-results-and-motors-of-global-change-
2   Unfortunately we are not able to predict the future state of open far-from-equilibrium systems such as the city. As Allen (1984) has shown, the state of our city may bifurcate to a range of potential solutions owing to the non-linearities involved. Perhaps though, by simulating the systems' response to uncertainties in input variables, we may be able to predict a reasonably probable future system state.
3   Let us suppose, for simplicity, that public bodies are a special case of a firm, in which the financial decisions are taken not by directors or shareholders but by government. All non-residential buildings may thus be considered as firms.

References

Allen, P. (1984) 'Towards a new synthesis in the modelling of evolving complex systems', *Environment and Planning B*, vol 12, pp65–84

Baccini, P. and Brunner, P. (1991) *Metabolism of the Anthroposphere*, Springer Verlag, Berlin

Erkman, S. (1998) *Vers une écologie industrielle*, Charles Léopold Mayer, Paris

Nicolis, G. and Prigogine, I. (1977) *Self-Organization in Non-equilibrium Systems*, Wiley-Interscience, New York

Odum, E. P. (1953) *Fundamentals of Ecology*, Saunders, Philadelphia

Robinson, D. and Quiroga, C. (2009) 'Sustainable masterplanning in practice: Evaluation and synthesis', *Proc. CISBAT 2009*: Lausanne, Switzerland

Sachs, J. D. (2008) *Common Wealth: Economics for a Crowded Planet*, Penguin, New York

Schneider, E. D. and Kay, J. J. (1994) 'Complexity and thermodynamics', *Futures*, vol 26, no 6, pp626–647

Schrödinger, E. (1944) *What is life?*, Cambridge University Press, Cambridge

UN (United Nations) (2004) *World Urbanization Prospects: The 2003 Revision*, Department of Economic and Social Affairs/Population Division, United Nations, New York

Wegener, M. (1994) 'Operational urban models', *Journal of the American Planning Association*, vol 60, no 1, pp17–29

Part I

Climate and Comfort

2

The Urban Radiant Environment

Darren Robinson

2.1 Introduction

All surfaces in the urban environment absorb solar radiation in the spectrum 0.3 micron (μm) to 3μm; we tend to refer to this as shortwave radiation exchange. These urban surfaces also transfer heat to other surfaces by radiation exchange in the spectrum 3–4μm to 100μm (i.e. the infrared part of the electromagnetic spectrum). This we tend to refer to as longwave radiation exchange.[1] These surface radiation exchange processes are an important determinant of the temperature of our urban surfaces, which correspondingly influences (and is influenced by) convective heat transfer to the air in contact with these surfaces as well as the transfer of heat by conduction into the material from which the surface is composed. The former transfer of heat by convection plays a key role in determining the urban climate, which may vary considerably in both space and time from that experienced in an adjacent rural context. We address this in detail in Chapter 4. For surfaces that represent a boundary between the outdoor and indoor environments of buildings, the transfer by conduction plays a key role in determining a building's energy balance and thus the energy consumed within the urban environment due to buildings. In the case of transparent surfaces, transmitted shortwave energy may be converted into heat, or electricity in the case of thermal or photovoltaic solar collectors, or contribute directly to buildings' energy balances.

It is thus important to be able to predict radiation exchange with a good degree of accuracy. But relative to rural environments, radiation exchange in urban environments is complicated considerably by the presence of other (predominantly built) surfaces. These other surfaces may obscure views to the sun and the sky as well as contribute reflected shortwave radiation or the absorption/emission of longwave radiation.

In this chapter we describe the key mathematical models, of varying complexity, that have been developed to predict this urban radiation exchange. But first it is necessary to introduce models for predicting the position of the sun and the angle of incidence from the sun onto a receiving surface, as well as models for predicting the distribution of radiant energy throughout the celestial vault. In doing so, we also introduce some of the early techniques that were developed to predict the availability of solar radiation within the urban environment.

2.2 Solar geometry

The earth's magnetic poles are not vertically aligned, to the extent that the axis of the earth's rotation is inclined from the vertical by approximately 23.45°. During summer months, the axis of rotation is tilted towards the sun, with the effect that the apparent solar altitude in the celestial vault is greater at noon than is the case in winter months when the axis is tilted away from the sun (Figure 2.2.1). Likewise, a line from the centroid of the earth to that of the sun cuts the earth's surface above the equator in summer and below in winter. We refer to this angle as the solar declination angle δ (rad).

This solar declination angle is given by the following Fourier series, after Spencer (1971):

$$\delta = 0.006918 - 0.399912\cos\tau + 0.070257\sin\tau - 0.006758\cos 2\tau + 0.000907\sin 2\tau - 0.002697\cos 3\tau + 0.00148\sin 3\tau \qquad [2.2.1]$$

in which, for the jth Julian day (with all days from 1 January being sequentially numbered, so that $j31$ corresponds to 31 January) $\tau = 2\pi(j-1)/365$ (rad).

As the earth rotates (in the clockwise direction), the sun first appears at the horizon towards the east, reaching its maximum altitude when due south, from which it again descends towards (and beyond) the horizon in the west. A useful observation is that the maximum altitude $\hat{\gamma}$ (rad) at latitude λ is simply $\pi/2 - (\lambda - \delta)$ radians. At other times, however, the spherical geometry is a little

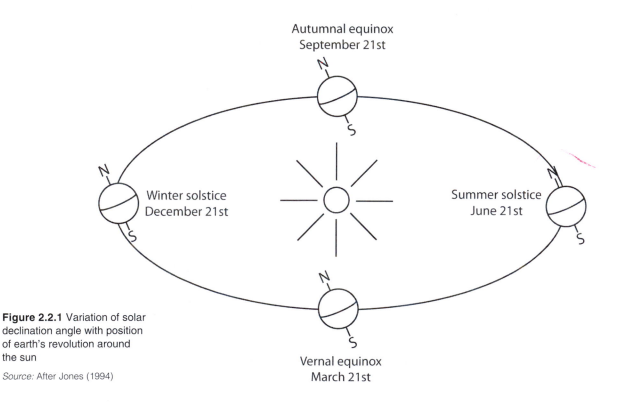

Figure 2.2.1 Variation of solar declination angle with position of earth's revolution around the sun

Source: After Jones (1994)

more complicated. In the general case, the solar altitude is given by the following expression:

$$\sin\gamma = \sin\lambda\,\sin\delta + \cos\lambda\,\cos\delta\,\cos\omega \qquad [2.2.2]$$

in which ω is the solar hour angle (rad), that is the angular distance between the current position of the earth's rotation and that corresponding to solar noon. Since we know that at sunrise and sunset the solar altitude (and its sine) will be zero and furthermore that the tangent of an angle is equal to the quotient of its sine and cosine, we may rearrange [2.2.2] above to determine the solar hour angle at sunrise/sunset:

$$\cos\omega = -\tan\lambda\,\tan\delta \qquad [2.2.3]$$

the corresponding time is simply $12 \pm 12\omega/\pi$. At other times the solar hour angle is simply $\omega = 12t/\pi$, where t is *solar time*. This solar time differs from the local clock time t' that is used at a given location for several reasons:

- The longitude $\frac{1}{M}$ (rad) at our site of interest may vary from the reference longitude that corresponds to our time zone, z (h).
- Our clocks may have been adjusted according to daylight savings time, d (h).
- The earth's orbit around the sun is elliptical, so that the apparent longitude of the sun changes faster when the earth is closer to the sun (in winter) than when it is farther (in summer). Furthermore, apparent solar time is measured as a projection of the sun's (apparent) motion onto the equator and this changes throughout the year as the projection cuts above and below the equator.[2] The effect that these two influences have on observed differences between clock and solar time is calculated by what we refer to as the equation of time, ε.

Combining the above influences we are able to calculate the equivalent solar time:

$$t = t' + (l - 15z)/60 + \varepsilon + d \qquad [2.2.4]$$

where $d = [0,1]$ and the equation of time ε may be calculated from the following Fourier series, also due to Spencer (1971):

$$\varepsilon = 229.2 \left(\begin{array}{l} 0.00008 + 0.00187\cos\tau - 0.0321\sin\tau - \\ 0.0146\cos 2\tau - 0.0409\sin 2\tau \end{array} \right) \Big/ 60 \qquad [2.2.5]$$

The proportion of the earth's revolution of the sun that has already been completed for the current year τ is found using the same expression as that used when calculating the solar declination angle, as presented above.

Now that we are able to calculate the solar altitude for any given local clock time and location, we are also able to calculate the corresponding solar azimuth α[3] (rad):

$$\alpha = \arccos\left(-\sin\lambda\,\sin\gamma + \sin\delta\,/\cos\lambda\,\cos\gamma\right), \ \omega \le \pi \qquad [2.2.6a]$$

$$\alpha = 2\pi - \arccos\left(-\sin\lambda\,\sin\gamma + \sin\delta\,/\cos\lambda\,\cos\gamma\right),\ \omega > \pi \qquad\qquad [2.2.6b]$$

and the corresponding cosine of the angle of incidence $\cos\theta$ of solar radiation onto our receiving surface:

$$\cos\theta = \cos\gamma\cos\alpha'\sin\beta + \sin\gamma\cos\beta \qquad\qquad [2.2.7]$$

where α' is the difference in azimuth between our receiving surface α_w and that of the sun: $\alpha' = \min\left(0, |\alpha - \alpha_w|\right)$, this being set to zero for azimuth differences exeeding $\pi/2$, and β is the tilt of this surface, where 0 corresponds to a horizontal surface facing up, $\pi/2$ is vertical and π is horizontal facing down, so that $0 \le \beta \le \pi$. Now solar radiation (radiant energy in the range 0.3µm to 3µm) is normally measured using a radiometer, which consists of two discs, a white disc with a hole in which there is a black disc, both covered by a glass hemisphere. The temperature difference between these discs, which at a given instant in time is proportional to the incidence solar irradiance (W.m^{-2}), is measured by a thermopile. An unobstructed horizontally positioned radiometer measures global horizontal solar irradiance I_{gh}; that is the irradiance due to both the sun and the sky. It is also possible to position a band above the radiometer so that the sun is obstructed along its trajectory from sunrise to sunset. A correction can then be made to calculate the diffuse horizontal solar irradiance I_{dh}; that is the irradiance due to the sky alone. Given these two measurements we can now finally calculate the direct solar irradiance that is incident on a given surface $I_{b\theta}$:

$$I_{b\theta} = \left(I_{gh} - I_{dh}\right)\cos\theta\big/\sin\gamma \qquad\qquad [2.2.8]$$

Note that considerably more sophisticated algorithms are available to calculate the position of the sun (for example Michalsky, 1988; Grena, 2008). However, the precision of that above is more than adequate for the purposes of urban environmental modelling.

2.2.1 Radiation availability: Simplified geometric methods

A very convenient way of visualizing the path that the sun takes across the celestial vault during the year is via the use of a sunpath diagram. In Figure 2.2.2 for example, we plot in thick black the sunpaths from the winter solstice (21 December) through to the summer solstice (21 June) at monthly intervals, passing through the vernal equinox (21 March). In this diagram the outer black circle corresponds to the horizon. Progressively smaller (and partially complete) grey circles correspond to $20°$ steps in altitude, with the zenith of the vault at the centre of the diagram. Radial lines represent $45°$ steps in azimuth. The dashed black curves correspond to solar time from sunrise in the east, through noon (due south) to sunset in the west.

Given the equations for solar altitude [2.2.2] and azimuth [2.2.6] above, it is relatively straightforward to create such a sunpath diagram, for any site latitude. This is achieved simply by translating these angular coordinates into planar x,y coordinates, whereby $x = (\pi/2 - \gamma)\sin\alpha$ and $y = (\pi/2 - \gamma)\cos\alpha$.

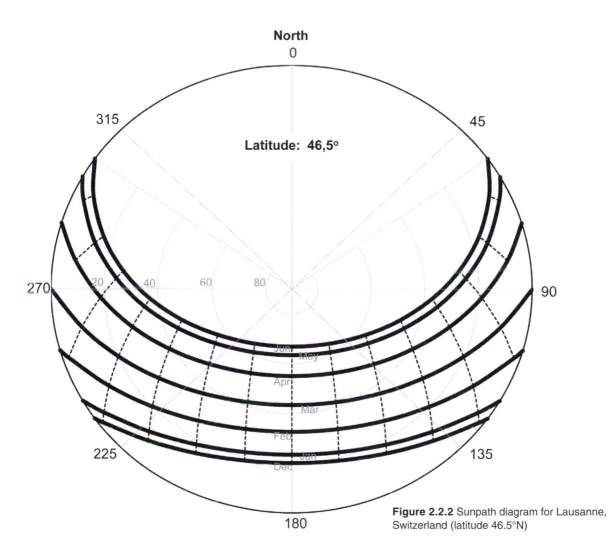

Figure 2.2.2 Sunpath diagram for Lausanne, Switzerland (latitude 46.5°N)

Setting γ to 0, 20...80 and discretizing the circle into sufficiently small steps in azimuth, we can readily create the iso-altitude lines. We can likewise plot the sunpaths, starting at sunrise and proceeding towards sunset at whole hour intervals. We can also connect the points at these whole hours from the winter through to the summer solstice, to plot the iso-time lines. Finally, we can plot iso-azimuth lines between the horizon and the zenith at 45° (or smaller) to complete the diagram.

It may also be useful to replace the iso-**solar**-time lines above with those corresponding to clock time, using [2.2.4] above. These iso-**clock**-time lines should resemble a figure of eight.

Now, if we have a three dimensional representation of an urban scene, for example by taking a photograph with a view direct to the zenith using a fish-eye lens,[4] we can create an image in which the surfaces are directly superimposed onto a sunpath diagram and so readily visualize the year during which views to the sun from our view point are obstructed by these surfaces. In Plate 4 we present such an image for a point in front of the Solar Energy and Building Physics Laboratory at the École Polytechnique Fédérale de Lausanne in Switzerland. Note that views to the sun from this point are only obstructed at the boundaries of the day during the winter and intermediate seasons. Such applications of shading masks have been in use for decades, partly due to their great simplicity.

Another method based purely on geometric considerations of solar availability was Everett's (1980) Shadowprint, which involved, based on interpolation of cumulative hours of solar visibility computed throughout a grid of points, the plotting of contours corresponding to equal reductions in solar visibility (10 per cent, 20 per cent etc.) arising from parallelepiped buildings of predefined orientation.

Such techniques, involving the use of computer models to produce graphical design tools, supported the preparation of some of the early guidelines for site layout and planning to ensure daylight and solar access to residential buildings (Littlefair, 1991; Littlefair et al, 2000).

With improvements in computer processing power it gradually became more usual to use computer models interactively. One early example is the computation of solar envelopes (Knowles, 1981, 2003), defined as the volume that a building can occupy on a given site without overshading adjacent buildings during a specified period of time. Such envelopes are created by projecting the vertical boundaries of the site of a potentially obstructing development, as seen from one or several viewpoints, along the opposite vector of the sun for the days/times of interest. A union of these images, in which the lower projection surfaces (or parts of them) take precedent over those above them, defines a volume within the site boundaries that does not obstruct the point(s) of interest.

With the introduction of Townscope (Teller and Azar, 2001) – or rather its predecessor CAM-UR (Dupagne, 1991) – it also became possible to automatically create shadow masks, by converting planar coordinates into spherical coordinates for the surfaces of a 3D urban model (Plate 5).

In a similar vein to the shadow footprints of Everett, the software 'shadows' automatically calculates iso-shadow contours (corresponding to 10 per cent, 20 per cent ...90 per cent of time spent in the building's shadow) for cuboid-shaped buildings of arbitrary location and orientation (Kristl and Krainer, 2001). On a similar basis, 'shadowpack' produces ground irradiance isopleths based on point calculations of direct irradiance in urban settings (Peckham, 1985).

2.3 Sky models

With the algorithm for determining the position of the sun relative to a point on a receiving surface presented in Section 2.2 above, it is straightforward to determine the incident direct irradiance, taking into account whether the sun is visible or not. As we have seen, it is furthermore possible to determine the reduction in incident direct solar energy due to shading obstructions. But as we discussed in Section 2.1, the diffuse radiation due to both the sky and obstructions must also be taken into account if we are to predict the total incident solar radiation with a reasonable degree of precision. In this section we therefore introduce some of the principle models that exist for calculating the distribution of radiant energy throughout the sky vault as well as the corresponding incident irradiance at a point on a receiving surface. In this we consider models for both shortwave and longwave exchange.

2.3.1 Shortwave exchange

Early models for predicting the irradiance incident at a point on a surface tended to assume that the sky was isotropic – that it had the same brightness, or rather radiance ($W.m^{-2}.sr^{-1}$), in all directions. In such cases, it is straightforward to predict the irradiance incident at a point on a receiving surface of tilt β due to diffuse sky radiation $I_{d\beta}$ ($W.m^{-2}$) as a function of the diffuse irradiance on the horizontal plane I_{dh}:

$$I_{d\beta} = I_{dh}\left(1+\cos\beta\right)/2 \qquad\qquad [2.3.1]$$

It is equally straightforward to predict the reflected irradiance from the ground $I_{\rho G\beta}$ of reflectance ρ as a function of the global irradiance on the horizontal plane I_{gh}:

$$I_{\rho G\beta} = \rho_G I_{gh}\left(1-\cos\beta\right)/2 \qquad\qquad [2.3.2]$$

assuming of course that neither our receiving surface, nor any other obstruction, significantly influences the total irradiance incident on the ground. The total irradiance incident on our receiving surface I_β is then the sum of the contributions from [2.2.6], [2.3.1] and [2.3.2].

We know from experience, however, that real skies are not isotropic. Even under perfectly overcast conditions, which are a relatively rare occurrence, the radiance of the sky vault increases with altitude relative to that at the zenith, such that $R_\gamma = R_z(1+2\sin\gamma)/3$ (after Moon and Spencer, 1942). In clear conditions, the radiance is high in the vicinity of the sun due to the local forward scattering of solar radiation, as well as at the horizon due to the back-scattering of energy reflected from beyond the horizon. We refer to this as circumsolar and horizon brightening, respectively. Many anisotropic sky models have been developed over the years to account for these phenomena. These may broadly be classified as two component (background + circumsolar) models, such as that due to Hay (1979), and three component models (background + circumsolar + horizon), such as those of Klucher (1979) and Reindl et al (1990). One such model that has gained widespread acceptance is that due to Perez et al (1987). This statistical model, which is based on a large number of scans of the sky radiance distribution at different locations, has performed rather well in independent empirical validation tests (Mardaljevic, 1995) and has been included in numerous building and solar energy conversion system simulation programs.

The three terms in brackets in [2.3.3] correspond to an isotropic background component, a circumsolar component and a horizon brightening component respectively:

$$I_{d\beta} = I_{dh}\left[\left(1-F_1\right)\left(1+\cos\beta\right)/2 + F_1 a_0/a_1 + F_2\sin\beta\right] \qquad\qquad [2.3.3]$$

In which the coefficients a account for the angle of incidence of the circumsolar component [$a_0 = \max(0, \cos\theta)$ and $a_1 = \max(\sin 5\pi/180, \sin\gamma)$], which is effectively treated as a point source placed at or above a limiting altitude of $5\pi/180$ (rad). $F_{1,2}$ in [2.3.3] are circumsolar and horizon brightness functions. These depend on the solar zenith angle Z (which is constrained to a minimum value of $5\pi/180$ radians), the sky brightness Δ and a set of statistical coefficients f for eight bins of sky clearness ε (see Table 2.3.1):

$$F_1 = \max\left(0, f_{11} + f_{12}\Delta + f_{13}Z\right) \qquad [2.3.4a]$$

$$F_2 = f_{21} + f_{22}\Delta + f_{23}Z \qquad [2.3.4b]$$

The sky brightness is the product of the number of optical air masses that direct solar radiation passes through, which is inversely proportional to the solar altitude ($m \approx \gamma^{-1}$) and the quotient of the diffuse solar irradiance on the horizontal plane I_{dh} and the extraterrestrial irradiance, also on the horizontal plane I_{eh}:

$$\Delta = mI_{dh}/I_{eh} \qquad [2.3.5]$$

This extraterrestrial horizontal irradiance is essentially the solar constant G (1367Wm^{-2}) adjusted to account for the eccentricity of the earth's orbit around the sun:

$$I_{eh} = G\left(1 + 0.033\cos[2\pi j/365]\right) \qquad [2.3.6]$$

Finally, the sky clearness index ε, with which we are able to select the corresponding statistical coefficients for the circumsolar and horizon brightness functions in [2.3.4] above, is given by the following expression:

$$\varepsilon = \frac{\left(I_{dh} + I_{bh}\right)/I_{dh} + 5.535E6 \cdot Z^3}{1 + 5.535E6 \cdot Z^3} \qquad [2.3.7]$$

Table 2.3.1 Statistical coefficients of circumsolar and horizon brightness functions

ε bin	f_{11}	f_{12}	f_{13}	f_{21}	f_{22}	f_{23}
1 (ε < 1.065)	−0.008	0.588	−0.062	−0.060	0.072	−0.022
2 (1.065 ≤ ε < 1.230)	0.130	0.683	−0.151	−0.019	0.066	−0.029
3 (1.230 ≤ ε < 1.500)	0.330	0.487	−0.221	0.055	−0.064	−0.026
4 (1.500 ≤ ε < 1.950)	0.568	0.187	−0.295	0.109	−0.152	−0.014
5 (1.950 ≤ ε < 2.800)	0.873	−0.392	−0.362	0.226	−0.462	0.001
6 (2.800 ≤ ε < 4.500)	1.132	−1.237	−0.412	0.288	−0.823	0.056
7 (4.500 ≤ ε < 6.200)	1.060	−1.600	−0.359	0.264	−1.127	0.131
8 (6.200 ≤ ε)	0.678	−0.327	−0.250	0.156	−1.377	0.251

The total incident irradiance is then the sum of the direct [2.2.8], ground reflected [2.3.2] and anisotropic sky [2.3.3] contributions.

It is useful to determine whether and to what extent this increase in modelling complexity improves the quality of predictions. To this end we plot, in Figure 2.3.1, irradiation surface plots (contour plots of sky irradiation for 5° bins of receiving surface tilt and azimuth) for the isotropic and Perez anisotropic models as well as the percentage difference between the two. From the latter, it is evident that for a surface tilt of around 70° (i.e. 20° from the vertical) the anisotropic model predicts that around 15 per cent more energy is received when oriented south and 20 per cent less when oriented north – with corresponding implications for a building's energy balance or for solar energy conversion. The relatively modest increase in complexity in accounting for the anisotropy of the distribution of radiant energy in the sky vault appears therefore to be warranted.

An alternative to these simple two and three component models for predicting the irradiance incident on a tilted surface, is to explicitly model the radiance distribution throughout the sky vault – typically as a continuous function of the angular location of a sky point relative to the zenith or the sun, and predict the contribution to incident irradiance from the region of the sky that is visible to our receiving surface.

Numerous models exist that enable us to do this, most of which have been developed to support daylight predictions; the earliest of these being the overcast sky luminance distribution model due to Moon and Spencer (1942), mentioned above. Other models include early formulations of the Commission International de l'Eclairage (CIE) clear sky model (Kittler, 1967) through more recent clear sky models (CIE, 1973, 1996) to more general sky definitions (Perez et al, 1993; CIE, 2002) that cover the range of sky types from overcast through to intermediate to clear. Once again the model due to Perez et al (1993), which provides a straightforward basis for the selection of each of the eight possible sky types, has won rather widespread acceptance.

Using the Perez luminance distribution model, we first calculate the *relative* luminance (lm.m^{-2}.sr^{-1}) at a given sky point (that is, the ratio of the luminance at this point relative to the luminance at an arbitrary reference point), which depends on the zenith angle to the considered sky element z and the angular distance from this point to the sun ξ: $\lambda = f(z,\xi)$. In particular this model takes the form:

$$\lambda = \left(1 + a\exp[b/\cos z]\right) \cdot \left(1 + c\exp[d \cdot \xi] + e\cos^2 \xi\right) \qquad [2.3.8]$$

The angular distance ξ is given by the expression $\cos\xi = \cos\gamma\cos\gamma'\cos|\alpha' - \alpha| + \sin\gamma\sin\gamma'$, where angles denoted by prime refer to the sky point and unprimed angles to the position of the sun. Functions a,b represent the magnitude and gradient of brightening/darkening at the horizon and between the zenith and the horizon; whereas c,d represent the magnitude and angular cone width of the circumsolar region. Finally, e represents the relative intensity of back-scattered light received at the earth's surface. In common with the tilted surface model, these functions[5] $a,b...e = \varphi$ depend on the solar zenith angle Z, sky clearness ε and sky brightness Δ, such that:

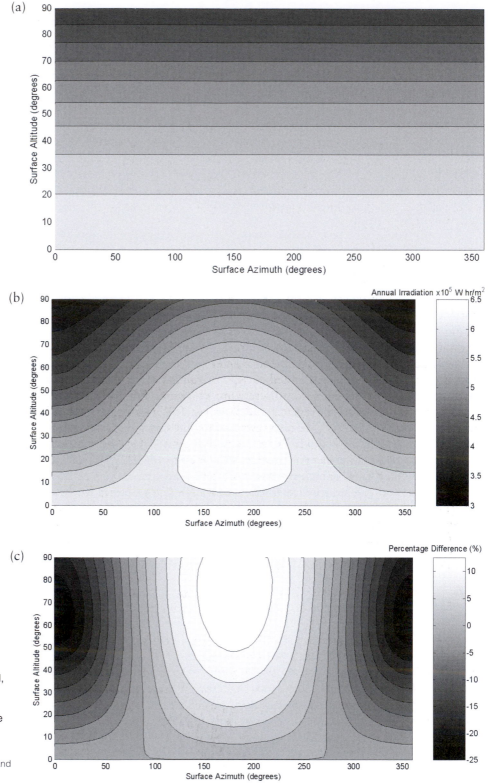

Figure 2.3.1 Annual diffuse sky irradiation surface plots for (a) the isotropic model, (b) the anisotropic models for Kew, UK, and (c) the percentage difference between the two

Source: After Robinson and Stone (2004a)

$$\varphi = \varphi_1 \varepsilon + \varphi_2 \varepsilon Z + \Delta \left(\varphi_3 \varepsilon + \varphi_4 Z \right) \tag{2.3.9}$$

but where the sky clearness is defined somewhat differently to that in [2.3.7] so that:

$$\varepsilon = \frac{\left(I_{db} + I_{bb} \right) / I_{db} + 1.041 Z^3}{1 + 1.041 Z^3} \tag{2.3.10}$$

The corresponding values of coefficients $\varphi_1, \varphi_2 ... \varphi_4$ are presented in Table 2.3.2.

To obtain the corresponding *absolute* luminance L (or indeed radiance), it is necessary to apply some form of normalization, using either a prediction of zenith luminance (so that $L = L_z \cdot \lambda(z, \xi) / \lambda(0, Z)$) or diffuse horizontal illuminance. However, it is equally appropriate to normalize using diffuse horizontal irradiance, in which case we obtain the absolute radiance of our sky element directly, as follows:

$$R = I_{db} \lambda(z, \xi) \bigg/ \int_0^{2\pi} \int_0^{\frac{\pi}{2}} \lambda(z, \xi) . d\gamma d\alpha \tag{2.3.11}$$

In which the dominator is essentially an equivalent diffuse horizontal illuminance (lm.m^{-2}), so that the quotient of the irradiance in the numerator and this illuminance produces a normalization factor χ, which corresponds to the reciprocal of an absolute luminous efficacy (W.lm^{-1}), so that $R = \lambda(z, \xi) \chi$.

For practical reasons it is useful to discretize the sky vault into a set of patches of constant radiance, defined by that calculated at the patch centroid. There are numerous schemes for discretizing the vault, but for the present purposes the method due to Tregenza and Sharples (1993) is appropriate. With this method the sky vault is split into seven azimuthal strips, each spanning an altitude range of 12°, and in which the azimuthal range ($\Delta \alpha$, radians) of the patches within these strips increases towards the zenith (12°, 12°, 15°, 15°, 20°, 30°, 60°) at which there is a single patch, so that there are 145 in total. The intention is that all patches subtend similar solid angle Φ, this being determined by the azimuthal range of the ith patch and the corresponding maximum and minimum patch altitude, so that $\Phi_i = \Delta \alpha_i \left(\sin \gamma_{i,max} - \sin \gamma_{i,min} \right)$ steradians. Now, given the mean altitude of each of our p patches we can calculate an approximate normalization from the summation: $\chi = I_{db} \bigg/ \sum_{i=1}^{p} \left(\lambda(z, \xi) \Phi \bar{\gamma} \right)_i$: the product of this and the relative luminance calculated at the ith patch centroid provide a good approximation of the mean radiance of the ith patch ($R_i = \lambda(z, \xi)_i \chi$).

Now, half of the sky vault will be obscured by a vertical receiving plane. To account for this we may estimate a patch view factor σ_i based on the proportion of the patches, azimuthal range that lies within 90° of our receiving surface normal ($0 \leq \sigma \leq 1$). We may then calculate the incident irradiance on our receiving plane by summing the contributions from each of the p patches from which our sky is constructed (Robinson and Stone, 2004a):

$$\chi = I_{db} \bigg/ \sum_{i=1}^{p} \left(\ell(z, \xi) \Phi \bar{\gamma} \right)_i \tag{2.3.12}$$

Table 2.3.2 Statistical coefficients of anisotropy functions

ε bin	a_1	a_2	a_3	a_4	b_1	b_2	b_3	b_4	c_1	c_2	c_3	c_4
1 (ε < 1.065)	1.353	-0.258	-0.269	-1.437	-0.767	0.001	1.273	-0.123	2.800	0.600	1.238	1.000
2 (1.065 ≤ ε < 1.230)	-1.222	-0.773	1.415	1.102	-0.205	0.037	-3.913	0.916	6.975	0.177	6.448	-0.124
3 (1.230 ≤ ε < 1.500)	-1.1	-0.252	0.895	0.016	0.278	-0.181	-4.5	1.177	24.22	-13.08	-37.70	34.84
4 (1.500 ≤ ε < 1.950)	-0.585	-0.665	-0.267	0.712	0.723	-0.622	-5.681	2.630	33.34	-18.30	-62.25	52.08
5 (1.950 ≤ ε < 2.800)	-0.6	-0.347	-2.5	2.323	0.294	0.049	-5.681	1.842	21.00	-4.766	-21.59	7.249
6 (2.800 ≤ ε < 4.500)	-1.016	-0.367	1.008	1.405	0.288	-0.533	-3.85	3.375	14.00	-0.999	-7.14	7.547
7 (4.500 ≤ ε < 6.200)	-1.0	0.021	0.503	-0.512	-0.3	0.192	0.702	-1.632	19.00	-5.000	1.243	-1.91
8 (6.200 ≤ ε)	-1.05	0.029	0.426	0.359	-0.325	0.116	0.778	0.003	31.06	-14.50	-46.11	55.37

ε bin	d_1	d_2	d_3	d_4	e_1	e_2	e_3	e_4
1 (ε < 1.065)	1.874	0.630	0.974	0.281	0.035	-0.125	-0.572	0.994
2 (1.065 ≤ ε < 1.230)	-1.580	-0.508	-1.781	0.108	0.262	0.067	-0.219	-0.428
3 (1.230 ≤ ε < 1.500)	-5.00	1.522	3.923	-2.62	-0.016	0.160	0.420	-0.556
4 (1.500 ≤ ε < 1.950)	-3.50	0.006	1.148	0.106	0.466	-0.33	-0.088	-0.033
5 (1.950 ≤ ε < 2.800)	-3.50	-0.155	1.406	0.399	0.003	0.077	-0.066	-0.129
6 (2.800 ≤ ε < 4.500)	-3.40	-0.108	-1.075	1.57	-0.067	0.402	0.302	-0.484
7 (4.500 ≤ ε < 6.200)	-4.00	0.025	0.384	0.266	1.047	-0.379	-2.452	1.466
8 (6.200 ≤ ε)	-7.23	0.405	3.35	0.623	1.500	-0.643	1.856	0.564

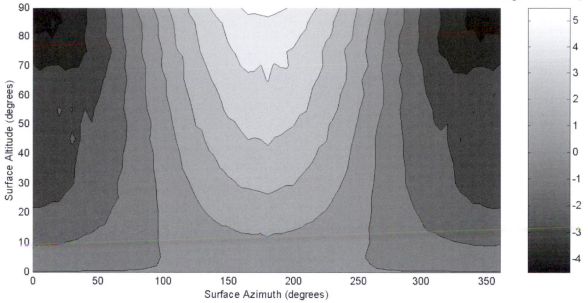

Figure 2.3.2 Surface plot illustrating percentage difference in annual irradiation between the Perez tilted surface model and the radiance distribution model

Source: Robinson and Stone (2004a)

From [2.2.7] above, it is apparent that the cosine of the angle of incidence from the ith patch centroid to a point on our receiving surface is $\cos\theta_i = \cos\overline{\gamma}_i \cos\overline{\alpha}_i \sin\beta + \sin\overline{\gamma}_i \cos\beta$. Note that for partially obscured patches, $\overline{\gamma}, \overline{\alpha}$ should relate to the visible proportion.

With a more rigorous treatment of sources of sky isotropy (and additional sources within the horizon band and due to background scattering) we find that, once again for Kew (London), this radiance distribution model predicts an increase of a maximum of 5 per cent of irradiation for surfaces oriented south and a 4 per cent reduction for those oriented north, relative to the Perez tilted surface model [2.3.3] (Figure 2.3.2).

It is questionable, in the case of an isolated surface, whether the increase in model complexity associated with the radiance distribution model is warranted. However, we show in Section 2.4 that the effects of obstructions to the sky (and sun) as well as the contributions from obstructions to reflected radiation may be added to this model in a rather convenient way. We will also see how such effects may be incorporated into the alternative tilted surface models. But first we conclude the treatment of sky models by considering the prediction of absorption and emission of longwave radiation.

2.3.2 Longwave exchange

Assuming that our surface is grey (that its longwave absorptivity equals its emissivity, ε) and that it is surrounded by an isotropic background (of some mean temperature) then, from the Stefan-Boltzmann law, we may write that the longwave irradiance I_L (W.m^{-2}) is:

$$I_L = \varepsilon \sigma \left(T_{env}^4 - T_s^4 \right) \qquad [2.3.13]$$

in which σ is the Stefan-Boltzmann constant ($\sim 5.67 \times 10^{-8}$), T_s is external surface temperature (K) and T_{env} is an effective surface temperature for the surrounding environment (K). For an isolated site, this is a combination of views to the ground and the sky, such that:

$$T_{env}^4 = T_{sky}^4 \left(1 + \cos\beta \right)/2 + T_g^4 \left(1 - \cos\beta \right)/2 \qquad [2.3.14]$$

All that remains is to estimate the relevant temperatures T_{sky}, T_g.

The temperature of the sky is dependent upon atmospheric molecules, aerosols and cloud cover, the last of these varying in terms of both type and height. While first-principles programs exist that simulate the range of absorption and emission processes, such as the commercially available MODTRAN (Acharya et al, 1998), they are computationally demanding and require inputs that are not widely available. Consequently, a plethora of simplified empirical methods have been developed that relate sky temperature to standard ground-based measurements, such as those of Angstrom (1915), Brunt (1932), Berdahl and Martin (1984) and Unsworth and Monteith (1975). A comprehensive study by Skartveit et al (1996) compared longwave irradiance predictions from 34 such empirical formulae to those from MODTRAN and to measurements, to identify those with the widest range of applicability. From this it was concluded that the formula due to Berdahl and Fromberg (1982), which expresses *cloud free* emittance as a linear function of dew point temperature (T_d) [2.3.15], performs adequately over a wide range of temperature and humidity:

$$\varepsilon_0 = I_{L\downarrow}/\theta T_{sky}^4 = 0.741 + 0.00062 T_d \qquad [2.3.15]$$

The increase in atmospheric emittance beyond its cloudless value ε_0 due to clouds, which after Berdahl and Martin (1984) can be phrased as $(\varepsilon - \varepsilon_0)/(1 - \varepsilon_0)$, is a function of cloud cover, emittance, base height and temperature gradient. Fortunately, in the absence of the relevant measurements, this emittance increase can be expressed to a good approximation (Skartveit et al, 1996), as: $(\varepsilon - \varepsilon_0)/(1 - \varepsilon_0) \approx n^{2.5}$ given the fractional cloud cover n ($n = C/8$, where C is cloud cover in Oktas); so that $\varepsilon_{sky} = \varepsilon_0 + (1 - \varepsilon_0)n^{2.5}$ and $T_{sky}^4 = T_a^4 \varepsilon_{sky}$.

Concerning the ground, a considerable approximation would be to assume that its temperature is similar to that of the local building surfaces, so that it can be ignored and the second term in equation [2.3.14] drops out. A more realistic approach might be to use a form of sol-air temperature; that is a fictitious temperature calculated for a film at the boundary of a solid surface, which considers the key surface thermal exchanges but ignores conduction into the solid. With this approach we have:

$$T_g^4 = \left(T_a + \left(I_\beta + I_L \left\{ +I_E \right\} \right)/h_{co} \right)^4 \qquad [2.3.16]$$

where the optional term in curly brackets I_E corresponds to the surface heat flux due to evapotranspiration from plants (for example grass) and h_{co} is an external surface convective heat transfer coefficient. A correlation often used by the Chartered Institution of Building Services Engineers (CIBSE) is that $h_{co} = 5.8 + 4.1v$, where v is the approximate local air velocity (m.s^{-1}). Now, continuing for the moment with the hypothesis that our surface is isolated, the longwave irradiance in [2.3.16] may be calculated from [2.3.13], where T_{env}^4 simply reduces to T_{sky}^4. However, an initial estimation of surface temperature is required (likewise for our built surface, for which we use output from a dynamic thermal model). For this we may take the air temperature, without introducing considerable error.

2.4 Simplified radiation exchange models

In this section we discuss in some detail a technique based on the processing of images to account for the effects of urban obstructions in diminishing views to the sun and sky. We go on to present simplified models that explicitly account for these effects, as well as the contributions of reflected radiation from obstructions, in their predictions of surface irradiance.

First, however, we briefly discuss some of the earlier attempts to handle the effects of obstructions in reducing incident diffuse sky irradiation. One such technique was 'Skymap', which involved dividing the sky, in the range $\gamma \leq 50$ deg and $|\Delta\alpha| \leq 70$ deg, into tiles and associating with each a pre-computed annual global solar irradiation (kWh/m^2) contribution (we see in Section 2.5.2 how to calculate such maps). By manually plotting the urban scene onto such a diagram it was then possible to estimate the solar irradiation available at a given point (ETSU, 1987), with the contribution from obstructions either not considered or estimated as some fraction of that of the obscured patch.

The first attempts to explicitly model obstructions to the sky seem to be due to Niewenda and Heidt (1996) and Quaschning and Hanitsch (1998), who calculated a sky view factor based on testing intersections with surfaces from rays spawned along a constant set of vectors that span the half of the sky vault that is in front of the receiving surface. Solar obstructions were accounted for by projecting obstructions onto the receiving surface along the sun vector. Neither model accounted for the reflected radiation from obstructions.

Shortly afterwards, however, Teller and Azar (2001) developed an elegant alternative method for predicting irradiation due to the sun and sky as well as a single diffuse reflection at an arbitrary point in 3D space, using their software Townscope. This involves using a stereographic projection of the 3D scene onto a sunpath diagram (Plate 5) to account for direct solar access and isoaire projection (projection that respects the solid angle) to account for sky access (the proportion of white space (sky) being equivalent to the sky factor). Marsh (2004) employs a similar technique, using an isotropic sky but with real sun positions to predict direct and diffuse, though not reflected, annual irradiation in his software Ecotect.

2.4.1 Digital elevation models and image processing

Another elegant result of an exercise in lateral thinking was the method of image processing of digital elevation models (DEMs) introduced by Richens (1997). A DEM is an image in which each pixel corresponds to position in x,y coordinates and the z coordinate is represented on a greyscale ($0 \leq z \leq 255$) (Figure 2.4.1). Each pixel is also associated with a *scale 's'*, which defines the pixel width, and a *calibration 'c'*, which defines the height difference represented by an integer in the greyscale. A 512×512 image in which the pixel scale corresponds to 1m and the calibration parameter to 0.2m represents an urban scene size of $512 \times 512 \times 51$m.

Richen's central algorithm computes shadows, given a sun position. Each pixel is translated and lowered along the opposite vector, so that $\Delta x = \cos \alpha$, $\Delta y = \sin \alpha$ and $\Delta z = c \tan \gamma / s$, each of which are of course rounded to the nearest integer. This process continues until all heights are zero or the remaining pixels have been translated and lowered to the outer limits of the image. If the original DEM is deducted from the union of each of these individual shadow images, after each have been converted to b/w, then we have a projection of the shadows for our urban scene, as shown in Figure 2.4.1c.

If we repeat this process for each hour for the central day of each month of the year, and divide the pixel value by the total number of images (144), then the union of these weighted images indicates the proportion of the year that a given horizontal (floor/roof) surface spends in shade: Figure 2.4.1d.

Richens also used this shadow casting algorithm to compute sky view factors. This simply involves distributing light sources throughout the sky vault and repeating the shadow casting algorithm in a similar manner as to that used for producing the mean shadow image in Figure 2.4.1d. For accuracy reasons, 255 light sources are used (distributed into regions of similar solid angle), corresponding to each pixel's maximum value, so that a value of 0 corresponds to a sky view factor of 1 (and 255 to 0) (Figure 2.4.1e).

Richens (1997) goes on to suggest a procedure by which incident shortwave irradiance due to direct, diffuse sky and first order reflection contributions may be accounted for, for both horizontal *and* vertical surfaces, assuming a simple overcast sky radiance distribution. Diffuse sky irradiance is simply the product of sky view factor and diffuse horizontal irradiance, but the direct and first-order reflected components require additional image processes (see Richens, 1997). However, the vertical irradiance, which also affects the reflected contribution to horizontal irradiance, relates only to parts of walls immediately adjacent either to the floor or to the roof. The accuracy of predictions in both counts is therefore somewhat questionable.

Ratti (2002) and Ratti et al (2003) subsequently used sky view factor as an indicator of incident shortwave and emitted longwave irradiation (as well as heat island intensity) in urban settings. However, as Robinson (2006) demonstrates, the errors in assuming an isotropic sky radiance distribution and in ignoring reflections significantly impair the accuracy of these predictions. Modelling techniques that resolve these limitations are described in the following sections.

In addition to this work, Ratti (2002, 2005) applied the image processing of DEMs to space syntax analysis with rather more success and Ratti et al

(a)

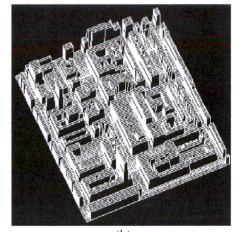

(b)

(c)

(d)

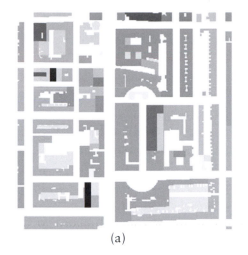

(e)

Figure 2.4.1 (a) DEM of part of central London, (b) corresponding axonometric projection, (c) b/w shadow image in which black pixels are shaded and white are exposed ground/ roof surfaces, (d) the inverse (for ease of interpretation) of a mean shadow image – where pixel value is inversely proportional to the fraction of the year spent in shade, and (e) a sky view factor image

Source: a, b and e Cambridge University, The Martin Centre for Architectural and Urban Studies; c and d Author

(2000) used geometric parameters derived from DEMs as input to a domestic energy model to explore relationships between urban texture energy consumption in non-domestic buildings (see Chapter 5).

2.4.2 Canyon models

An alternative approach to Richens' image processing, this time due to Robinson and Stone (2004a), is to abstract the geometry of buildings in the vicinity of our receiving plane, to represent an equivalent street canyon, for which the angle of elevation of the opposing canyon wall (its urban horizon angle) u produces the same obstruction view factor as the real skyline (Figure 2.4.2); and likewise the wall of the canyon of our receiving plane, as seen from the centre of the opposing canyon wall.

Isotropic canyon model

Now from inspection of [2.3.1] above it is apparent that, in the isotropic case, the incident irradiance on a surface of slope β is simply the product of diffuse horizontal irradiance and the view factor to the sky from this surface. We may thus define an equivalent sky view factor for the case in which views to the sky are additionally diminished by obstructions and not just due to the receiving surface's slope. Indeed if we can abstract our adjacent obstructions into an equivalent obstruction skyline (Figure 2.4.2) we may represent our obstructions as an increase in slope. This combination of skyline and slope could be derived by numerical integration of results from tests of obstructions to discrete regions of the sky of known solid angle, thus:

$$\frac{1}{2}\cos(\beta + u) = \frac{1}{\pi}\iint_{S}\cos\theta.d\omega \qquad\qquad [2.4.1]$$

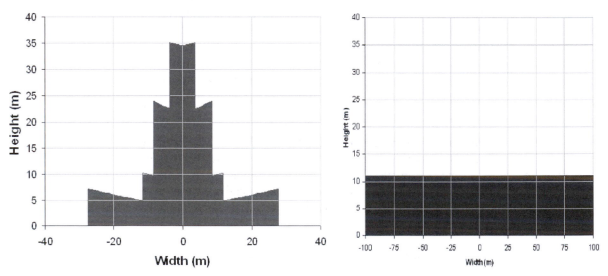

Figure 2.4.2 (a) Hypothetical skyline and (b) equivalent abstracted canyon

Alternatively one could attempt to visually estimate the urban horizon angle.

From [2.4.1] it is clear that the irradiance incident at a point on our receiving plane due to the sky is simply:

$$I_{d\beta} = I_{db}\left(1 + \cos(\beta + u)\right)/2 \qquad [2.4.2]$$

Thus we have a straightforward way of diminishing the sky irradiance that is incident at our receiving point due to the presence of urban obstructions. To this we need to add the contributions due to diffuse reflections from these urban obstructions. Now these obstructions may be classified in terms of those that lie above the horizontal plane relative to our calculation point and those that lie below (Figure 2.4.3). The reflected irradiance due to upper obstructions $I_{\rho U,\beta}$ of diffuse surface reflectance ρ and incident global irradiance $I_{g\beta}$ is:

$$I_{\rho U,\beta} = I_{g\beta}\rho\left[\cos\beta - \cos(\beta + u)\right]/2 \qquad [2.4.3a]$$

And that due to lower obstructions $(I_{\rho L\beta})$ is:

$$I_{\rho L,\beta} = I_{g\beta}\rho\left[\cos(\beta - u^*) - \cos\beta\right]/2 \qquad [2.4.3b]$$

The final contribution to the irradiance of our receiving surface is due to reflections from the ground $(I_{\rho G\beta})$:

$$I_{\rho G,\beta} = I_{g\beta}\rho\left[1 - \cos(\beta - u^*)\right]/2 \qquad [2.4.4]$$

Equations [2.4.2] to [2.4.4] can be applied to determine the irradiance incident on both walls of this hypothetical canyon due to the sky and diffuse reflections from the canyon walls. For the first reflection, the incident global irradiance terms in [2.4.3] to [2.4.4] result from the sky and sun only. When dealing with the sky contribution it may be reasonable to assume that the irradiance incident at a point at the centre of a receiving surface is a good approximation of the average that it received over the whole surface. This is not necessarily the case for the direct contribution, which may easily be an order of magnitude greater than that due to the sky. It is thus useful to determine the proportion of the receiving surface that is directly insolated, so that the mean direct irradiance is $I_{b\beta} = \sigma_t I_{bh}\cos\theta/\sin\gamma$. This sun view factor σ_t at time t may be found by discretizing the surface and checking for intersections between the *real* skyline and the sun so that σ_t is the ratio of the number of cells at which there is an unobstructed view to the sun to the total number of cells. $I_{g\beta}$, for this first reflection, is then found from this view factor-weighted direct contribution and that due to [2.4.2] above.

The diffuse irradiance incident on the ground is a special case, in that knowledge of both sides of the canyon is required. For this the irradiance is given by:

$$I_{d,gnd} = I_{db}\left(\cos\delta_1 + \cos\delta_2\right)/2 + \rho_1 I_{g\beta,1}\left(1 - \cos\delta_1\right)/2 + \rho_2 I_{g\beta,2}\left(1 - \cos\delta_2\right)/2 \qquad [2.4.5]$$

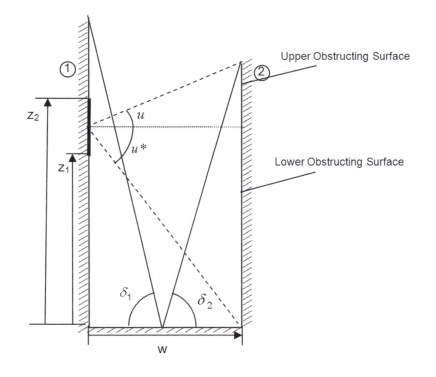

Figure 2.4.3 Geometry of an abstracted canyon for the diffuse reflection calculation

Note: The canyon is comprised of a vertical reflecting plane 2, a sloped plane 1 which includes a receiving surface and the ground of the canyon, of width w.

For subsequent reflections the irradiance on each canyon surface depends on that of the other surfaces, so that an iterative technique is required.

There are, however, some geometric exceptions to this model, which limit its applicability for non-vertical receiving surfaces, as discussed by Robinson and Stone (2004a).

Anisotropic canyon model

As noted in Section 2.3.1, the Perez tilted surface model consists of three components: isotropic background, circumsolar brightening and horizon brightening. Each of these terms may be adjusted in turn, as follows:

- The background term may be adjusted in a similar fashion as with the isotropic model [2.4.2].
- The circumsolar term may be multiplied by a Boolean operator B to account for whether views to the sun are obstructed or not by the real skyline relative to our calculation point.
- A scaling factor S may be introduced into the final term to account for the proportion of the horizon band that is visible from our calculation point[6]:

$$S = \min\left[0, (b - \bar{u})/b\right], \text{ where } \bar{u} = \frac{2}{\pi} \int_{\alpha_w}^{\alpha_w - \pi/2} u \cos\alpha \, . d\alpha, \text{ where } b \text{ is the elevation}$$

of the horizon band, normally taken to be $5\pi/180$ (rad).

The Perez tilted surface model then takes the form:

$$I_{d\beta} = I_{db} \left[\left(1 - F_1\right) \cdot \left[1 + \cos\left(\beta + u\right)\right] \middle/ 2 + B \cdot F_1\, a_0/a_1 + S \cdot F_2 \sin\beta \right] \qquad [2.4.6]$$

Contributions from reflecting surfaces may be solved using the procedure described above for the isotropic canyon model ([2.4.3] to [2.4.5]). Although [2.4.5] does not account for any horizon and circumsolar sources that may be visible, the associated errors in this approximation are not likely to be significant.

Accuracy

The principal source of error in these simple canyon models is that sky vault anisotropy is either ignored or concentrated into a circumsolar point source and a horizon band. Since much of the horizon band is likely to be obscured in urban settings, treatment of anisotropy tends to be restricted to whether or not the solar point source is visible. In reality the absence of background scattering, and the fact that the circumsolar region may be large in bright sky conditions, may be such that these errors are significant. Of less significance is the fact that, although we can derive a canyon geometry of equivalent view factor to the real scene geometry, the uniform radiance of this geometry is calculated for the surface centroid. In this way neither the true obstruction radiance nor the angle of incidence from elements of the real geometry to our receiving point are respected.

In order to judge this, Robinson and Stone (2004a) prepared a simple scene composed of two identical parallel planes of varying height separated by a reflecting street (as in Figure 2.4.1 above). They compared predictions for this scene using the canyon models with those of a detailed Monte Carlo ray tracing program called RADIANCE[7] (see Section 2.5), using the add-in RADIANCE module *gendaylit* (Figure 2.4.4).

From this it is clear that in both cases the above simplifications have a rather profound impact on the quality of predictions. These discrepancies are exaggerated in the case of a north-facing surface in which the contribution of direct solar irradiance (which may readily be predicted with good accuracy) is limited.

Root mean squared (RMS) errors in the two cases are between 10 and 25 per cent.

2.4.3 Simplified radiosity algorithm (SRA)

As noted in Section 2.3.1, if we have some set of p sky patches, each of which subtends a solid angle Φ (Sr) and has radiance R (Wm^{-2}Sr^{-1}) then, given the mean angle of incidence θ (radians) between the patch and our plane, together with the proportion of the patch that can be seen σ ($0 \leq \sigma \leq 1$), we have a general solution for direct sky irradiance (Wm^{-2}) in the form of [2.3.12]. Note that the quantity $\Phi\sigma\cos\theta$ in [2.3.12] may be treated as a single quantity obtained by numerical integration of $\cos\theta \cdot d\Phi$ throughout each sky patch, for example by post-processing rendered scenes from each receiving point (as in Robinson and Stone, 2005). Similarly, views may be rendered from the sun

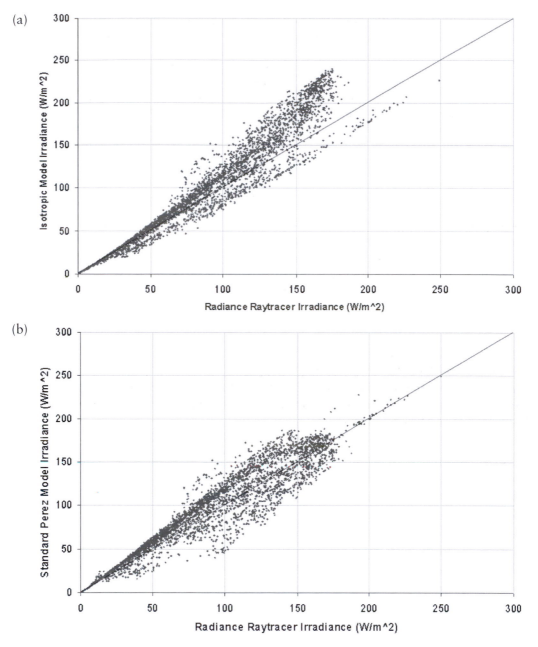

Figure 2.4.4 (a) Comparison of hourly results of anisotropic and (b) isotropic canyon models with RADIANCE for a north-facing receiving surface in hypothetical urban scene

position and the images processed to determine the proportion of each surface that is visible (defined approximately as the ratio of the number of pixels that are visible, to the number that would be visible if the surface was unobstructed) to calculate the corresponding solar contribution to surface irradiance (see

Section 2.4.2) (Plate 6). With the sky and solar contributions defined, all that remains is to account for the contributions from reflecting surfaces $I_{\rho\beta}$. For this we have a similar form of equation that is used for the sky contribution, with the exception that now we sum the contributions from the obscured proportions of patches from two hemispheres (so that there are $2p$ patches): a vault for occlusions that lie above the horizontal plane and an upside-down vault for occlusions that lie below the horizontal plane:

$$I_{\rho\beta} = \sum_{i=1}^{2p} \left(R^* \Phi \omega \cos\theta \right)_i \qquad [2.4.7]$$

Note that ω in [2.4.7] corresponds to the obstruction view factor and R^* to the corresponding surface radiance. In fact it is here that we see the key simplification in this algorithm: the obstruction radiance in [2.4.7] corresponds to that of the *dominant* obstruction – defined simply as that which contributes the most to $\Phi\omega\cos\theta$ (note that $\Phi\omega\cos\theta$ is also obtained by numerical integration of $\cos\theta \cdot d\Phi$ throughout the obstructed region of each patch). This assumption, that the radiance distribution within the obstructed region of a patch is uniform and may be represented by that of the dominant surface, significantly improves the computational efficiency of the algorithm – reducing the number of energy exchange pathways from $O(n^2)$ to $O(n)$.

The dominant surface itself can be readily identified by performing a scene rendering in which every surface is uniquely coloured (so that for all *r,g,b* permutations we have 256^3-1 available combinations; with one of these colours being reserved for the sky). The radiance of this and every other obstruction is obtained, assuming that our surfaces are Lambertian (they reflect uniformly throughout the hemisphere), from:

$$R = \left(I_{b\beta} + \sum_{i=1}^{p} \left(R\Phi\sigma\cos\theta \right)_i + \sum_{j=1}^{2p} \left(R^*\Phi\omega\cos\theta \right)_j \right) \rho \Big/ \pi \qquad [2.4.8]$$

where the three terms in brackets are the solar, sky and reflected contributions to the incident surface irradiance. For the first reflection we need solve only for the first two terms in [2.4.8], but for subsequent reflections the radiance of our receiving surface depends on that of other surfaces, which themselves may depend on our receiving surface.

Now, combining [2.3.11], [2.3.12], [2.4.7] and [2.4.8] above, we may write that:

$$\underline{I_d} = A\underline{I_g} + B\underline{R} \qquad [2.4.9]$$

where $\underline{I_d}$ and $\underline{I_g}$ are vectors of incident diffuse and global irradiance, $\underline{R}$ is a vector giving the radiance of each sky patch and $\underline{I_g} = \underline{I_b} + \underline{I_d}$, in which $\underline{I_b}$ is a vector of incident beam irradiance ($I_{b\beta}$ for each surface).

The matrix A in [2.4.9], which is square and has a dimension of n^2, describes how the irradiance incident on each surface is eventually distributed to the other n surfaces in the scene:

$$A = \begin{bmatrix} \dfrac{\rho_1 k_{1,1}}{\pi} & \dfrac{\rho_2 k_{1,2}}{\pi} & \cdots & \dfrac{\rho_n k_{1,n}}{\pi} \\[2mm] \dfrac{\rho_1 k_{2,1}}{\pi} & \ddots & & \vdots \\[1mm] \vdots & & \ddots & \vdots \\[1mm] \dfrac{\rho_1 k_{n,1}}{\pi} & \dfrac{\rho_2 k_{n,2}}{\pi} & \cdots & \dfrac{\rho_n k_{n,n}}{\pi} \end{bmatrix} \qquad [2.4.10]$$

where ρ_i is the reflectance of surface i, and $k_{i,j}$ describes a scaling factor for the contribution of the energy reflected *from* surface j *to* surface i. If surface j is the dominant surface obstructing m sky patches when viewed from surface i, denoted by $x_1, x_2 \ldots x_m$, then $k_{i,j} = \sum_{k=1}^{m} \Phi_{i,x_k} \left(1 - \sigma_{i,x_k} - \omega_{self,x_k} \right) \cos\theta_{i,x_k}$, where σ_{i,x_k} is the view factor from surface i to sky patch x_k and Φ_{i,x_k} is the solid angle of sky patch x_k, as seen by surface i. ω_{self,x_k} is the obstruction view factor to sky patch x_k, due to full or partial occlusion of this patch by the receiving surface itself (some or all of the patch may be behind the receiving surface).

Matrix B describes the contribution from each sky patch (of unit radiance) to the irradiance incident on each surface within the scene and thus has a dimension of n × p:

$$B = \begin{bmatrix} \Phi_{1,1}\sigma_{1,1}\cos\theta_{1,1} & \Phi_{1,2}\sigma_{1,2}\cos\theta_{1,2} & \cdots & \Phi_{1,p}\sigma_{1,p}\cos\theta_{1,p} \\[1mm] \Phi_{2,1}\sigma_{2,1}\cos\theta_{2,1} & \ddots & & \vdots \\[1mm] \vdots & & \ddots & \vdots \\[1mm] \Phi_{n,1}\sigma_{n,1}\cos\theta_{n,1} & \Phi_{n,2}\sigma_{n,2}\cos\theta_{n,2} & \cdots & \Phi_{n,p}\sigma_{n,p}\cos\theta_{n,p} \end{bmatrix} \qquad [2.4.11]$$

In principle [2.4.9] can be reformulated and solved by matrix inversion (as explained by Robinson and Stone, 2004a). But matrix A is extremely sparse, containing less than n × p non-zero elements; potentially significantly less since some surfaces may act as dominant obstructions to multiple patches (represented by the coefficient $k_{i,j}$). Matrix B is likewise sparse, containing fewer than 145n non-zero elements, depending upon the number of fully occluded sky patches. Since matrix-vector multiplications are relatively inexpensive in these cases, it is more efficient to solve for [2.4.9] iteratively. Initially the vector I_b should be calculated; likewise the product $B\underline{R}$, so that for the first reflection [2.4.9] reduces to: $I_g = I_b + B\underline{R}$, whereas for subsequent reflections the contribution of I_d to I_g will contain reflected contributions.

Finally, it is worth noting that by replacing I_x by E_x and R by L in [2.4.9] we can also predict the incident diffuse illuminance throughout our scene.

Accuracy

This model is considerably more complex and is thus more computationally demanding than the previous models. But it is also potentially far more accurate, because the true geometry of the urban scene is retained in the calculation, not only with respect to sky and direct solar irradiance, but also for the reflected irradiance (for which we account for infinite reflections if we solve our matrices by inversion). The only key simplifications made in this algorithm are that: the surfaces are Lambertian (diffusely reflecting); and the average radiance of the occluded region of a sky patch is equal to that calculated at the centre of the main (largest) occluding surface within this patch.

The implications of the above simplifications were tested by Robinson and Stone (2004a) for a simple scene composed of two identical parallel planes of varying height separated by a reflecting street (as in Figure 2.4.1 above), by once again comparing predictions with those of the detailed Monte Carlo ray tracing program RADIANCE.[8] Presented in Figure 2.4.5 is a comparison of

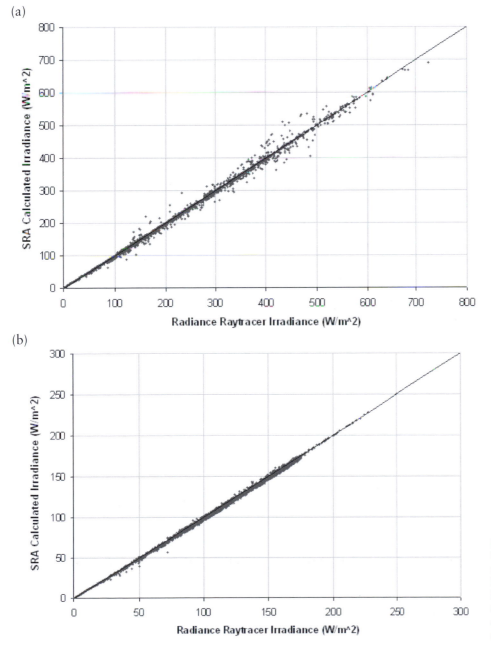

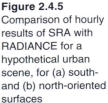

Figure 2.4.5
Comparison of hourly results of SRA with RADIANCE for a hypothetical urban scene, for (a) south- and (b) north-oriented surfaces

hourly results at a point in this scene, using UK climate data. From this it is clear that the agreement is excellent in both cases (and far superior to the results obtained from the simple canyon models), but that there is slightly more discrepancy for the south-oriented surface, due principally to the approximate way in which the solar view factors are calculated.[9] However, these modest errors are acceptable for most urban environmental modelling purposes.

Nevertheless, in more complex urban scenes the second source of error mentioned above may be exaggerated in the case of surfaces (especially large surfaces) for which the radiance varies significantly. Such spatial variations in surface radiance can be particularly prevalent for large surfaces that oppose a complex urban skyline. For this reason it is sensible to institute some form of pre-process, in which we have an approximate calculation of direct (solar and sky) surface irradiance distribution throughout a surface, to inform a process of splitting this surface into the smallest possible number of sub-surfaces that pass some criteria according to which surfaces are split. Using a simplistic procedure in which surfaces are split to yield sub-surfaces of acceptable vertical and horizontal sky view factor, Robinson and Stone (2005) achieve the following result as compared with RADIANCE (Figure 2.4.6 and Plate 7).

(a)

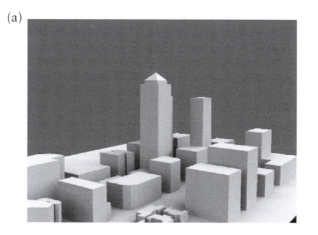

Annual Irradiance (MWh)

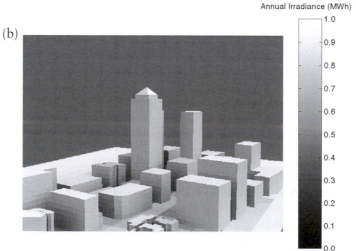

(b)

Figure 2.4.6 Annual shortwave irradiation (MWh.m⁻²) throughout a model of Canary Wharf in London, UK. (a) Results from RADIANCE and (b) the SRA for artificially split 10m × 10m surface

The RADIANCE simulations take more than five orders of magnitude longer, so that for urban-scale simulations in which surfaces are predominantly diffuse-reflecting the SRA appears to perform considerably better. Crucially in the context of this book, the SRA is more appropriate for integration with simulation tools dedicated to the modelling of urban-scale resource (energy, water and waste) flows. Furthermore, although the SRA is mathematically more sophisticated than either of the canyon models, the additional computational overhead is reasonably small, so that the increase in modelling complexity is warranted.[10]

Longwave irradiance

In Section 2.3.2 we presented a simplified model for the prediction of longwave radiation exchange, based on the difference in surface and environmental temperature, each expressed to the fourth power. But [2.3.14] for calculating environmental temperature supposes that the receiving surface has a completely unobstructed view of the sky, which is seldom the case in the urban context.

Fortunately, we may use the view information calculated for shortwave radiation exchange calculations (above) to calculate this effective environmental temperature thus:

$$T^{*4} = \frac{1}{\pi}\left(T_{sky}^4 \sum_{i=1}^{p}\left(\Phi\sigma\cos\theta\right)_i + \sum_{j=1}^{2p}\left(\Phi\omega\cos\theta T_s^4\right)_j \right) \qquad [2.4.12]$$

This then is a solid-angle weighted effective environment temperature, with the first term in brackets representing the sky temperature and the second term the adjacent surface temperature. The former may be estimated using [2.3.15] and the second term using an estimate of ground surface temperature [2.3.16] and/or of the surface temperature of the building envelope. Given the small relative temperature difference between the emitting and receiving surfaces, we may use the surface temperature predicted by a dynamic building thermal model for the preceding time step for the latter.

2.5 Simulation techniques

A more general approach to the analysis of daylight and solar radiation potential in urban settings involves the use of detailed simulation programs. Using such programs, the direct solar and sky contributions may be resolved with similar accuracy to the SRA, but the contributions from surface reflections, both specular and diffuse, may be accurately resolved for scenes of arbitrary complexity and detail. There are two approaches to numerical simulation of radiation exchange: radiosity and ray tracing.

The former essentially involves discretizing the surfaces within the computational domain and solving initially for exchanges between light source(s) and receiving cells and then for successive exchanges between these cells, assuming diffuse reflection characteristics (see Cohen and Wallace (1993) for a detailed explanation). The basis is similar to that of the SRA but without the simplification that obstructions to obscured regions of sky are lumped and represented by the radiance of the dominant surface in this region of sky.

Ray tracing techniques may be either forward or backward. In the backwards case, rays are spawned from surfaces within an observer's visual field (the image to be rendered) initially towards light sources and subsequently within the ambient environment, based on Monte Carlo sampling. This is a recursive process, so that once a reflecting surface is encountered, this too spawns rays. The process continues according to predefined image quality settings (such as minimum distance between sample points – affecting interpolation – and number of ambient bounces) (see Ward Larsen and Shakespeare (1997) for a detailed explanation). Numerous software tools have evolved that utilize radiosity and ray tracing algorithms and, in fact, hybrids of them. Several studies have compared the more commonly used programs on the basis of accuracy (Mardaljevic, 1995) and usability (Ashmore and Richens, 2001), from which the open source ray tracing program RADIANCE (Ward Larsen and Shakespeare, 1997), and interfaces to it, consistently emerges as the best performer, on the basis of accuracy and versatility.

The power of numerical simulation has recently been exploited to excellent effect in the current context in the form of predicting solar irradiation. In one early study, this was based on performing hourly simulations (Kovach and Shmid, 1996), but subsequent work focussed on ways of reducing the computational expense of this useful form of analysis. These are based either on statistical sky reduction and the extrapolation of results (by post-processing) to create a full hourly results set or by pre-processing of a cumulative sky radiance distribution.

2.5.1 Statistical sky reduction

Inspired by his earlier work on the use of daylight coefficients as an efficient means for producing time-series interior daylighting predictions (Mardaljevic, 1999), Mardaljevic introduced a related technique to facilitate the prediction of surface irradiation in urban settings (Mardaljevic and Rylatt, 2000, 2003).

First, the sky is discretized into bins of equal range in azimuth and altitude (8° by default). Then the number N of occasions that the sun is within each bin is calculated for the period of interest (for Leicester in the UK this results in b=179 active bins for a year, based on a 15 minute time resolution). A RADIANCE simulation is then performed for a *unit radiance* light source located at each of these sun positions. A similar process to that described above is repeated for the anisotropic diffuse sky calculation. Since the region of circumsolar brightening is large relative to the sun, a cruder discretization is appropriate (for example 16°). A RADIANCE simulation is performed for a sky radiance distribution (using the CIE intermittent sky model) based on the mean sun position in each bin and *unit diffuse horizontal irradiance*. One final simulation is performed to account for overcast sky conditions, also with respect to unit diffuse horizontal irradiance. The total irradiation I^T (Wh) for the period of interest is then determined, for each pixel in the simulation image, as follows:

$$I^T = \Delta t \sum_{b=1}^{n}\left[\left(I_s R\right) + \left(I_{an}\, f I_{dh}\right) + I_{ov}\left(1-f\right)I_{dh}\right]_b \qquad [2.5.1]$$

where R is the radiance of the sun, n corresponds to the total number of time steps, f is a clearness factor that governs a blending between intermittent and overcast skies (equivalent to $C/8$ as used in the longwave model described in Section 2.3.2 above), I (s, an, ov) is the irradiance from the three unit (ir)radiance simulations (sun, anisotropic and overcast, respectively) and Δt is the integration interval (for example 0.25h).

One of the attractions of this approach is that it is relatively straightforward to construct time series results for the scene being simulated, and these may even be split into solar and sky components.

2.5.2 Cumulative sky modelling

The method of statistical sky reduction involves the extrapolation of results from separate simulations for the direct and diffuse contributions to incident irradiance to build up a set of results for each time step throughout the period of interest – typically a year. If our purpose is simply to predict the total incident irradiation during this period, so that we are not interested in the temporal distribution of results, then an alternative is simply to perform a single simulation using a sky that represents the cumulative annual radiance distribution ($Wh.m^{-2}.Sr^{-1}$): a pre-process as opposed to a post-process.

This approach was first introduced by Compagnon and Raydan (2000) and Compagnon (2004) to study the potential for the use of solar energy conversion technologies in cities. Compagnon's technique involved creating a virtual sky vault defined by a series of round light sources. This is beneficial in the sense that only RADIANCE's direct calculation is used, so that it is efficient. A downside is that the means for subdividing partially obscured light sources in RADIANCE is a little crude, with corresponding implications for accuracy. An alternative technique of defining a conventional sky in which the radiance distribution is discretized (Robinson and Stone, 2004b) may thus be preferable.

For the diffuse component of the sky radiance distribution, this simply involves using available climate data as input to a radiance distribution model to calculate the sky radiance at the centre of each patch into which the sky is discretized, according to some scheme. In line with the SRA in Section 2.4.3, Robinson and Stone discretized the sky according to the method of Tregenza and calculated the radiance at the centre of each of the 145 patches using the model due to Perez et al (1993) according to [2.3.11] above. These results are then aggregated for each of the n hours in the year in which there is a non-zero global horizontal irradiance, so that for the ith patch, $R_i^T = \sum_{b=1}^{n} R_{i,b}$ (Figure 2.5.1a). The format of the RADIANCE files that describe such a sky is presented in Appendix A2.1.

For the direct component there are two possibilities. One option is to create a global as opposed to solely diffuse discretized sky radiance distribution. This simply involves adding to the total diffuse radiance that is due to the sun, in which case we have that $R_i^T = \sum_{b=1}^{n} R_{i(sky),b} + \sum_{b=1}^{n} I_b / \Phi_i$ in which the second term

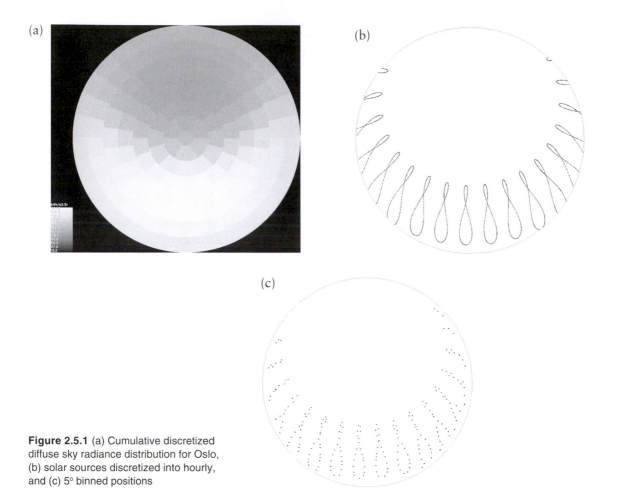

Figure 2.5.1 (a) Cumulative discretized diffuse sky radiance distribution for Oslo, (b) solar sources discretized into hourly, and (c) 5° binned positions

corresponds to the quotient of the beam irradiance $I_b = \left(I_{gh} - I_{dh}\right)/\sin\gamma$ and the patch solid angle – so that the radiance of the sun is essentially smeared over the entire patch.

The alternative is to define the position of a set of light sources, each corresponding to the position and radiance of the sun. In reality this aggregate solar source would be a continuous band (as the earth rotates *continuously* about the sun). It is more convenient, however, to discretize the sunpath, for example according to hourly sun positions (Figure 2.5.1b) or to bins in range of altitude and azimuth (5° in Figure 2.5.1c). The coordinates are defined by a 3D vector and the source radiance is defined in the same way as that for the direct component of the sky patch (so that $R_{sun} = I_b/\Phi_{sun}$), with the exception that the solid angle of the sun is ~0.222Sr.

2.5.3 Applications

From the above it should be apparent that the two most accurate approaches for simulating shortwave radiation exchange in urban environments are the

SRA and detailed simulation tools. The SRA was designed for integration with building and urban energy simulation programs, which do not require very fine spatial resolution in their treatment of solar irradiation incident on building envelopes or solar energy conversion systems, but do require fast calculation times. For such applications, the SRA reaches a very good balance between accuracy and computational cost. Detailed simulation programs, by contrast, are not constrained in the spatial resolution with which they simulate radiation exchange and most of them can simulate both diffusely and specularly reflecting surfaces, but these programs are significantly more computationally expensive than the SRA. But for applications that require fine spatial resolution – particularly where visualization is important – and/or the treatment of specularly reflecting materials, there really is no alternative.

As noted above, the most popular detailed simulation program is the ray tracing program RADIANCE, because it is both open source and highly versatile. In the following we therefore present some applications of RADIANCE to evaluate the potential for solar radiation utilization in urban settings using cumulative skies to accelerate the computational task.

Irradiation distributions

As part of an applied research project funded by the Swiss Federal Office of Energy to investigate the potential for investments in solar energy conversion systems to reduce net urban energy demands, three Swiss city districts were chosen as case studies. These included the densely populated 59ha district of Matthäus in Basel, the 36ha district of Bellevaux in Lausanne and the low density 998ha district of Meyrin in Geneva (Robinson et al, 2005) (Figure 2.5.2).

Using a cumulative sky, it is relatively straightforward and inexpensive to simulate the annual solar irradiation distribution throughout an urban scene, with respect to a given view point and direction, and to visualize renderings of the corresponding results. Indeed the RADIANCE program *falsecolour* can be used to output images in which each pixel corresponds to a radiation quantity (Plate 8). We can also control the way in which falsecolour does this. In Plate 8b for example, pixels that have a value of below $800kWh/m^2$ are plotted on a greyscale, whereas those exceeding this threshold are coloured yellow. This irradiation threshold is thought to correspond well to the condition at which photovoltaic panels become economically viable for integration with the building envelope.

But as well as being able to visualize which surfaces exceed a given threshold, it is also useful to be able to quantify the total area of surface throughout a given scene that exceeds this threshold. For this, Compagnon (2004) developed a very useful accompaniment to RADIANCE. Called PPF this discretizes the surfaces describing our scene into a simple Cartesian mesh. A calculation point is placed at the centre of each cell and slightly offset from the surface. This point, which is oriented along the normal vector of this surface, is also associated with the cell surface area. PPF then calls the RADIANCE program *rtrace*, to which it parses the coordinates of each viewpoint and view direction vector, and aggregates the results.

Shown in Figure 2.5.3, for example, are irradiation histograms corresponding to our three city districts. From these it is immediately apparent that roof

(a)

(b)

(c)

(d)

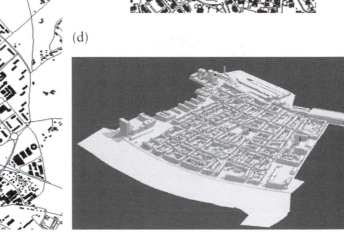

(e)

(f)

Figure 2.5.2 The city districts of (a) Matthäus (Basel), (b) Bellevaux (Lausanne) and (c) Meyrin (Geneva); and 3D models of (d) Matthäus (Basel), (e) Bellevaux (Lausanne) and (f) Meyrin (Geneva)

Source: Robinson et al (2005)

(a)

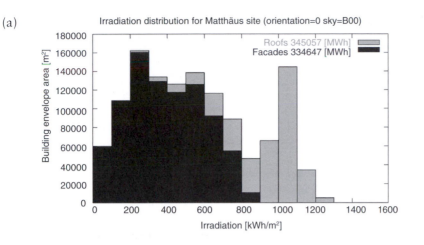

(b)

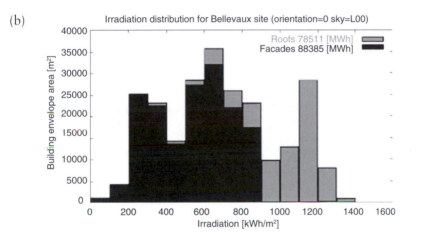

(c)

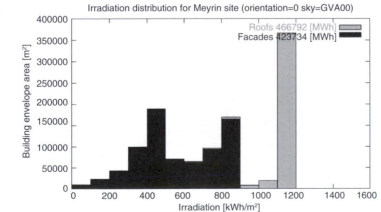

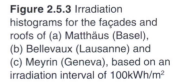

Figure 2.5.3 Irradiation histograms for the façades and roofs of (a) Matthäus (Basel), (b) Bellevaux (Lausanne) and (c) Meyrin (Geneva), based on an irradiation interval of 100kWh/m²

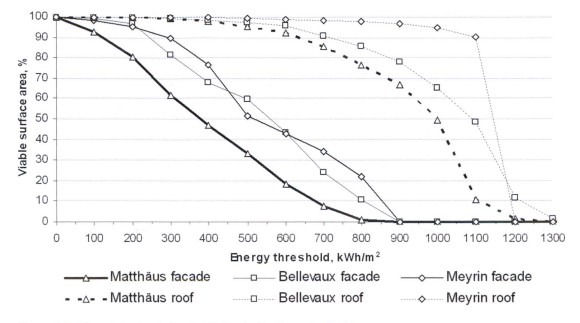

Figure 2.5.4 Cumulative irradiation distribution for the three city districts

surfaces have considerably greater potential for the exploitation of available solar energy than do façades, as one would expect. It also seems as though the solar energy potential of the densely populated district of Matthäus, whether for façades or for roofs, is considerably more constrained relative to that of the low density district of Meyrin.

The situation is clearer if we plot the cumulative surface area, expressed as a percentage of total, for which our irradiation bins are exceeded (Figure 2.5.4). For example, the theoretical potential for the conversion of energy using solar cells is around 1 per cent, 11 per cent and 22 per cent of the available façade area in Matthäus, Bellevaux and Meyrin respectively; whereas this increases to 77 per cent, 86 per cent and 98 per cent for roofs. Site density therefore has an important impact on the potential to utilize available solar radiation, particularly with respect to façades (with corresponding implications for a building's thermal energy balance) (see Robinson et al (2005) for further discussion).

2.6 Conclusions

In this chapter we described the range of methods that have been developed during the last three decades to model the availability of solar radiation in the urban context as well as the potential to utilize this available solar radiation. We examined simple geometric models for calculating sky and solar access, projected shadows and the irradiance incident on receiving surfaces. We also described considerably more elaborate models for predicting the incident shortwave irradiance (and indeed emitted longwave irradiance) that account for the anisotropy of the sky vault as well as occlusions to this vault and the contributions of occlusions to the sun and sky to the reflected radiation incident on receiving surfaces.

The two most accurate approaches for simulating shortwave radiation exchange in urban environments are the SRA and detailed simulation programs, whether radiosity or ray tracing based. The SRA is well suited for integration into building and urban energy simulation software and such an example is described later in this book (Chapter 5); whereas detailed simulation programs are more suitable for standalone applications where a detailed representation of the spatial distribution of incident irradiation is of interest.

Appendix A2.1

As with any RADIANCE simulation in which we make use of an ambient light source, it is necessary to describe a sky in a .rad file. In Figure A2.1 we see the three basic components: the first is the function that is used to define the radiance distribution; the second defines the glow material from which the sky is composed, with each of the RGB (red, green, blue) channels set to unity (this equal weighting produces a grey sky); the third simply defines the geometry of our hemispheric sky vault.

```
void brightfunc skyfunc
2 skybright ./cumulativesky.cal
0
0
skyfunc glow sky_glow
0
0
4 1 1 1 0
sky_glow source sky
0
0
4 0 0 1 180
```

Figure A2.1 Definition of sky.rad for cumulative sky modelling using RADIANCE

The file sky.rad refers to a RADIANCE.cal file, which contains a set of instructions written using a programming language that is native to RADIANCE. This .cal file, cumulativesky.cal (Figure A2.2), first converts the vector of the outgoing ray (one that has been spawned from a particular surface and intersected the sky vault) into an azimuth and an altitude. This information is then used to identify the corresponding patch, according to its range in azimuth and the relevant band in altitude (or *row* in this context). The cumulative radiance is then associated with this ray (or rather the skybright function).

A module for RADIANCE called *gencumulativesky* can be used to create the above .cal file given an appropriately formatted climate file. A tutorial

```
skybright=row0+row1+row2+row3+row4+row5+row6+row7;

row0=if(and(alt-0, 12-alt),select(floor(0.5+az/12.00)+1,
        147487.5,
        148490.2,
        .
        .
        .
row6=if(and(alt-72, 84-alt),select(floor(0.5+az/60.00)+1,
        143473.5,
        155179.4,
        184145.3,
        201720.8,
        183553.0,
        154574.5,
        143473.5),0);

row7=if(alt-84,165902.9,0);

alt=asin(Dz)*180/PI;

az=if(azi,azi,azi+360);
azi=atan2(Dx,Dy)*180/PI;
```

Figure A2.2 Definition of cumulativesky.cal

describing the use of gencumulativesky is described in Robinson (2011) and gencumulativesky itself can be downloaded from the website: https://documents. epfl.ch/groups/u/ur/urbansimulation/www/GenCumSky/GenCumSky.zip. It is also available as part of a plugin to the 3D modelling software Rhino developed by Lagios et al (2010) at: www.DIVA-for-Rhino.com

Notes

1   So that we essentially have a two-band (shortwave and longwave) model of radiation exchange.
2   For a comprehensive explanation of these phenomena the reader is referred to the following excellent website: www.analemma.com
3   In physics it is normal to use the symbols to θ, ϕ represent the coordinates of some emitting surface relative to some point on a receiving surface, where theta is the zenith angle and phi the azimuth. In architecture and engineering it is more common to use γ, α where gamma is altitude and alpha the azimuth [or occasionally vice versa]. We adopt the latter convention γ, α = altitude, azimuth in this book.
4   Alternatively, and more laboriously, we can manually draw our obstructions onto such a diagram, taking care to perform cosine correction of the obstructions' altitude.
5   With the exception that the functions c,d for the first bin are calculated directly thus:

$$c = \exp\left[\left(\Delta\left(c_1 + c_2 Z\right)\right)^{c_3}\right] - c_4 \text{ and } d = \exp\left[\Delta\left(d_1 + d_2 Z\right)\right] + d_3 + \Delta d_4.$$

6   Note that the function F2 in the Perez tilted surface model may be negative under overcast conditions, corresponding not to a negative energy contribution from the horizon but rather to a reduction in zenith brightness. In such circumstances it is not appropriate to use the above scaling factor. Instead Robinson and Stone suggest an alternative scaling based on an overcast sky luminance distribution integrated over the visible range of the vault:

$$S = \frac{\int_u^{\pi-\beta}(1+2\sin\gamma)d\gamma}{\pi-\beta-u} \cdot \frac{\pi-\beta}{\int_0^{\pi-\beta}(1+2\sin\gamma)d\gamma} = \frac{(\pi-\beta-u)+2(\cos\beta+\cos u)}{(\pi-\beta)+2(\cos\beta+1)} \cdot \frac{\pi-\beta}{\pi-\beta-u}$$

7   In fact the surfaces in the RADIANCE model were also defined as Lambertian (i.e. the specularity and roughness were set to zero), so that comparisons concentrated on the quality of approximations in the radiosity calculation. This was deemed reasonable as surfaces in urban settings do tend to be mainly diffusely reflecting.

8   See note 7.

9   In this early version of the SRA, the scene was rendered and the solar view factors calculated at hourly intervals (based on solar time) but only for the central day of each month. Two-dimensional Lagrangian interpolation was used to extrapolate to local time for all days in each month.

10   There is also considerable potential for accelerating the radiation model, particularly in respect of the pre-processing of view factors, by parallelizing the code.

References

Acharya, P. K., Berk, A., Bernstein, L. S., Matthew, M. W., Adler-Golden, S. M., Robertson, D. C., Anderson, G. P., Chetwynd, J. H., Kneizys, F. X., Shettle, E. P., Abreu, L. W., Gallery, W. O., Selby, J. E. A., Clough, S. A. (1998) *MODTRAN User's Manual Versions 3.7 and 4.0*, Air Force Research Laboratory, Space Vehicles Directorate, Air Force Material Command, Hanscom AFB, MA 01731-3010

Angstrom, A. (1915) 'A study of the radiation of the atmosphere', *Smithsonian Inst. Misc. Coll.*, vol 65, pp1–159

Ashmore, J. and Richens, P. (2001) 'Computer simulation in daylight design: Comparison', *Architectural Science Review*, vol 44, no 1, pp33–44

Berdahl, P. and Fromberg, R. (1982) 'The thermal radiance of clear skies', *Solar Energy*, vol 29, no 4, pp299–314

Berdahl, P. and Martin, M. (1984) 'Emissivity of clear skies', *Solar Energy*, vol 32, no 5, pp663–664

Brunt, D. (1932) 'Notes on radiation in the atmosphere', *J. R. Met Soc*, vol 58, pp389–418

CIE (Commission Internationale de l'Eclairage) (1973) *Standardisation of Luminous Distribution on Clear Skies*, CIE publication no. 022, CIE, Vienna

CIE (1996) *Spatial Distribution of Daylight – CIE Standard Overcast Sky and Clear Sky*, CIE S 003/E-1996, CIE, Vienna

CIE (2002) *Spatial Distribution of Daylight – CIE Standard General Sky*, CIE DS 011.2/E-2002, CIE, Vienna

Cohen, M. and Wallace, J. (1993) *Radiosity and Realistic Image Synthesis*, Academic Press Professional, Boston

Compagnon, R. (2004) 'Solar and daylight availability in the urban fabric', *Energy and Buildings*, vol 36, pp321–328

Compagnon, R. and Raydan, D. (2000) 'Irradiance and illuminance distributions in urban areas', *Proc. PLEA 2000*, pp436–441

Dupagne A. (1991) 'A computer package to facilitate inhabitants participation in urban renewal', *Environment and Planning B: Planning and Design*, vol 18, pp119–134

ETSU (Energy Technology Support Unit) (1987) 'Passive solar design programme', *Leaflet 19: Housing Estate Layout: A Design Aid*, ETSU, Harwell

Everett, R. (1980) *Passive Solar in Milton Keynes*, Open University Energy Research Group, Milton Keynes

Grena, R. (2008) 'An algorithm for the computation of the solar position', *Solar Energy*, vol 82, no 5, pp462–470

Hay, J. (1979) 'Calculation of monthly mean solar radiation for horizontal and inclined surfaces', *Solar Energy*, vol 23, no 4, pp301–307

Jones W. P. (1994) *Air Conditioning Engineering*, 4th edition, Arnold, Hodder Headline Group, London

Kittler, R. (1967) 'Standardisation of the outdoor conditions for the calculation of the Daylight Factor with clear skies', in *Proc. Conf. Sunlight in Buildings*, Bouwcentrum, Rotterdam, pp273–286

Klucher, T. M. (1979) 'Evaluation of models to predict insolation on tilted surfaces', *Solar Energy*, vol 23, no 2, pp111–114

Knowles, R. L. (1981) *Sun, Rhythm, Form*, MIT Press, MA

Knowles, R. L. (2003) 'The solar envelope: its meaning for energy and buildings', *Energy and Buildings*, vol 35, pp15–25

Kovach, A. and Schmid, J. (1996) 'Determination of energy related output due to shading of building-integrated photovoltaic arrays using a ray tracing technique', *Solar Energy*, vol 57, no 2, pp117–124

Kristl, Z. and Krainer, A. (2001) 'Energy evaluation of urban structure and dimensioning of building site using iso-shadow method', *Solar Energy*, vol 70, no 1, pp23–34

Lagios, K., Niemasz, J. and Reinhart, C. F. (2010) 'Animated Building Performance Simulation (ABPS): Linking Rhinoceros/Grasshopper with Radiance/Daysim', *Proceedings of SimBuild 2010*, New York

Littlefair, P. J. (1991) 'Site layout and planning for daylight and sunlight: A guide to good practice', *BRE Report 209*, BRE, Watford, UK

Littlefair, P. J., Santamouris, M., Alvarez, S., Dupagne, A., Hall, D., Teller, J., Coronel, J. F. and Papanikolaou, N. (2000) 'Environmental site layout planning: Solar access, microclimate and passive cooling in urban areas', *BRE Report 380*, CRC Limited, London

Mardaljevic, J. (1995) 'Validation of a lighting simulation program under real sky conditions', *Lighting Research and Technology*, vol 27, no 4, pp181–188

Mardaljevic, J. (1999) 'Daylight simulation: Validation, sky models and daylight coefficients', unpublished PhD thesis, DeMontfort University, Leicester

Mardaljevic, J. and Rylatt, M. (2000) 'An imagebased analysis of solar radiation for urban settings', in *Proc. PLEA 2000*, Cambridge, p442–447

Mardaljevic, J. and Rylatt, M. (2003) 'Irradiation mapping of complex urban environments: An image-based approach', *Energy and Buildings*, vol 35, pp27–35

Marsh, A. (2004) 'Non-uniformity in incident solar radiation over the facades of high rise buildings', in *Proc. PLEA 2004*, Eindhoven

Michalsky, J. (1988) 'The astronomical almanac's algorithm for approximate solar position (1950–2050)', *Solar Energy*, vol 3, no 40, pp227–235

Moon, P. and Spencer, D. E. (1942) 'Illumination from a non-uniform sky', *Illuminating Engineering*, vol 37, no 10, pp707–726

Niewenda, A. and Heidt, F. D. (1996) 'Sombrero: A PC tool to calculate shadows on arbitrary oriented surfaces', *Solar Energy*, vol 48, no 4, pp253–263

Peckham, R. (1985) 'Shading evaluations with general three dimensional models', *Computer-aided Design*, vol 17, no 7, pp205–310

Perez, R., Seals, R., Ineichen, P., Stewart, R. and Menicucci, D. (1987) 'A new simplified version of the Perez diffuse irradiance model for tilted surfaces', *Solar Energy*, vol 39, no 3, pp221–231

Perez, R., Seals, R. and Michalsky, J. (1993) 'All-weather model for sky luminance distribution – preliminary configuration and validation', *Solar Energy*, vol 50, no 3, pp235–243

Quaschning, V. and Hanitsch, R. (1998) 'Irradiance calculations on shaded surfaces', *Solar Energy*, vol 62, no 5, pp369–375

Ratti, C. (2002) 'Urban analysis for environmental prediction', unpublished PhD thesis, University of Cambridge, Cambridge

Ratti, C. (2005) 'The lineage of the line: Space syntax parameters from the analysis of urban DEMs', *Environment and Planning B: Planning and Design*, vol 32, pp547–566

Ratti, C., Robinson, D., Baker, N. and Steemers, K. (2000) 'LT Urban – the energy modelling of urban form', in *Proc. PLEA 2000*, Cambridge, pp660–666

Ratti, C., Raydan, D. and Steemers, K. (2003) 'Building form and environmental performance: Archetypes, analysis and an arid climate', *Energy and Buildings*, vol 35, pp49–59

Reindl, D. T., Beckmann, W. A. and Duffie, J. A. (1990) 'Evaluation of hourly tilted surface radiation models', *Solar Energy*, vol 45, no 1, pp9–17

Richens, P. (1997) 'Image processing for urban scale environmental modelling', *Proc. Fifth International IBPSA Conference: Building Simulation '97*, Prague

Robinson, D. and Stone, A. (2004a) 'Solar radiation modelling in the urban context', *Solar Energy*, vol 77, no 3, pp295–309

Robinson, D. and Stone, A. (2004b) 'Irradiation modelling made simple – the cumulative sky approach and its applications', in *Proc. PLEA 2004*, Eindhoven

Robinson, D. and Stone, A. (2005) 'A simplified radiosity algorithm for general urban radiation exchange', *Building Services Engineering Research and Technology*, vol 26, no 4, pp271–284

Robinson, D., Scartezzini, J. L., Montavon, M. and Compagnon, R. (2005) *Solurban: Solar Utilisation Potential of Urban Sites*, Final Report, Swiss Federal Office of Energy, (www.bfe.admin. ch/php/modules/enet/streamfile.php?file=000000008944.pdf&name=000000250027.pdf)

Robinson, D. (2006) 'Urban morphology and indicators of radiation availability', *Solar Energy*, vol 80, no 12, pp1643–1648

Robinson, D. (2011) 'Integrated resource flow modelling of the urban built environment', in Hensen, J. L. M. and Lamberts, R. (eds) *Building Performance Simulation for Design and Operation*, Taylor & Francis, London

Skartveit, A., Olseth, J. A., Czeplak, G. and Rommel, M. (1996) 'On the estimation of atmospheric radiation from surface meteorological data', *Solar Energy*, vol 56, no 4, pp349–359

Spencer, J. W. (1971) 'Fourier series representation of the position of the sun', *Search*, vol 2, no 5, p172

Teller, J. and Azar, S. (2001) 'TOWNSCOPE II – a computer rendering system to support solar access decision making', *Solar Energy*, vol 70, no 3, pp187–200

Tregenza, P. and Sharples, S. (1993) 'Daylighting Algorithms', *ETSU S 1350-1993*, ETSU, Harwell

Unsworth, H. M. and Monteith, J. L. (1975) 'Longwave radiation at the ground – I. Angular distribution of incoming radiation', *Q. J. R. Met. Soc.*, vol 101, pp13–24

Ward Larsen, G. and Shakespeare, R. (1997) *Rendering with Radiance – The Art and Science of Lighting Visualisation*, Morgan Kauffmann, San Francisco

3

The Urban Climate

Adil Rasheed and Darren Robinson

3.1 Introduction

Urban terrain, in which built and natural forms are extruded from the ground, is often highly geometrically complex, having greater rugosity than is found in rural settings where the climatic measurements that form the basis of standard meteorological databases tend to be made. Due to inter-reflections between the surfaces constituting this terrain, its albedo tends to be lower, so that shortwave radiation is more efficiently absorbed relative to rural terrain. Furthermore, obstructions between surfaces diminish views to the sky, so that heat is less efficiently transferred at night by longwave exchange to the relatively cold sky. In consequence, more heat is absorbed and retained in urban than in rural terrain. Added to this is the heat gain due to anthropogenic sources, for example due to transport systems and heat sources in buildings, although this may be partially offset by evapotranspiration from vegetation.

In consequence, the mean temperature tends to be higher in urban than in rural terrain, with the intensity of the 'urban heat island (UHI) effect' tending towards a maxima at the centre of a city, as the air entrained into the buoyant plume (which may be both deflected and diluted by wind) is successively heated. This type of behaviour has been observed in numerous experimental field studies (Santamouris, 1998; Palmer et al, 2000; Graves et al, 2001). However, urban surfaces also tend to have greater thermal inertia than do rural surfaces. Indeed Swaid and Hoffmann (1989) estimate the difference in time constant to be six to eight hours. The urban temperature profile is thus shifted in phase with respect to the rural profile so that the UHI profile (the difference between the two: $T_{urban}(t) - T_{rural}(t)$) tends to reach a minima in the late afternoon/early evening (to the extent that this instantaneous UHI may be negative) and a maxima during the night. Due to the above mechanisms, the measured intensity of the London UHI varies from –2°C to +6°C, with corresponding implications for buildings' energy performance. This UHI therefore needs to be considered in predictions of buildings' energy demands (Chapter 6). These differences in air temperature, radiant temperature, relative humidity and local air velocity between urban and rural terrains also impact upon pedestrians' comfort (Chapter 4).

We begin this chapter by outlining the different approaches to modelling the climate of cities, before selecting the class of numerical models. We then discuss the difficulties involved in modelling the climate of cities due to the diverse time and length scales involved. The length scale for example can vary from a few metres (buildings) to a few kilometres (mountains) and the timescale from a few seconds (gusts) to seasonal variations lasting months. It is practically impossible to resolve all the scales in a single model with the present computational power available. A way to overcome this problem is to couple different models capable of resolving different scales. We go on therefore to present such a multi-scale approach to modelling the urban climate as well as some first applications of it.

3.2 Atmospheric flow modelling

The problem can be expressed through its fundamental equations (of which more in Section 3.5):

$$\frac{\partial \rho}{\partial t} + \vec{\nabla}.(\rho \vec{u}) = 0 \quad \text{Mass} \tag{3.2.1}$$

$$\rho \left(\frac{\partial \vec{u}}{\partial t} + \vec{u}.\nabla \vec{u} \right) = -\vec{\nabla}p + \mu \nabla^2 \vec{u} + \vec{f} \quad \text{Momentum} \tag{3.2.2}$$

$$\rho \left(\frac{\partial C_p T}{\partial t} + \vec{u}.\nabla T \right) = \mu \nabla^2 T + Q_T \quad \text{Energy} \tag{3.2.3}$$

There are three fundamental methods for modelling atmospheric flows: physical, analytical and numerical. With the first technique, scale model replicas of observed ground surface characteristics (for example topographic relief, buildings) are constructed and inserted into a chamber such as a wind tunnel (water tanks are also used). The flow of air or other gases or liquids in this chamber is adjusted so as to best represent the larger-scale observed atmospheric conditions. Analytical modelling, in contrast, utilizes such basic analysis techniques as algebra and calculus to solve directly all or a subset of [3.2.1] to [3.2.3] for constrained cases. The third approach, numerical modelling, is the most flexible of them all and can be used to simulate complex fluid flow. The following subsections describe them in a little more detail.

3.2.1 Physical modelling

Physical modelling involves conducting experiments in wind tunnels on a scaled down model (in our case: a city or part of it). This calls for some physical modelling criteria (popularly known as similarity criteria) to be satisfied. These similarity criteria are derived by writing the governing flow equations for the city and the scaled-down model. Both these sets of equations are then non-dimensionalized using the characteristic length, velocity and temperature scales of the city and the model. These two sets of non-dimensionalized equations will be identical when the coefficients of each term of these two sets of equations match. These coefficients are known as the Reynolds Number, Froud Number, Richardson Number, Prandtle Number, Eckert Number, Rossby Number and the Schmidt Number. Matching these numbers ensures that the results from the experiment are independent of the scale of the model. Complete similarity of the flow requires, in addition to matching the foregoing parameters for the small and full-scale system, similarity of the external boundary conditions. These external conditions include the distribution of surface temperature, the turbulence characteristics above the atmospheric boundary layer, the surface roughness and there should be no pressure gradient in the mean flow direction. Of these, it is almost impossible to have control over the first two. For sloping or irregular ground surfaces, a geometrically similar topographical model is required to match the roughness and the modelled upwind fetch must be sufficiently long as to ensure that flow approaching the modelled urban area is in equilibrium with the upwind boundary conditions to minimize the upwind pressure gradient. With all these requirements, physical modelling has been primarily limited to stably stratified flows over regular terrains. Even in this case, however, such observed features of the real atmosphere as the veering of winds with height and buoyancy-driven flow cannot be satisfactorily reproduced. Thus the possibility of using a physical model to understand the urban heat island does not appear to be feasible.

3.2.2 Analytical modelling

The system of equations presented in Section 3.2 is a set of nonlinear partial differential equations. The nonlinear characteristics of the equations occur because products of the dependent variables are included in the relationships. To obtain exact solutions to the conservation relationships, it is necessary to remove the nonlinearities in the equations. This can be achieved by making some considerable simplifications, but such simplified situations rarely occur in reality. Nevertheless, results from such simplified, linear equations are useful for the following reasons. First, the exact solutions of the simplified linear differential equations give some idea as to the physical mechanisms involved in specific atmospheric circulations. Because exact solutions are obtained, an investigator can be certain that the results are not caused by computational errors, as can be the case with numerical models.

Second, results from these linearized equations can be contrasted with those obtained from a numerical model in which the magnitude of the nonlinear terms is small relative to the linear terms. An accurate nonlinear numerical model would give good agreement with the linear results when the products of the dependent variables are small. Linear representations of the conservation relations have been used to investigate wave motions in the atmosphere, as well as to represent actual meso-scale circulations. Kurihara (1976), for example, applied a linear analysis to investigate spiral bands in a tropical storm. Klemp and Lilly (1975) used such an approach to study wave dynamics in downslope wind storms to the lee of large mountain barriers. Other linear models of airflow over mountain barriers include the model of Wang and Lin (1999).

Similar approaches have also been made by the building physics community to develop a model for predicting the temperature in an urban canopy (Swaid and Hoffman, 1990; Elnahas and Williamson, 1997). However, in their implementation Robinson and Stone (2004) were unable to produce convincing results (Robinson et al, 2007): these simplified models, which are not derived from the governing flow equations, do not adequately respect the physics of atmospheric flow. Indeed the complex nature of the nonlinearities involved in real atmospheric phenomena effectively prohibits the development of an elegant analytical model of the urban climate.

3.2.3 Numerical modelling

Because of the aforementioned limitations of physical and analytical models we choose a third approach in which the governing nonlinear differential equations are solved numerically on a computer. The governing equations are discretized in time and space and solved using finite volume, finite element or a finite difference approach. A complete description of these methods can be found in Chung (2002). The equations, when solved numerically with appropriate boundary conditions, can be used to compute velocity, pressure and temperature profiles on a predefined numerical grid.

3.3 Problems in urban climate modelling

The main complexities in atmospheric flow modelling arise due to the chaotic nature of turbulence and the presence of a large variety of spatio-temporal scales. These are explained in detail in the following subsections.

3.3.1 Turbulence modelling

In fluid dynamics, turbulence or turbulent flow is a fluid regime characterized by chaotic, stochastic property changes. This includes high momentum convection and rapid variation of pressure and velocity in space and time. Turbulence causes the formation of eddies of many different length scales. Most of the kinetic energy of the turbulent motion is contained in large-scale structures. This energy 'cascades' from these large-scale structures to smaller-scale structures by an inertial and essentially inviscid mechanism. This process continues, creating smaller and smaller structures that produce a hierarchy of eddies. Eventually, this process creates structures that are small enough so that molecular diffusion becomes important and viscous dissipation of energy finally takes place. The scale at which this happens is known as the Kolmogorov length scale. Important features of turbulence can be enumerated as:

- Turbulence is irregular and seemingly random (chaotic). Statistical methods should be used for extracting useful engineering information.
- Turbulence is highly diffusive. Rapid mixing significantly increases momentum, heat and mass transfer.
- Turbulence is a rotational and 3D motion.
- Turbulence is associated with high levels of vorticity fluctuation. Smaller scales are generated by the vortex stretching mechanism.

- Turbulence is highly dissipative. It needs a source of energy to be maintained.
- Turbulence is a continuum phenomenon. The smallest scale of turbulence is much larger than the molecular scales of certain engineering applications.
- Turbulence is a manifestation of the flow and not of the fluid.

Spectral analysis

Turbulence has a wide range of length (time) scales. A typical energy spectrum (Fourier decomposition of energy) is shown in Figure 3.3.1. Here *En(k)* is the energy spectrum and *k* is the wavenumber (the inverse of wavelength ($1/\Lambda$)). Fluctuation energy is produced at the large eddies (with low wave numbers). A vortex stretching mechanism then generates smaller and smaller eddies and energy flows down the spectrum to the high wave number region. Energy is mainly dissipated into heat at the smallest eddies (of the Kolmogorov scales). Depending upon the production and dissipation of turbulent kinetic energy, the spectrum can be divided into the energy containing range, the inertial subrange and the dissipation subrange.

Energy containing range – this is the range of large-scale eddies that contain most of the energy. At this scale, energy is converted from the mean flow into turbulent kinetic energy (TKE). The forcing mechanisms that extract TKE from the mean flow are shear, buoyancy and potentially pressure perturbations (which may produce TKE in smaller ranges, see McBean and Elliott (1975)). The energy containing range is dominated by the integral length scale ι. *En(k)*

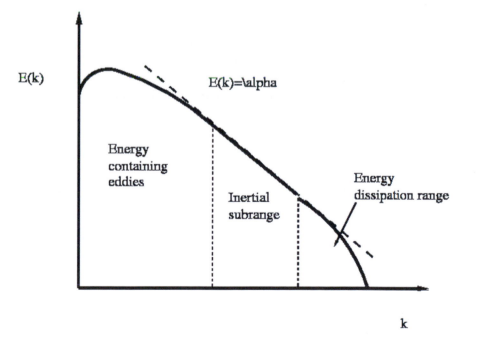

Figure 3.3.1 Turbulent kinetic energy spectrum En (k), or E(k) as indicated here, as a function of turbulent eddy wave number

Source: Schiestel (2007)

reaches its maximum at a wavenumber roughly corresponding to this Eulerian integral length scale.

Inertial subrange – this is the range of wavenumbers that are smaller than the smallest energy input ($\approx 10^1 m$) but larger than the Kolmogorov microscale λK ($\approx 10^{-3} m$). In this range, TKE is neither produced nor dissipated. Eddies no longer interact with the mean flow, and turbulence at this scale is statistically uncorrelated to the mean flow. It is isotropic and does not contribute to turbulent flux densities. Energy is passed down from larger scales to smaller ones, and according to Kolmogorov (1941) the inertial subrange is characterized by a straight line, known as Kolmogorov's –5/3 law: $En(k) = \alpha \varepsilon^{2/3} \kappa^{-5/3}$ where α is a constant.

Dissipation subrange – in the dissipation subrange, TKE is transformed by dissipation into heat. Dissipation of TKE starts roughly at wavenumbers that are smaller than the Kolmogorov microscale λ_κ: $\lambda_\kappa = \left(\dfrac{\nu^3}{\varepsilon} \right)^{1/4}$ where ν is the kinematic molecular viscosity and ε the dissipation rate of TKE. With ultrasonic anemometers, this part of the spectra cannot be measured directly because the frequency response of these instruments is too slow and the measurement volume is too large. Dissipation can be indirectly calculated from the inertial subrange slope.

Reynolds decomposition

Reynolds decomposition splits any instantaneous variable $a(x, t)$ at a given location and time t into a resolved mean value (denoted by on overhead bar) and an unresolved fluctuating part (denoted by a prime): $a = \bar{a} + a'$.

The splitting is performed commonly in the time domain with a, the temporal average over an averaging time t_a, which fulfils the assumption of (1) stationarity and (2) the condition that t_a lies in the region of the spectral gap:

$$\bar{a} = \frac{1}{t_a} \int_{t=0}^{t_a} a(t) dt \, .$$

The condition of stationarity, which results in $\partial / \partial t = 0$, is seldom fulfilled, since superscale forcing (for example inactive turbulence, diurnal and synoptic effects) results in continuously changing boundary conditions. For the same reason, the presence of the spectral gap, which theoretically results from an energetic separation of the energy input at the synoptic scale and the energy produced at the turbulent scale (Oke, 1988), is in doubt.

Turbulence models

The problem of turbulence may be solved to a greater or a lesser extent using a turbulence model. All of the existing turbulence models lie in one of the three categories: direct numerical simulation (DNS), large eddy simulation (LES) or Reynolds-Averaged Navier-Stokes (RANS).

DNS – in DNS the Navier Stokes system of equations is solved directly with refined meshes capable of resolving all turbulence length scales including the Kolmogorov microscales, $\lambda_k = (v^3 / \varepsilon)^{1/4}$.

All turbulence scales ranging from the large energy-containing eddies to the dissipation scales, $0 \leq k\lambda_k \leq 10$ with k being the wavenumber that must be resolved (Figure 3.3.1). To meet this requirement, the number of grid points required is proportional to $L / \lambda_k \approx \mathrm{Re}^{3/4}$, where L is the characteristic length and Re is the Reynolds number, referenced to the integral scale of the flow. This leads to the number of grid points in 3D being proportional to $\mathrm{Re}^{9/4}$. Similarly the time step is limited by the Kolgomorov timescale, $\tau = (v/\varepsilon)^{1/2}$, as $\delta_t = 0.003H/u_T \, \mathrm{Re}_T^{1/2}$. These restrictions are clearly too severe for DNS to be a practical tool for urban-scale applications, in view of currently available computing resources.

LES – LES is a compromise between accurate modelling of turbulence and available computing resources. Here, by using more refined meshes than are usually required for the RANS system of equations (see below), large eddies are calculated (resolved) whereas the diffusion of small eddies is modelled. The rigor of LES in terms of performance and ability is somewhere between RANS and DNS. There are two major steps involved in LES analysis: filtering and subgrid modelling. Traditionally, filtering is carried out using the box function, Gaussian function or Fourier cut-off function. Subgrid modelling includes the eddy viscosity model, the structure function model, the dynamic model, the scale similarity model and a mixed model, among others.

RANS – RANS equations are the conventional approach to turbulence modelling. An ensemble version of the governing equations is solved, which introduces new apparent stresses known as Reynolds stresses, resulting in a greater number of unknowns than there are equations. This problem is known as the problem of closure. It adds a second order tensor of unknowns for which various models can provide different levels of closure. It is a common misconception that the RANS equations do not apply to flows with a time-varying mean flow because these equations are 'time-averaged'. In fact, statistically unsteady (or non-stationary) flows can equally be treated. This is sometimes referred to as URANS. There is nothing inherent in Reynolds averaging to preclude this, but the turbulence models used to close the equations are valid only as long as the timescale of these changes in the mean is large compared to the timescales of the turbulent motion containing most of the energy.

3.3.2 Spatial and temporal scales

As noted earlier, in addition to turbulence, urban climate modelling is also confounded by the diverse spatial and temporal scales involved. Most atmospheric processes are characterized by certain spatial and temporal scales that are reflected in their classification as global, meso or micro-scale processes. But the demarcation of these scales is not strictly defined so that overlaps may arise between them. Nevertheless, it is the chosen scale of interest and the magnitude of a process that together determine whether this process should be resolved explicitly, modelled implicitly (parameterized) or ignored completely. It is also important to understand that all of these scales are interdependent. For example, turbulent kinetic energy is passed down from larger scales to smaller scales and at the smallest scales it is dissipated as heat. However, smaller-scale processes might initiate and evolve larger-scaled structures and pattern.

In the context of a numerical model, the domain size, grid resolution and filtering operators decide what scales can be handled. Thus these models have a limited lower and upper resolution. Unresolved processes that are below the lower limit of the chosen scale are called subscale processes while the ones above the upper limit are called superscale processes. Accounting for both these types of processes is the key to a reasonable climatic prediction. Generally, the subgrid scale processes are modelled under certain closure assumptions or by parameterization, while unresolved superscale processes are forced through a variable boundary condition using a model that is capable of handling these larger-scale processes. This is a classical one-way nesting, or multi-scale modelling, approach.

Before proceeding further it is helpful to consider more closely the different scales that are encountered in urban climate modelling. Britter and Hanna (2003) suggest four conceptual ranges of length scales in the urban context: street canyon scale (<100m), neighbourhood scale (1–2km), city scale (10–20km) and regional scale (100–200km).

Street canyon scale (urban canyon)

This is the scale that directly impacts micro-scale pollutant dispersion, pedestrian comfort, wind loading on buildings and building ventilation. The nature of the urban roughness sublayer is a direct consequence of heterogeneity at this scale. The flow at this scale can either be modelled by detailed CFD simulations or by wind tunnel experimentation using a reduced-scale model, the former being more practical and flexible, though not necessarily as accurate (indeed wind tunnel results may be highly valuable for benchmarking numerical codes). Nearly all surface measurements for wind and urban fluxes are conducted at this scale, although their results are interpreted to be representative of larger scales. Results from experimentation at this scale are also used extensively for developing urban parameterization schemes (such as the Urban Canopy Models described later) to be used to handle the subscale processes in models handling city or regional scales.

Neighbourhood scale

The neighbourhood scale restores horizontal homogeneity of the surface at a larger scale by horizontal averaging over a homogeneous area of the city, large enough to filter out (repetitive) surface inhomogeneities at the street canyon scale. In other words, such a model has a similar effect on the bulk flow characteristics as if the small-scale inhomogeneities were explicitly modelled.

The formation of an inertial sublayer is a consequence of the (assumed) homogeneity at the neighbourhood scale (for example a regular array of parallelepipeds). The neighbourhood scale is the preferred level of detail where urban Lagrangian near-field pollution dispersion models are run (for example Rotach, 2001; Hanna et al, 1993). The restored horizontal homogeneity allows for many simplifications, but also requires parameterizations in order to model the underlying urban roughness and canopy sublayer. Finally, the neighbourhood scale is also the scale of choice for turbulent flux monitoring sites. In short it can be said that the spatially averaged results of simulation, experiment or observation will be representative at this scale.

City scale and regional scale (meso-scale)

These scales focus on the modification of the whole boundary layer. This is of interest in climate modelling since today's weather forecasting models already include many grid cells that are 100 per cent urban; and these urban areas modify the whole boundary layer, its stability, thermodynamic properties and the mixed layer height. To account for these mechanisms, and thereby the urban heat island effect mentioned in Section 3.1, there have been several attempts to simply alter the surface exchange parameterization of models to incorporate the effects of the city scale (for example Taha, 1999). Sophisticated urban parameterizations have also been developed to model the subgrid scales at this resolution (for example Masson, 2000; Martilli et al, 2002; Otte et al, 2004). The numerical grids used in such meso-scale simulations have a typical resolution ranging from a few hundred metres to a few kilometres.

In this section we have focussed on the spatial scales influencing urban climate modelling but different temporal scales may also be involved. For example there can be seasonal changes that take place over a few months and then there are gusts and hurricanes that can last for not more than a few seconds or minutes. For a robust simulation of the urban climate, all of these scales should be taken into account.

3.4 Proposed solution: Multi-scale modelling

We introduced above the different scales encountered in urban climate modelling. Unfortunately, it is not possible to satisfactorily resolve all of these scales in a computationally tractable way using a single model. It is, however, possible to tackle this problem by coupling different models, each targeting different climatic scales. Here we describe one such approach (Figure 3.4.1).

First, freely available results from a global model are input to a meso model at a slightly larger scale than that of the city in question. Then a meso model is run as a pre-processor to interpolate the macro-scale results at progressively finer resolutions until the boundary conditions surrounding our city are resolved at a compatible resolution. Since the meso-scale model itself is used to interpolate the results to different grids, the conservation of mass, momentum and energy is automatically satisfied. It should be stressed that for the purpose

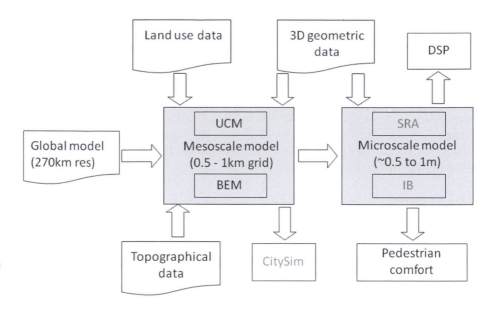

Figure 3.4.1 Schematic of multi-scale modelling approach

of interpolation we assume a 100 per cent rural surface in all meso-scale model grids. The meso model with subscale parameterization is then run in a normal way. In the rural context this may simply involve associating topography and average land-use data with each cell, the former affecting temperature as pressure changes with height; the latter affecting temperature due to evapo(transpir)ation from water bodies or vegetated surfaces.

In the urban context, however, it is important to account for the energy and momentum exchanges between the built surfaces and the adjacent air, which implies some representation of 3D geometry. For this we use a new urban canopy model in which the velocity, temperature and scalar profiles are parameterized as functions of built densities, street orientation and the dimensions of urban geometric typologies. These quantities are then used to estimate the sources and sinks of the momentum and energy equations.

Even at the micro-scale the use of conventional CFD modelling is unattractive because of the time involved in grid generation/tuning and the definition of boundary conditions. Furthermore, even the simplest geometry may require hundreds of millions of grid cells for a domain corresponding to a single meso model cell, particularly if unstructured grids are used, which are attractive for productivity reasons but suffer from numerical instabilities. To overcome this problem we use a new approach based on immersed boundaries in which the flow around any complex geometry can be computed using a simple Cartesian grid, so that users benefit from both improved productivity and accuracy.

Thus, a completely coupled global, meso and micro model can be used to predict the temperature, wind and pressure field in a city taking into account not only the complex geometries of its built fabric but also the scales that are bigger than the city scale. In this way the effects of superscales in a given model are captured through the boundary conditions that are fed by a model handling superior scales while the effects of subgrid scales are parameterized. For the meso-scale two such parameterizations have been developed: an urban canopy model (UCM) and a building energy model (BEM).

The result from such a multi-scale model can be used to evaluate pedestrian comfort (Chapter 4) or can be fed to an urban resource flow modelling tool (Chapter 6).

In summary, our multi-scale urban climate model consists of a meso-scale model (with UCM and BEM embedded within it), a micro-scale model based on the Immersed Surface Technique (IST) and using an SRA for the computation of radiation incident on built surfaces. In the following sections we present these new techniques and evaluate their reliability for making urban climate predictions in a reasonable amount of time.

3.5 Meso-scale model

In this first implementation of the multi-scale urban climate model we use the meso-scale finite volume model (FVM), which was partly developed at the Soil and Air Pollution Laboratory of EPFL (Clappier et al, 1996).

3.5.1 Conservation of mass

The conservation of mass is expressed as follows:

$$\frac{\partial \rho}{\partial t} + \vec{\nabla}.(\rho \vec{v}) = 0 \qquad [3.5.1]$$

where v is the wind velocity and ρ the air density. On typical scales of velocity and length for the motion in the meso-scale range $\frac{\partial \rho}{\partial t}$ is much smaller than $\vec{\nabla}.(\rho \vec{u})$ and can therefore be neglected (anelastic approximation). Here, and in the following sections, variables are Reynolds-averaged. Primed letters stand for their respective turbulent fluctuations.

Equations [3.5.3] to [3.5.4] hereafter have been written in advection form using the Lagrangian time derivative for a more compact representation of the basic conservation laws. Because total mass is conserved, the rate of change of any mass-specific quantity ψ can be formulated by:

$$\rho \frac{d\psi}{dt} = \frac{\partial(\rho\psi)}{\partial t} + \vec{\nabla}.(\rho \vec{v} \psi) \qquad [3.5.2]$$

Using the budget operator $\partial(\rho...)/\partial t + \vec{\nabla}.(\rho\vec{v}...)$. $\partial(\rho\psi)/\partial t$ can be interpreted as the storage of ψ and $\vec{\nabla}.(\rho\vec{v}\psi)$ as its mean transport (advection).

3.5.2 Conservation of momentum

The conservation of momentum is expressed as follows:

$$\rho \frac{d\vec{v}}{dt} = -\vec{\nabla}\bar{p} + \rho \frac{\theta'}{\theta_0} \vec{g} - 2\vec{\Omega} \times (\vec{v} - \vec{v}^G) - \frac{\partial \overline{\rho \vec{v}' v_z'}}{\partial z} + \vec{D}_u \qquad [3.5.3]$$

in which p is the pressure, θ_o is the potential temperature of the reference state, $\theta' = \theta - \theta_o$ is the fluctuation relative to this state, $\vec{g}$ is acceleration due to gravity, $\vec{\Omega}$ is the earth's rotational angular velocity and $\vec{v}^G$ is the geostrophic wind velocity. The interpretation of the individual terms of [3.5.3] is as follows:

$\vec{\nabla}\overline{p}$ is the pressure gradient force, $\rho \dfrac{\theta'}{\theta_0} \vec{g}$ is the vertical action of gravity (buoyancy), $2\vec{\Omega} \times (\vec{v} - \vec{v}^G)$ is the influence of the earth's rotation (Coriolis effects), $\dfrac{\partial \rho \overline{v'v'_z}}{\partial z}$ is turbulent transport and $\vec{D}_u$ represents the forces induced by interaction between solid surfaces and airflow.

Equation [3.5.3] is the non-hydrostatic form of the momentum conservation equation and the buoyancy term is written using the Boussinesq approximation (see Section 3.5.7).

3.5.3 Conservation of energy

The conservation of energy is expressed as follows:

$$\rho \frac{d\theta}{dt} = \frac{\partial \rho \overline{\theta v'_z}}{\partial z} - \frac{1}{C_p} \left(\frac{p_o}{\overline{p}} \right)^{R/C_p} \frac{\partial R_{lw}}{\partial z} + D_\theta \qquad [3.5.4]$$

where θ is potential temperature, C_p is the specific heat capacity at constant air pressure, R is the gas constant, p_o is the reference pressure (1000mb) and R_{lw} is the long wave radiation flux. D_θ denotes the impact of the sensible heat fluxes from the solid surfaces (ground or buildings) on the potential temperature budget. The interpretation of the various terms is as follows: $\dfrac{\partial \rho \overline{\theta v'_z}}{\partial z}$ represents turbulent transport of heat, $\dfrac{1}{C_p} \left(\dfrac{p_o}{\overline{p}} \right)^{R/C_p} \dfrac{\partial R_{lw}}{\partial z}$ expresses loss through longwave emissions.

D-terms in [3.5.3] and [3.5.4] arise from the consideration of urban elements, and are solved by the urban canopy parameterization module presented later (Section 3.7).

3.5.4 Poisson equation for pressure

In its numerical resolution, the mass equation [3.5.1] is combined with the momentum equation [3.5.3] to yield the following Poisson differential equation for pressure:

$$\vec{\nabla}^2 \overline{p} = \nabla.\vec{F} \qquad [3.5.5]$$

Where $\vec{F}$ is defined as:

$$F_i = -\vec{\nabla}.(\rho \vec{v} v_i) + \left[\rho \frac{\theta'}{\theta_0} \vec{g} - 2\vec{\Omega} \times (\vec{v} - \vec{v}^G) - \frac{\partial \rho \overline{v'v'_z}}{\partial z} + \vec{D}_u \right].\vec{e}_i \qquad [3.5.6]$$

This Poisson equation actually expresses the propagation of acoustic waves through the domain. A study of orders of magnitude shows that this propagation is practically instantaneous. Equations [3.5.3] and [3.5.4] are solved explicitly, except for the pressure, which is solved implicitly.

3.5.5 Turbulent fluxes

Unfortunately, by introducing prognostic equations for the previously unknown second moments in [3.2.2] and [3.2.3], we obtain new third-order terms in [3.5.3] and [3.5.4], which we are still not able to predict. With each higher order set of equations, we have even more unknown terms than equations. This is called the closure problem. Practically, the process of continuously introducing new prognostic equations for even higher moments has to be stopped at a certain level of detail. Any turbulence closure scheme considers only a finite set of equations and approximates the missing higher order moments in terms of known moments. There are local and non-local closure schemes. Local closure schemes approximate any unknown parameter by known parameters at the same point in space. A common local scheme is the K–$theory$, which approximates turbulent transports with a transfer coefficient Kz, that is proportional to the local mean gradient, as follows:

$$\overline{u_i a'} = -K_{zi}\frac{\partial \overline{a}}{\partial x_i} \tag{3.5.7}$$

where a is the mean part and a' the turbulent part of the variable, that may be either the potential temperature or a velocity component depending on the equation to be solved and K_{zi} is the diffusion coefficient. The vertical-transfer coefficient K_{zi} is parameterized with a $k - l$ closure from Bougeault and Lacarrere (1989). For that, the following prognostic equation for turbulent kinetic energy is solved:

$$\frac{\partial \rho e}{\partial t} + \frac{\partial e u_j}{\partial x_j} + \frac{\partial \rho \overline{e' u'}_j}{\partial x_j} = -\overline{u'_i u'_j}\frac{\partial u_i}{\partial x_j} + g\frac{\overline{u'_i \theta'}}{\theta_o}\delta_{i3} - \frac{\rho C_\varepsilon e^{3/2}}{l_\varepsilon} + Q_\varepsilon \tag{3.5.8}$$

The interpretation of the various terms in [3.5.8] is as follows: $\dfrac{\partial \rho e}{\partial t}$ is the time variation of TKE, $\dfrac{\partial e u_j}{\partial x_j}$ is the advection of TKE, $\dfrac{\partial \rho \overline{e' u'}_j}{\partial x_j}$ is the turbulent transport of TKE, $-\overline{u'_i u'_j}\dfrac{\partial u_i}{\partial x_j}$ is the shear production of TKE, $g\dfrac{\overline{u'_i \theta'}}{\theta_o}\delta_{i3}$ is the buoyant production of TKE, $\dfrac{\rho C_\varepsilon e^{3/2}}{l_\varepsilon}$ is the dissipation of TKE, and Q_e represents sources/sinks of TKE.

The vertical diffusion coefficient can then be calculated using the following relation:

$$K_{zi} = c_i C_k l_k e^{1/2} \tag{3.5.9}$$

where c_i, C_k are numerical constants and l_k and l_- are the turbulent and dissipative length scales and are computed as follows:

$$\int_{z}^{z+l_{up}} \beta(\theta(z)-\theta(z'))dz' = E(z) \qquad [3.5.10]$$

$$\int_{z-l_{down}}^{z} \beta(\theta(z')-\theta(z))dz' = E(z) \qquad [3.5.11]$$

$$l_{\varepsilon} = (l_{up}l_{down})^{1/2} \qquad [3.5.12]$$

$$l_{k} = \min(l_{up}, l_{down}) \qquad [3.5.13]$$

where, l_{up} and l_{down} refer to the distance that a parcel originating from level z, and having a TKE of the level $e(z)$ can travel upwards and downwards before being stopped by buoyancy effects. Close to the surface, the maximum value of l_{down} is limited by the height above the ground l_{ground}. In the standard meso-scale model, at the ground, turbulence fluxes of momentum and heat are computed using Monin–Obukhov Similarity Theory according to the formulation of Louis (1979). The solar radiation at the surface is computed using the formulation of Schayes (1982), including a specific aerosol absorption factor, variable earth–sun distance, dry air Rayleigh scattering and water vapour absorption. The longwave radiation flux is computed with the Sasamori (1999) scheme, which takes into account water vapour and carbon dioxide concentration in the atmosphere. The same formulation is used for the evaluation of the infrared flux divergence in [3.5.4]. Further details regarding shortwave and longwave radiation modelling in the meso-scale FVM can be found in Martilli et al (2002) and Krpo (2009).

3.5.6 Meso-scale grid

The meso-scale model uses a terrain-following (deformed) mesh (Figure 3.5.1) and is thus able to take into account the topography of the domain. The model is typically applied over areas of 200km by 200km horizontally and reaches up to heights of 10km above the earth's surface, so as to cover the entire troposphere. The volume thus defined is discretized to provide a horizontal resolution with cells of 1km to 5km and a vertical resolution of typically 10m close to the ground, where high accuracy is needed, to 1000m at the top of the domain, near the tropopause.

3.5.7 Simplifying hypotheses

Boussinesq approximation

The Boussinesq approximation is applied in the field of buoyancy-driven flow. It states that density differences are sufficiently small to be neglected, except where they appear in terms multiplied by g, the acceleration due to gravity. The essence of the Boussinesq approximation is that the difference in inertia is negligible but gravity is sufficiently strong to make the specific weight appreciably different between two fluids. The approximation's advantage arises

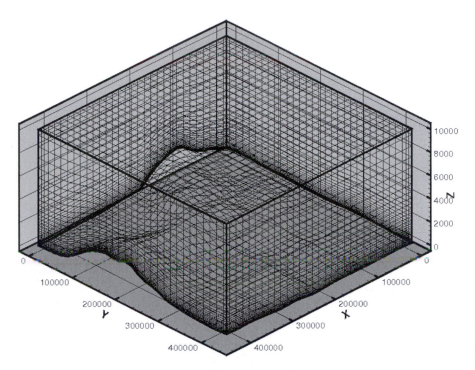

Figure 3.5.1 The terrain following mesh in FVM

Source: Authors

because when considering a flow of, say warm and cold air of densities ρ_1 and ρ_2, one needs only to consider a single density ρ: we assume that the difference $\rho_1 - \rho_2$ is negligible. Dimensional analysis shows that, under these circumstances, the only sensible way that acceleration due to gravity g should enter into the equations of motion is via a reduced gravity g' where:

$$g' = g \frac{\rho_1 - \rho_2}{\rho_1} \qquad [3.5.14]$$

Furthermore, neglecting the pressure variation in comparison to the potential temperature variation yields:

$$\frac{\rho_o - \rho}{\rho_o} \approx \frac{\theta - \theta_o}{\theta_o} \qquad [3.5.15]$$

in which ρ_1 and ρ_2 have been replaced by ρ_0 (the density at hydrostatic state) and by ρ, respectively. Equations [3.5.14] and [3.5.15] give rise to the buoyancy term in the momentum conservation equation [3.5.3].

Anelastic approximation

The objective of the anelastic approximation is similar to that of the Boussinesq approximation, but it can be applied to non-acoustic atmospheric motions. The key point of the approximation is to drop the time derivative term in the continuity equation:

$$\frac{\partial \rho}{\partial t} = \vec{\nabla}.(\rho\vec{v})$$
[3.5.16]

This assumption also implies that the atmospheric fluid is incompressible.

3.5.8 Numerical methods

In the meso-scale model the mass, momentum, energy and turbulent kinetic energy conservation equations are solved using an FVM. Advection of the aforementioned quantities is very important in such a model. This is handled using a multiple order Crowley method (Crowley, 1968) with a Universal Limiter (Thuborn, 1996). As explained in Leveque (2002), this numerical scheme is very efficient as it leads to small diffusive errors and prevents non-physical oscillations. The algorithm has also been corrected for multidimensional applications (Clappier, 1998). For the complete resolution of the meso-scale problem, the acoustic equation has been derived from the mass and momentum conservation laws and solved implicitly with a bi-conjugate gradient method, preconditioned in the vertical direction. The spatial discretization is based on a finite volume approach, with the pressure gradients and the velocity fluxes estimated at the faces of the cells (finite volumes), while the velocity components, temperature, density, humidity and pressure are computed at the centre. The model was tested for several well-known problems to evaluate its efficiency and accuracy. The results can be found in Krpo (2009).

3.6 Micro-scale models

In CFD, the quality of mesh very often dictates the accuracy of the results and the computational time. This is important for micro-scale modelling, since we require a relatively fine mesh if we are to *resolve* the flow around buildings. A wisely chosen mesh can significantly improve the accuracy of the result without incurring any increase in computational costs. Several types of grid are available for spatially discretizing the computational domain: structured, unstructured or block structured.

Structured grids (Figure 3.6.1a) are built with a repeating geometric and topological structure. They are usually composed of hexahedra or bricks. These grids are very simple to deal with, especially in terms of application development, computation and visualization. This simple structure often simplifies the computational connectivity of the grid, allowing for very efficient computation on modern computers.

Block-structured grids are a collection of structured grids that together fill complex domains. They inherit most of the computational efficiency of a structured grid, but a difficulty is introduced of communication between the blocks. Nevertheless, it is easier to grid a complicated geometry with a multi-block than with a structured grid, but filling in complex geometry intersections and building blocks that properly share boundary surfaces usually requires significant expertise and partially offsets the benefits of the multi-block approach.

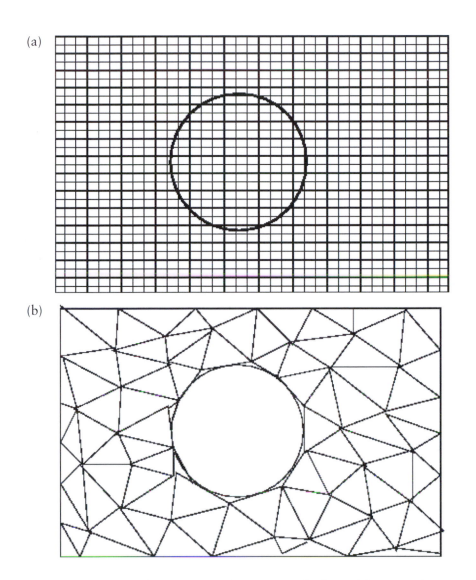

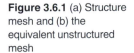

Figure 3.6.1 (a) Structure mesh and (b) the equivalent unstructured mesh

Unstructured grids (Figure 3.6.1b) are typically formed from simplexes such as tetrahedra. The fact that they have no repeating structure can make it very difficult to create and compute the necessary cell-to-cell connectivity required in CFD applications. The random orientation of an unstructured grid can also lead to awkward interfaces within the grid, possibly reducing the final accuracy of the solution. Despite these complications, unstructured grids have become popular due to their potential to mesh even the most complex geometric forms, and in a way that readily permits variations in spatial resolution to be accommodated within a given domain.

In summary then, the use of a Cartesian structured grids not only provides simplicity in grid generation but also makes available efficient algorithms for CFD simulations. This is therefore our desired solution, provided of course that we can fit this grid to the complex geometries found in real cities. For this we use a method called the IST.

3.6.1 Immersed Surface Technique

The term 'Immersed Surface Technique' was first used in reference to a method developed by Peskin (1977) to simulate cardiac mechanics and associated blood flow. The distinguishing feature of this method was that the whole simulation was carried out on a Cartesian grid that did not conform to the geometry of the heart; a novel procedure was formulated for imposing the effects of the immersed boundary on the flow. The IST used in this work is a variant of that method. With this IST, solid walls are represented by a level set function representing the exact distance to the surface; it is zero at the surface, positive in the fluid and negative in the solid. Both the liquid and solid have different thermophysical properties based on this level set function. The Navier-Stokes equations are modified to account for the presence of the solid level set function. The treatment of viscous shear at the solid surface is handled in very much the same way as in conventional CFD codes; as explained below.

3.6.2 Governing equations of the IST

As noted earlier, the immersed surface is represented on the fluid grid by a level set function (ϕ_s), where $\phi_s = 0$ represents the fluid–solid interface. ϕ_s is a signed distance function that is positive in the solid phase and negative in the fluid phase. The equations in the solid and fluid domain are combined using a smooth Heaviside function $H(\phi_s)$ that has value 1 in the fluid phase and 0 in the solid phase, thus:

$$H(\phi_s) = \frac{1}{2}\left(1 - \tanh\left(\frac{2\phi_s}{\delta_{sf}}\right)\right) \qquad [3.6.1]$$

where, δ_{sf} is the solid–fluid finite interface thickness. The following mass and momentum equations are used for the solid phase:

$$\frac{\partial \rho^s}{\partial t} + \frac{\partial}{\partial x_j}\left(\rho^s u_j^s\right) = 0 \qquad [3.6.2]$$

$$\frac{\partial \rho^s u_i^s}{\partial t} + \frac{\partial}{\partial x_j}\left(\rho^s u_i^s u_j^s\right) = 0 \qquad [3.6.3]$$

For the case of non-moving immersed surfaces, the solid phase velocity is set to zero ($u_i^s = 0$). The standard Navier-Stokes equations are used for the fluid phase:

$$\frac{\partial \rho^f}{\partial t} + \frac{\partial}{\partial x_j}\left(\rho^f u_j^f\right) = 0 \qquad [3.6.4]$$

$$\frac{\partial \rho^f u_i^f}{\partial t} + \frac{\partial}{\partial x_j}\left(\rho^f u_i^f u_j^f\right) = -\frac{\partial p^f}{\partial x_i} + \frac{\partial}{\partial x_j}\left(2\mu^f \frac{\partial S_{ij}^f}{\partial x_j}\right) + \rho^f g_i \qquad [3.6.5]$$

Combining the solid and fluid equations into a single equation by multiplying the phase equations by the respective Heaviside functions and summing up, we obtain the following equations:

$$\frac{\partial \rho}{\partial t} + \frac{\partial}{\partial x_j}\left(\rho u_j\right) = 0 \tag{3.6.6}$$

$$\frac{\partial \rho u_i}{\partial t} + \frac{\partial}{\partial x_j}\left(\rho u_i u_j\right) = -H(\phi_s)\frac{\partial \rho^f}{\partial x_i} + \frac{\partial}{\partial x_j}\left(2\mu\frac{\partial S_{ij}}{\partial x_j}\right) + H(\phi_s)\rho^f g_i - 2\mu^f S_{ij}^f n_j \delta(\phi_s) \tag{3.6.7}$$

where, the composite quantities ρ and u_i are defined as:

$$\rho = H\rho_f + (1-H)\rho_s \tag{3.6.8}$$

$$\rho u_i = H\rho_f u_i^f + (1-H)\rho_s u_i^s \tag{3.6.9}$$

the last term in the right hand side of equation 3.6.7 is a viscous shear at the wall, where n_j is the normal to the fluid–solid interface and $\delta(\phi_s)$ is the Dirac delta function representing the location of the interface. The wall shear itself is modelled (after Beckermann et al, 1999) as:

$$2\mu^f S_{ij}^f n_j = 2\mu^f\left(\frac{\rho}{\rho_f}\right)u_i \delta(\phi_s) \tag{3.6.10}$$

When used in combination with RANS turbulence modelling with wall functions, the wall shear is calculated using the logarithmic law of the wall.

3.6.3 IST in an urban context

This new technique, in contrast with the conventional CFD approach, offers us the possibility of simulating relatively large urban-scale domains of the order of several hundred metres. Construction of city geometry with a 3D modelling tool is trivially complex and can be reasonably quick depending on the availability of existing data. Such geometries can be quickly converted into an STL (stereolithography) CAD (computer-aided design) file. An STL file is a triangular representation of a 3D surface geometry. The surface is tessellated logically into a set of oriented triangles (facets). Each facet is described by the unit outward normal and three points listed in counter clockwise order representing the vertices of the triangle. While the aspect ratio and orientation of individual facets are governed by the surface curvature, the size of the facets is driven by the tolerance controlling the quality of the surface representation in terms of the distance of the facets from the surface. Depending upon the chosen geometric tolerance, highly complex geometries can be represented and stored in STL format.

3.7 Urban canopy model

In order to more accurately model the physics of an urban canopy, new concepts in surface modelling have been developed. These models aim to solve the surface energy balance (SEB) for a realistic 3D urban canopy. Almost all of them share the following characteristics in their constructions:

- 3D shapes of the buildings and their impacts on drag and shear forces are represented.
- A distinction is made between roof, street and wall surfaces.
- Radiative interactions between streets and walls are accounted for, albeit in a crude way.
- Cities are represented by a regular array of parallelepipeds.

These models consist of horizontal and vertical representations of urban structures. The vertical surfaces represent building walls and horizontal surfaces represent streets and roofs. Since a clear distinction between these surfaces is made, it is appropriate to assign the correspondingly different values of thermophysical parameters to them. Such simple models use a highly simplified approach to compute complex radiation exchanges, as in the work by Noihan (1981) that is based on view factors between different surfaces or facets comprising those surfaces. Solar reflections and occlusion to the sun and the (normally isotropic) sky are also explicitly resolved. Surface temperatures, energy exchanges with the surroundings and energy storage in the built material are computed by solving a set of one dimensional conduction equations for different types of surfaces. These models can be separated into two main categories: those where the canopy air is parameterized, as in Masson's (2000) town energy balance (TEB) and those that use a drag approach, as for forests, but here with buildings (Martilli et al, 2002). The first type is normally referred to as a single-layer model because there is a direct interaction with only one atmospheric layer above the uppermost roof level. The second category is called a multilayer model because several air layers are explicitly influenced by the buildings between the ground surface and the lowest atmospheric layer.

Single-layer models – in these models, exchanges between the surfaces and atmosphere occur only at the top of the canopies and roofs. This results in simplicity and computational efficiency but since no equation is solved to compute the velocity, humidity and temperature profiles inside the canopies, some assumptions are to be made. Generally, a logarithmic law for wind is assumed to apply down to the buildings' roof level, and an exponential decay law is used below (Swaid, 1993). Some models even use a constant velocity profile inside the canopy. Furthermore, air humidity and temperature is assumed to be uniform inside the canopy. The simplest of these models is the TEB by Masson (2000), which makes use of just one generic roof, wall and street. Other models falling into this category include those of Mills (1997), which consists of building blocks with streets intersecting each other at right angles, and Kusaka et al (2001), which is similar to TEB but allows for several canyons to be treated separately. Despite the many arguments (principally revolving around computational efficiency) in favour of single-layer models, the basic underlying assumption that the temperature, humidity and wind velocity can be represented by a single value inside the canopy seems unreasonable (as shown later).

Multi-layer models – in these models, velocity, temperature and humidity profiles are computed on a vertical grid. The vertical resolution opens up the possibility of treating the roofs, walls and ground surfaces independently. Distinction can even be made between different points (depending upon the resolution) on the same vertical surfaces. These models thus allow for a more detailed and accurate treatment of multi-storied buildings (Salamanca et al, 2009). Among these models, that of Martilli et al (2002) models the effects of street orientation and variations in building heights. This model, tested against wind turbulence data from Rotach (2001) and Roth (2000), is able to represent the differential heating of the wall surfaces due to the shading effects of local obstructions. Two other models of this type have been developed, one by Vu et al (1999) and another by Kondo and Liu (1998). They are based on similar principles except that only one surface energy balance per wall is possible (there is no vertical resolution). In the Vu et al model (1999) the volume occupied by the buildings is more accurately taken into account. However, this comes at the cost of significant modifications to the atmospheric flow equations.

The above models suffer from the drawback that there is no way of ensuring that the (limited) quantities predicted by these models faithfully represent the real (invariable complex inhomogeneous) urban geometric forms that are being modelled. For this a new technique has been developed (of which more in Section 3.7.2) but this requires an urban canopy model in which energy and momentum fluxes are parameterized in terms of a wider range of geometric variables than those previously published; in particular building widths and street widths in two directions along with the building height variation and street orientation. To this end, and informed by results from comprehensive LES simulations of flow over regular arrays of cuboids, we have also developed a new theoretically rigorous 1D momentum diffusion equation that satisfies these requirements.

3.7.1 New urban canopy model

The space averaged equations, after slight modifications suggested by Kondo et al (2005), take the following form and constitute our 1D model for predicting the velocities and potential temperature profiles inside a canopy:

$$\frac{\partial <U_c>}{\partial t} = \frac{1}{\Lambda}\frac{\partial}{\partial z}\left(K_{zu}\Lambda\frac{\partial <u>}{\partial z}\right) - a_1 C_d <U_c>\sqrt{<U_c>^2 + <V_c>^2} \qquad [3.7.1a]$$

$$\frac{\partial <V_c>}{\partial t} = \frac{1}{\Lambda}\frac{\partial}{\partial z}\left(K_{zu}\Lambda\frac{\partial <v>}{\partial z}\right) - a_1 C_d <V_c>\sqrt{<U_c>^2 + <V_c>^2} \qquad [3.7.1b]$$

$$\frac{\partial <\theta_c>}{\partial t} = \frac{1}{\Lambda}\frac{\partial}{\partial z}\left(K_{z\theta}\Lambda\frac{\partial <\theta>}{\partial z}\right) + <Q_\theta> \qquad [3.7.1c]$$

$<U_c>$ and $<V_c>$ are the wind velocity components in the stream-wise and span-wise directions inside the canopies. θ_c is the space averaged potential temperature. The subscript c is added to stress the fact that these quantities are computed on the one dimensional urban canopy grid. Λ can be defined as volume porosity. The heights of buildings may be non-uniform and can be described using a variable $Pb(z)$ such that $0 \leq Pb(z) \leq 1$. $Pb(z) = 1$ means that the entire building area at z is actually occupied by buildings.

In this the drag forces offered by the cubes are taken to be proportional to the square of the local velocity field and the turbulent and dispersive fluxes have been combined (they are similar in nature for $W_1/B_1 > 1$). The coefficients a are geometric parameterisations of the simplified building layout (Figure 3.7.1):

$$a_1 = \frac{B_1 P_b(z)}{(B_1 + W_1)(B_2 + W_2) - B_1 B_2 P_b(z)} \qquad [3.7.2a]$$

$$a_2 = \frac{B_2 P_b(z)}{(B_1 + W_1)(B_2 + W_2) - B_1 B_2 P_b(z)} \qquad [3.7.2b]$$

It should be noted, that in the expression of a_1 and a_2, any plane area can be approximated to an area with infinitely wide streets. In such a situation the variables a_1 and a_2 become zero, leading to a no drag situation, as one would expect. Similarly if the variable $P_b(z)$ takes on a value of zero for all z we also have a plane.

Λ, also defined as volume porosity, is calculated as follows:

$$\Lambda = 1 - \left(\frac{B_1 B_2}{(B_1 + W_1)(B_2 + W_2)} \right) P_b(z) \qquad [3.7.3]$$

For our 1D case, this is also the surface permeability. As with the atmosphere (except for the surface layer), turbulent diffusion coefficients are used. In particular the Gambo (1978) formula is used for $R_f \leq R_{fc}$, where R_f is the flux Richardson number and $R_{fc} = 0.29$ is the critical Richardson number, so that:

$$K_{zu} = L^2 \left| \sqrt{\left(\frac{\partial U_c}{\partial z} \right)^2 + \left(\frac{\partial V_c}{\partial z} \right)^2} \right| \frac{S_m^{3/2}}{\sqrt{C}} (1 - R_f)^{1/2} \qquad [3.7.4]$$

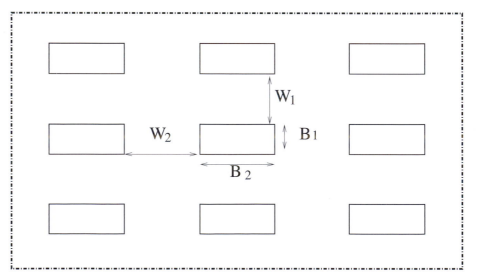

Figure 3.7.1 Regular array of parallelepipeds in an aligned configuration

A complete derivation of the expression for K_{zu} can be found in Gambo (1978). The length scale L is given by Watanabe and Kondo (1990) and was derived from consideration of a forest canopy:

$$L(z) = \frac{2\kappa^3}{ca}(1 - \exp(-\eta))$$ [3.7.5a]

where η is $\eta = \frac{caz}{2\kappa^2}$, and above the canopy we use the interpolation formula of Blackadar (1968):

$$L(z) \leq \frac{\kappa z}{1 + \frac{\kappa z}{L_o}}$$ [3.7.5b]

which interpolates between two limits $L \approx \kappa z$ as $z \to 0$ and $L \approx L_o$ as $z \to \infty$. In this study we have used a value of $L_o = 70m$. When $R_f = R_{fc}$:

$$K_{zu} = L^2 \left| \sqrt{\left(\frac{\partial U_c}{\partial z}\right)^2 + \left(\frac{\partial V_c}{\partial z}\right)^2} \right|$$ [3.7.6]

Surface fluxes

In order to compute our surface temperatures the following heat diffusion equation is solved for walls, roofs and ground surfaces (Figure 3.7.1):

$$\frac{\partial \rho_{mat} C_{pmat} T_{mat}}{\partial t} = \frac{\partial}{\partial x}\left[K_{mat} \frac{\partial T_{mat}}{\partial x} \right]$$ [3.7.7]

where T_{mat} is the temperature of the different layers inside the material, ρ_{mat} is the density, C_{pmat} is the specific heat capacity and K_{mat} is the thermal conductivity of the built material. At the external surface the following time varying heat flux boundary condition is applied:

$$q_{ext} = (1 - \alpha_{ext})Rs_{ext} + \varepsilon_{ext}Rl_{ext} - \varepsilon_{ext}\sigma T_n^4 - h_{ext}(T_n - T_{amb})$$ [3.7.8]

where α_{ext} and h_{ext} are respectively the albedo and emmisivity of the external layer, σ the Boltzmann constant, Rs_{ext} the incident external shortwave radiation, Rl_{ext} the longwave radiation received by the external surface and h_{ext} is the external surface heat transfer coefficient. In particular this value is determined by the expression (Clarke, 2001):

$$h_{ext} = c_c\left[a_c + b_c\left(\frac{U^{hor}}{d_c}\right) \right]$$ [3.7.9]

where a_c, b_c, n_c, d_c are constants deduced from laboratory studies, respectively equal to 1.09, 0.23, 5.678 and 0.3048. The term U^{hor} corresponds to the horizontal wind component.

The classical Monin–Obukhov theory is used for estimating the flux (Kondo, 1975) from horizontal and vertical surfaces when the surface temperature is below the ambient temperature. The treatment of the internal surface boundary condition is similar to that of the external albeit with a different correlation for the heat transfer coefficient and using a fixed internal temperature.

3.7.2 The equivalent geometry problem

The urban canopy parameterisation that we presented in the previous section can only be applied with confidence to those urban geometries that can be faithfully represented by a regular array of cuboids. This is problematic because in real cities we tend to encounter complex geometries that do not obviously match such simplified geometries. Yet all of the urban parameterizations thus far developed share the assumption that a city is made up either of a regular array of cuboids or of infinitely long canopies. The inputs to these models, which include street width, building width, building density and a statistical representation of the buildings' heights, are generally obtained through quantitative field surveys (which are very slow and time consuming to perform) or qualitative estimates. But in performing this geometric abstraction there is no way to ensure that the total built surfaces and volumes of the simplified geometry match those of the actual city that we intend to model or more importantly that the energy and momentum exchanges are equivalent. In this section we aim to test the central hypothesis underlying all urban canopy parameterizations, that cities can be accurately represented by a regular array of cuboids or canopies. For this we investigate, for a particular scenario, the effects of complexity in urban geometry on the spatially averaged drag forces and shortwave radiation exchange. For drag computation we used the IST (Section 3.6), while for computing the incident radiation we used the SRA (Chapter 2). After testing the above hypothesis we propose a new approach for fitting an array of cubes to any complex (realistic) geometry, so that new or existing urban parameterisation schemes can be used with confidence.

Testing the underlying hypotheses

For this study we have chosen a part of the city of Basel, the chosen part having a dimension of 1000m by 750m. A good approximation of the real geometry was sketched assuming that all the buildings have a uniform height of H=15m (Figure 3.7.2a). In fact, many of the buildings in this part of Basel, a very dense city, have been constructed to this maximum height, although they do not necessarily all have flat roofs. However, our objective here is not to attempt to reproduce reality. Rather it is to test whether a simplified abstract representation of urban geometry can be used to reproduce similar energy and momentum exchanges to its real (complex) counter part. For this, a simplification of the third dimension of our geometry should not undermine the relevance of our study. The total built vertical and horizontal surface areas are presented in Table 3.7.1. Three simplified representations of this geometry are also considered in the present investigation. These we refer to as long canopies, simple cuboids 1 and simple cuboids 2.

The long canopies representation of the city consists of ten rows of terraced buildings each of dimension 500m × 30m with an interspacing of 67m as shown in Figure 3.7.2b. Simple cuboids 1 consists of 20 × 18 cuboids each of

(a)

(b)

(c)

(d)

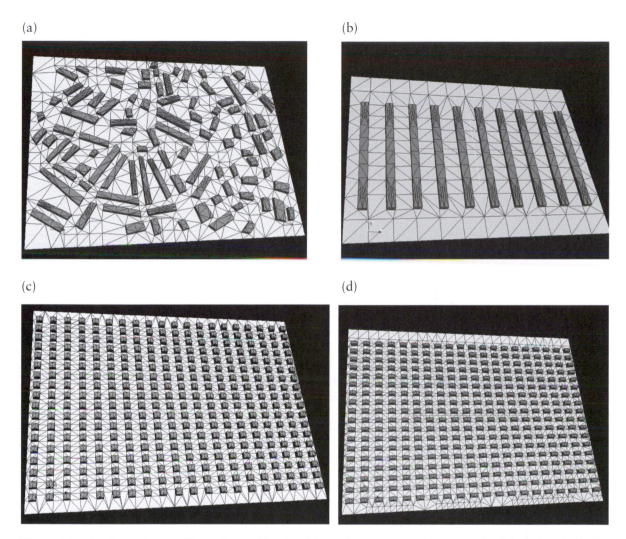

Figure 3.7.2 Four types of geometries under consideration: (a) complex geometry, (b) long canopies, (c) simple cuboids 1 and (d) simple cuboids 2

dimension 20m × 20m × 15m and aligned in a regular array with a spacing of 30m in the stream-wise direction and 20m in the span-wise direction (Figure 3.7.2c). Similarly, the simple cuboids 2 representation consists of 20 × 18 cuboids each of dimension 26.7m × 15m × 15m aligned in a regular array with a spacing of 23.3m in the stream-wise direction and 25m in the span-wise direction (Figure 3.7.2d). For clarity we present in Table 3.7.2 some associated geometric quantities: the building plan area fraction (λ_p) and the building wall area fraction (λ_w). Here $\lambda_p = A_r/A_d$ and $\lambda_w = A_w/A_d$ where A_r is the total roof area, A_w is the total wall area and A_d is the total domain area. It should be noted that the building plan area fraction for all the representations under

Table 3.7.1 Geometric characteristics of built
surfaces in the domain of interest

Horizontal built area (roofs)	144,000m²
Vertical built area (walls)	432,000m²
Horizontal built area (ground)	606,000m²
Building height	15m
Total built volume	2,160,000m³

consideration are similar (approximately 0.2). However, the wall area fraction for the long canopy varies significantly from the other representations. The intention here is to show that even when the built volume and roof area are conserved, the vertical wall area can be very different and this can have a significant impact on radiation exchange and air flow. In reality (from surveys) even basic quantities such as the built volume are hardly conserved. Thus by ensuring the equivalence of these quantities in our different representations, we focus on testing our underlying hypothesis, that real geometries can be modelled with reasonable accuracy by their simplified representations.

Radiation analysis

The magnitude of incident irradiation varies with the type of surface (wall, roof and ground) due to differences in surface tilt, orientation and occlusion. This tends to result in different surface temperatures, which in turn affects the quantity of energy being exchanged with the surroundings. To better understand this problem, we investigate in this section the differences in incident irradiation for our simplified geometries of equivalent volume.

For radiation computation, the surfaces in each of the representations are tessellated into smaller surfaces (Figure 3.7.2). The details of the tessellation are shown in Table 3.7.2. This simulation was conducted for 7 January.

Now, all domains of the same size will have the same quantity of solar radiation entering them. However, for meso-scale modelling, the correct calculation of the *distribution* of the radiation among the wall, roof and ground surfaces is important, as this determines the total absorption of radiation

Table 3.7.2 Roof area A_r, domain area A_d, wall area A_w, building plan area fraction λ_p and wall area fraction λ_w

	A_r (m^2)	A_d (m^2)	A_w (m^2)	λ_p	λ_w
Long canopies	150,000	750,000	159,000	0.200	0.21
Simple cuboid 1	144,000	750,000	432,000	0.192	0.57
Simple cuboid 2	144,180	750,000	450,360	0.192	0.60
Real morphology	144,000	750,000	432,000	0.192	0.57

within our domain and the corresponding energy that is transferred to the adjacent air. Variations in the spatial distribution of absorbed solar energy may also modify momentum transfers. From Figure 3.7.3 we make the following observations:

- Roofs – since the horizontal roof surface areas in all four of our representations are the same and all the buildings are of the same height (and hence there is no obstruction to the sky), the amount of radiation absorbed during the whole day is similar, as expected.

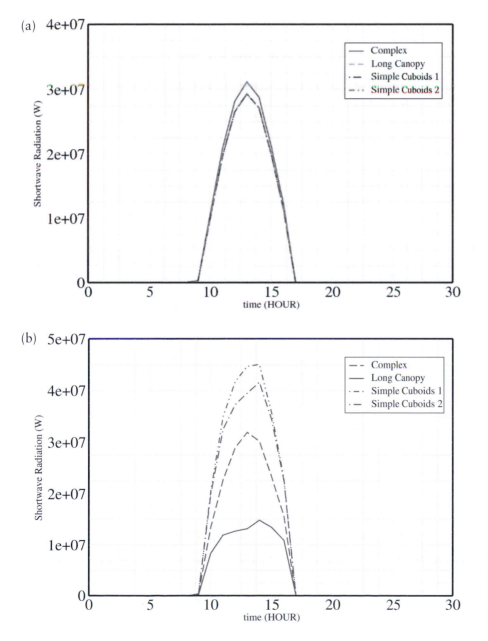

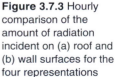

Figure 3.7.3 Hourly comparison of the amount of radiation incident on (a) roof and (b) wall surfaces for the four representations

- Ground – in the particular case of long canopies the ground receives more solar radiation than either of the cube layouts, as views to the sun and sky are relatively unobstructed. In the complex representation these views are relatively obstructed so that the radiation incident on the ground decreases. In the case of the two cuboid representations, views are even further obstructed, so that even less solar radiation is incident on the ground of our domain.
- Walls – the two simplified cuboid representations receive more shortwave radiation than the complex and long canopy representations. This is due to an increased reflected contribution and an increased south facing surface area. Thus, for this particular day, the walls in the simplified representation will be warmer than in the complex one. The opposite will be true for the ground surfaces. This will result in different surface temperatures for the walls and ground with a corresponding influence on surface energy exchanges.

CFD analysis

For the present analysis the geometrical representations are the same as those used for radiation calculations. However, the domain has been extended at all four boundaries by an additional distance of 13H, resulting in a total distance of 15H from the inlet to the start of the built area. Finally the top boundary is specified at a height of 5H. The domain is discretized into 175 × 175 × 40 cells (stream wise × span wise × vertical). For the complex geometry, two more simulations were conducted using 150 × 150 × 40 and 225 × 225 × 60 cells. Very little difference was observed in the velocity and turbulent kinetic energy field, implying grid independence, so that subsequent simulations for other geometries were conducted using the former resolution (175 × 175 × 40).

For the inlet boundary condition on the left side of the domain a standard logarithmic profile is used, given by $U = u_* \ln(z/z_0)/\kappa$ for the wind in the stream-wise direction. A surface roughness value of $z_0 = 0.3mm$ and a friction velocity of $u_* = 0.06$ has been chosen; the latter to give a free stream velocity of 1m/s. A turbulent kinetic profile is generated using the above value for U in the expression $K = (0.01U^2)$ and for the eddy dissipation rate we use a profile given by $\varepsilon = \rho C_\mu K^2 / \mu_t$, where ρ is the density of the air, $C_\mu = 0.09$ is a constant and μ_t, the turbulent viscosity, is given by $\mu_t / \mu = 20$, where μ is the viscosity of air. An outlet boundary condition was applied on the right side. For the bottom side, a wall boundary condition is specified and for the rest of the domain surfaces a symmetry boundary condition was imposed. The turbulence model used in this simulation is the standard $k - \varepsilon$ model, the advection scheme used for density and velocity is the HYBRID and a preconditioned (multi-grid) GMRES (Generalized Minimal Residual Method) solver is used for computing the pressure field. All CFD simulations were conducted for an isothermal (neutral atmosphere) stationary case. Convergence criteria of 10^{-5} for velocity and turbulent kinetic energy and 10^{-4} for dissipation were imposed for all simulations.

In Plate 9 we present the velocity field for all four geometric representations at a height of 5.6m (0.37H) above the ground plane. The more complex (real) representation is characterized by the formation of large vortices in the inter-building spaces. There is also a tendency for the flow to be deflected in the span-wise direction, due to the irregular orientation of the buildings. Long canopies strongly retard the flow, which tends to stagnate within the canopies. There is also an acceleration of flow at the ends of the long canopies. Within the other simplified representations, vortices are formed on the leeward side of the cuboids, which are small and well isolated from each other. Also, because these obstructions are non-continuous, the fluid motion remains essentially unidirectional in the stream-wise sense. These observations (in Table 3.7.3) are also evident from the magnitude of the total drag and shear forces (obtained by integrating the pressure field over the building surface vectors) imposed by the buildings contained in the domain.

Finding the equivalent geometry

From the previous section it appears to be clear that the form and layout of buildings (that have a similar cumulative volume) have important implications on the imposed drag forces and the distribution of absorbed radiant energy that might lead to differential heating of surfaces and hence to differences in the total energy exchange with the surrounding air. It is thus important to identify an arrangement of a simplified geometry (as used in the urban parameterization scheme) for which these two quantities (drag and radiation absorption) are roughly equivalent to those experienced by the corresponding real geometry. For this purpose we propose a technique for fitting such an equivalent simplified geometry. In this we define an equivalent geometry as 'that geometry which has the same built volume, horizontal and vertical built area, offers the same drag and absorbs the same radiation on vertical and horizontal surfaces as the complex/real representation' (Rasheed et al, 2010 and Rasheed, 2009; Rasheed and Robinson, 2009).

To find the equivalent geometry a digitalized 3D representation is sketched and parsed to the solver. In this a constraint is applied; that the total built surface area and volume of the two geometries should be equivalent. Mathematically:

$$S_{complex} = S_{simplified} \qquad [3.7.10]$$

$$V_{complex} = V_{simplified} \qquad [3.7.11]$$

where S represents vertical or horizontal built surface area and V the total built volume. This ensures that the building plan area fraction (λ_p) and wall area fraction (λ_w) do not change because of the mapping. This constraint is more

Table 3.7.3 Space averaged drag (*Fx, Fy*) and shear forces (*Sx,Sy*)

–	Fx (N)	Fy (N)	Sx (N)	Sy (N)	Fx+Sx (N)	Fy+Sy (N)
Complex	8207	157	985	2.5	9194	160
Long canopies	14093	38.52	1424	1.95	15507	40.5
Simple cuboids 1	4931	−46	754	1.3	5658	−45
Simple cuboids 2	2911	−35	665	−3	3577	−38

important in those urban parameterizations where the atmospheric equations are modified for the built volume. The objective functions to be minimized are then defined by the following equations:

$$f_1 = Radiation_{complex}^{wall} - Radiation_{simplified}^{wall} \qquad\qquad [3.7.12]$$

$$f_2 = Radiation_{complex}^{ground} - Radiation_{simplified}^{ground} \qquad\qquad [3.7.13]$$

$$f_3 = Drag_{complex} - Drag_{simplified} \qquad\qquad [3.7.14]$$

To demonstrate the methodology, we have chosen the three most obvious quantities: shortwave radiation incident on wall and ground surfaces and the total drag force experienced in the domain, but other parameters such as the spatially averaged velocity or turbulent kinetic energy profiles could also be chosen.

Algorithm

The algorithm for finding the equivalent geometry involves the following steps:

1. A 3D geometry of the part of the city corresponding to the meso-scale tile of interest is sketched and used as the complex representation. This geometry is saved in STL format. If digital elevation models are available, then they can be used instead.

2. The STL files are converted into GTS (GNU's Not Unix Triangulated Surface) format using open source GTS Library (2010). The volume and surface area (both horizontal and vertical) of the buildings in the domain are computed. This representation is referred to as the complex representation.

3. The daily total shortwave irradiation incident on the different surfaces ($Radiation_{complex}^{wall}$, $Radiation_{complex}^{ground}$) and the total drag forces ($Drag_{complex}$) offered by the buildings in the domain are computed using the SRA and IST respectively.

4. Using the number of buildings sketched in Step 1, together with the maximum and minimum permissible dimensions of buildings and streets found in the domain and the total built volume and surface areas computed in Step 2, a simplified representation (in terms of B_1, B_2, W_1, W_2 and street width) of the urban area is constructed.

5. For the simplified representation constructed in Step 4, the total incident shortwave irradiation on the two types of surface ($Radiation_{simplified}^{wall}$, $Radiation_{simplified}^{ground}$) together with the total drag forces ($Drag_{simplified}$) are computed.

6. The objective functions (f_1, f_2, f_3) are evaluated. If the functions are below the convergence criteria we have our equivalent simplified representation; otherwise Steps 4–6 are repeated.

It should be noted here that in the present work the choice of B_1, B_2, W_1, W_2 and street width is based on intuition and results from the previous iteration. For example, if we observe that the radiation incident on the walls in our simplified representation is considerably less than in its complex counterpart then the parameters are adjusted in such a way as to increase the south facing surfaces. Similarly, if the drag force is less in the steam-wise direction then the obstruction normal to the flow direction is increased.

Result

After several iterations we have identified a geometry that satisfies our definition of 'equivalent geometry' (Figure 3.7.4) for our case study of Basel. We can see from Table 3.7.4 that the stream-wise drag forces for both geometric models are comparable. Although the forces in the span-wise direction do differ, their magnitudes compared to the stream-wise forces are negligible.

(a)   (b)

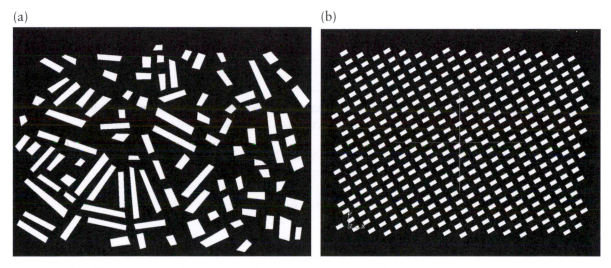

Figure 3.7.4 (a) Complex geometry and (b) its equivalent form

Table 3.7.4 Drag, shear and total force (in Newtons)

–	Fx (N)	Fy (N)	Sx (N)	Sy (N)	Fx+Sx (N)	Fy+Sy (N)
Complex	8207	157	985	2.5	9194	160
Equivalent	7731	−346	894	5.8	8625	−340

Furthermore, from Figure 3.7.5 we see that the profiles of radiation incident on the ground and wall surfaces for the complex and equivalent representations are now precisely superimposed. The radiation incident on the roof surfaces is not presented: it is proportional to the horizontal roof surface areas, which are identical for both representations. Each cube in the equivalent (simplified) representation has a dimension of 26.7 × 15 × 15m (width × breadth × height). The east–west street width is 23.3m and it is aligned at an angle of 30° to the

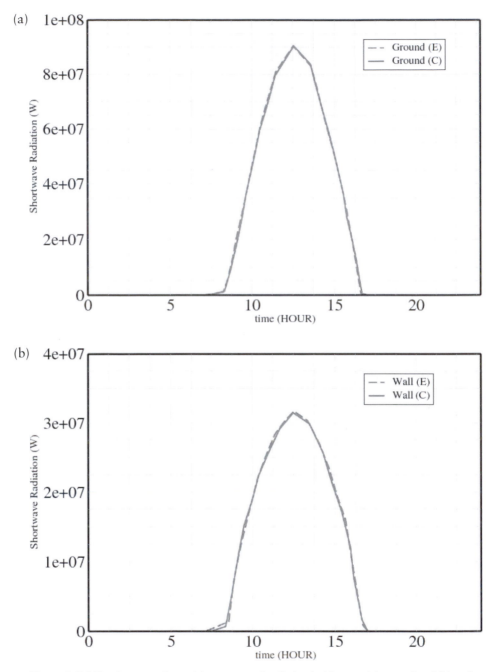

Figure 3.7.5 Hourly comparison of the amount of radiation incident on (a) ground and (b) wall surfaces

east, while the north–south street width is 25m and is aligned orthogonal to the other street.

Although these results are convincing, a potential shortfall of this methodology is that we suppose that drag and shortwave radiation are *fully* sufficient in themselves to judge the quality of fit between real and simplified geometries for urban climate prediction. This of course is not necessarily the case. We have focussed on these two for reasons of parsimony, but further work would be warranted to confirm or disprove this hypothesis and in the latter case to select alternative or additional parameters. Finally, a process of manual trial and error has thus far been employed in fitting our simplified geometries by minimizing differences in drag and radiation predictions. Subject to computational constraints the use of evolutionary algorithms would be more appropriate, enabling the available parameter space to be explored in a far more rigorous way.

3.8 Applications of the multi-scale urban climate model

To demonstrate the capabilities of our multi-scale model we have chosen the city of Basel in Switzerland. Basel is located at the border with Germany and France, at a latitude and longitude of 47° 00'N and 8° 00'E, respectively.

To conduct a realistic simulation, input data such as the topography and land use are required. We also need some means for forcing the superscale effects on our meso-scale model. For this latter we use data from the NCEP (National Centers for Environmental Prediction) global model, from which simulation data (velocity, humidity, temperature, pressure) are available via a web portal[1] at a spatial resolution of 270km. To force these boundary conditions onto the meso-scale model, we first construct a domain with a resolution of 15 × 15km assume it to be 100 per cent rural, and run a simulation to generate an output file. This output file is then used to force another smaller domain with a higher resolution and so on until we are able to interpolate the boundary conditions onto a grid of 0.5km to 1km (Plate 10).

A meso-scale domain, representing a city and its immediate hinterland, may span several tens or even hundreds of kilometres, over which the topography may vary significantly. This we can take into account using topographical data from the US geological survey[2] that is available in digital elevation model format for a horizontal resolution of 30 arc seconds (approximately 1km). This simply requires processing to extract the data relating to our domain of interest and convert it to the appropriate format (Plate 11 left). As noted in Figure 3.4.1 above, we also require land-use data: we need to know, for each grid cell, the proportion of that cell which corresponds to an urban land use. For this the Global Vegetation Monitoring Unit of the European Commission's Joint Research Centre provides a harmonized global land cover database for the year 2000. Extracting the data relating exclusively to our domain we have the remaining input data that is necessary for our meso-scale simulation (Plate 11 right), to account for ground thermophysical properties and possible evapotranspiration.

Except of course that we also need to account for the energy and momentum exchanges within the urban canopy for each of our fully or partially urban grid cells. For this we have gone through the procedure outlined above for each cell, creating an approximate 3D model of the buildings and deriving the equivalent simplified geometry. The corresponding parameters are then associated with the urban canopy model for each cell and the meso-scale simulations are carried out.

Plate 12 contrasts the results at 5m above ground level for 13:00H on 25 June for the Basel region with and without properly representing the urban context within the meso-scale model. Here one can clearly see a rise in temperature in and around the city. This can be attributed to the increased absorption of radiation by the urban structures, to the change in surface thermophysical properties and a damping of air flow within the city. The UHI intensity is around 5–6°C. This has significant implications for buildings' space conditioning energy demands.

These meso-scale simulation results are useful in their own right and as input to urban-scale resource flow modelling tools such as CitySim (Chapter 6). But these meso-scale simulation results may also be used to force the boundary conditions of a local micro-scale model, so that good quality local urban climate predictions may be achieved while accounting for large-scale climatic tendencies such as the UHI effect. This can be of value for more accurate building and urban-scale energy simulation as well as for the simulation of pedestrian comfort.

By way of example we present in Plate 13 microclimate IST simulation results relating to the district of Matthäus in Basel, for which the boundary conditions have been forced using the meso-scale model. The ambient temperature tends to be higher in the regions where the velocity is lower (Plate 13 right); the more a packet of air circulates around a built structure, the more time it has to exchange energy with the buildings, thus becoming warmer. As can be observed in Plate 13 (left) streams of air flowing through the city attain a higher temperature compared to the stream that avoids contact with built surfaces.

3.9 Conclusions

The urban climate is substantially different from the rural environment in which the majority of meteorological measurements are made and these differences can have significant implications not only for buildings' energy demands but also for the comfort of pedestrians. This therefore needs to be accounted for in such energy and comfort predictions. The only viable method for doing so is by numerical modelling. But the task is complicated by the diverse spatial and temporal scales involved. In this chapter we introduced the difficulties involved in numerical urban climate modelling and introduced a new multi-scale approach by which they may be overcome. We also applied this methodology to simulate the climate of Basel in Switzerland and in more detail the district of Matthäus.

This multi-scale modelling methodology simulates the features that we expect of the urban climate. The city is on average warmer than its rural hinterland and this warming reaches its maximum as we approach the centre of the city; though this epicentre may be deflected by wind. The temperature profile is also shifted in phase relative to the rural profile, so that the difference between the two is at its maximum at night and minimum during the day; indeed the difference may be negative during the afternoon. This gives us confidence in the predictive accuracy of the model, as do comparisons with measurements for the city of Basel (Rasheed, 2009). But we should not be complacent. This model has yet to be rigorously validated against a comprehensive empirical dataset; largely because high quality spatially and temporally fine datasets do not yet exist. Our assumption that drag forces and shortwave irradiation are sufficient to calibrate the parameterization of the urban canopy model also remains to be verified. But perhaps the biggest challenge facing us is to simulate the climate of the city for an entire year, as required by urban resource flow models of the CitySim variety (Chapter 6). This will require that as much advantage as possible be taken of processes that may be computed in parallel.

Notes

1   www.cdc.noaa.gov/cdc/reanalysis/reanalysis.shtml
2   http://edc.usgs.gov/products/elevation/gtopo30/gtopo30.htm

References

Beckermann, C., Diepers, H-J., Steinbach, I., Karma, A., Tong, X. (1999) 'Modeling melt convection in phase-field simulations of solidification', *Journal of Computational Physics*, vol 154, pp468–496

Blackadar, A. K. (1968) 'The Vertical Distribution of Wind and Turbulent Exchange in Neutral Atmosphere', *Journal of Geophysical Research*, vol 67, pp3085–3102

Bougeault, P. and Lacarrere, P. (1989) 'Parametrization of Orography-Induced Turbulence in a Mesobeta-Scale Model', *Monthly Weather Review*, vol 117, pp1872–1890

Britter, R. and Hanna, S. (2003) 'Flow and dispersion in urban areas', *Annual Review of Fluid Mechanics*, vol 35, pp469–496

Chung, T. (2002) *Computational Fluid Dynamics*, Cambridge University Press, Cambridge

Clappier, A. (1998) 'A correction method for use in multidimensional time-splitting advection algorithms: Application to two- and three-dimensional transport' *Monthly Weather Review*, vol 126, pp232–242

Clappier, A., Perrochet, P., Martilli, A., Muller, F. and Krueger, B. (1996) 'A new non hydrostatic mesoscale model using a cvfe (control volume finite element) discretization technique', *EUROTRAC Symposium 17*, Computational Mechanics Publications, Southampton, pp527–531

Clarke, J. (2001) *Energy Simulation in Building Design*, Butterworth-Heinemann, Oxford

Crowley, W. (1968) 'Numerical advection experiments', *Monthly Weather Review*, vol 96, pp1–11

Elnahas, M. M. and Williamson, T. J. (1997) 'An improvement of the CTTC model for predicting urban air temperatures', *Energy and Buildings*, vol 25, pp41–49

Gambo, K. (1978) 'Notes on the turbulence closure model for atmospheric boundary layers', *Journal of the Meteorological Society of Japan*, vol 56, pp466–480

Graves, H., Watkins, R., Westbury, P. and Littlefair, P. (2001) *Cooling Building in London: Overcoming the Heat Island*, BRE Report BR 431, CRC Ltd, London

GTS Library (2010) available at http://gts.sourceforge.net, last accessed 16 December 2010

Hanna, S. R., Chang, J. C. and Strimaitis, D. G. (1993) 'Hazardous gas-model evaluation with field observations', *Atmos. Environ. A-Gen.*, vol 23, pp2265–2285

Klemp, J. B. and Lilly, D. (1975) 'The dynamics of wave-induced downslope winds', *Journal of Atmospheric Science*, vol 32, pp320–339

Kolmogorov, A. (1941) 'A local structure of turbulence in incompressible viscous fluid for very large reynolds numbers', *Doklady ANSSSR*, vol 30, pp301–304

Kondo, J. (1975) 'Air–sea bulk transfer coefficients in diabetic conditions', *Boundary-Layer Meteorology*, vol 9, vol 91–124

Kondo, H. and Liu, F. (1998) 'A study on the urban thermal environment obtained through one-dimensional urban canopy model', *J. Jap. Soc. Atmos. Environ.*, vol 33, pp179–192

Kondo, H., Genchi, Y., Kikegawa, Y., Ohashi, Y., Yoshikado, H. and Komiyama, H. (2005) 'Development of a multi-layer urban canopy model for the analysis of energy consumption in a big city: Structure of the urban canopy model and its basic performance', *Boundary-Layer Meteorology*, vol 116, pp395–421

Krpo, A. (2009) 'Development and application of a numerical simulation system to evaluate the impact of anthropogenic heat fluxes on urban boundary layer climate', PhD thesis, Swiss Federal Institute of Technology Lausanne, Lausanne

Kurihara, Y. (1976) 'On the development of spiral bands in a tropical cyclone', *Journal of Atmospheric Science*, vol 33, pp940–958

Kusaka, H., Kondo, H., Kikegawa, Y. and Kimura, F. (2001) 'A simple single-layer urban canopy model for atmospheric models: Comparision with multi-layer and slab models', *Boundary-Layer Meteorology*, vol 101, pp329–358

Leveque, R. (2002) *Finite Volume Method for Hyperbolic Problems*, Cambridge University Press, Washington DC

Louis, J. (1979) 'A parametric model of vertical eddies fluxes in the atmosphere', *Boundary Layer Meteorology*, vol 17, pp187–202

Martilli, A., Clappier, A. and and Rotach, M. (2002) 'An urban surface exchange parametrization for mesoscale models', *Boundary Layer Meteorology*, vol 104, pp261–304

Masson, V. (2000) 'A physically-based scheme for the urban energy budget in atmospheric models', *Boundary Layer Meteorology*, vol 94, pp357–397

McBean, G. and Elliott, J. (1975) 'Vertical transport of kinetic energy by turbulence and pressure in boundary-layer', *Journal of Atmospheric Science*, vol 32, pp753–766

Mills, G. (1997) 'An urban canopy-layer climate model', *Theoretical Applied Climatology*, vol 57, pp229–244

Noihan J. (1981) 'A model for the net total radiation flux at the surfaces of a building', *Building and Environment*, vol 16, pp259–266

Oke, T. (1988) *An Introduction to Boundary Layer Meteorology*, Kluwer Academic Publisher, Dordrecht

Otte, T., Lacser, A., Dupont, S. and Ching, J. (2004) 'Implementation of an urban canopy parametrization in a mesoscale meteorological model', *Journal of Applied Meteorology*, vol 43, pp1648–1665

Palmer, J., Littlefair, P., Watkins, R. and Kolokotroni, M. (2000) 'Urban heat islands', *Building Services Journal*, vol 5, pp55–56

Peskin, C. (1977) 'Numerical analysis of blood flow in the heart', *Journal of Computational Physics*, vol 25, pp220–238

Rasheed, A. (2009) '*Multiscale modelling of urban climate*', PhD Thesis, École Polytechnique Fédérale de Lausanne, Lausanne

Rasheed, A. and Robinson, D. (2009) 'On the effects of complex urban geometries on mesoscale modeling', in *Proc. Int. Conf. Urban Climatology*, Yokohama, International Association for Urban Climate

Rasheed, A., Robinson, D., Clappier, A., Chidambran, N. and Lakehal, D. (2010) 'Representing complex urban geometries in mesoscale modelling', *International Journal of Climatology*, available online at DOI: 10.1002/joc.2240

Robinson, D. and Stone, A. (2004) 'Thermal microclimate modelling', Deliverable Report 7a, Project SUNtool, BDSP Partnership London for European Commission, Brussels, June

Robinson, D., Campbell, N., Gaiser, W., Kabel, K., Le-Mouele, A., Morel, N., Page, J., Stankovic, S. and Stone, A. (2007) 'SUNtool – a new modelling paradigm for simulating and optimising urban sustainability', *Solar Energy*, vol 81, no 9, p1196–1211

Rotach, M. (2001) 'Simulation of urban-scale dispersion using a lagrangian stocastic dispersion model', *Boundary Layer Meteorology*, vol 99, pp379–410

Roth, M. (2000) 'Review of atmospheric turbulence over cities', *Q. J. R. Meteorological Society*, vol 126, pp941–990

Salamanca, F., Krpo, A., Martilli, A. and Clappier, A. (2009) 'A new building energy model coupled with an urban canopy parameterization for urban climate simulation – part I: Formulation, verification and sensitivity analysis of the model', *Theoretical and Applied Climatology*, vol 99, pp331–344

Santamouris, M. (1998) 'The Athens urban climate experiment', in *Proceedings of the 15th International Conference on Passive and Low Energy Architecture* (PLEA), Lisbon, Passive and Low Energy Architecture, London

Sasamori, T. (1999) 'Radiative cooling calculation for application to general circulation experiments', *Journal of Applied Meteorology*, vol 16, pp721–729

Schayes, G. (1982) 'Direct determination of diffusivity profiles from synoptic reports', *Atmospheric Environment*, vol 16, pp1407–1413

Schiestel, R. (2007) *Modeling and Simulation of Turbulent Flows*, Wiley-Blackwell

Swaid, H. (1993) 'The role of radiative/convective interaction in creating the microclimate of urban street canyons', *Boundary Layer Meteorology*, vol 64, pp231–259

Swaid, H. and Hoffman, M. E. (1989) 'The prediction of impervious ground surface temperature by the Surface Thermal Time Constant (STTC) model', *Energy and Buildings*, vol 13, no 2, pp149–157

Swaid, H. and Hoffman, M. E. (1990) 'Prediction of urban air temperature variations using the analytical CTTC model', *Energy and Buildings*, vol 14, pp313–324

Taha, H. (1999) 'Modifying a mesoscale meteorological model to better incorporate urban heat storage: A bulk parametrization approach', *Journal of Applied Meteorology*, vol 38, pp446–473

Thuborn, J. (1996) 'Tvd schemes, positive schemes and universal limiters', *Monthly Weather Review*, vol 125, pp1990–1993

Vu, T. C., Asaeda, T. and Ashie, Y. (1999) 'Development of a numerical model for the evaluation of the urban thermal environment', *Journal of Wind Engineering and Industrial Aerodynamics*, vol 81, pp181–191

Wang, T. A. and Lin, Y.-L. (1999) 'Wave ducting in a stratified shear flow over a two dimensional mountain. Part ii: Implications for the development of high drag states for severe downslope windstorms', *Journal of Atmospheric Science*, vol 56, pp437–452

Watanabe, T. and Kondo, J. (1990) 'The influence of the canopy structure and density upon the mixing length within and above vegetation', *Journal of Meteorological Society of Japan*, vol 68, pp227–235

4
Pedestrian Comfort

Darren Robinson and Michael Bruse

4.1 Introduction

As we strive to improve the sustainability of urban developments, so there will be increasing pressure on urban areas to intensify their use of personal (walking, cycling) and public (buses, trams, trains) means of transport. In consequence, a greater fraction of the urban realm can be expected to be designed to favour pedestrians and cyclists as they walk or cycle to and from their destinations, perhaps via modes of public transport. They will thus be expected to spend more time outdoors. It is important then that this outdoor experience be pleasant, if this strategy is to succeed.

But there are myriad factors that influence pedestrians' perception of, and thus satisfaction with, the outdoor environment. Broadly we may think of these as being environmental, influenced by the stimuli received by our thermal, visual, aural and olfactory receptors as well as our desire to remain dry and to perform our tasks even in the presence of wind. We are also influenced by sociological factors. For example do we feel safe? Is the route crowded? Do we like the appearance of this environment? Are the amenities that we desire sufficiently close by? Ideally we would have some means for evaluating these diverse factors to arrive at an overall judgement regarding pedestrians' satisfaction.

In the following sections we review the progress that has been made in evaluating pedestrians' environmental comfort, with a particular emphasis on mechanical wind comfort and thermal comfort. We then discuss attempts that have been made to provide for an integrated assessment of environmental comfort before finally speculating as to how we might develop a unified index of pedestrians' overall comfort, considering both environmental and sociological factors.

4.2 Environmental comfort

As noted above, pedestrians' environmental comfort is influenced by the physical stimuli received by their thermal, visual, aural and olfactory receptors. In the case of thermal comfort these stimuli, which include air temperature, relative air velocity, surface temperature, radiant temperature and relative humidity, influence the heat that is transferred between the human body and the ambient environment by convection (23 per cent),[1] conduction (9 per cent), radiation (35 per cent) and a combination of evaporation and respiration (33 per cent), respectively.

In the urban context, the physical stimuli driving these heat transfers may vary significantly in time and space, according to the mechanisms influencing the urban climate discussed in Chapter 3. For example, depending upon the time of day and on the construction materials used, the air temperature may be higher or lower than in a local rural setting, likewise the surface temperature that influences heat conduction through our footwear as well as radiant exchanges. Radiant exchanges may also be influenced by the provision of shade at pedestrian level. If this shade is provided by vegetation, there may also be an influence on local air temperature (due to evapotranspiration) as well as on relative humidity. Water features may also be a source of evaporative cooling.

Following from the above heat exchanges, receptors located within our skin record a sensation of relative warmth or cold. Corresponding messages are then transmitted to the hypothalamus. To prevent our core body temperature from rising, messages are sent to effectors to dilate our blood vessels and to start sweating. In the inverse case, our effectors may be instructed to constrict blood vessels and start shivering (leading to an increase in heart and therefore metabolic rate).

The thermal sensation recorded by our skin receptors and the relative effectiveness of the associated physiological thermoregulatory control mechanisms influences our thermal satisfaction (or comfort). But unlike our thermoregulatory mechanisms, the mapping from thermal sensation (skin or core temperature) to satisfaction is not common to all human beings. Indeed, we express considerable diversity depending upon our personal expectations, the opportunities available to us to adapt our environment and possibly also age and gender.[2]

This mechanism of receptor sensation, effector adaptation and mapping to satisfaction is shared by our sense of sight, but in the case of smell and sound we are more limited in that we are not able to employ intrinsic effectors. We may, however, extrinsically close our nostrils or cover our ears to prevent unpleasant or harmful odours or noise levels!

As noted above, pedestrian comfort is also influenced by rain and wind, both of which influence thermal comfort by increasing the conductivity of our clothing and hence the convection of heat from its outer surface, and/or by increasing the rate of convection and evaporation from our skin and clothing. Our clothing also tends to become less supple when wet and high wind speeds tend to impair our ability to conduct basic outdoor tasks such as reading, walking or sitting.

Research on pedestrians' environmental comfort has thus far focussed on thermal and mechanical wind comfort. In this, both empirical and numerical methods have been employed in an attempt to characterize these aspects of comfort as well as to produce predictive models.

4.3 Empirical methods

Empirical methods are based on the analysis of results from field surveys of pedestrians' environmental comfort. Informed by a considerable body of work on *indoor* environmental comfort, these normally involve soliciting candidates to complete a questionnaire while simultaneously recording measurements of the local physical environment. These surveys may be transverse, in which a broad cross section of respondents are solicited one time only, or longitudinal, in which a smaller set of respondents are requested to participate in the survey at regular intervals for an extended period of time. The format of the questionnaire as well as the physical measurements that are recorded depend upon the field survey objectives.

4.3.1 Mechanical wind comfort

The earliest systematic attempt to relate wind speed to peoples' comfort was devised by Admiral Sir Francis Beaufort in 1806. Originally designed for use at sea, the Beaufort scale has since been extended for use on land and refined by Penwarden (1973) by integrating results from observations of the effects of wind on pedestrians (Table 4.3.1). For this Penwarden also performed the first quantitative tests of the effects of wind force on the human body, the rate of work when walking against wind and on the effects of wind on thermal comfort. From these analyses he concluded that a mean wind speed of 5m/s marks the onset of discomfort, that 10m/s may be defined as unpleasant and that speeds of around 20m/s are dangerous. This work was prompted by fatal accidents, particularly involving elderly persons, in the vicinity of tall buildings.

Table 4.3.1 Beaufort's wind speed and the corresponding effects

Beaufort Number	Speed (m/s)	Effects
0,1	0–1.5	Calm, no noticeable wind
2	1.6–3.3	Wind felt on face
3	3.4–5.4	Wind extends light flag; hair is disturbed; clothing flaps
4	5.5–7.9	Raises dust, dry soil and loose paper; hair disarranged
5	8.0–10.7	Force of wind felt on body; drifting snow becomes airborne; limit of agreeable wind on land
6	10.8–13.8	Umbrella used with difficulty; hair blown straight; difficult to walk steadily; wind noise on ears unpleasant; airborne snow above head height
7	13.9–17.1	Inconvenience felt when walking
8	17.2–20.7	Generally impedes progress; great difficulty with balance in gusts
9	20.8–24.4	People blown over by gusts

Source: Penwarden (1973)

This is due to the relatively high velocity flow incident at the upper parts of tall buildings being deflected down to pedestrian level. In such situations the gradient of wind speed approaching a corner of a tall building may be particularly significant, causing pedestrians to lose their balance.

This seminal work prompted further experimental studies (Hunt et al, 1976; Murakami and Deguchi, 1981) to develop more rigorous wind comfort criteria based on observed phenomena under different steady wind conditions. Meanwhile there was a growing realization that threshold wind speeds for different types of pedestrian activity should be associated with a limiting probability of occurrence; in other words that the concept of risk of discomfort, or indeed of danger, should be introduced. Following from this rationale Penwarden and Wise (1975), Lawson and Penwarden (1975), Isyumov and Davenport (1975) and Melbourne (1978) proposed alternative criteria based on limiting frequencies of occurrence of wind speed, see Figure 4.3.1 from which it is clear that there is considerable diversity among these criteria.

Furthermore, and as Murakami et al (1986) claim, these diverse criteria tended not to be based on strong empirical or theoretical foundations.[3] Indeed Ratcliff and Peterka (1990) conclude that there is no ideal set of criteria

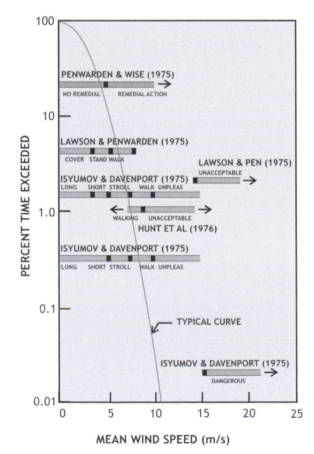

Figure 4.3.1 Pedestrian wind comfort criteria based on the percentage of time that mean wind speeds are exceeded

Source: Ratcliff and Peterka (1990)

available in published form and a more recent comparison of criteria used by different public research laboratories (Sanz-Andres and Cuerva, 2006) suggests that there remains a need to harmonize the disparate wind comfort criteria; or indeed to supplement those that exist.

Irrespective of these conclusions, Lawson's criteria seem to have gained popularity,[4] despite Ratcliff and Peterka's suggestion that these are too lenient, especially for dangerous locations. In their current usage (Ratcliff and Peterka, 1990) these take the form shown in Table 4.3.2.

To apply these criteria, we may either use numerical or physical modelling techniques to predict the wind speeds within a particular urban development. As noted in Chapter 3, the correct modelling of turbulent kinetic energy production and dissipation in the vicinity of bluff bodies, which tend to dominate in urban settings, is non-trivial. Indeed these bluff bodies are poorly represented by the conventional temporal averaging of the three dimensional Navier-Stokes equations (we call this a RANS model) in CFD software. For these situations LES models are preferred, in which the production, transport and diffusion of larger eddies is explicitly modelled and smaller eddies are isotropically diffused. But these models are highly computationally demanding. Indeed with currently available resources, the computational cost tends to be prohibitive for simulations of urban domains of the size of several hundred metres. Much more practical is the use of wind tunnels, in which the flow regime is assumed to be isothermal.[6]

A physical model placed in a wind tunnel should explicitly represent the local urban scene up to a distance of at least five times the largest dimension of the scene of interest. Beyond this, the roughness of the approach for a given wind direction should be adjusted to match the local terrain. Now as mentioned in previous chapters, meteorological measurements are usually recorded at rural locations, typically airports, and at a standard height, usually of 10m. Using a reference velocity at this height (v_{ref}), the coincident speed within the atmospheric boundary layer may be estimated. The incoming flow within the wind tunnel should then be adjusted until the scaled speed above the model's boundary layer matches this corrected reference wind speed for the wind direction of interest. Wind speeds may then be measured at a range of pedestrian

Table 4.3.2 Wind comfort criteria of Lawson and Penwarden (1975)

Situation	Limiting criteria[5]
Covered area	$\bar{U} > 3.35$ m/s for T < 4% and $\hat{U} > 5.7$ m/s for T < 4%
Standing area	$\bar{U} > 5.45$ m/s for T < 4% and $\hat{U} > 9.3$ m/s for T < 4%
Walking area	$\bar{U} > 7.95$ m/s for T < 4% and $\hat{U} > 13.6$ m/s for T < 4%
Unacceptable	$\bar{U} > 13.85$ m/s for T < 2% or $\hat{U} > 23.7$ m/s for T < 2%
Uncomfortable	In excess of unacceptable

Source: Lawson and Penwarden (1975)

locations of interest within an urban scene for this wind direction and the process repeated for all directions of interest; for example 16, so that we have wind direction intervals of 22.5°. For the ith direction and jth observation point within the model, the local wind speed at the kth hour is then $v_{ijk} = v_{ik} \cdot v_{ij}/v_{ref}$. Repeating this for each hour, it is then a straightforward matter to determine a cumulative distribution of wind speeds and thus which of the comfort criteria are satisfied for each point within an urban pedestrian scene. In Plate 14 for example results from wind tunnel measurements have been used to identify which pedestrian activities are acceptable for a proposed urban development in Islington, London.

But these mechanical wind comfort criteria are not in themselves sufficient to judge pedestrians' overall comfort. As discussed above, this depends not only on their ability to conduct mechanical tasks without difficulty but also on achieving this within a comfortable range of environmental stimuli, thermal in particular.

4.3.2 Thermal comfort

In a first attempt to quantify relationships between relevant physical variables and their influence on human thermal comfort outdoors, Tacken (1989) conducted a transverse survey involving some 210 subjects of varying age and gender located at Delft in The Netherlands. For each test involving two people, participants were seated for 20 minutes before completing a questionnaire. During this time the coincidental temperature (t, °C), wind speed (v, m/s) and solar irradiance (I, W/m²) were recorded; these having been identified from literature as the dominant physical variables influencing human thermal comfort. From these results the following multiple linear regression equation[7] was derived to predict thermal satisfaction (TS): $TS = -0.329 + 0.215t - 0.600v + 0.002I$. Tacken also suggested that areas designed for outdoor relaxation should be well oriented to the sun and that the mean wind speed should not exceed 2.5m/s – though higher wind speeds may be tolerated if compensated by relatively high solar irradiance (exceeding 700W/m²).

A similar procedure was later followed by Givoni et al (2003) in Tokyo, Japan. For this longitudinal survey, three pairs of individuals of varying age and gender were asked to remain seated in three different types of environment (exposed to the sun and wind; exposed to the sun, reduced wind; exposed to wind, shaded from the sun) on several occasions throughout the four seasons. From these results the following multiple linear regression equation[7] was derived to predict thermal satisfaction (TS): $TS = -0.329 + 0.215t - 0.600v + 0.002I$. Although Givoni et al warn that the sample size from which this equation is derived is very small, the fit with observed thermal satisfaction is extremely good (the slope is almost unity: $T_{pred} \approx T_{obs}$).

In a prior summertime study in Osaka, Japan, college students were asked to record their thermal satisfaction at specific positions while walking predefined routes: one beginning in an air-conditioned underground space and ending out of doors, the other starting outside and ending within the underground space (Nagara et al, 1996). From these results it was evident that students walking outdoors that were previously indoors, in a cooled environment, systematically reported warmer thermal sensation than those that began their tour outdoors; in other words 'thermal sensation …is effected by the history of (environmental) exposure'.

Despite Nagara et al's assertion that one must consider the history of pedestrians' exposure (a complication that had been avoided by Tacken (1989) and Givoni et al (2003) since occupants had been sedentary outdoors for some time before reporting their sensation), Nikolopoulou et al (2001) asked respondents to report their satisfaction immediately upon interrupting their prior activity. In common with the previous surveys, coincidental environmental measurements were also recorded; likewise their clothing and prior activity. The actual sensation vote (ASV) was then compared with the predicted mean vote (PMV) obtained using a steady state thermal comfort model (see Section 4.4), assuming participants to now be sedentary. From this the corresponding predicted and actual percentage of people dissatisfied (PPD and APD) was estimated, with the PPD for the entire dataset being 66 per cent as compared to a total APD of 11 per cent. The authors (Nikolopoulou and Steemers, 2003) later suggested that this discrepancy 'could not be (explained) by physical parameters …(that) psychological adaptation is also an important factor', going on to suggest that the discrepancy between PMV and ASV is explained by the following psychological factors that are not taken into account in the PMV model: naturalness, expectations, experience, time of exposure, perceived control and environmental stimulation. While this is plausible, an alternative explanation might be that the scales used in determining PMV and ASV are incompatible[8] and that the thermal history (c.f. Nagara et al's findings) had in fact been ignored, although accounting for the latter would require a dynamic model.

Nikolopoulou et al (2001) also observed the number of people that were using outdoor spaces and related these observations to average globe temperature for each of the sites surveyed. In all cases these were found to be positively correlated, as one would expect.

Based on the results from a much larger European field survey campaign (Nikolopoulou and Lykoudis, 2006), and following a similar methodology to that adopted in her earlier doctoral work, Nikolopoulou (2004) presents regression models of thermal sensation for a variety of European cities as well as a single regression model for the whole of Europe. These models are linear functions of air temperature, solar irradiance and wind speed as well as relative humidity. Using these regression equations in conjunction with simplified models of shortwave and longwave irradiance as well as wind speed, Katzschner et al (2004) predict the spatial distribution of pedestrians' sensation. Provided that the models used are valid, this is a potentially powerful tool.

4.4 Numerical methods

4.4.1 Stationary models

Numerical methods for evaluating pedestrians' comfort have thus far been limited to thermal comfort. As noted in Section 4.2, heat is transferred between humans and their ambient environment principally by, convection C, radiation R and evaporation E. Indeed we may write, for a given metabolic rate M and rate of work W, that the change in energy storage S, from which we may derive the core temperature, is $M - W - E - C - R = S$. From this observation and using results from carefully controlled climate chamber experiments involving college students, Fanger (1970) derived the following equation to predict the mean vote of a large population of subjects (on a seven point scale ranging from −3 to +3: cold, cool, slightly cool, neutral, slightly warm, warm, hot):

$$PMV = \left(0.303\exp\left(-0.036M\right)+0.28\right)\cdot \text{coefficient for change in metabolic rate}$$

$$\{M - W \quad \text{heat production in human body at rest}$$

$$-3.05\cdot 10^{-3}\left(5733 - 6.99(M-W) - p_a\right) \quad \text{heat loss by vapour diffusion through skin}$$

$$-0.42\left(M - W - 58.15\right) \quad \text{heat loss by sweat evaporation from skin}$$

$$-1.7\cdot 10^{-5}M\left(5867 - p_a\right) \quad \text{heat loss by latent respiration}$$

$$-0.0014M\left(34 - t_a\right) \quad \text{heat loss by dry respiration}$$

$$-3.96\cdot 10^{-8}f_{cl}\left[\left(t_{cl} + 273\right)^4 - \left(\overline{t_r} + 273\right)^4\right] \quad \text{heat loss by radiation}$$

$$-f_{cl}h_c\left(t_{cl} - t_a\right)\} \quad \text{heat loss by convection} \quad [4.4.1]$$

and from this the percentage of people that are thermally dissatisfied (PPD). Thus an empirical model is used to translate the results from a numerical steady state heat balance to a group's thermal sensation and their corresponding (dis) satisfaction ((dis)comfort). This simple empirical numerical model has since become enshrined in international standards for the prediction of human thermal comfort in indoor environments (ISO, 1984, 1994).

But it is only really appropriate to use this model to predict thermal satisfaction when the human body is expected to be at thermal equilibrium with its environment. In indoor environments such conditions are encountered when a person's activity and clothing level have been constant for a sufficiently long time within an environment that is maintained at constant temperature (air and radiant), velocity and relative humidity,[9] as in air-conditioned environments. Clearly this is unlikely to be the case in outdoor spaces, in which pedestrians tend to move at a non-constant rate within a microclimate that is highly varied – both spatially and temporally – with the feedback to perceived comfort possibly leading to actions to adapt their activity, walking route and clothing levels. Given that we are typically outside for relatively short periods of time, a steady state model would thus give a false result – typically a pessimistic one (Höppe, 2002).

As noted earlier, it is likely for this reason that Nikolopoulou et al's (2001) ASVs differed so markedly from the PMVs: a steady state model was applied within a non-steady environment, neglecting the participants' recent history.

4.4.2 Dynamic models

An alternative to the approach adopted by Fanger (1970) is to model the dynamic human thermoregulatory responses to environmental stimuli and thus to map in some way from sensation to satisfaction. This was the approach adopted by Arens and Bosselmann (1989) in their seminal work that was conceived to support the design of comfortable outdoor spaces. First, they used physical modelling techniques with which to adapt hourly rural climate data to the urban context. In particular, wind speed data was modified using velocity ratios measured at chosen points within a physical model placed within a boundary layer wind tunnel. The incidence or otherwise of solar irradiance at these points was determined by appropriately orienting and tilting the physical model with respect to a parallel light source.[10] The modified hourly data were then input, along with time and location-dependent assumptions of activity and clothing level, to a simplified two-node dynamic model of the human thermoregulatory system (Gagge et al, 1970) in which the human body is represented as two concentric cylinders representing both skin and core for which all major heat transfers are simulated, including blood flow regulation and perspiration.

In cold conditions, the model determines comfort using the skin temperature and in hot conditions this is achieved using the fraction of the skin that is covered by unevaporated perspiration (skin wettedness) (ASHRAE, 1981). In this way it was possible to predict the proportion of the time, during normal pedestrian hours, that pedestrians would be comfortable at the chosen reference points, enabling designers to make informed decisions as to how to improve the design of outdoor spaces.

The need for dynamic models for pedestrian thermal comfort evaluation was further underlined by Höppe (2002), based on simulations of the time required to reach thermal equilibrium under a range of initial conditions (prior indoor temperature) and outdoor activities, using a more sophisticated human thermoregulatory model.[11] But Höppe goes on to point out that for dynamic models, the thermal history of the pedestrian is also important. Neither the earlier regression models nor the numerical models mentioned above consider the transient heat transfer between pedestrians and their environment *for their recent activities and the environments in which these took place*. This latter is a subtle but important point – it implies that pedestrians' movement needs to be tracked. A coherent approach to this might be to simulate the pedestrians' movement (as multiple agents) while simultaneously simulating the transient microclimate conditions encountered by them. Environmental, activity and clothing characteristics could then be parsed to a transient human thermoregulatory model to predict our agent-pedestrians' thermal sensation. In such a way we may also be able to simulate agents' preferred routes and activities within their urban landscape.

4.4.3 Combined movement and comfort modelling

In this excellent progress has been made by Bruse (2002, 2007) (Figure 4.4.1). The distribution of air temperature, mean radiant temperature, wind speed and relative humidity for a given urban scene and period of time are predicted using ENVI-met (Bruse, 1999), simplified urban microclimate modelling software (see Chapter 3).[12] The digital 3D model of the urban scene that was generated for the ENVI-met microclimate simulations can be directly imported into the

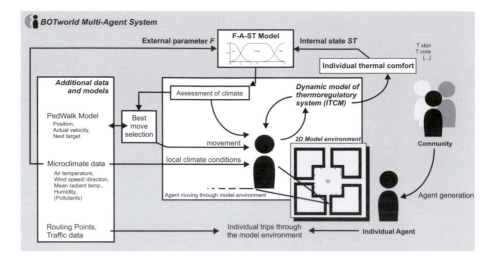

Figure 4.4.1 Multi-agent simulation of pedestrians' comfort-influenced movement

Source: Bruse (2007)

Multi-Agent Simulation software BOTworld. In BOTworld, this scene is reduced to a discrete 2D horizontal cellular landscape that is populated with pedestrian agents (or BOTs) that are designated with targets to move towards. A route-finding algorithm then determines the best route to the agent's next target destination. Normally the best route through an urban setting is equal to the shortest route. However, when subject to discomforting stimuli other aspects may influence agents' routing decisions. For example, if pedestrians feel uncomfortably hot they might prefer a shaded street even if this means a (small) increase in path length. To take into account such quality aspects, BOTworld uses a 'virtual' quality-weighted distance, rather than the absolute distance of standard route finding algorithms.

While the agents move through the virtual environment they are exposed to a range of factors that influence their perception, from simple dynamic conflicts such as congestion due to other agent-pedestrians, to (dis)comforting stimuli arising from the microclimate and air pollution. The former are handled by straightforward operations such as acceleration, deceleration and/or local deviations. The latter are more complex. First, the environmental conditions (or factors, F) at agents' actual positions are parsed, along with each agent's personal and physiological characteristics, to a simplified dynamic two-node human thermoregulatory model (Bruse, 2005) to predict the agents' thermal state (ST). The agents' responses depend on their preference. If the preferred microclimate factor and the internal state resulting from the actual experienced microclimate coincide, a location is evaluated positively (up to +1); otherwise it is perceived as uncomfortable (down to −1). Acknowledging the uncertainties in predictions from microclimate and comfort models, a system of Fuzzy Logic rules (Zadeh, 1965) are used to predict these agent assessments. The main advantage of Fuzzy Logic is that there are no discrete thresholds for assessing a value as 'low' or 'high'. Rather, Fuzzy Logic rules allow for shades of grey or 'uncertainties' where a value can be for example 'low' with a level of 70 per cent, leaving an uncertainty of 30 per cent that it is in fact a low value.

This essentially involves evaluating the truthfulness of statements such as 'X is high' or 'X is low', for both X='ST' and X='F'. Plate 15 shows an example of a rule set that is used to evaluate the combination of the radiant temperature t_r as an external factor (F) and the agent's skin temperature t_{sk} as an internal state (ST). In this case, we have a *high–low* relationship: a high skin temperature (hot state) favours a low radiant temperature and dislikes high t_r values. The truthfulness that the internal state is 'hot' is calculated as 0.97 (97 per cent true) and the statement that the microclimate factor is uncomfortable in terms of t_r is 100 per cent (the charts on the right show the organization of the 'low', 'average' and 'high' classes). Linking both factors together via the fuzzy rule system, the statement 'The assessed location is uncomfortable' is A=0.97 or 97 per cent true (see left side Plate 15). These comfort assessments (A values) can then be used to plot distribution maps and to modify the agents' routing decisions. Note that situations in which high–high combinations are preferred are also possible; for example a high skin temperature accompanied by a high wind speed for evaporative cooling.

By way of example, Plate 16 shows a BOT route through a part of a south German city. The small window to the left presents a time series plot of the microclimate stimuli experienced by the agent during this trip (top chart), while the bottom plot shows the agent's simulated thermoregulatory system response to this sequence of microclimate stimuli. The most significant thermal comfort parameter is the skin temperature, as this is where the human thermoreceptors are located.

Simulated route choices from applications of this pedestrian modelling environment to a range of hypothetical urban movement problems suggest that the agents' rule base is reasonable. However, and as Bruse (2002) admits, 'empirical observations are needed to adjust the different model parameters and validate the model'. It may also be desirable to integrate evolutionary algorithms (see Chapter 7) with this modelling environment to simulate agents' learning mechanisms – so that over time they choose the consistently most comfortable routes between origins and destinations, which may ultimately be handled by a general urban transport model (see Chapter 8). It may also be desirable to substitute the simplified human thermoregulatory model with a more sophisticated model, such as Fiala's 19 segment model (Fiala et al, 1999), to account for radiant and wind asymmetry.

Another promising approach would be to integrate developments from Space Syntax research (Hillier and Hanson, 1984) into the BOTworld system. Space Syntax theory was established in the late 1970s as a first attempt to understand why urban spaces that were considered to offer 'breathtaking architecture' were either ignored by pedestrians or rated as unpleasant by them. Space Syntax theory assumes that there are two views of the same city: a physical one, described by the buildings and the spaces connecting them, and a social one that represents the activities of the citizens and the use of the urban space, both being linked by space. This work has since matured into a set of numerical and visual tools to analyse how place or space is integrated with the urban realm. It seems sensible to make use of these advances in the coding of pedestrians' routing choices as part of a more comprehensive multi-agent pedestrian simulation system.

4.5 Integrated analyses

Using Europe-wide field survey results, Nikolopoulou and Lykoudis (2007) related observations of pedestrian activity to microclimate variables, finding that pedestrians' environmental preferences vary depending upon the time of day and of the year (which itself affects the strength of thermal comfort stimuli). They go on to suggest that 'appropriate microclimatic treatment of different spaces, offering the *environmental diversity* required at different seasons, with appropriate solar exposure or shading and wind protection or exposure ... (can ensure that the) use of open spaces is feasible throughout the year'. From this observation, Steemers et al (2004) exploited techniques for the processing of digital elevation models (see Chapter 2) to produce a map of environmental diversity (Plate 17). In this, areas indicated in yellow (and the corresponding percentage) correspond to open space with high sky and sun availability, in cyan to high sun and wind availability and in magenta to high sky and wind availability; white corresponds to high availability of sky, sun and wind and black to the opposite.

Environmental diversity D is defined as a sample standard deviation of the proportion of open space p that lies within each of the $N=8$ available categories, normalized so that $D \in [0;1]$: $D = 1 - 2.8571 \left(\dfrac{1}{N-1} \sum_{i=1}^{N} (p - \bar{p})^2 \right)^{1/2}$. In this, a value of 1 corresponds to the absence of diversity, so that one parameter dominates, and 0 corresponds to perfect diversity, so that the proportion of open space in each parameter is evenly distributed. But this concept of diversity supposes that we consistently wish to have wind and sun rather than protection from them. In response to this, the concept of desirability ranks the microclimates from worst *1* to best *8* for a given season (for example winter, summer) and type of climate (for example temperate, cold, hot-humid). For instance in a temperate climate, an open area with high sun and sky availability would be more desirable in winter than it would be in summer, when an area with high availability of both sun and wind would be more desirable (Plate 17c – lower right). In addition to maps of desirability, which can help with identifying which types of urban design response may be preferable throughout a given urban area, a global desirability index D' can also be calculated. This is defined simply as the mean of the proportion of open space within each category p, weighted according to its desirability ranking r, so that

$$D' = \frac{1}{N} \sum_{i=1}^{N} p \cdot r .$$

Spatial diversity and desirability are both interesting and useful notions, but further work is required to determine whether they truly correspond to pedestrians' expectations. Nevertheless, the technique is a simple and potentially powerful one, provided that the appropriate attributes are appropriately weighted. Such techniques may also in the future be used in conjunction with results from more rigorous modelling methods.

In the introduction to this chapter we noted that, as well as being influenced by mechanical wind and thermal comfort, pedestrians' satisfaction with outdoor space also depends on visual, olfactory and aural comfort, the protection from rain as well as sociological factors, such as whether we like the look of a place, whether we feel safe, whether we feel crowded and whether a space has the amenities we desire.

Now good progress has been made in respect of predicting the visual, thermal and aural environment. Radiosity or ray tracing software may be used to predict the visual environment (Chapter 2) as well as the aural environment (Kang, 2007) and CFD models may be used, with certain simplifications, to predict the thermal and olfactory environment, while also considering larger-scale phenomena. It is also possible to use particle tracking algorithms in CFD software to simulate rain; this can in principle also be achieved in a simplified way by image processing DEMs. So we are approaching the point at which it would be meaningful to develop some integrated assessment of pedestrians' environmental comfort, whether as a single index or as a set or indicators.[13]

A truly holistic basis of assessing pedestrians' satisfaction would, however, also consider sociological factors. Integrating and perhaps further developing advances made within the Space Syntax community (Hillier and Hanson, 1984) with research to address the range of environmental factors into a unified basis for evaluating pedestrians' comfort would appear to be a significant but fascinating challenge for the coming years.

4.6 Conclusions

In this chapter we have seen that pedestrians' comfort is influenced by myriad factors, both environmental and sociological, not all of which are currently well understood. Given the nature of this book, we have concentrated in this chapter on the environmental factors that influence comfort. In this particular progress has been made with respect to mechanical wind comfort and thermal comfort. Based on a range of empirical studies, a consensus seems to have emerged in favour of one particular criterion (that of Lawson and Penwarden, 1975).

Both empirical and numerical approaches have been employed to evaluate the thermal comfort of pedestrians. A range of multiple linear regression equations have been derived from different field survey campaigns, which include a common set of variables but which have widely different coefficients. There are many reasons for these discrepancies including differences in the experimental procedure (for example whether participants were sedentary or not), in the sample size and distribution (age, gender) as well as the absence of consideration of personal variables such as clothing level. For these and other reasons, it seems that the prospect of having a generally applicable and rigorously founded empirical model seems implausible. It is entirely plausible, however, that we will be able to predict pedestrians' comfort, with due regard for their thermal history, using a dynamic human thermoregulatory model in conjunction with a model of pedestrians' movement and a record of their personal characteristics. Indeed good progress has already been made in this respect, though further work is necessary to calibrate the rule base according to which pedestrian agents move as well as to improve the accuracy of the thermoregulatory model used.

But how and under what circumstances should these criteria be used? Arens and Bosselmann (1989) sensibly suggest that thermal comfort criteria be applied at lower wind speeds and mechanical wind comfort criteria at the high speeds at which mechanical buffeting becomes the primary cause for discomfort. But this is just a part of the picture. We should also be capable of considering visual, aural and olfactory causes of (dis)comfort as well as rainfall, ideally in some integrated way. Achieving this as well as integrating sociological factors influencing pedestrians' satisfaction is a particularly interesting challenge for the coming years!

Notes

1   The figures in parentheses indicate the (approximate) associated proportion of steady state heat loss at standard indoor room conditions, clothing and activity levels.

2   Which may influence our metabolic rate as well as the skin temperature, which depends upon the degree of skin insulation as well as upon environmental conditions.

3   This prompted Murakami et al to undertake a long-term longitudinal survey of pedestrians' comfort in which subjects were requested to complete a daily diary of the wind environment over a period of two years, during which time local wind speeds were also recorded. Based on analyses of these results, comprehensive wind comfort criteria were proposed and compared with those of Isyumov and Davenport, with generally good agreement. Unfortunately, however, Murakami et al's new criteria were based on peak daily gust speed – a quantity that is not readily available directly but can be derived from measured or predicted maximum average wind speed, given an estimated gust factor. But this introduces uncertainty into the application of the procedure.

4   See www.rwdi-anemos.com/downloads/comfort_criteria.pdf

5    $\bar{U}$ = mean wind speed, $\hat{U}$ = peak wind speed ($\hat{U} - \bar{U} + 2.7U_{rms}$) and T = time.

6   This assumption is normally reasonable for outdoor simulations in which wind pressure tends to be orders of magnitude greater than buoyancy pressure.

7   Note that since the questionnaire scale ranged from +1 to +7, this equation may give the absurd predictions that TS < 0, for example at night (I = 0) and when the air temperature and/or air velocity are relatively low.

8   Although the same definition for dissatisfied ($PMV \geq |1|$) appears to have been used in conjunction with the actual sensation vote, the scale size differed: a five point, as opposed to a seven point, scale was used.

9   It is for this reason that there is a move away from the Fanger model towards what is becoming known as the 'adaptive model' of thermal comfort for use in conjunction with transient (for example naturally ventilated) indoor environments in which occupants are able to adapt their personal and environmental characteristics.

10   Even reflected direct solar radiation received at a point of interest was handled in a simplified way – multiplying reflected beam radiation by the contributing surface reflectance.

11   In Gagge's model, thermal gradients within the compartments are assumed to be uniform – reducing the model's reliability in strongly asymmetric wind/radiation conditions. Also there is no distinction between clothed and unclothed parts, so that local discomfort may not be well handled.

12   Note that alternative software may also be employed to generate the necessary climate predictions.

13   One possibility might be to weight each indicator according to its importance I, the cumulative total summing to unity. If each indicator is associated with a satisfaction [$S \in [0,1]$], then the mean satisfaction $\bar{S} = \sum_i I_i S_i$. The problem here is that the relationships

between all indicators are assumed to be linear, which may not necessarily be the case; such indicators also run the risk of information loss. A unified basis of assessment should thus retain the information of each contributing factor while also accounting for non-linear relationships between factors in producing a single indicator.

References

Arens, E. and Bosselmann, P. (1989) 'Wind, sun and temperature – predicting the thermal comfort of people in outdoor spaces', *Building and Environment*, vol 24, no 4, pp315–320

Arup (2004) 'Masterplan for City Road Basin, Islington, Planning Guidance for Development Control Purposes, Appendix E – Environmental Impact: Wind', www.islington.gov.uk/ DownloadableDocuments/Environment/Pdf/crbmp_appx_e.pdf

ASHRAE (American Society of Heating, Refrigerating and Air-Conditioning Engineers) (1981) ASHRAE-Standard 55–81: Thermal environmental conditions occupancy, ASHRAE, Atlanta, GA

Bruse, M. (1999) 'Simulating microscale climate interactions in complex terrain with a high-resolution numerical model: A case study for the Sydney CBD Area', in *Proc. Int. Conf. Urban Climatology & International Congress of Biometeorology*, International Association for Urban Climate, Sydney, pp8–12

Bruse, M. (2002) 'Multi-agent simulations as a tool for the assessment of urban microclimate and its effect on pedestrian behaviour', in *Proc. iEMS*, Lugano, available at www.envi-met.com/ scidocs.htm, last accessed 16 December 2010

Bruse, M. (2005) 'ITCM – a simplified dynamic 2-node model of the human thermoregulatory system and its application in a multi-agent system', *Annals of Meteorology*, vol 41, pp398–401

Bruse, M. (2007) 'Simulating human thermal comfort and resulting usage patterns of urban open spaces with a Multi-agent System', *Proc. 24th Int. Conf. Passive and Low Energy Architecture (PLEA)*, Passive and Low Energy Architecture, Singapore, pp699–706

Fanger, P. O. (1970) *Thermal comfort: Analysis and Applications in Environmental Engineering*, Danish Technical Press, Copenhagen

Fiala, D., Lomas, K.J., Stohrer, M. (1999) 'A computer model of human thermoregulation for a wide range of environmental conditions: The passive system', *Journal of Applied Physiology*, vol 87 (5), pp1957–1972

Gagge, P., Stolwijk, J. and Nishi, Y. (1970) 'An effective temperature scale based on a simple model of human physiological regulator response', *ASHRAE Transactions*, vol 70, pp247–260

Givoni, B., Noguchi, M., Saaroni, H., Pochter, O., Yaacov, Y., Feller, N. and Becker, S. (2003) 'Outdoor comfort research issues', *Energy and Buildings*, vol 35, pp77–86

Hillier, B. and Hanson, J. (1984) *The Social Logic of Space*, Cambridge University Press, Cambridge, UK

Höppe, P. (2002) 'Different aspects of assessing indoor and outdoor thermal comfort', *Energy and Buildings*, vol 34, pp661–665

Hunt, J. C. R., Poulton, E. C. and Mumford, J. C. (1976) 'The effects of wind on people: new criteria based on wind tunnel experiments', *Building and Environment*, vol 11, pp15–28

ISO (International Organization for Standardization) (1984) 'Moderate thermal environments – determination of the PMV and PPD indices and specification of the conditions for thermal comfort', ISO 7730:1984, ISO, Geneva

ISO (1994) 'Moderate thermal environments – determination of the PMV and PPD indices and specification of the conditions for thermal comfort', ISO 7730:1994, ISO, Geneva

Isyumov, N., and Davenport, A. D. (1975) 'The ground level wind environment in built-up areas', in *Proc. 4th Inc. Conf. Wind Effects on Buildings and Structures*, Cambridge University Press, Cambridge, pp403–422

Kang, J. (2007) *Urban Sound Environment*, Taylor & Francis incorporating Spon, London

Katzschner, L., Bosch, U. and Roettgen, M. (2004) 'Thermal comfort mapping and zoning', in Nikolopoulou, M. (ed) *Designing Open Spaces in the Urban Environment: A Bioclimatic Approach*, Centre for Renewable Energy Sources, Attiki, Greece, pp22–26

Lawson, T. V. and Penwarden, A. D. (1975) 'The effects of wind on people in the vicinity of buildings', in *Proc. 4th Inc. Conf. Wind Effects on Buildings and Structures*, Cambridge University Press, Cambridge, pp605–622

Melbourne, W. H. (1978) 'Criteria for environmental wind conditions', *Journal of Industrial Aerodynamics*, vol 2, pp241–249

Murakami, S., and Deguchi, K. (1981) 'New criteria for wind effects on pedestrians', *Journal of Wind Engineering and Industrial Aerodynamics*, vol 7, pp289–309

Murakami, S., Iwasa, Y. and Morikawa, Y. (1986) 'Study on acceptable criteria for assessing wind environment at ground level based on residents' diaries', *Journal of Wind Engineering and Industrial Aerodynamics*, vol 24, pp1–18

Nagara, K., Shimoda, Y. and Mizuno, M. (1996) 'Evaluation of the thermal environment in an outdoor pedestrian space', *Atmospheric Environment*, vol 30, no 3, pp497–505

Nikolopoulou, M. (2004) 'Thermal comfort models for open urban spaces', in Nikolopoulou, M. (ed) *Designing Open Spaces in the Urban Environment: A Bioclimatic Approach*, Centre for Renewable Energy Sources, Attiki, Greece

Nikolopoulou, M. and Lykoudis, S. (2006) 'Thermal comfort in outdoor urban spaces: Analysis across different European countries', *Building and Environment*, vol 41, pp1455–1470

Nikolopoulou, M. and Lykoudis, S. (2007) 'Use of outdoor spaces and microclimate in a Mediterranean urban area', *Building and Environment*, vol 42, pp3691–3707

Nikolopoulou, M. and Steemers, K. (2003) 'Thermal comfort and psychological adaptation as a guide for designing urban spaces', *Energy and Buildings*, 35, p95–101

Nikolopoulou, M., Baker, N. and Steemers, K. (2001) 'Thermal comfort in outdoor urban spaces: understanding the human parameter', *Solar Energy*, vol 70, no 3, pp227–235

Penwarden, A. D. (1973) 'Acceptable wind speeds in towns', *Building Science*, vol 8, pp259–267

Penwarden, A. D. and Wise, A. F. E (1975) 'Wind environment around buildings', BRE Report, HMSO, London

Ramos, M. (2010) unpublished PhD, University of Cambridge Department of Architecture, University of Cambridge, Cambridge

Ratcliff, M. A. and Peterka, J. A. (1990) 'Comparison of pedestrian wind acceptability criteria', *J. Wind Eng. Ind. Aerodynamics*, vol 36, pp791–800

Sanz-Andres, A. and Cuerva, A. (2006) 'Pedestrian wind comfort: Feasibility study of criteria homogenisation', *J. Wind Eng. Ind. Aerodyn*, vol 87, pp93–110

Steemers, K., Ramos, M. C. and Sinou, M. (2004) 'Urban Morphology', in Nikolopoulou, M. (ed) *Designing Open Spaces in the Urban Environment: A Bioclimatic Approach*, Centre for Renewable Energy Sources, Attiki, pp17–21

Tacken, M. (1989) 'A comfortable wind climate for outdoor relaxation in urban areas', *Building and Environment*, vol 24, no 4, pp321–324

Zadeh, L. (1965) 'Fuzzy sets', *Information Control*, vol 8, pp338–353

Part II

Metabolism

5

Building Modelling

Darren Robinson, Frédéric Haldi, Jérôme Kämpf and Diane Perez

5.1 Introduction

In the introduction to this book (Chapter 1, Section 1.2) we briefly described how cities function from an environmental perspective. From these considerations we can identify a set of requirements for a comprehensive model of buildings' metabolism. For example, such a model should predict: (1) the consumption of products having short (for example food, water and clothing; the associated production of waste), medium (for example furnishings) and long (for example constructional materials) residence times; (2) buildings' energy demands for space conditioning, with due regard for the urban climate (thermal and radiant) as well as occupants' presence and their interactions with buildings' envelopes and space conditioning systems; (3) the energy demands due to the activities accommodated within buildings, such as automated or occupant-controlled use of mechanical and electrical equipment; (4) the supply of energy to buildings either from embedded energy conversion systems or from those integrated with decentralised energy centres, possibly derived from buildings' waste products; and (5) the exchanges of energy and mass between buildings, for space conditioning and to support the activities accommodated. In this chapter we describe the progress that has been made in the development of such a comprehensive model and the work that remains to achieve it.

5.2 Brief review of methods[1]

Models of buildings' energy demands are not new. The first generation of dynamic building simulation programs was developed during the 1970s and early 1980s (for example Clarke, 1977; Gough, 1982). These were essentially command-line interfaces to routines to calculate the dynamic thermal energy exchanges within a building and between this and the outside rural environment. Subsequent work concentrated on improving the usability of these routines and extending the scope of the programs' core capabilities, for example to incorporate coupled plant (Tang, 1984) and mass flow (Hensen, 1991) modelling. With improved functionality and amidst growing demand for their use by the more pioneering design consultants, attention shifted to proving the validity of their core thermal energy exchange models (Bland, 1992; Judkoff and Neymark, 1995; Lomas et al, 1997). By the mid-1990s, with results from these validation studies taken on board and with improved usability, attention then focused upon the addition of further modelling functionality. This included the addition of 3D conduction modelling (Nakhi, 1995), links with ray tracing programs for improved lighting modelling (Janak, 1997), electrical power flow modelling (Kelly, 1998) and embedded CFD (Beausoleil-Morrison, 2000). The results are programs such as ESP-r (Clarke, 2001) with a transient finite difference heat flow solver at the core, supporting simultaneous solutions of plant, fluid, electrical power and CFD equation sets.

Thus, at the dawn of the new millennium, we had at our disposition some very sophisticated models for predicting buildings' demands. But these models represented occupants' presence and behaviour, using deterministic rules or profiles, they ignored the UHI, and used very simplistic models of urban radiation exchange. They were also focussed on the modelling of individual buildings. But attention has since started to shift from the modelling of single buildings to the modelling of urban developments comprised of many buildings. These early models focussed mainly on energy use for space conditioning.

Broadly speaking, those methods that are based on a physical rather than on a statistical model,[2] may be categorized into those that model many buildings individually and those that extrapolate from results of modelling a statistical sample of buildings. Models of the latter type predominate, inspired by progress made in national building stock modelling.

A prime example is the Building Research Establishment Housing Model for Energy Studies, BREHOMES (Shorrock and Dunster, 1997). Using a combination of national UK statistical data, for example based on family expenditure and house conditions, and dedicated survey data, a representation of the stock is developed in a form compatible with the BRE's Domestic Energy Model (BREDEM). Indeed over a thousand categories of dwelling are used for historical stock analysis, but the testing of future scenarios (based on the forecasted national uptake of energy efficiency measures) is based on the definition of an average dwelling. Johnston et al (2005) have since used a similar approach to investigate future CO_2 emissions due to the UK housing stock, but based on the use of two dwelling types (for pre- and post-1996) to account for the increased uptake of certain improvement options among older buildings. More recently, Natarjan and Levermore (2007) have refined this approach, allowing forecasts based on an elegant disaggregated representation of the stock comprised of a potentially large number of building categories.

A further example is N-DEEM (Pout, 2000). Using a detailed database of the UK non-residential building stock (Bruhns et al, 2000) to define categories of building and their attributes, this calculates the energy and environmental performance of the non-residential building stock, and can also be used for the testing of scenarios to support the formulation of national policy.

In what follows we first describe approaches that have been developed to model the energy needs of (and in certain cases the energy supply to) residential and then non-residential buildings at the district or city scale, before describing progress in the integrated modelling of the resource flows of arbitrary groupings of buildings.

5.2.1 Residential energy demand modelling

The energy and environmental prediction (EEP) model

The main aim of EEP is to provide an auditing tool for quantifying energy use and emissions for the city, to aid in its more sustainable development (Jones et al, 1998). Models currently available support local planning authorities to evaluate the energy use and CO_2 emissions of their housing stock and to support investment decisions regarding improvements in the performance of this stock (Jones et al, 1999, 2007).

In this a description of the urban area of interest is held in a geographical information system (GIS). This involves the acquisition of digital ordnance survey maps (of appropriate format) from which building outlines may be deduced. The following attributes are then associated with each individual building: age, building type (terraced, detached etc), number of storeys, storey height, frontal window area and number of chimneys. Obtained from a combination of historical records and visual surveys, this information is held in a GIS database.

Using the above information a set of representative model typologies (or clusters) are then defined (based on heated ground floor area, exposed façade area, glazing ratio and age). Using a stationary domestic energy model, the energy use and CO_2 emissions of these typologies are then estimated and the results extrapolated to estimate the energy performance of the entire housing stock.

Results may then be analysed using the GIS system, at a user-defined spatial granularity (for example at a 'post code' level of around 30 houses or the 'ward' level of around 1300 houses) (Plate 18).

Work is underway (Jones et al, 2007) to automate part of the process of data acquisition using a combination of satellite imagery and image processing techniques. Furthermore, it is planned to extend the capabilities of EEP to include the modelling of non-domestic buildings as well as of industrial activities and of transport systems.

Shimoda's model

Also based on extrapolation of results from simulations of a statistical sample, Shimoda et al (2003) developed a rather sophisticated model for predicting the energy demands of cities' housing stock. Using Osaka as their case study they used some 460 combinations of model representing ten types of detached house, ten types of apartment and for each, 23 configurations of household composition (single, couple, one and two parent family etc.).

For each model combination, the household composition is used to deduce the ownership of appliances that, in combination with time-use survey statistics related to occupants' occupation, is used to predict (average) hourly lighting and appliance electrical demand profiles, as well as heating and cooling schedules. This also helps to determine the demand for hot water that, together with estimations of inlet and outlet temperature, is used to predict the associated energy demand. A response-factor based thermal model then takes heat gains from the appliance and hot water models as input, together with climate data, a description of housing type and the space conditioning schedules, to predict heating and cooling loads. These loads are then divided by a system coefficient of performance to determine the associated electrical energy use.

With a reasonably favourable comparison of measured with simulated energy use for the residential stock (it is within 18 per cent), the model was applied to test the effectiveness of improvements to space conditioning system efficiency as well as to the fabric of buildings. In later work, Taniguchi et al (2007) used the model to test the implications of occupants' investments in more efficient electrical and space conditioning appliances as well as behavioural changes to reduce residential energy demands. Examples included relaxed space conditioning set-points and communal use of televisual entertainment.

The solar energy planning (SEP) model

The purpose of SEP is to help municipalities determine the potential for reducing residential building energy use by better passive solar design and through the use of solar thermal and photovoltaic collectors. In contrast to EEP and Shimoda's model, this is based on the modelling of individual buildings in the study area (which may in principle extend to an entire city, though the scale in practice has to date been considerably more modest), rather than extrapolation from a cluster of buildings.

SEP is developed around proprietary GIS software and includes several internal utilities for the derivation of geometric data, in particular a 'footprint tool' to derive enclosed building polygons from standard ordnance survey data (Rylatt et al, 2001), as well as links with a relational database and several energy modelling tools (Gadsden et al, 2003). Initially, GIS-based tools may be invoked to filter the buildings according to their viability for use of solar collectors; based on geometric and socio-economic parameters. A monthly stationary energy model may then be called to predict the baseline energy demands for heating and hot water for the shortlisted residential buildings, using both geometric and attribution data. The latter is available at a variety of levels of granularity – from default assumptions based on statistics from periodic national house condition survey data to building-specific data arising from field surveys. For proposed new buildings, hypotheses may then be tested for reducing energy use by better passive solar design. In the more usual case of existing buildings, other models may be called upon to determine the extent to which energy use is reduced using solar thermal and photovoltaic collectors. The purpose of this then is to help target buildings for financial subsidy of solar collector installations or to interest the public in self-financing such installations.

Critique of models

In calculating the performance of the urban stock from the extrapolation of results for statistically averaged descriptions of buildings in each category, the EEP and Shimoda models fail to consider the urban context in which their buildings are placed. Specifically, there is no consideration of the local climate, either radiant or thermal, or the possibility of supplying energy using local energy centres. A similar criticism may be levelled at SEP, although the obstructions to direct and diffuse irradiation due to opposing buildings are handled in an approximate way. None of the above attempt to model the stochastic presence and behaviour of occupants. Finally, and perhaps most importantly for building and urban designers, none of the above models is truly amenable for *designers* to use as a *tool* for modelling and optimizing the performance of new or existing urban developments.

5.2.2 Non-residential energy demand modelling

LT-Urban

Conceived to examine relationships between urban texture and energy use, LT-Urban (Ratti et al, 2000; 2005) is a coupling between image processing techniques (discussed in Section 2.4) for the derivation of urban geometric parameters and a simplified energy model for predicting the energy use of non-domestic buildings (Robinson and Baker, 2000). In this, the geometry of an urban scene, say 1km², is first represented as a DEM: a 2D image in which each pixel has x,y coordinates and height (z) may be represented by the pixel value: 0 to 255 for a greyscale image, with 0 representing unbuilt space (see Section 2.4.1). Geometric operations are then performed on these DEMs, using MATLAB's image processing toolbox, to determine for each pixel:

- whether each built pixel corresponds to a non-passive or a passive zone (i.e. it is within twice the floor-to-ceiling height of the façade);
- the orientation of the façade associated with each passive zone pixel;
- the mean angle of elevation of the urban skyline with respect to each passive zone pixel (the mean urban horizon angle);
- the mean angle of elevation from the opposing skyline towards the target pixel (the mean obstruction sky view).

Note that the above process may be repeated by progressively reducing pixel values by building floor-to-ceiling height, so that results for each floor of each building may be obtained. A file containing the above urban parameters, along with a further file describing the default characteristics of the buildings to be modelled may then be parsed to the lighting and thermal (LT) model that then outputs a results file that is in turn read by MATLAB. But rather than repeat this process for each built pixel of each floor of each DEM, energy use results may be pre-computed for an appropriately discretized five-dimensional matrix (corresponding to each of the above four urban parameters plus façade glazing ratio) to facilitate rapid energy use estimates for a given climate/set of default building properties.

Using DEMs relating to parts of London, Berlin and Toulouse, in combination with the corresponding pre-computed energy use matrices, Ratti et al (2000, 2005) compared the energy effectiveness of different types of urban form to identify optimum façade characteristics (for example glazing ratio) for each context (Plate 19).

Yamaguchi's model

Yamaguchi et al's (2003) energy model for non-residential buildings is based on a similar approach to Shimoda's model for residential buildings. In the absence of time-use survey data, a basic stochastic model simulates occupants' weekday presence (arrival, lunch and then departure) and, while present, whether they are using one or two PCs or none at all (this depending upon their type of job). Other electrical loads (including lighting) are deterministically predicted on the basis of installed capacity and schedule of use. Heat gains from these electrical loads are then input to a space conditioning demand model, using a 'weighting factor' method. Given a system coefficient of performance, this load is then translated into an energy use. Results from all buildings within a given case study zone are then aggregated and input to a district energy supply model, which simulates district heating, cooling and co/tri-generation systems as well as thermal distribution losses. Initial applications of this model focussed on the effectiveness of district energy supply options as well as basic measures to reduce the energy use of two modelled buildings (including relaxed set-points, the use of heat exchangers and more efficient glazing and lighting systems). Yamaguchi et al (2007a) later applied their model to simulate the energy use of and supply to 55 large commercial buildings in a district of the city of Osaka (Japan) and scenarios according to which these may evolve through to the year 2050. From this they concluded that the CO_2 emissions of commercial buildings could be reduced by some 60 per cent.

Yamaguchi et al (2007b) also experimented with increasing the scale of their analysis from that of the city district to the entire city. First, the city is discretized into $500m^2$ grid cells for which the built floor area of each of six categories of non-residential building is defined from statistical data. Representative cells within which each of the building categories dominates are then selected. Basic field surveys are then conducted in each of these cells to define key characteristics of a sample of buildings (those $>1000m^2$) to be modelled. Based on this information some 612 prototype building models were prepared, representing four building uses, four or five ranges in size, nine configurations of building form and four types of heating system. The performance of these buildings was then simulated to determine a per unit area energy use that, when multiplied by the distribution of built area for each building category within each city grid cell, gives an estimation of total city energy use for non-residential buildings. Yamaguchi et al (2007c) further outline how this approach may be adapted to model the entire national stock of non-residential buildings.

Finally, the Shimoda and Yamaguchi models have also been run in tandem to simulate the energy use of both residential and non-residential buildings (that is the entire built stock) for the city of Osaka (Shimoda et al, 2007) based on a similar principle of extrapolation from simulations of a statistical sample. The purpose of this study was to examine the implications of increased tele-commuting within the city of Osaka (albeit ignoring the implications for transport energy use).

Critique of models

One of the key objectives of LT-Urban was to understand whether and to what extent urban texture evolves as a deliberate response to the desire to optimize

urban densification, microclimate and the utilization of ambient energy resources –
in particular daylight and solar radiation. The effects of urban obstructions on
reducing direct shortwave and visible radiation and in contributing reflected
radiation were therefore explicitly modelled (albeit using a crude form of canyon
model, see Section 2.4.2). However, the urban thermal microclimate was entirely
ignored. Similarly, there was no attempt to model occupants' behaviour in
buildings in any detail or to model energy supply using high efficiency or
renewable energy conversion systems. But these latter omissions are reasonable
given the focus on relationships between texture and microclimate.

Yamaguchi, by contrast, does model a subset of efficient energy conversion
systems (combined heat and power (CHP) and co/tri-generation) and occupants'
presence and their interactions with PCs (although this represents a small
subset of the behaviours influencing buildings' energy demands). But the effects
of adjacent buildings on either the radiant or thermal climate are completely
ignored.

Remedying these shortfalls in the form of a general urban resource flow
model (i.e. for energy, water and waste flows) for the range of building types
was part of the motivation behind SUNtool.

5.2.3 Integrated resource flow modelling (SUNtool)

An acronym for Sustainable Urban Neighbourhood modelling **tool**, SUNtool
was conceived as a decision support system for designers to optimize the
environmental sustainability of master planning proposals (Robinson et al,
2003, 2007), based on integrated resource (energy, water and waste) flow
modelling.

Now, a master plan may be composed of many buildings, potentially several
hundred, and these may support a variety of uses (residential, commercial,
schooling, healthcare etc), not to mention adjacent obstructions, external
landscaping and services (such as street lighting). For manageable predictions,
we therefore need a rapid way of describing the geometric form of our master
plan and of attributing the described objects according to characteristics that
influence the flows of resources. The solution of the flows of resources should
also be arrived at quickly, so that the user is swiftly guided towards a reasonably
optimal solution. Furthermore, the set of resource flows should respect their
sensitivity to the urban microclimate, to human behaviour and to possible
couplings between buildings and between buildings and systems, which may be
embedded or centralized (Robinson, 2005). These were the guiding principles
for the development of SUNtool – the conceptual structure of which is outlined
in Figure 5.2.1.

On starting a master plan modelling project, the user first chooses/enters the
geographical location to set the site coordinates and associate the site with
climate data. The user is then invited to select a relevant 'iDefault' dataset; that
is, a database of default attributes (occupancy, constructional, plant systems etc)
for the range of building types. The software's sketching tool may then be used
to prepare a 3D description of the site. Building objects are assigned a default
use (residential) but this may be overridden, so that the appropriate characteristics
are assigned to the building. Likewise any building or façade-specific
characteristics may be easily overridden by clicking on the corresponding

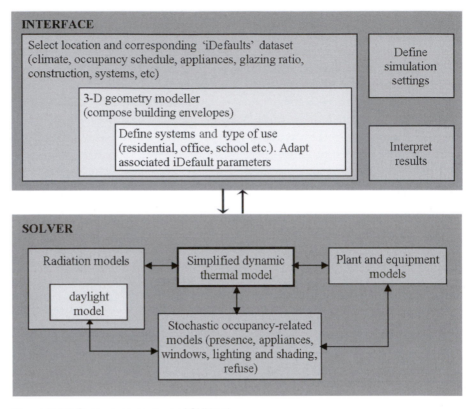

Figure 5.2.1 Conceptual structure of SUNtool

Source: Robinson et al (2007)

object. Solar (thermal or electric) collectors may be associated with building surfaces in a similar fashion. Specific buildings may also be selected for association with a district energy centre.

When a site description is complete this is parsed to the SUNtool solver, in which there are four principal families of model: radiation, thermal, stochastic and plant. Note that there is potential feedback between these families of model. The radiation model influences the internal space conditions predicted by the thermal model and this in turn influences the calculation of external longwave radiation exchange. The magnitude of transmitted daylight (as well as the position and radiance of the sun) influences users' behaviour relating to lights and blinds, which in turn influences the prediction of interior daylight levels. The thermal inputs arising from occupants' behaviour influence the internal space conditions predicted by the thermal model and this in turn may influence their behaviour (for example in respect of window opening). The thermal energy demands for space conditioning may be adjusted by psychrometric processes within air handling plant. Furthermore, plant systems (whether air handling or otherwise) may not have the necessary capacity to meet the buildings' demands, with implications for the indoor thermal environment. The basis of these models is described in Robinson et al (2007).

Batches of simulations may be prepared, relating to a selected group of buildings and for a chosen period of time. Alternatively, parametric studies may be performed. For the latter, certain parameters may be varied between user-defined lower and upper limits according to some chosen increment. When complete, line graphs and tabular summaries of results may be interrogated and buildings may be false-coloured according to the magnitude of certain variables. Animations of the evolution of these parameters may also be displayed; otherwise results may be exported for analysis using third-party tools.

Limitations

SUNtool is the most complete of the models reviewed in Chapter 7 (Section 7.2), but it does have some weaknesses of its own. The thermal model lacks generality (although this has since been improved by Stone, 2008), somewhat rudimentary stochastic models of lighting, blinds and window use have been integrated, not all key energy conversion systems are modelled, there is no model of energy storage associated with building or district energy centres and modelling of water and waste flows is limited.

5.3 CitySim

Developed at the LESO-PB at EPFL, CitySim is a successor to SUNtool for simulating and optimizing the sustainability of urban developments of various scales, from a small neighbourhood to an entire city. It is heavily inspired by its predecessor SUNtool, but it does include many refinements, particularly in terms of its modelling algorithms.

In common with SUNtool, the CitySim graphical user interface (GUI) is an object-oriented application written in Java, but using JavaOpenGL as the 3D rendering engine. When the 3D model of a project has been defined or imported, its objects fully attributed and the simulation parameters defined, an XML file describing this project is written and parsed to the solver. Simulation results are then parsed back to the GUI for interpretation.

In the following we focus on describing the models that are integrated with the CitySim solver and their application to some urban modelling problems.

5.3.1 Thermal model

For the purposes of urban-scale simulation, it is important to find a good balance between modelling accuracy, computational overheads and data availability. From these criteria, which have been applied throughout the development of the CitySim solver, it was decided to develop a refined version of Nielsen's (2005) two-node electrical circuit analogy model.

In this model (Kämpf and Robinson, 2007) (Figure 5.3.1), an external air temperature node[3] T_{ext} is connected with an outside surface temperature node T_{os} via an external film conductance K_e, which varies according to wind speed and direction. T_{os}, which also experiences heat fluxes due to shortwave (Q_{sun1}) and longwave (Q_{ir}) exchange, is connected to a wall node T_w of capacitance C_w via a conductance defined by the external part of the wall. In fact this node

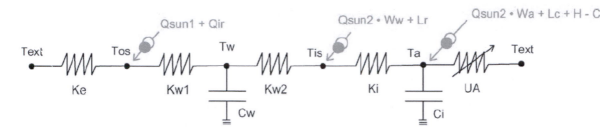

Figure 5.3.1 Monozone form of the CitySim thermal model

Source: Authors

resembles a mirror plane, so that we have similar connections to an internal air node T_a of capacitance C_i via an internal surface node T_{is}. T_{is} may also experience (wall-weighted) shortwave flux due to transmitted solar radiation $(Q_{sun2}W_w)$ and a longwave flux due to radiant heat gains from internal sources (L_r) and T_a may experience convective gains due to absorbed (air-weighted) shortwave radiation $(Q_{sun2}W_a)$, internal casual gains (L_c) and heating (H) / cooling (C) systems. Finally, our internal air node may be connected with our external air temperature node via a variable conductance due to infiltration and ventilation.

Such a model can be expressed by a differential equation of the form $C \cdot \vec{T}'(t) = A(t) \cdot \vec{T}(t) + \vec{u}(t)$, where $\vec{T}(t)$ denotes the temperature vector at the n nodes, $\vec{T}'(t)$ is its derivative upon time and $\vec{u}(t)$ represents the source terms at each node. C is a positive diagonal thermal capacity matrix and $A(t)$ is the symmetric heat transfer matrix. With respect to our simplified model, in which the building's capacitance is represented by just two nodes, that for the walls C_w and that for air and internal furnishings C_p, this model can be represented as follows:

$$\begin{pmatrix} C_i & 0 \\ 0 & C_w \end{pmatrix} \cdot \begin{pmatrix} T_a'(t) \\ T_w'(t) \end{pmatrix} = \begin{pmatrix} -UA(t) - k_2 & k_2 \\ k_2 & -k_2 - k_1(t) \end{pmatrix} \cdot \begin{pmatrix} T_a(t) \\ T_w(t) \end{pmatrix} + \begin{pmatrix} u_a(t) \\ u_w(t) \end{pmatrix} \quad [5.3.1]$$

where the air and wall source terms are:

$$\begin{pmatrix} u_a(t) \\ u_w(t) \end{pmatrix} = \begin{pmatrix} UA(t) \cdot T_{ext}(t) + k_2(Q_{sun2}(t) \cdot w_w + L_r(t))/k_{w2} \\ k_2(Q_{sun2}(t) \cdot w_w + L_r(t))/k_i \end{pmatrix}$$

$$+ \begin{pmatrix} Q_{sun2} \cdot w_a + L_c(t) + H(t) - C(t) \\ k_1(t)(k_e(t) \cdot T_{ext}(t) + Q_{sun1}(t) + Q_{ir}(t)) \end{pmatrix} \quad [5.3.2]$$

with $k_1(t)$ and k_2 being the conductance between $T_{ext}(t)$ and T_w (left part of Figure 5.3.2) and between T_a and T_w respectively:

$$k_1(t) = \left(\frac{k_e(t) \cdot k_{w1}}{k_e(t) + k_{w1}} \right), \qquad k_2 = \left(\frac{k_i \cdot k_{w2}}{k_i + k_{w2}} \right) \quad [5.3.3]$$

See Kämpf and Robinson (2007) and Kämpf (2009) for a detailed explanation of the implementation of this model, its extension to solve for a building of an arbitrary number of zones as well as results from verification tests.

5.3.2 Plant and equipment models

As indicated in Figure 5.3.1, given the surface radiation balance, infiltration and internal solar and casual heat gains, the thermal model predicts an energy demand for heating and possibly cooling. If air is used as the medium for delivering this energy, so that a HVAC system is installed, then an additional energy demand may be incurred due to the treatment of outside air. In either case, the demand for energy needs to be satisfied using some form of energy conversion system; perhaps a boiler for a water-based heating system or a heat pump in the case of an air-based mechanical cooling system. Now these energy conversion systems may or may not have the capacity necessary to meet the predicted energy demands. In this case, with or without intermediate HVAC plant, insufficient energy will be supplied to the thermal zone so that a corrected internal state is calculated: the indoor temperature drifts above or below the set-point temperature.

We describe briefly below the approach used in calculating adjusted energy demands and the supply of energy.

HVAC systems

For the purposes of urban-scale energy simulation, a pragmatic solution to the prediction of HVAC system demands is simply to model the required change in the psychrometric state (enthalpy) of air which is input to HVAC plant (outside air or the exhaust air from a heat/moisture exchanger) to absorb the sensible and latent heat gains within the supply zone to maintain that zone within a defined comfort envelope (Figure 5.3.2) at the required mass flow rate.

Thus, if we have air at 30°C and 0.02kg/kg (dry air) input to our HVAC plant (state T_2, w_2 in Figure 5.3.3), we will need to sensibly cool this air, then dehumidify it and possibly also to reheat it, depending upon the magnitude of the sensible gains to be absorbed within the target zone at the required mass flow rate, so that that zone is maintained within the limits of its comfort envelope (to achieve the state T_s, w_s in Figure 5.3.3). Thus the total energy load, due to the n processes that change the air enthalpy h, is: $Q = \sum_{i=1}^{n} \dot{m}(h_i - h_{i-1})$, where $\dot{m} = \max\left(\dfrac{Q}{C\Delta T}, \rho_a n_p v_p 10^{-3}\right)$ is the larger of the mass flow rates needed to satisfy the target zone's *sensible* heating/cooling demands (first term) and that required to satisfy the occupants' fresh air requirements (second term). A detailed description of this HVAC model and its implementation can be found in Kämpf (2009).

Energy conversion and storage systems

As with HVAC systems, the purpose of CitySim is not to support detailed system design and control, but rather to support the choice of the most

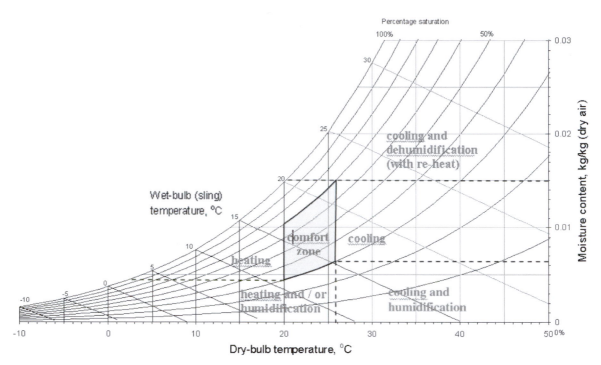

Figure 5.3.2 Psychrometric processes required on air supplied to HVAC plant

Source: Authors

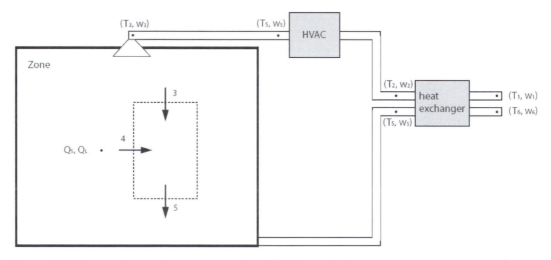

Figure 5.3.3 Stages in the psychrometric processing of HVAC supply air

Source: Authors

appropriate system(s) to be integrated within a given building or urban development and the approximate dimension(s) and corresponding implications of energy use and/or emissions. To this end, it is reasonable to use simplified empirically based models. At present, models of the following are integrated with CitySim:

- Solar collectors: both thermal (air/water) and photovoltaic.
- Wind turbines.
- Boilers, with different types of fuel.
- Heat pumps.

Cogeneration systems (possibly combined with heat pumps)

Models of wind turbines, boilers and cogeneration systems are simply based on performance curves. In the former case the power output may be expressed as a function of the mean wind speed at the hub of the turbines, corrected for the height of the hub and the terrain rugosity relative to that at which the wind speed was measured. In the latter cases the power output is a function of the partial load factor.

In the case of solar photovoltaic panels, we use a simplified model due to Duffie and Beckman (1991): $P = A_c I_{g\beta} \eta_{mp} \eta_e$, where A_c is the collector area, $I_{g\beta}$ the total incident shortwave irradiance, and $\eta_{mp} \eta_e$ are the combined efficiencies of the panel at maximum power point and of the power conditioning equipment. Note that the former accounts for degradations in conversion efficiency at elevated cell temperatures and is calculated relative to measured performance at standard operating conditions. Solar thermal collectors are modelled using an empirical quadratic equation (www.solarkeymark.org) of the form:

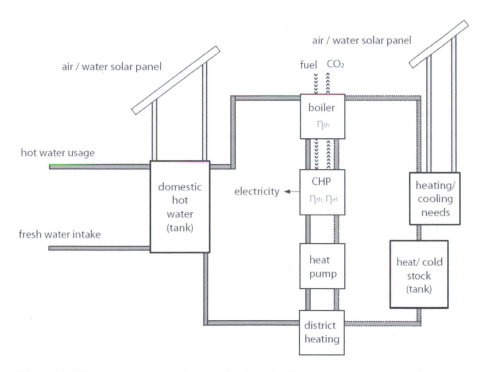

Figure 5.3.4 Storage tanks as the intermediary between thermal consumers and producers, showing one possible configuration

Source: Authors

$P_{th} = A_c \left(\eta_0 I_{g\beta} + \alpha_1 \left(T_f - T_a \right) - \alpha_2 \left(T_f - T_a \right)^2 \right)$, in which η_0 is the optical efficiency of the glazed cover, α_1, α_2 are first and second order heat loss coefficients and T_f is the mean fluid temperature. Finally, for heat pumps the thermal power output is simply the product of the electrical power input, the system technical efficiency and the Carnot efficiency at target and source temperatures: $P_{th} = P_{el} \eta_{tech} \eta_{Carnot}$. Clearly this expression may be rearranged to give the power demand for a given thermal output. Furthermore, the source temperature used in calculating the Carnot efficiency may relate to air temperature or ground temperature, the latter depending upon the depth and position of a ground source heat exchanger (whether horizontal or vertical) using an expression due to Labs (1982).

In CitySim, buildings and domestic hot water services are connected with energy conversion systems via storage tanks (Figure 5.3.4). Note that these tanks, which are assumed to be at uniform temperature, may store both sensible and latent heat, the latter using some form of phase change material.

A more detailed description of these energy conversion and storage system models can be found in Kämpf (2009).

5.3.3 Behavioural models

Occupants' presence has a direct impact on buildings' energy flows due to their emissions of sensible and latent heat. These energy flows are also affected by occupants' interactions with building fabric, lights and appliances. But these processes (presence and interactions) are stochastic in nature: they include both deterministic and random responses to input variables, which reflect variations in behaviours between people or indeed of one person's behaviour, even for identical times and/or environmental stimuli. For example we do not always arrive at work at 9am, or open a window when the temperature exceeds 25°C, or lower a blind when the incident solar irradiance exceeds 50W/m².

The errors arising from treating occupants' presence and behaviour as being deterministic can be highly significant (Page, 2007), particularly with respect to aggregate resource profiles when such assumptions are repeated for many buildings. It is thus important that we use stochastic models of presence and behaviour for urban-scale resource flow modelling.

Occupants' presence

The key behavioural model in CitySim relates to occupants' presence, not only because this leads directly to emission of metabolic heat gains and pollutants, but because all subsequent behaviours depend on occupants' presence.

Our model assumes that occupants may be modelled independently of one another and that, while not in the midst of a long absence (either from home or from work), their current presence depends only on their immediate past presence. Under this Markov condition we need only model transitions between the states present and absent: $P \left(X_{t+1} = i \mid X_t = j, X_{t-1} = k, ..., X_{t-N} = l \right)$

$= P\left(X_{t+1} = i\,|\,X_t = j\right) =: T_{ij}\left(t\right)$. Thus, the probability of an occupant being present at time $t+1$ is equal to the probability of presence at t multiplied by the transition probability present to present T_{11} plus the probability of absence at t and the transition probability absent to present T_{01}:

$$P(t+1) = P(t) \cdot T_{11}(t) + (1 - P(t)) \cdot T_{01}(t) \qquad [5.3.4]$$

For this we use a 15 minute occupancy presence probability profile $P(t)$, but to determine the transition probabilities we need a little more information. In particular we use a mobility parameter μ – the ratio of the probability of changing state to not changing state:

$$\mu(t) := \frac{T_{01}(t) + T_{10}(t)}{T_{00}(t) + T_{11}(t)} \qquad [5.3.5]$$

so that the transition absent to present is found from:

$$T_{01}(t) = \frac{\mu - 1}{\mu + 1} \cdot P(t) + P(t + 1) \qquad [5.3.6]$$

and that of present to present from:

$$T_{11} = \frac{1 - P(t)}{P(t)} \cdot T_{01} + \frac{P(t+1)}{P(t)} =$$
$$\frac{1 - P(t)}{P(t)} \cdot \left[\frac{\mu - 1}{\mu + 1} \cdot P(t) + P(t+1) \right] + \frac{P(t+1)}{P(t)} \qquad [5.3.7]$$

The remaining transitions are simply: $T_{10} = 1 - T_{11}$ and $T_{00} = 1 - T_{01}$. For further details on the implementation and validation of this model, we refer the reader to Page (2007) and Page et al (2007).

But as mentioned above, we also need to consider long absences, for example due to work-related absence, illness or vacation. Further work (in particular data) is required here, but our approach is currently to use a time dependent profile of the probability that a long absence will start in conjunction with a time dependent probability distribution for the duration of this long absence. Thus, during a pre-process, we determine, at a daily resolution, whether our occupant is on vacation. Then, while not on vacation we simulate their short-term presence/absence.

Window opening

When modelling occupants' behaviour (or actions) once present, we essentially have three options. We can model occupants' actions as a Bernoulli process, as an occupancy-dependent Markov chain or as a continuous time process.

In the first of these we predict the probability that the device being controlled will be found in a particular state, formulated as a logistic model. In the case of windows we might predict the probability that a window would be found to be open as:

$$P_{open}\left(x_1,...,x_p\right) = \frac{\exp\left(a + \sum_{k=1}^{p} b_k x_k\right)}{1 + \exp\left(a + \sum_{k=1}^{p} b_k x_k\right)} \qquad [5.3.8]$$

where x_i are the retained explanatory variables and a, b_k the corresponding logistic regression parameters – respectively the intercept and slope.

In the case of a Markov chain, we explicitly model the dynamics of occupants' interactions, by simulating transitions between the states i and j of the device being controlled:

$$P_{ij}\left(x_1,...,x_p\right) = \frac{\exp\left(a + \sum_{k=1}^{p} b_k x_k\right)}{1 + \exp\left(a + \sum_{k=1}^{p} b_k x_k\right)} \qquad [5.3.9]$$

where P_{ij} is the probability of transition from state i to state j, which may depend on whether an occupant has just arrived (potentially representing strong changes in environmental stimuli), whether they are in a state of intermediate occupation (so that environmental stimuli change relatively modestly) or whether they are about to leave (perhaps evoking some kind of predictive control action – for example for nocturnal cooling of an office).

Although modelling state transitions as an occupancy-dependent Markov chain faithfully encapsulates occupants' interaction dynamics, this also potentially leads to many redundant calculations (predictions of no state transition), particularly during periods of intermediate occupation. The third type of model is a solution to this dilemma, explicitly modelling the duration with which a particular device will *survive* in a particular state. The density of the probability distribution of survival in state i, depending upon explanatory variable x is given by a Weibull distribution, thus:

$$f_i(t) = \lambda\alpha(\lambda t)^{\alpha-1}\exp\left(-(\lambda t)^\alpha\right), \ \lambda = 1/\exp(a + bx) \qquad [5.3.10]$$

After having tested different variants of the above types of model, Haldi and Robinson (2009) developed a hybrid: an occupancy-dependent Markov chain, extended to a continuous time process for window opening durations. The retained explanatory variables x_i are indoor (θ_{in}), outdoor (θ_{out}) and daily mean outdoor ($\theta_{out,dm}$) temperature, the occurrence of rain (f_R), occupant presence (T_{pres}) and expected absence duration (f_{abs}). Action probabilities P_{ij} from state i to state j ($i,j = 0,1$) are formulated as logistic models [5.3.9] with parameters a and b_k, as displayed in Table 5.3.1.

While windows are open, a total airflow rate (Q_t) is calculated by combining the volume flow rates due to wind (Q_v) and buoyancy (Q_b) pressures in quadrature ($Q_t = \left(Q_v^2 + Q_b^2\right)^{1/2}$, m³/s.). This volume flow rate is then used to calculate the variable conductance ($UA = \rho Q_t C_p\left(T_i - T_o\right)$) for CitySim's thermal model (Figure 5.3.1).

Table 5.3.1 Regression parameters for probabilities of actions on windows

Windows: Variables	Opening Prob. P_{01}	Closing Prob. P_{10}
Arrival		
a	-13.88 ± 0.37	3.97 ± 0.37
θ_{in}	0.312 ± 0.016	-0.286 ± 0.017
θ_{out}	0.0433 ± 0.0033	-0.0505 ± 0.0045
$f_{abs,prev}$	1.862 ± 0.044	
f_R	-0.45 ± 0.11	
During pres.		
a	-12.23 ± 0.28	-1.64 ± 0.22
θ_{in}	0.281 ± 0.013	-0.0481 ± 0.0098
θ_{out}	0.0271 ± 0.0024	-0.0779 ± 0.0020
T_{pres}	$(-8.78 \pm 0.53)\cdot 10^{-4}$	$(-1.62 \pm 0.06)\cdot 10^{-3}$
f_R	-0.336 ± 0.081	
Departure		
a	-8.75 ± 0.22	-8.54 ± 0.48
		0.213 ± 0.022
$\theta_{out,dm}$	0.1371 ± 0.0075	-0.0911 ± 0.0061
$f_{abs,next}$	0.84 ± 0.12	1.614 ± 0.069
f_{GF}	0.83 ± 0.13	-0.923 ± 0.068

Source: Authors

Blind use

The model for the prediction of actions on blinds (Haldi and Robinson, 2010) is also based on a Markov chain, predicting lowering and raising probabilities. The model takes pre-processed occupancy states, outdoor illuminance $E_{gl,hoz}$ and indoor illuminance E_{in} as inputs (requiring coupling with a daylight model – see Section 5.3.5). The following action probabilities determine lowering and raising actions:

$$P_{act}\left(E_{in}, B_L\right) = \frac{\exp(a + b_{in}E_{in} + b_L B_L)}{1 + \exp(a + b_{in}E_{in} + b_L B_L)} \qquad [5.3.11]$$

where B_L is the current unshaded fraction, with parameters a, b_i displayed in Table 5.3.2. If an action is predicted, the probabilities of adjusting blinds to their fully (un)shaded position are:

$$P_{full,act}\left(E_{in}, B_L\right) = \frac{\exp(a + b_{out}E_{gl,hoz} + b_L B_L)}{1 + \exp(a + b_{out}E_{gl,hoz} + b_L B_L)} \qquad [5.3.12]$$

But if a partial raising action is predicted, the deduced shaded fraction is drawn from a uniform distribution and in the case of partial lowering, the increase in shading ΔB is drawn from the Weibull distribution:

$$f(\Delta B) = \lambda\alpha(\lambda\Delta B)^{\alpha-1}\exp\left(-(\lambda\Delta B)^{\alpha}\right) \qquad [5.3.13]$$

with $\alpha = 1.708$ and $\lambda = 1/\exp(-2.294+1.522B_{L,init})$. The incident shortwave irradiance is then multiplied by the unshaded fraction to obtain the transmitted irradiance.

Table 5.3.2 Regression parameters for probabilities of actions on blinds

Blinds: Variables	Lowering Prob. P_{lower}	Raising Prob. P_{Raise}
Arrival		
a	-7.41 ± 0.16	-1.520 ± 0.051
E_{in}	$(10.35 \pm 0.19) \cdot 10^{-4}$	$(-6.54 \pm 0.46) \cdot 10^{-4}$
B_L	2.17 ± 0.16	-3.139 ± 0.068
During pres.		
a	-8.013 ± 0.086	-3.625 ± 0.030
E_{in}	$(8.41 \pm 0.13) \cdot 10^{-4}$	$(-2.76 \pm 0.22) \cdot 10^{-4}$
B_L	1.270 ± 0.086	-2.683 ± 0.040
Full lowering or raising		
a	-0.27 ± 0.14	0.435 ± 0.062
$E_{gl,hor}$	$(0.91 \pm 1.33) \cdot 10^{-6}$	$(-2.31 \pm 0.11) \cdot 10^{-5}$
B_L	-2.23 ± 0.16	1.95 ± 0.11

Source: Authors

Ongoing work

CitySim's behavioural modelling is at present limited to the above. In the absence of further experimental results, a reasonable approach to the modelling of occupants' interactions with lights would be to use the models of Hunt (1979, 1980) for the probability of switching lights on at arrival, Reinhart and Voss (2003) for intermediate switching and Pigg et al (1996) for switch-off at departure; as integrated by Reinhart (2004) into his tool *Lightswitch-2002* (and later into the software *DaySim*). This approach will shortly be implemented.

At present there is a dearth of research relating to the modelling of occupants' interactions with electrical appliances. Following from a review of literature, Page (2007) proposed a bottom-up model in which sources of randomness were separated into the ownership of appliances, occupants' presence and, while present, their use of appliances, focussing particularly on the last of these. In this, appliances were categorized as those that are: (1) always on (for example refrigerators) or are switched on/off (for example water heaters) automatically, (2) switched on by the occupant and off automatically (for example washing machines), (3) switched on and off by the occupant (PCs, cookers), and (4) are too small or used too infrequently to warrant individual modelling. The last category is thus to be modelled as a time varying aggregate. The challenge here is that, in the case of appliance types (2) to (4), individual appliances and their use by their owners vary considerably. Developing and calibrating a robust model would thus require a very considerable measurement campaign. Unfortunately, the necessary data are not currently available; at least, not to this author's knowledge.

The modelling of occupants' interactions with the HVAC system settings (for example the choice of heating system set-point) is also in need of further investigation and supporting data.

Finally, the regression parameters presented above in relation to the window and blind use models are based on the analysis of aggregate data for an entire population of building occupants. But the form of these models, and that of occupancy, is directly amenable for the modelling of individuals' behaviours; indeed these models have each been successfully applied in this respect. Thus, we are heading towards the implementation of an agent-based model of individual occupants' presence and behaviour. This is a theme that will be further developed in Chapter 6 on transport modelling.

5.3.4 Radiation models

Shortwave and longwave radiation exchange

In CitySim, the SRA of Robinson and Stone (2004, 2005), as described in Section 2.4.3, is used to calculate the shortwave irradiance incident on and transmitted through buildings' envelopes. In the latter case, the transmitted contribution to a thermal zone's energy balance is diminished in proportion to the fraction of glazing that is shaded by blinds (Section 5.3.3).

But we may wish to model the presence of both relatively nearby buildings that bound our urban site and far away mountainous obstructions. In the former case we simply associate each building with a tag, indicating whether this building participates exclusively in the SRA or whether a full energy simulation is to be conducted. In the latter case a modified sky radiance distribution (Section 2.3.1) is calculated, where for each patch we have that:

$$R_i = fR_i + (1-f)\left(I_{b\beta} + \sum_{j=1}^{p}(R\Phi\sigma\cos\theta)_j\right)\rho\Big/\pi \qquad [5.3.14]$$

in which f corresponds to an unoccluded fraction of the ith patch and ρ to the reflectance of the mountainous surface (which in principle may also be time varying, to account for snow cover) that is occluding this patch. The second term in brackets corresponds to the solar and sky irradiance incident on this occluding surface.

For longwave radiation exchange, the view information used by the SRA for shortwave irradiance calculations is reused, as described in Section 2.4.3.

Daylight modelling

As noted in Section 5.3.3, one of the inputs to the model of occupants' use of blinds is indoor illuminance which would also be input to a model of artificial lighting use.

As indicated in Section 2.4.3, it is relatively straightforward to use the SRA (see Robinson and Stone, 2006) to predict the illuminance E incident on the external surfaces of our urban scene. Thus we can readily obtain their luminance from the relation: $L = E\rho/\pi$. We can now calculate the illuminance received due to both the sky (E_s) and external occlusions (E_s) at a point within a room of a building:

$$E_s = \sum_{i=1}^{p}(L\Phi\sigma\cos\theta\tau)_i \qquad [5.3.15a]$$

$$E_o = \sum_{i=1}^{2p}(L^*\Phi\omega\cos\theta\tau)_i \qquad [5.3.15b]$$

For this we require additional renderings from each internal calculation point, from which we simply process the information within the visible extremities of external openings (of transmittance τ) to define the sky and external surface view factors and for the latter to identify the dominant obstructions. Note that while solar illumination may contribute to internal and external surface luminance, it is assumed that users will interact with blinds if there is a risk of direct insolation in the vicinity of our calculation points, so that there is no direct solar contribution to internal illumination.

All that remains is to calculate the contribution due to internal reflections. For this there are two obvious alternatives: to perform an additional radiosity calculation to determine the luminance of the (discretized) surfaces bounding our room and the contribution of these surfaces to the illuminance of our internal calculation points (as in Robinson and Stone, 2005), or to use a diffusing sphere approximation, as with the BRS split flux equation of Hopkinson et al (1966) (as in Robinson and Stone, 2006). The former approach is more physically realistic, but it is also more complex to implement and more computationally demanding. The latter is straightforward to implement and is computationally efficient. But it can also lead to considerable errors in the handling of internally reflected light when the external luminous field is strongly anisotropic. Fortunately, this tends not to be the case in the range $0 < E_{in} \leq 1000$ Lux in which lights tend to be switched on and off, so that the simplification inherent in the split flux equation seems to be reasonable (Robinson and Stone, 2006). In this case this final contribution to internal illumination is calculated as follows:

$$E_i = \left(F_D \rho_L + F_U \rho_U \right) / A \left(1 - \overline{\rho} \right) \qquad [5.3.16]$$

where the incoming luminous fluxes in the downwards F_D and upwards F_U directions are reflected initially by surfaces having an area-weighted mean reflectance of the lower and upper halves of the room respectively, ρ_L, ρ_U and are subsequently diffused throughout the room of surface area A and area-weighted mean reflectance $\overline{\rho}$. The corresponding incoming fluxes are calculated as follows:

$$F_D = \sum_{i=1}^{n} A_{g,i} \left(I_{b\theta} \eta_b \tau + \sum_{j=1}^{p} \left(L \Phi \sigma \cos \theta \tau \right)_j + \sum_{k=1}^{p} \left(L^* \Phi \omega \cos \theta \tau \right)_k \right)_i \qquad [5.3.17a]$$

$$F_U = \sum_{i=1}^{n} A_{g,i} \left(\sum_{j=p+1}^{2p} L^* \Phi \omega \cos \xi \tau \right)_i \qquad [5.3.17b]$$

In determining F_D and F_U, we may reuse information from renderings executed at the external surface of the ith glazed element of surface area $A_{g,i}$. Note that η_b corresponds to a beam luminous efficacy.

5.3.5 Models' implementation

As noted earlier, a scene description is parsed from the CitySim GUI to the solver in XML format. In the solver, this scene is decomposed into one or more districts, each composed of one or more buildings that may themselves be composed of one or more zones (Figure 5.3.5). Each zone is enclosed by walls,[4]

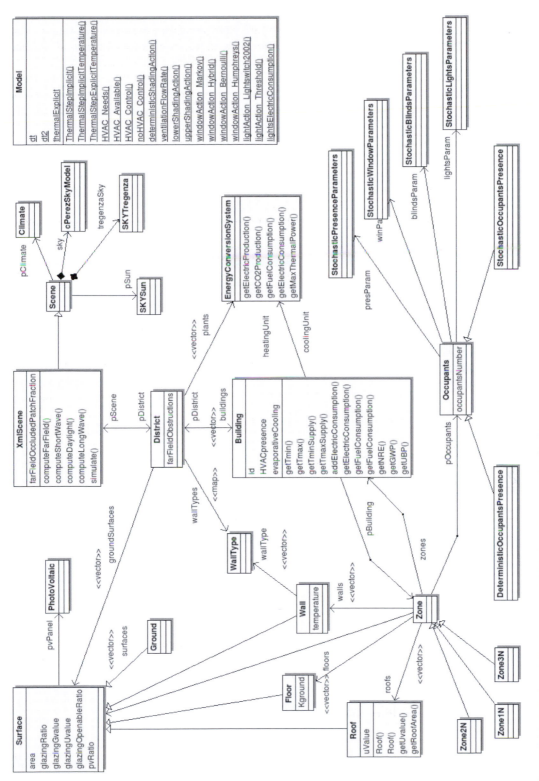

Figure 5.3.5 Unified modelling language (UML) class diagram of the CitySim solver

Source: Authors

which may or may not be thermally active (they may be used by the radiation model, but not by the thermal model). Each zone may also contain occupants, whose behaviours may be simulated and whose presence may be either simulated or associated with a deterministic profile.

For the purposes of calculating shortwave radiation exchange a radiation scene is prepared from the XML scene. This scene is composed of surface data, a sky discretization scheme and a sky radiance distribution model, likewise the view factor calculations. The sun and climate data also depend on this scene.

Separately shown in Figure 5.3.5 is the class model, which contains a variety of methods relating to the implicit and explicit solution schemes of the thermal model as well as of the modelling of HVAC plant. In all cases these model methods depend solely on buildings, whereas energy conversion systems (ECSs) may depend on either a district or a building (ECSs may be building embedded or district wide).

In terms of calculation sequence (Figure 5.3.6), the radiation model first predicts the shortwave irradiation incident on the building envelope (starting with a preconditioning period of several days), of which part is absorbed by the opaque surfaces and part is transmitted through the transparent surfaces, from where it is absorbed by the air and the internal surfaces. The zone's heating and cooling demands are then calculated using an implicit solution scheme. If there is no mechanical ventilation (HVAC) equipment the ECS models are called. As noted in Section 5.3.2, if these systems have insufficient power, a new zone temperature is calculated using the thermal model; likewise if the ECSs have

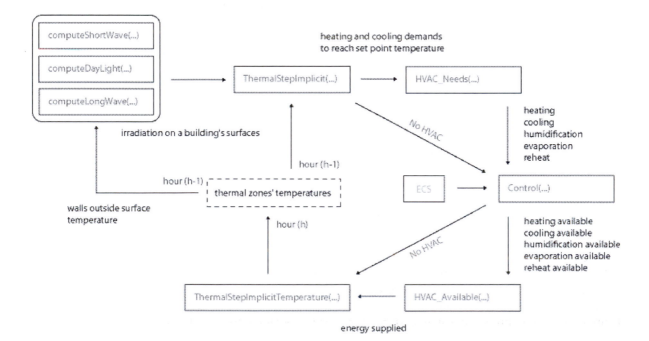

Figure 5.3.6 Calculation sequence of the CitySim solver

Source: Authors

insufficient capacity to meet the revised power demands following from the conditioning of air using HVAC plant. Finally, an external surface temperature is used for the calculation of external surface longwave exchange at the next time step (a guess being used for the first time step of the first day of preconditioning).

5.3.6 Applications of CitySim

At the time of writing, CitySim remains under development, so that not all of the intended functionality is currently fully implemented. Nevertheless, the following two examples provide some indication of the potential scales of its application, from an individual building focussing on the impact of occupants' behaviour – an important issue when supplying energy to multiple buildings – to an entire urban district. Note that an example application at the intermediate scale of a city block is presented in Section 8.5, in the context of optimizing an urban block refurbishment strategy. We begin by describing the larger-scale application.

District scale modelling

As has been noted on several occasions throughout this book, urban-scale energy modelling poses challenges concerning the acquisition of data describing the urban scene under investigation, the time required to manage this data and the time and resources required to perform the computations of interest. These challenges become more acute as we increase our scale of analysis from a few tens of buildings (as in Section 8.5) to an urban district of several hundred buildings. In this section we focus on the methods employed for acquiring and managing data to handle relatively large-scale urban simulations. For this we use a case study district in the City of Neuchâtel in Switzerland (46°59'31"N, 6°55'44"E; altitude 430m; population 34,000), which forms the focus for the European Commission-funded project HOLISTIC (HOListic Integration of Sustainable Technologies In Cities), that is supporting the development of CitySim.[5]

Broadly speaking, the scene description that is parsed to the CitySim solver is comprised of: (1) geometry: 3D building and adjacent shading objects, 2D ground surfaces and far-field horizon coordinates, (2) attributes: building construction, occupation, HVAC systems and embedded energy conversion systems, district energy conversion and storage systems, and (3) simulation settings.

Geometry
When applied to relatively small-scale applications of a few tens of buildings, we may either use the basic 3D modelling functions that are available from within the CitySim graphical user interface or import a 3D drawing exchange format (.dxf) file prepared using a third party 3D modelling tool such as Google SketchUp. But this is not convenient when modelling several hundred buildings. For this we need to reuse, as far as possible, existing data sources. Fortunately most municipalities have digital cadastral maps describing their

territory, the boundaries of land ownership and the footprints of buildings accommodated on this land.

In Neuchâtel, the territorial information system manages all geographical data using GIS software; from which buildings' footprints may be exported in a variety of formats including .dxf, the shapefile format that is common to most GIS software (.shp) and the geography markup language (.gml) format – the XML grammar defined by the Open Geospatial Consortium (OGC) to express geographical features.

But we still require information describing the third dimension of our building envelopes. Fortunately the Swiss Federal Office of Topography has prepared a numerical surface model for the whole country. Based on airborne LIDAR (Light Detection And Ranging) measurements, point heights are available at a density of 1 point per $2m^2$ and an average altitude accuracy of 0.5m. Using standard GIS software functions, it is thus possible, by processing the surface model points which lie within building footprints, to determine a mean building height. Thus we can extrude 3D volumes from our building footprints to create a 2.5D model of our urban district (Plate 20) with a reasonably high degree of accuracy. Such a geometric description was prepared for our district in Neuchâtel and exported in keyhole markup language (.kml) format using the GIS software Manifold. This is essentially an XML file format for which a vertex listing of the buildings' footprints was supplemented with a name (a numerical building ID) and a mean building height.

For the present time, a standard OpenGL algorithm tessellates the ground plane in CitySim so that adjacent building footprint vertices are linked by triangular planes. Regarding the far-field obstruction profile, an input that can be particularly important in Switzerland, this can be readily exported from the climate modelling and database software Meteonorm.[6] Hourly climate data is readily available from the Swiss meteorological organization MeteoSwiss.

Unfortunately the building layers of Neuchâtel's GIS model include all solid constructions, from unheated shelters and garages to waste water treatment plant and swimming pools. Further data regarding buildings' use is therefore required to identify those for which we wish to simulate their energy demands and use.

Attributes

In Switzerland several types of census are issued (normally every ten years) by the Swiss Federal Office of Statistics to individuals, households and residential (or mixed use) building owners. In combination, these census returns provide for a relatively detailed description of residential buildings and their inhabitants, in particular regarding the buildings' location; the type of owner (private individual, insurance company etc); the number of building floors and the number of apartments and their surface area; dates of construction and last major renovation; household composition, age and occupation per apartment; the type of heating system and fuel source; rental costs and so on. In addition, companies are required to return an 'enterprise census' that provides details regarding companies' location, the number of employees and the type of activity performed.

These data are provided to municipalities who are responsible for maintaining detailed building and inhabitants registers. Now, we were initially interested only in (wholly or partially) residential buildings, so that we could compare predicted with measured heating energy use for residential buildings that were connected to the city's district heating network. Using the building register we were able to filter our buildings to enable such a comparison. But first we required additional attributes describing our buildings, in particular with respect to the composition of their envelopes.

For this a visual survey was conducted for the entire case study district, consisting of some 440 individual buildings. For each building the following were observed: type of building (individual house, semi-detached, terrace, apartment building); age category; number of floors; external façade material, state and orientation; glazing ratio and type of glazing system; presence of balcony; type of solar shading; type (whether occupied or not) and state of roof. We also prepared, in collaboration with the city architect, standard building façade element compositions that we could match to the corresponding observations. It certainly is not our intention that such surveys be conducted each time we wish to model an existing urban district, but by carrying out these kinds of survey initially, we are able to build up relatively accurate default characteristics that we can associate with a given type of building and category of age; or indeed to prepare a cumulative probability distribution for a given characteristic that we can randomly assign to a building. In this way we will be able to reduce future modelling effort.

Thus we were able, in principle, to develop a relatively detailed description of the buildings within our case study zone by supplementing existing data with visual observations. But this requires that (1) each building has a known and unique identifier that is consistently applied in relation to all data sources, and (2) that all data are reliable. Unfortunately neither is the case.

Data from the Swiss Federal Office of Statistics are associated with a unique building identity (called an EGID), which is also associated with x,y coordinates. Unfortunately these x,y coordinates do not always fit within a building's footprint, and occasionally we have more than one EGID for one building's footprint. This may be perfectly legitimate: there may be more than one owner of a single building envelope. Other data sources may be associated with a street address. Furthermore, the individuals completing their census questionnaires may make simple blunders when completing them or may simply be mistaken, for example concerning a buildings' age, number of floors, type of heating system or fuel source. For some of these we were able to identify inconsistencies using our visual field survey results, but for others we needed the help of local experts. Thus we do not have a foolproof approach, but we do nevertheless have a labour saving one, the results of which are parsed to the CitySim GUI in comma separated value (.csv) format.

Nevertheless, this part of the work has proven to be the most time consuming. It is also the least addressed by research, with few available tools designed to help in this task at this scale. For the time being we have used GIS software to provide a visual access to data, a geographical representation of the scene and some helpful geometrical functions.

Simulation settings

For the present time, we have relatively few simulation settings to adjust when launching a simulation with CitySim. We may distinguish those buildings for which we want full energy simulations from those that should only participate in calculations of shortwave radiation exchange (for example they simply act as occlusions to the sun and sky to our buildings of interest) and declare whether we wish to perform full energy simulations or restrict ourselves to shortwave radiation exchange modelling (for example to assist with siting solar collectors) (see for example Plate 21).

Results

In addition to having acquired relatively comprehensive data regarding the geometry and attribution of the buildings describing our urban scene, we have also been able to acquire measured energy use, albeit temporally crude. This is largely because, in common with several other local municipalities, the City of Neuchâtel is a shareholder of the energy supply company (called Viteos).

In general these results are promising, but occasionally we have very large discrepancies owing to the sources of uncertainty outlined above, in particular regarding the extent of the building to which energy is supplied. Work is ongoing to minimize the difference between measured and predicted energy consumption to correct these data mismatches and also to formally calibrate our models.

Sensitivity to occupants' behaviour

This study (for further details see Haldi and Robinson, forthcoming) of a hypothetical *shoebox* building was conceived to focus on the influence of occupants' behavioural diversity on building energy demand and indoor conditions, in particular with respect to their use of windows and shading devices. For this we have described a single office building, which corresponds to a typical office of LESO-PB at EPFL in Switzerland, which has a volume of $44.1m^3$ (Figure 5.3.7). For this the heating system is a boiler of maximum power $P = 1$ kW. Real data monitored from the LESO-PB building are used to define the occupant's presence profile, which is associated with a sensible metabolic heat gain of 90W.

An insulated timber clad construction is assumed for the walls and roof (U-Value = 0.44 $W/m^2.K$), whereas the floor is insulated concrete (0.7 $W/m^2.K$). The

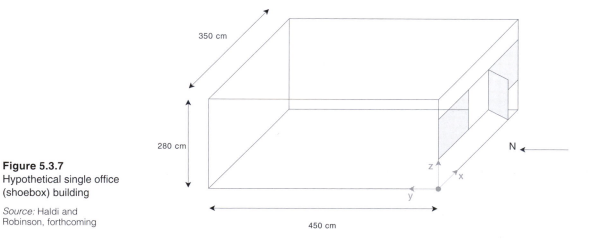

Figure 5.3.7
Hypothetical single office (shoebox) building

Source: Haldi and Robinson, forthcoming

glazing is assumed to have a U-value and G-value of 1.4 W/m².K and 0.7 respectively, while air leakage is represented by a constant infiltration rate of 0.2/h.

Parameters studied

The influence of the following parameters has been evaluated:

- Glazing ratio of the south façade: G = 0.10 and 0.05; this glazing is assumed, for simplicity, to be fully openable.
- Set-point temperatures for heating H = 18°C and 21°C, and cooling: C = 26°C and 30°C. The cases of no heating and no cooling are also investigated.
- Individual behaviours, denoted by P (set to 0, 1, ..., 22, 23, D), linked with corresponding regression parameters, where 0 denotes the models based on the aggregated data (Tables 5.3.1, 5.3.2) and D a deterministic control strategy (window opening if θ_{in} > 26°C, closing if θ_{in} < 20°C; blind lowering if E_{in} > 2500 (lux), raising if E_{in} < 300 (lux)).

To model individuals' behaviours P, we use regression parameters similar to those found in Tables 5.3.1 and 5.3.2, but derived from the analysis of actions on windows and shading devices performed by individuals rather than from aggregate data. These individuals' regression parameters values are presented in Haldi and Robinson (2009, 2010).

As noted earlier, the model of shading device behaviour requires internal illumination as an input. For this we use the SRA, as described in Section 5.3.4, that predicts illuminance E_{in} at two penetration distances (H/2 and 3H/2, where H is the room height). In this study we use the value closest to the window (H/2 = 1.5m by default). A proportionality constant accounts for the effect of shaded fraction.

We have studied the influence of the above building and behavioural parameters on both total heating and cooling energy demand. Note that in this, the use of stochastic behavioural models suggests the replication of simulations for the assessment of the variability between predictions. In each considered case, simulations are repeated 50 times, which allows us to study the distribution of results rather than relying on fixed mean values.

Results

Replicates of simulations with identical design and behavioural inputs display significant variability in their results. This is in line with our expectations: a given occupant will not always behave identically even for similar environmental conditions. Figure 5.3.8 illustrates this fact for 50 simulations of the case G0.10-H21-C26-P0, where, for instance, the heating load ranges from 2417 to 4496kWh/year for 95 per cent of cases. The degree of this dispersion also varies between design variants, as shown in Figure 5.3.9, in which the distributions of simulation results for the above mentioned levels of glazing ratio and set point temperature (yielding 2 × 3 × 3 × 50 = 900 replicates) are also presented. These simulations show that an increased glazing/window opening ratio raises heating demands but lowers cooling demands (the rejection of heat by ventilation outweighing the solar gains).

Due to the large number of required simulations, the impact of different individuals' behaviours was investigated exclusively for the configuration

G0.10-H18-C30, which corresponds to relatively distant set-point temperatures and a large window opening area. Figure 5.3.10 shows the distributions of heating and cooling loads with respect to the simulated individual behaviours. Compared to the model P0 of an 'average occupant', the dispersion of the results is strongly reduced, which is a consequence of higher slopes in the regression parameters (and thus more deterministic behaviour) in the case of models for individuals.

However, the overall spread of results between occupants outweighs by far the spread initially noticed in the case of the aggregated behavioural model. The explicit simulation of behavioural diversity thus brings a more realistic

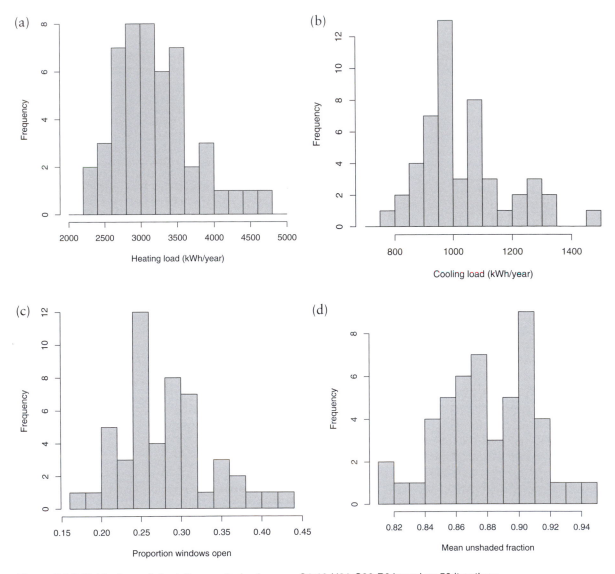

Figure 5.3.8 Distributions of simulation results for the case G0.10-H21-C26-P0 based on 50 iterations

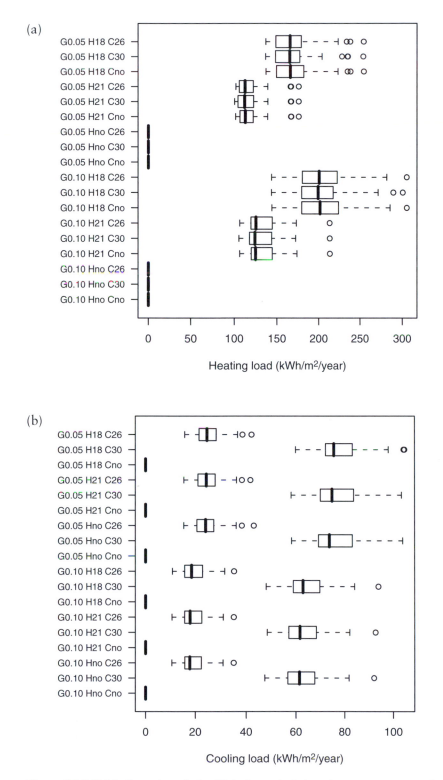

Figure 5.3.9 Distributions of results for 18 design variants based on average occupant behaviour (P0)

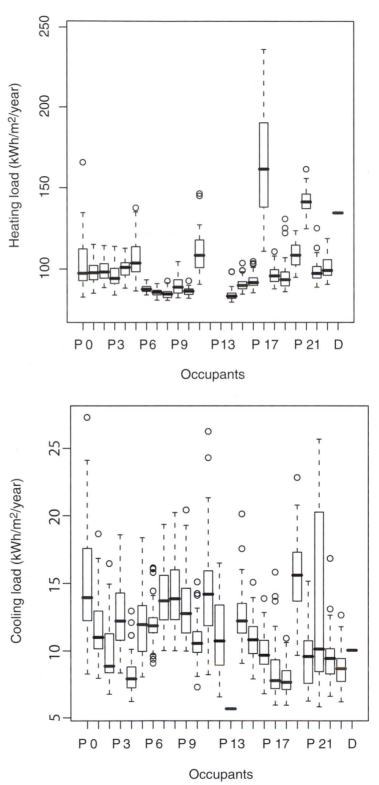

Figure 5.3.10 Distributions of (a) heating and (b) cooling loads with respect to behavioural diversity

estimation of the distribution of outcomes in building simulation, particularly when simulating urban developments in which many occupants are accommodated. Finally, the failure of deterministic rules D to properly represent occupants' behaviour is clear – stochastic variations and occupants' diversity are ignored, so that the single fixed result is wholly unrepresentative of the observed range of behaviour and corresponding impacts on energy demand.

5.4 Conclusions

The purpose of this chapter was to address the considerable challenge of modelling urban-scale resource flows due to buildings. In the chapter introduction we suggested that to achieve this an ideal model should predict: (1) the consumption of products having short (for example food, water and clothing; the associated production of waste), medium (for example furnishings) and long (for example constructional materials) residence times; (2) buildings' energy demands for space conditioning, with due regard for the urban climate (thermal and radiant) as well as occupants' presence and their interactions with buildings' envelope and space conditioning systems; (3) the energy demands due to the activities accommodated within buildings, such as automated or occupant controlled use of mechanical and electrical equipment; (4) the supply of energy to buildings either from embedded energy conversion systems or from those integrated with decentralized energy centres, possibly derived from buildings' waste products; and (5) the exchanges of energy and mass between buildings, for space conditioning and to support the activities accommodated.

To date the majority of models, whether bottom-up or based on the extrapolation of results from representative building typologies, focus on buildings' energy demands for space conditioning (item 2), though not necessarily accounting explicitly for occupants or the urban climate. In certain cases the modelling of energy storage and supply to buildings from a relatively broad range of technologies is also considered (item 4). But thus far, none of the models predict the energy demands due to the activities (for example commercial, industrial or healthcare) accommodated within buildings (item 3); likewise the consumption of matter in its broad sense (item 1) or the exchanges of energy and matter between buildings (item 5).

Models of urban resource flows due to buildings are thus very much in their infancy. But resolving these gaps in modelling capability will also require advances in the acquisition, sharing and management of data; particularly as the scale of the more detailed models increases towards that of the city, at which advances in computing methods are also required. These issues are discussed further in Chapter 10. In the meantime, an exciting challenge is to couple detailed building and transport models to more reliably account for the flows of goods and people between buildings (Chapter 6).

Acknowledgements

Financial support received from the Swiss National Science Foundation and the European Commission's DG-TREN for the development of CitySim is gratefully acknowledged. The contributions to CitySim from the following members, either past or present, of the Sustainable Urban Development research group at LESO-PB/EPFL are also very gratefully acknowledged: Deepak Angrula, Fei He, Rishab Jain, Anikhet Jha, André Kostro, Jessen Page and Urs Wilke.

Notes

1   This section is a further developed version of the very brief review presented in Section 15.3 of Robinson (2011, forthcoming).
2   Filchakova et al (2009) have developed, for example, a statistical model of the residential stock of the city of Basel. This is a useful model that enabled its users to identify whether assumed renovation scenarios would achieve the city's energy demand reduction targets. But this model gives no information regarding the tangible renovation strategies that should be implemented.
3   This is defined in a climate file, for which the air temperature column may in principle be defined by a meso-scale atmospheric flow model in which the effects of the urban canopy on energy and mechanical exchanges between air and surfaces are parameterized (see Chapter 4).
4   Note that roofs may be alternatively defined for the thermal model so that they are associated only with a total conductance rather than as a composite of elements having specific thermophysical properties for use within the dynamic thermal model.
5   www.holistic-ne.ch.
6   www.meteotest.ch.

References

Beausoleil-Morrison, I. (2000) 'The adaptive coupling of heat and airflow modelling within dynamic whole-building simulation', PhD Thesis, University of Strathclyde, Strathclyde
Bland, B. H. (1992) 'Conduction in dynamic model: analytical tests for validation', *Building Services Engineering Research and Technology*, vol 3, no 4, pp197–208
Bruhns, H., Steadman, P. and Herring, H. (2000) 'A database for modelling energy use in the non-domestic building stock of England and Wales', *Applied Energy*, vol 66, pp277–297
Clarke, J. A. (1977) 'Environmental systems performance', PhD Thesis, University of Strathclyde, Strathclyde
Clarke, J. A. (2001) *Energy Simulation in Building Design*, 2nd edition, Butterworth Heinemann, London
Duffie, J. A. and Beckman, W. A. (1991) *Solar Engineering of Solar Processes*, 2nd edition, Wiley, Chichester
Filchakova, N., Wilke, U. and Robinson, D. (2009) 'A model of whole-city housing stock and its temporal evolution', in *Proc. Eleventh Int. IBPSA Conf: Building Simulation 2009*, Glasgow, pp1068–1074, available at www.ibpsa.org/m_papers.asp, last accessed 17 December 2010
Gadsden, S., Rylatt, M., Lomas, K. and Robinson, D. (2003) 'Predicting the urban solar fraction: A methodology for energy advisers and planners based on GIS', *Energy and Buildings*, vol 35, no 1, pp37–48
Gough, M. C. B. (1982) 'Modelling heat flow in buildings: An eigenfunction approach', PhD Thesis, University of Cambridge, Cambridge
Haldi, F. and Robinson, D. (2009) 'Interactions with window openings by office occupants', *Building and Environment*, vol 44, no 12, pp2378–2395
Haldi, F. and Robinson, D. (2010) 'Adaptive actions on shading devices in response to local visual stimuli', *Journal of Building Performance Simulation*, vol 3, no 2, pp135–153
Haldi, F. and Robinson, D. (forthcoming) 'The impact of occupants' behaviour on urban energy demand', *Journal of Building Performance Simulation* (submitted)
Hensen, J. L. M. (1991) 'On the thermal interaction with building structure and heating and ventilating systems', PhD Thesis, University of Eindhoven, Eindhoven

Hopkinson, R. G., Petherbridge, P. and Longmore, J. (1966) *Daylighting*, Heinemann, London

Hunt, D. R. G. (1979) 'The use of artificial lighting in relation to daylight levels and occupancy', *Building and Environment*, vol 14, pp21–33

Hunt, D. R. G. (1980) 'Predicting artificial lighting use: A method based upon observed patterns of behaviour', *Lighting Research and Technology*, vol 12, no 1, pp7–14

Janak, M. (1997) 'Coupling building and lighting simulation', in *Proc. Building Simulation '97* 5th Int IBPSA Conf, Prague, available at www.ibpsa.org/m_papers.asp, last accessed 17 December 2010

Johnston, D., Lowe, R. and Bell, M. (2005) 'An exploration of the technical feasibility of achieving CO_2 reductions in excess of 60% within the UK housing stock by the year 2050', *Energy Policy*, vol 33, pp1643–1659

Jones, P., Williams, J. and Lannon, S. (1998) 'An energy and environmental prediction tool for planning sustainability in cities', in *Proc. 2th European Conf. REBUILD*, Florence, April

Jones, P., Patterson, J., Lannon, S. and Prasad, D. (1999) 'An energy and environmental prediction tool for planning sustainable cities', *Proc. Passive and Low Energy Architecture 99*: Brisbane, pp789–794, available at www.arct.cam.ac.uk/PLEA/home.aspx, last accessed 17 December 2010

Jones, P., Patterson, J. and Lannon, S. (2007) 'Modelling the built environment at an urban scale – energy and health impacts in relation to housing', *Landscape and Urban Planning*, vol 83, pp39–49

Judkoff, R. and Neymark, J. A. (1995) 'A testing and diagnostic procedure for building energy simulation programs', in *Proc. Building Environmental Performance Analysis Club (BEPAC)*, York, pp103–116

Kämpf, J. (2009) 'The modelling and optimisation of urban resource flows', unpublished PhD (Dr és Science) Thesis, EPFL, Lausanne

Kämpf, J. and Robinson, D. (2007) 'A simplified thermal model to support analysis of urban resource flows', *Energy and Buildings*, vol 39, no 4, pp445–453

Kelly, N. (1998) 'Towards a design environment for building integrated energy systems: The integration of electrical power flow modelling with building simulation', unpublished PhD Thesis, University of Strathclyde, Strathclyde

Labs, K. (1982) 'Regional analysis of ground and above-ground climate conclusion', *Underground Space*, vol 7, no 1, pp37–65

Lomas, K. J., Eppel, H., Martin, C. J. and Bloomfield, D. P. (1997) 'Empirical validation of building energy simulation programs', *Energy and Buildings*, vol 26, no 3, pp253–267

Nakhi, A. (1995) 'Adaptive construction modelling within whole building dynamic simulation', PhD Thesis, University of Strathclyde, Strathclyde

Natarjan, S. and Levermore, G. J. (2007) 'Predicting future UK housing stock and carbon emissions', *Energy Policy*, vol 35, pp5719–5727

Nielsen, T.R. (2005) 'Simple tool to evaluate energy demand and indoor environment in the early stages of building design', *Solar Energy*, vol 78, no 1, pp73–83

Page, J. (2007) 'Simulating occupant presence and behaviour in buildings', unpublished Ph.D. (Dr ès Sciences), EPFL

Page, J., Robinson, D., Morel, N. and Scartezzini, J.-L. (2007), 'A generalised stochastic model for the prediction of occupant presence', *Energy and Buildings*, vol 40, no 2, pp83–98

Pigg, S., Eilers, M. and Reed, J. (1996) 'Behavioural aspects of lighting and occupancy sensors in private offices: A case study of a university office building', in *ACEEE Summer Study on Energy Efficiency in Buildings*, vol 8, pp161–171

Pout, C. (2000) 'N-DEEM: The national nondomestic buildings energy and emissions model', *Environment and Planning B: Planning and Design*, vol 27, no 5, pp721–732

Ratti, C., Robinson, D., Baker, N. and Steemers, K. (2000) 'LT Urban – the energy modelling of urban form', in *Proc. PLEA 2000*, James and James, London, pp660–666

Ratti, C., Baker, N. and Steemers, K. (2005) 'Energy consumption and urban texture', *Energy and Buildings*, vol 37, no 7, pp762–776

Reinhart, C. F. (2004) 'Lightswitch-2002: A model for manual and automated control of electric lighting and blinds', *Solar Energy*, vol 77, no 1, pp15–28

Reinhart, C. and Voss, K. (2003) 'Monitoring manual control of electric lighting and blinds', *Lighting Research and Technology*, vol 35, pp243–260

Robinson, D. (2005) 'Decision support for environmental master planning by integrated flux modelling', in *Proc. CISBAT 2005*, EPFL, Lausanne, pp533–538

Robinson, D. (forthcoming) 'Integrated resource flow modelling of the urban built environment', in Hensen, J. L. M. and Lamberts, R. (eds) *Building Performance Simulation for Design and Operation*, Taylor & Francis, London

Robinson, D. and Baker, N. (2000) 'Simplified modelling: Recent developments in the LT Method', *Building Performance*, vol 3, no 1, pp14–19

Robinson, D. and Stone, A. (2004) 'Solar radiation modelling in the urban context', *Solar Energy*, vol 77, no 3, pp295–309

Robinson, D. and Stone, A. (2005) 'A simplified radiosity algorithm for general urban radiation exchange', *Building Services Engineering Research and Technology*, vol 26, no 4, pp271–284

Robinson, D. and Stone, A. (2006) 'Internal illumination prediction based on a simplified radiosity algorithm', *Solar Energy*, vol 80, no 3, pp260–267

Robinson, D., Stankovic, S., Morel, N., Deque, F., Rylatt, M., Kabele, K., Manolakaki, E. and Nieminen, J. (2003) 'Integrated resource flow modelling of urban neighbourhoods: Project SUNtool', in *Proc. Building Simulation 2003*, IBPSA, Eindhoven, pp1117–1122, available at www.ibpsa.org/m_papers.asp last accessed 17 December 2010

Robinson, D., Campbell, N., Gaiser, W., Kabel, K., Le-Mouele, A., Morel, N., Page, J., Stankovic, S. and Stone, A. (2007) 'SUNtool – a new modelling paradigm for simulating and optimising urban sustainability', *Solar Energy*, vol 81, no 9, pp1196–1211

Rylatt, M., Gadsden, S. and Lomas, K. (2001) 'GIS-based decision support for solar energy planning in urban environments', *Computers, Environment and Urban Systems*, vol 25, pp579–603

Shimoda, Y., Fujii, T., Morikawa, T. and Mizuno, M. (2003) 'Development of residential energy end-use simulation model at city scale', in *Proc. Building Simulation 2003*, IBPSA, Eindhoven, pp1201–1208, available at www.ibpsa.org/m_papers.asp, last accessed 17 December

Shimoda, Y., Yamaguchi, Y., Kawamoto, K., Ueshige, J., Iwai, Y. and Mizuno, M. (2007) 'Effect of telecommuting on energy consumption in residential and non-residential sectors', *Proc. Building Simulation 2007*, IBPSA, Beijing, pp1361–1368, available at www.ibpsa.org/m_papers.asp, last accessed 17 December 2010

Shorrock, L. D. and Dunster, J. E. (1997) 'The physically-based model BREHOMES and its use in deriving scenarios for energy use and carbon dioxide emissions of the UK housing stock', *Energy Policy*, vol 25, no 12, pp1027–1037

Stone, A. M. (2008) 'Energy simulation of urban masterplans', unpublished EngD Thesis, University College London, London

Tang, D. (1984) 'Modelling of heating and air-conditioning systems', PhD thesis, University of Strathclyde, Strathclyde

Taniguchi, A., Shimoda, Y., Asahi, T., Yamaguchi, Y. and Mizuno, M. (2007) 'Effectiveness of energy conservation measures in residential sector of Japanese buildings', in *Proc. Building Simulation 2007*, IBPSA, Beijing, pp1645–1652, available at www.ibpsa.org/m_papers.asp, last accessed 17 December 2010

Yamaguchi, Y., Shimoda, Y. and Mizuno, M. (2003) 'Development of district energy simulation model based on detailed energy demand model', in *Proc. Building Simulation 2003*, IBPSA, Eindhoven, pp1443–1450, available at www.ibpsa.org/m_papers.asp, last accessed 17 December 2010

Yamaguchi, Y., Shimoda, Y. and Mizuno, M. (2007a) 'Transition to a sustainable urban energy system from a long-term perspective: Case study in a Japanese business district', *Energy and Buildings*, vol 39, pp1–12

Yamaguchi, Y., Shimoda, Y. and Mizuno, M. (2007b) 'Proposal of a modelling approach considering urban form for evaluation of city level energy management', *Energy and Buildings*, vol 39, pp1–12

Yamaguchi, Y., Shimoda, Y. and Mizuno, M. (2007c) 'Simulation support in designing the transformation of urban building stock and energy infrastructure', *Proc. Building Simulation 2007*, IBPSA: Beijing, pp1564–1571, available at www.ibpsa.org/m_papers.asp, last accessed 17 December 2010

6

Transport Modelling

Kay Axhausen

6.1 Introduction

Resources in urban settlements are consumed principally by buildings and the activities accommodated within them and by the transport of goods and people to and between them. While in recent years there has been a tendency for energy consumption in buildings to stabilize or even to reduce, the reverse is true in the case of transport. In the UK for example, transport is the sector that has experienced the greatest growth since the 1970s: its 19 per cent share in 1970, increased to 25 per cent in 1980, 33 per cent in 1990 and was 38 per cent in 2008 (DUKES, 2009). Given that most of this energy is non-renewable, there is an increasing desire to explore ways in which both the demand for travel and its energy intensity can be reduced. For this we need transport models.

Transport planning models have been under development for the past 60 years, since their first application to design the Detroit and Chicago regions freeway systems (DMATS, 1955; CATS, 1960). They have since seen remarkable conceptual, technical, algorithmic and statistical advances. This chapter discusses the key elements of these models and introduces the central statistical tool used to estimate the weights of the generalized cost functions on which travel choices are based. It illustrates the general framework sketched with the application of a state-of-the-art modelling framework to a major infrastructure investment in Switzerland: the western bypass around Zürich, the country's business centre.

6.2 The task

Travel is the minimum cost for participating in the desired or necessary out-of-home activities of daily life. This cost can be understood as the composite of the time and money resources required, weighted by the risks involved and the comfort in which the travel can be performed. These *generalized costs of travel* are at the centre of all formal transport modes. The definition of the generalized costs in terms of the variables considered, the functional form of the variables and their relative weights differ between studies and over the years.

Transport models focus on the questions of who is where, when, for what purpose and how they arrived there – using what mode along which connection/route. They model the scheduling of daily activities, i.e. daily life, which generally excludes longer journeys[1] outside of the immediate study area, or journeys involving an overnight stay. In their standard form they ignore the utility derived from participating in activities, or acknowledge it only indirectly by allowing the weights (parameters) of the generalized cost function to vary by the purpose of the activity at the end of the trip.

To obtain comparable and definable solutions, transport models calculate a consistent equilibrium between the demand for travel and the supply of slots offered by an existing or a planned transport system, i.e. infrastructures and the services offered by them (bus routes, train services, etc.). A *slot* is a path through the time-space system, which allows a traveller and her/his vehicle to travel at the desired, prescribed or emergent speed. In transport systems, these slots and their speeds are either emergent from the interaction of the users, such as the lower speeds arising from crowding on a motorway or the left/right division of a walkway in a crowded shopping centre, or they are the product of explicit control, such as a signal-controlled road or rail intersection, through airspace or at airports. The moment the demand approaches the capacity of the system, i.e. the currently available number of slots, the quality level of the service drops, for example speeds decrease or crowding levels increase, as in any other queuing system. This increase in the generalized cost of travel ensures equilibrium in space and time, as the travellers will start to avoid the most crowded parts of the network by shifting the timing, the route, the mode, the destination of his/her trip, or maybe foregoing the trip completely (see for example Downs, 1962, 2004 or Weis and Axhausen, 2009). It is this point, when the (perception of the) generalized costs of travel are consistent between the expectation of the travellers and the performance of the network, that defines the equilibrium in terms of the flows through the time–space network (where, when and with what mode to which destination).

While the equilibrium is unique for a given definition of the generalized costs, a given set of travellers and a given network, it should be of no surprise that there are various definitions of equilibrium. These need to be distinguished in the application of transport models. The differences in the scope within the given definition of the generalized costs (see below), the networks, the population distribution and the number and distribution of the activity facilities available are the policy focus of the application. The conceptual differences are more fundamental, as they reflect the policy objectives and the basic assumptions regarding the behaviour of the travellers. The first distinction that can be made is whether the traveller perceives the generalized costs with or without error. The second is whether the generalized costs include only the private elements or include all costs due to a trip, that is, if the externalities i.e. the impacts on third parties in terms of travel time, comfort, noise, emissions, safety, etc. are included. The resulting classification is shown in Table 6.2.1.

These Nash (1951) network equilibria were first formalized by Wardrop (1952), building on an earlier behavioural motivation by Knight (1924). He argued that drivers change routes as long as they can reduce their generalized costs and until all such possibilities are exhausted. He contrasted this deterministic user equilibrium (DUE) with the system optimum (SO), which occurs when the drivers follow routes to minimize their total collective

Table 6.2.1 Classification of the transport system equilibria

Perception of the travellers	Treatment of externalities	
	Included	Excluded
Error free	SO: system optimum	(D)UE: (deterministic) user equilibrium
With stochastic errors	----	SUE: stochastic user equilibrium

generalized costs, implying that some drivers accept higher costs to themselves to reduce the (congestion) externalities for everyone. Daganzo and Sheffi (1977) first proposed the stochastic user equilibrium (SUE) following Beckmann et al's (1956) formulation of the DUE as a mathematical optimization problem. In the DUE, all travellers between an origin and a destination (OD pair) have the same minimal generalized costs on all routes used. In SUE the share of users on the identified routes between an OD pair will be proportional to the generalized costs, implying that the users perceive the costs differently, i.e. with a specified stochastic error.[2]

Having set out the basic task of transport modelling above, the following sections discuss the two most prominent solution methods (aggregate flow-based models and agent-based disaggregate models) after a description of some key modelling tools and constructs. But before doing so we need to discuss some of the behavioural dimensions and whether they are considered endogenous or exogenous to the specific model application.

6.3 Endogenous choice dimensions and exogenous constraints

The main ambition of transport planning is to understand, capture and model the response of daily out-of-home behaviour to changes in exogenously given constraints (see below) or indeed to their removal through new capacity provided by new infrastructure and services. The boundary between the exogenous and the endogenous choices is fluid and depends on the policy context of the specific modelling exercise. While recent developments have broadened the scope of the modelling,[3] a standard practice has nevertheless emerged. This is detailed below.

Transport modelling applications take the following variables as exogenously given, meaning that these forecasts and scenarios are provided or established for the various years of the planning horizon independently from the transport model and its resources:

- Population change by age and sex (including in and out migration and natural change).
- Household numbers, size distribution by structure.
- Income by household size.
- Population distribution by location.
- Number of work places by location and (maybe) type.

- Spatial distribution of service facilities by type and size, for example schools, shops, stadia etc.
- Network structure and capacity by location.
- Transport services by frequency, capacity and route.
- Price levels by location, distance travelled and network type.

These variables define the policy of the local, regional or national government or the enterprise planning its future actions, who generally wish to retain control over the assumptions about these changes during the planning process. In any case, trustworthy working land-use models have not been easily available over the last 50 years (see Lee, 1975; Wegener, 2004 or more generally Parker et al, 2003) and models of spatially specific network growth were essentially missing in the literature until recently (see Xie and Levinson, 2009).

Within these constraints, the transport model distinguishes between the long-term choices of the household and the short-term choices of the individuals, from which this household is composed. The following long-term choices, which specify the spatially fixed reference points of the traveller (home, work, school), the available time budget after the fixed commitments of work and school and the speed and short run marginal monetary costs of travel, (i.e. the generalized costs of travel) are, or should be addressed.

Participation in the workforce is normally taken as given from demographic forecasts and economic scenarios. Nevertheless, it might be worthwhile to test the impact of accessibility change directly, as it has been shown to encourage (Fröhlich, 2008) or to suppress workforce participation, especially of low-income or other part-time workers.

Work place location given residential location; in many cases, the resulting matrix of flows is available from the most recent census and then only updated for the policy scenarios using incremental pivot-point approaches or iterative proportional fitting (see below).

School location given residential location is again taken from the census or established via applicable administrative rules. To the extent that these rules are becoming less relevant as parents and students have more choices, explicit models are required (see below).

Mobility tool ownership (cars, season tickets, driving licences) is normally reduced, following US practice and conditions, to car ownership modelling only. It has been shown, however, that neglecting public transport season ticket ownership strongly biases the car ownership models where these are available, leading to biased policy conclusions (Simma and Axhausen, 2003). Fortunately, the necessary discrete choice models are now available (see below) to forecast the set of tools consistently and completely.

Longer-term commitments, such as to clubs, churches or friendship networks. The impact of the spatial constraints imposed by these commitments is obvious, but transport planning has only recently started to address them. As such their inclusion in operational models is no more than a desire at this point in time (Carrasco, 2006; Arentze and Timmermans, 2008; Frei and Axhausen, 2008; Hackney, 2009).

The following short-term choices are, or should be, addressed.

Number and types of activities are normally allocated to the group or agent modelled by *trip generation* (cross-classification) models based on the available socio-demographic characteristics (Wootton and Pick, 1976). A real understanding of the dynamics and needs behind the activities is missing, although research is beginning to provide some first insights here (see Schönfelder and Axhausen, 2010 and references cited therein).

Sequence of activities is either ignored, as in the typical aggregate trip-based model (see below) or taken from observed activity chains. Neither the earlier (Recker et al, 1986a and b; Jones et al, 1983) nor more recent (Feil et al, 2009) sequence optimization models have as yet been considered in practical applications. Aggregate activity chain-based models are, however widely used (Fellendorf et al, 1997).

In the standard aggregate model the *timing* and *duration of activities* is ignored or drastically simplified by considering isolated peak hours or periods without allowing for shifts into or out of these. Although various dynamic models have recently started to address these interactions (Peeta and Ziliaskopoulos, 2001), it is with agent-based models that these dynamics can be treated most naturally (see below).

Group composition is an issue that has essentially been ignored so far, as current models ignore the group context of both travel and activity participation. The generally unsatisfactory models of sharing a ride as a car passenger are the only very limited exception. However, recent work on social networks has highlighted the importance of the group, and travel behaviour surveys are now starting to document joint travel and activity (Vovsha et al, 2003; Löchl et al, 2005).

Expenditure and *allocation of costs* between participants is neglected for the activities themselves, while for travel it is assumed that the driver takes on the marginal costs of the trip, allowing for exceptions such as company cars or parents paying for their children.

Location is a central dimension of every transport model and has received substantial attention. While the simple gravity model of *trip distribution* (see below) has conceptualized travel as a series of isolated and unrelated trips, more comprehensive models capture interaction within the activity chain (Axhausen, 1989; Fellendorf et al, 1997; Lohse, 2000). While the demand side of activity generation is addressed above, the supply side or receiving side of *trip attraction* is modelled using regression approaches, linking the size and type of the activity facilities to the number of expected trips to them (for example ITE, 2008). *Movement* related choices, the mode and route, are obviously the core of any transport model. Standard aggregate models use the trip as their unit of analysis, i.e. they allocate a main mode to the underlying sequence of stages and treat the intervening walk stages as access or egress times, while ignoring the location choices within the trip (parking location, first and last stop of a public transport trip). For mode choice, logit models are the standard today, while route choice is implicitly modelled through the *assignment* process (see below). At the present time group composition, expenditure and its allocation for a given trip is neglected, as described above.

The standard aggregate transport model addresses four elements (trip generation and attraction, trip distribution, mode choice and assignment) and is therefore often called the *four-stage process*; although car ownership models and the allocation of the trip matrices to the peak hour or period are two further models involved (see for example Martin et al, 1961; Creighton, 1970; Hutchinson, 1974; Ortuzar and Willumsen, 2001; Goulias, 2002).

6.4 Key modelling tools

Aggregate models consider flows arising from the aggregation of the choices of the individuals residing in a given part of the study area. The aggregation of the individuals occurs by market segments deemed relevant for the policies under consideration. Agent-based models, in contrast, retain the individual agent throughout and calculate any aggregate result needed afterwards. Both approaches by necessity share the mathematical abstractions and tools to describe the study area, the generalized costs and the decision making of the population, but apply them as appropriate. The most important ones are presented in the following subsections.

6.4.1 Networks (link, node, zone)

The spatially detailed transport models discussed here geo-reference the flows of interest using a mathematical abstraction of the built and operated networks. In these models the network consists of two types of element: links (arcs) and nodes to represent the roads, canals, rivers, routes or alignments and the junctions, stations, stops, airports or harbours respectively. The links have the following minimal set of attributes:

- Start node–end node.
- Direction, unless it is automatically assumed that both directions are available for traffic.
- Length.
- Capacity (maximum flow per unit time).
- The set of link-specific parameters of the function chosen to describe the impedance of the link as a function of flow and capacity.

In principle, any facility that serves travellers can be considered a link, not only roads, but also parking lots or buildings or shopping malls, as long as a corresponding impedance function can be formulated.

The nodes have a geo-reference and further attributes, which depend on the type of network being modelled. For road networks they will encode the permitted turning movements, or for public transport networks the permitted transfers between lines. Generally, the interactions within the node and the resulting impedance (costs) are ignored or approximated. An example of such an approximation is the use of an impedance function to calculate the additional travel time due to signal control. In simplified form, the function will only consider the flow volume of the turning movement, whereas the full calculation requires consideration of the total flow of all competing turning movements (Webster, 1958; IHT, 1987; Akcelic, 1994; FGSV, 2001; ITE, 2009).

A specialized type of node is the (zonal) centroid, which is the source and destination of all movements for a certain area/building/facility (zone). While most models (see below) divide their study area into spatially exhaustive zones, there is no reason to do so. For example, one could represent all off-street commercial parking facilities of an area with a centroid, which might or might not be consistent with the zoning system for on-street parking. No turning movements or other link-to-link movements are allowed in a centroid.

6.4.2 Impedance and generalized cost function

As mentioned above, the calculation of the equilibrium requires that the additional impedance offered by the flow along the links of the chosen route (time–space path) through the network is calculated. For aggregate models of flow, the bulk of the relevant work so far has focussed on changing travel times on motorways (see Greenshields, 1935 for the starting point of this literature and Leutzbach, 1988 and Helbing, 2001 for later reviews). For disaggregate models the focus has been on the description of the generalized costs of travel and its dependence on travel times and travel costs and, in turn, on the capacity of the network.

The aggregate impedance function of traffic flows links the volume of traffic q_s on link s with the associated travel time t for that link. The most widely used among many other functions is the Bureau of Public Roads (BPR) function (BPR, 1950):

$$t_s = t_{0s} \left(1 + \alpha \, (q_s/C_s)^\beta\right) \qquad\qquad [6.4.1]$$

with t_{0s} being the free-flow travel time on link s with the maximum allowed speed, C_s the capacity of the link and α and β empirically estimated parameters to describe a particular type of link, such as a motorway or a two-lane rural road. It implicitly averages over a time period, as it allows the flow to become larger than the link capacity, assuming that such peaks are of short duration and do not lead to infinite travel times (waiting times), as classical queuing theory would suggest (Gross et al, 2008). This lack of a singularity has the additional computational advantage of making the generally used iterative solutions schemes (see below) faster and more stable.

At the disaggregate level one tries to capture all relevant elements of the generalized costs of travel. The wider generalized costs of the activity schedule are discussed below. They are, as mentioned above, the risk- and comfort-weighted sums of the time and money expenditures for a particular movement. In general, they are formulated for trips i.e. the sequence of stages between activities, and account for the inherent differences between private and public modes of transport (see Table 6.4.1).

The time elements are mostly obvious and it is intuitively clear that they will be valued differentially by the travellers. The parentheses around the initial waiting time represents travellers' specific risk aversion level, which is outside of the control of the system operator. However, the reliability of the service interacts with the choices of the travellers, so that it might be appropriate to include a relevant variable (waiting time or headway) here. The schedule delay (whether early or late) (see Vickrey, 1969; Noland and Small, 1995) is an often overlooked but major element. In the case of public transport it is due to the timetabled nature of the services, which will hardly ever deliver the travellers at their destination at exactly the scheduled start of their activity. In the case of private modes or of unscheduled public modes, the schedule delay arises from the unpredictability of the travel times vis-à-vis the scheduled start time of the activity.

Transfers and transfer waiting times are additionally listed under the private modes, as they represent a possibility for car sharing.

Consistent with the intention of Table 6.4.1 to look at the short-term general costs of travel, the monetary costs are limited to the avoidable costs of travel. Fixed cost elements, such as the price of a monthly bus pass or the annual insurance premium, are omitted.

The discussion above has shown that reliability interacts with the travel time elements as an additional element in the generalized costs. Hensher et al (2009) show how difficult or ambiguous it is to capture reliability or punctuality in the generalized costs, especially as it is well known that travellers have difficulties to conceptualize distributions, i.e. variances. Nevertheless, time buffers chosen to avoid embarrassingly late arrivals must be a function of the expected variance in the door-to-door travel times, but the literature has not yet agreed on a preferred way of including this aspect of the travel experience either in surveys or in the models.

Similarly, comfort and physical safety aspects are pervasive. In their simplest form these are captured as constants for the different modes of transport, for example walking, car passenger, or within public transport (bus, tram, train à grande vitesse (TGV) or other high speed trains). Where possible, they should be included as interaction terms with the appropriate travel time or cost elements (see for example, Schüssler and Axhausen, 2010, for the differentiated travel time valuations on different road classes, which capture safety, comfort and reliability effects). In the same vein, it is usual to estimate different parameter weights for the travel time elements of the different modes.

Table 6.4.1 Time and monetary elements of the short-term generalized costs of travel

Elements	Private modes	Public modes
Time	Access	Access
	Preparing the vehicle	Acquiring ticket
		(Initial waiting time)
	In-vehicle (free-flow, congested)	In-vehicle (sitting, standing, crowded)
	(Transfer and transfer times)	Transfer and transfer times
	Parking search	
	Getting the vehicle ready to leave	
	Egress	Egress
	Schedule delay	Schedule delay
Avoidable monetary costs	Usage-related depreciation	(Single) fare
	Usage-related maintenance	
	Fuel	
	Parking fee	
	Toll	

6.4.3 Iterative proportional fitting

Iterative proportional fitting (IPF) is an algorithm which is used for many different purposes in aggregate travel demand modelling. It is also known as the Fratar (1954) or Furness (1965) method, but is primarily used in conjunction with the gravity models of trip distribution (see below). Proofs of convergence are provided by Fienberg (1970) and Bregman (1967) (cited in Lohse et al, 1997).

In its basic form its core task is to find the values of the $n_i * n_j$ cells in a 2D matrix for given and fixed values of the vectors of the marginal sums q_i and q_j so that the q_{ij} follow a given criterion or model. Find q_{ij} given:

$$q_i = \sum_{\forall j} q_{ij} = \text{Constant}$$
$$q_j = \sum_{\forall j} q_{ij} = \text{Constant}$$

[6.4.2]

Proceed with the following steps:

1 Initialize q_{ij}^0 with the model of interest, for example $q_{ij}^0 = q_i * q_j$

2

$$q_{ij}^{n+1} = \frac{q_{ij}^n \bullet q_i}{\sum_{\forall j} q_{ij}^n}$$

$$q_{ij}^{n+2} = \frac{q_{ij}^{n+1} \bullet q_j}{\sum_{\forall j} q_{ij}^{n+1}}$$

[6.4.3]

3 Repeat step 2 until the chosen error function $h() \leq \varepsilon$.

The error function might be the absolute error, the relative error or the root mean squared error of q_{ij} for succeeding iterations. The IPF converges quickly and is robust. It is therefore a popular workhorse for the solution of any problem that can be formulated in its terms.

6.4.4 Choice modelling

Basics of discrete choice modelling

Transport modellers seek to formulate travellers' behaviours as far as possible as discrete choices. They conceptualize travellers as choosing the best from among the set of discrete alternatives, for example modes, routes, departure times, locations etc. This micro-economic approach was developed by McFadden (1974) and demonstrated in a first large-scale application for the San Francisco Bay area by Domencich and McFadden (1975). It links travel behaviour with welfare theory and allows for the derivation of a theoretically consistent measure of welfare gain (Daly et al, 2005). Following from McFadden's original work on generalized extreme value (GEV) models (McFadden, 1981), a whole family of models has been formulated that addresses specific choice situations and overcomes some specific limitations of the basic GEV model. Nevertheless, this basic multinomial logit model (MNL) remains the reference for all of the more sophisticated models. This MNL predicts the likelihood that a traveller q chooses alternative i as a function of its utility for him or her (utility is inversely proportional to the generalized costs of that choice). The utility function U_{qi} has two parts:

$$U_{qi} = V_{qi} + \varepsilon_{qi} \qquad\qquad [6.4.4a]$$

V_{qi} describes the part that the analyst can describe and observe systematically, while ε_{qi} captures all the unobserved or idiosyncratic elements beyond the analyst's ability to capture.

Imposing the most restrictive conditions on the set of ε_{qi}, i.e. that they are independently and identically distributed (IID) for all alternatives and travellers, one obtains the probability P_{qi} with the MNL as:

$$P_{qi} = \exp(V_{qi}) \, / \, \Sigma_j \, \exp(V_{qj}) \qquad\qquad [6.4.4b]$$

where the denominator corresponds to the aggregate observable utility for the set of j alternatives. This model is symmetrical and the differences in probability are driven only by the differences in the utility (generalized costs).

The generalized cost function, as discussed above, is expanded with terms that describe on the one hand the traveller taking the decision, and on the other hand with terms that describe the situation in which the choice is taken: sex, age, income, weather, time of day, group size, availability of specific options. Generally, these terms are added as additional linear terms, effectively specifying the constant term in more detail and allowing the different segments in the market to be captured. Recently, more emphasis has been placed on the interaction between the socio-demographic and choice situation variables and the generalized cost variables, so as to capture more fully the heterogeneity of travellers' tastes (see Mackie et al, 2003; Axhausen, 2008; Hess et al, 2008).

To estimate the parameters of the utility function the analyst needs to describe both the chosen alternative as well as the non-chosen alternatives. Based on this choice set, the parameters are estimated using maximum likelihood estimation, which is suitable for discrete alternatives. Ben-Akiva and Lerman (1985), Train (1986) and Hensher and Johnson (1981) discuss this in detail, while Train (2003) provides an introduction to the alternative Bayesian estimation approach. Ortuzar and Willumsen (2001) also introduce this latter approach in their general textbook on transport modelling.

IIA and motivation of similarity

The independence of irrelevant alternative (IIA) property is the motivation for most of the work to remove the restrictions on the variance–covariance matrix of the errors imposed by the IID assumption of the MNL. It forces the MNL to offer unrealistic exchanges between pairs of alternatives in the presence of a third alternative, which is similar to one of the other two. The starting point is that the MNL assumes that the ratio of the probabilities of choosing two alternatives is constant and independent of the presence of any other alternative:

$$\frac{P_i}{P_j} = \frac{e^{V_i}}{\sum_{\forall k} e^{V_k}} \cdot \frac{\sum_{\forall k} e^{V_k}}{e^{V_i}} = \frac{e^{V_i}}{e^{V_j}} \quad \text{Constant} \qquad\qquad [6.4.5]$$

Due to this a third alternative, which is similar to one, but not the other alternative, will be allocated the same share from both alternatives to keep the ratio constant. Think of a red bus service identical in all other respects to a blue bus service that is already competing on equal terms in utility with the car. In the situation with three alternatives, the MNL allocates one third to each alternative although intuition tells us that one quarter, one quarter and one half is a more reasonable allocation. The key to avoid this unrealistic behaviour of the MNL is to devise further GEV models that allow for correlation of the error terms between the alternatives or that account for the similarity between them explicitly in the systematic part of the utility function.

Models accounting for similarities

Two ways forward have been pursued since the 1970s. One focuses on removing the restrictions of the IID assumption, but the resulting models are only suitable for small numbers of alternatives (see below). With the recent increase in interest in route and (facility-level) location choice, a second approach is gaining popularity. This captures the similarities explicitly in the systematic part of the utility function and is computationally feasible for the very large numbers of alternatives which are typical for these choice situations. Schüssler and Axhausen (2009b) review these approaches in detail, while the most prominent of the alternative models are discussed briefly below (see Ben-Akiva and Lerman, 1985; Hensher and Greene, 2003; Train, 2003 for more details).

Nested logit (NL) models group the alternatives into exclusive nests, which allows for correlation between nests but retains the IIA property within the nests. The resulting tree structure can have multiple levels. This and all other structures mentioned below have no behavioural interpretation. They only address the structure of the variance–covariance matrix of the errors. The cross-nested logit (CNL) or pairwise-cross-nested logit model (PCL) allows an alternative to belong in parts to multiple nests. The ordered logit accounts for the correlation between alternatives that have a natural order, such as departure times or fleet sizes.

The error-component logit (ECL) model, or its mathematically equivalent random parameter logit (RPL) model, belongs to the general class of mixed logit (ML) models. Here the correlation is captured by random error terms, which are shared between any number of the alternatives considered. In the RPL interpretation the random terms are used to describe the heterogeneity of the (taste) parameters between the different travellers. These models have, in contrast to the other models mentioned so far, no closed form solution and need to be estimated and applied using Monte Carlo simulation, which makes them computationally costly.

The explicit description of the similarity between alternatives can be motivated from a number of viewpoints: to measure inclusion into the choice set (visibility), to measure regret, to measure difference from a reference alternative, to measure super-visibility, to measure the impact of other travellers, to measure the collective impact of multiple similar options etc. The mathematical formulation remains the same: an additional term with its own parameters (weights, transformation and exponent) is added, which captures the mean similarity of the alternative vis-à-vis all others or against an *a priori* defined reference: the best alternative in case of regret; the prior choice in the case of Kahneman and Tversky's prospect theory (1979).

This short discussion cannot do full justice to choice modelling. Important issues, such as latent-class market segmentation or how to construct the choice sets, have necessarily been ignored. For these we refer the interested reader to the literature cited above.

6.5 Models of aggregate flows

This section introduces the key characteristics of the generally used four-step modelling process. Of the dimensions of activity scheduling mentioned above it focuses on the following:

- Trip production and attraction (number and location of activities).
- Destination choice (volume of trips, flows, between all locations or OD pairs).
- Mode choice (division of the flows among the relevant modal alternatives).
- Time-of-day choice (of the trips to predefined time slots, typically peak hours).
- Assignment, the allocation of the flows to the relevant routes to match one of the equilibrium criteria discussed above.

The long-term decisions are external as described above. The time-of-day choice is often just a trivial multiplicative factor applied to the modal OD matrices and is therefore not given proper attention. This discounting has led to the perception of there being only four steps.

6.5.1 Resolution (space, time)

Aggregate models resolve space (demand) as zones of a size suitable for the overall study area and matching the desired network resolution. As a rule of thumb, the network should include one level of the road hierarchy more than the level of interest (for a detailed discussion of network hierarchies see IHT, 1987; Marshall, 2005; ITE, 2009; FGSV, 2008). Say the model is interested in the national motorway system, then the network model will have to include all roads of regional interest as well, so that the zonal connectors can be linked with the lower level network isolating, as far as possible, the network of interest from any artefacts of these connections.

The network of the Swiss National Transport model, for example, has 3114 zones, 24,432 nodes and 61,132 links (Vrtic et al, 2005) and connects all Swiss municipalities with each other as well as with a ring of zones in the adjacent countries.

While one- or two-hour long peak hour models are the most common application, many applications are 24 hour models of a whole average working day. The scaling of the hourly measured capacities and impedance functions to 24 hours or any other multiple is a difficult operation, as a simple multiplication will lead to too much capacity. The factor has to consider indirectly the congestion generated during the peaks.

6.5.2 Demand generation

The three demand generation steps (trip production/attraction, distribution, mode choice) employ a variety of statistical approaches and vary from study to study and from country to country.

Trip production and attraction employ different approaches to calculate the aggregate totals for each zone. In the simplest form regression models are used to predict the (observed) number of trips from a travel diary survey as a function of the mean socio-demographic (and geographic) characteristics of a zone. In the most sophisticated form disaggregated NL models will be employed to capture all three elements in a coherent and market segmented approach (for example Shiftan, 1998; Bowman and Ben-Akiva, 2001). As a rule, cross-classification models at the household or person level are used to predict the number of trips by activity, by multiplying the number of households/persons with the average trip rates. On the attraction side one derives trip rates as a function of the different land uses using traffic counts and survey data (Bosserhoff, 2006; ITE, 2008). These models have little – in the case of the NL models – or no sensitivity to the overall level of generalized costs of travel, leaving a big gap in the modelling process. For a review of the issues and relevant results on induced demand (see Weis and Axhausen, 2009).

Given the predicted trip production and attraction, the distribution step links the origins and destinations to obtain the relevant flows. The doubly constrained gravity model (Ortuzar and Willumsen, 2001) or the related EVA model (Lohse, 2000) solve this underdetermined linear problem by imposing the idea of maximum entropy (Wilson, 1970) or maximum information gain (Lohse et al, 1997) to find the most likely set of flows. These flows are proportional to the generalized costs, but the exact form of the proportionality, and of the formulation of the generalized costs, varies. The most common combination is a negative exponential relationship based on uncongested (car) travel times between the zones.

In the case of the maximum entropy solution of Wilson (1970):

$$q_{ij} = \alpha_i^0 \alpha_j^0 q_i q_j e^{-\beta k_{ij}} \qquad [6.5.1]$$

with α_i, α_j the n balancing factors for the rows and columns and β the parameter for the generalized costs, which ensures that the observed mean generalized costs are reproduced by the resolved origin-destination matrix. The balancing factors are calculated using the IPF:

1   Initialize $\alpha_i^0 = 1$ and $\alpha_j^0 = 1$

2
$$\alpha_i^{n+1} = \frac{1}{\sum_{\forall j} \alpha_i^n \, q_j \, e^{-\beta k_{ij}}}$$

$$\alpha_j^{n+2} = \frac{1}{\sum_{\forall j} \alpha_i^{n+1} \, q_j \, e^{-\beta k_{ij}}}$$

3. Repeat step 2 until:

$$\sum_{\forall j} \frac{\left| \alpha_j^{k+1} - \alpha_j^k \right|}{\alpha_j^k} \leq \varepsilon$$

MNL or NL models are used to predict the market shares of each mode for the market segments distinguished in the study for the cross-classification in trip production. The generalized costs formulation of the choice models incorporate some or all of the elements discussed above.

6.5.3 Assignment

The travel demand calculations need to be repeated after the actual generalized costs are known once the first assignment has been performed. The number of feedback loops varies in practical application, but two or three is the minimum to ensure that no important feedback has been overlooked.

The basic elements of the assignment are the identification of the routes used and the distribution of the flows between them while achieving the desired equilibrium. The algorithms generally used identify the routes incrementally by updating the travel times on all links with the predicted flows from the last iteration and finding the current shortest paths (see Dijkstra, 1959 or variants thereof such as Lefebvre and Balmer, 2007). The flows are then updated using various smoothing algorithms (see Sheffi, 1985 or Patriksson, 1994 for overviews), which advance the overall set of flows towards the equilibrium chosen by the analyst.

The overall solution, found after multiple passes through the four-step process, is usually compared against independent evidence to assess the quality of reproduction of the current (or some past) situation. Traffic counts (car, public transport, air, cycling), number of persons boarding by stop or station, trip length distributions by mode and purpose and commuting matrices from a census are typical examples of such evidence.

6.6 Agent-based models

Agent-based models differ first and foremost in their resolution from the aggregate models presented above. The core is an agent, an artificial representation of a decision making unit in the modelled world: a traveller, a household, a firm etc. The software representation of the agents is given enough intelligence to represent the preferences of the agents and to let them act across the choice dimensions of interest. The resulting actions of the agents lead to interactions with other agents which in combination impact on the generalized costs of travel and may lead to new choices in the next iteration. The activity-based approach to travel demand modelling (see Jones et al, 1983; Carpenter and Jones, 1983; Jones, 1990; the books of the IATBR conference series[4]) and agent-based simulation were made for each other, as both put the individual (agent) and its choices under constraints and in the company of others at the centre of their attention.

There are currently a number of agent-based models of travel demand under development (see Bowman et al, 1999; Arentze et al, 2000; Vovsha et al, 2002; Bhat et al, 2004; Pendyala, 2004; Schnittger and Zumkeller, 2004 and related models to name only the most prominent ones). It is not possible to review each of these here. Rather, the focus will be on the MATSim toolkit developed jointly at TU Berlin and ETH Zürich[5] (Balmer, 2007; Rieser et al, 2007; Nagel et al, 2008; Meister et al, 2009 and others). MATSim is unique in its focus on the speed of computation and the scale of the applications it can cope with.

6.6.1 Search for the steady state

MATSim implements an evolutionary algorithm to obtain a steady-state solution, in which the agents cannot improve their utility (fitness) any further. This utility encompasses all elements of the schedule and is therefore wider than the usual generalized costs of travel that are addressed in the aggregate models. The utility function has to include both the gains from the activities performed, as well as the costs of travel between them. These generalized costs of the activity schedule therefore add the risk- and comfort-weighted times as well as the monetary expenditures on travel between activities.

In line with most other models, the Charypar and Nagel (2005) formulation of the utility function is not as comprehensive as outlined above. In its currently used form, employed in most MATSim applications, it includes only:

- activity time, in logarithmic form, with an optimal duration specific to each activity type;
- travel time in linear form;
- late arrival penalty, which requires the specification of the opening hours of each facility (type).

The parameters of these elements are fixed arbitrarily, but are in line with the experience of many Vickrey-type bottleneck models (see for example Small, 1982; Noland and Polak, 2002; de Palma and Picard, 2005) of the choice of arrival time.

However, in recent work Feil et al (2009) estimate a new formulation of the utility function, based on Joh's earlier (2004) work. In this formulation the utility of an activity follows an asymmetrical S-shaped curve, which gives one control over the total level of utility gained from any one activity. They show how one can empirically estimate the parameters of this model, which in its full form allows for mode-specific generalized cost (travel time, transfer, expenditure) parameters and late arrival penalties.

During each iteration, MATSim switches between the improvement of a set of activity schedules for each agent and the simulation of the physical execution of those schedules, in particular of the movement between the relevant locations. After each iteration, a randomly chosen set of agents optimizes a schedule along the dimensions deemed relevant for the application at hand.

Each agent has a small set of schedules (typically three to five), which are generated incrementally. The number depends on the available computer memory and the number of agents simulated. MATSim selects one of these for execution, choosing them randomly based on MNL-derived probabilities, which favours the better schedules. The worst schedule is removed.

6.6.2 Resolution

While agent-based simulations can be resolved at any resolution, MATSim is designed to describe behaviour in quasi-continuous time (seconds), for parcel-level address-fine locations (x,y coordinates), which are attached to complete navigation networks, i.e. all links in a region. Even at lower resolutions, the facilities, i.e. the locations at which activities can be performed (homes, work places, schools, shops etc.) are mapped uniquely to the appropriate link in the network used, so that MATSim has as many origins or destinations as there are links to which facilities are attached. This approach gives MATSim the flexibility to work with less finely resolved networks, such as a typical planning network of an aggregate model.

6.6.3 Demand generation

MATSim distinguishes between the generation of the initial demand, i.e. the initial schedules of the agents and the further improvement/optimization of these during the further iterations. The number of methods to initialize/improve the schedules for a given model configuration and time-dependent generalized costs is large; MATSim offers several methods for each of the dimensions discussed above in Section 6.3. This flexibility is a strength of the system, but makes the comparison of the results and of their computation times difficult, as the more sophisticated algorithms generally require substantially more computation time.

The initial schedules are constructed around schedules observed in the appropriate national or regional travel diary survey (Balmer, 2007). They are classified by the sequence of activities undertaken and their durations in hourly intervals. The number of activity types varies between implementations, but at least five are used (home, work, education, shopping, leisure). The schedule is drawn randomly, conditional on the socio-demographics of the agent, which already specifies the home location. For work and education activities, the location is determined randomly using the relevant census-commuter matrices as the conditional distribution of the locations. The modes are selected randomly using a subtour-specific random utility mode choice model, which accounts for the varying availability of the different modes for each tour and subtour (Ciari et al, 2008). Destination choice is performed, in the simplest implementation, by an exhaustive neighbourhood search and in the most advanced form, as a random utility-based choice, accounting for the access constraints imposed by the schedule, as well as the capacity constraint of the destination facilities (Horni et al, 2009, 2011). Route choice employs an optimized A*-shortest path algorithm, which accounts for the time-of-day-varying travel times (Lefebvre and Balmer, 2007).

During iterations, all dimensions are addressed partially or in full. The sequence and number of activities have been kept fixed in all major applications so far, but Feil et al (2010) have developed a tabu-search-based optimization approach for both issues. The activity durations and starting times can be altered randomly (Balmer, 2007) or optimized using a genetic algorithm-based optimization (Meister et al, 2006, 2005). The mode, destination and route choice possibilities have been discussed above.

6.6.4 Traffic flow modelling

The simultaneous execution of the schedules of all agents is carried out by the traffic flow models available within the MATSim framework. MATSim offers both time step and event oriented queue-based implementations, which vary in their scope with regards to the treatment of signal control, public transport vehicles and parallelization of the code.

Cetin (2005) and Raney and Nagel (2006) developed the initial MATSim time step oriented queue-based simulation. This approach trades speed of execution for behavioural detail by ignoring the interaction of vehicles on the links of the network and capturing the delays only at the junctions. The junction dynamics are also simplified and account for the occupation of the junction and the availability of space on the next link. Rieser (2010) expands this approach to include timetable-based public transport vehicles with entering and alighting drivers and passengers.

The time step oriented simulation is slow for the less congested time periods. The event oriented simulation of Charypar (2008) avoids this and adds a more realistic queue dynamic. Furthermore, its parallel implementation (Charypar et al, 2007) scales nearly linearly with the number of processors.

6.6.5 Coupled building and transport modelling

Transport models are used almost exclusively to inform transport infrastructure planning decisions; in particular relating to the routing and capacity of new or extensions to existing networks. The motive here is to maximize travellers' personal utility or rather to minimize their cost of travel expressed, as noted earlier, as the composite of the travel time and monetary resources required, weighted by the risks involved and the comfort in which the travel can be performed. But minimizing these costs may be in conflict with objectives to minimize the adverse environmental consequences of travel. There may be comfort, time and indeed cost advantages to independent car travel as opposed to the use of more environmentally benign public transport options. But until recently this environmental agenda has not been considered in transport modelling and so is not directly considered in the generalized cost of travel upon which most models are based. But this may be about to change. More and more municipalities are formally committing themselves to plans to reduce environmental emissions during the coming years. The city of Zürich, for example, has committed to the achievement of a 2kW society by the year 2050. This requires that average per capita primary energy consumption be reduced by almost a factor of three from its current average of 5.8kW. To achieve such commitments municipalities require comprehensive resource (particularly energy) flow models with which to test hypotheses to reduce net demands. These models need to simulate buildings, the activities accommodated within them and the transport of goods and people between them. Only then can the interrelationships between the location and timing of activities, and the modes of travel between them, be fully accounted for.

As a first step in this direction a current project is working on the coupling of MATSim and CitySim (described in Chapter 5) in order to evaluate strategies for achieving Zürich's objectives of a 2kW society. The means for achieving this will be through the exchange of occupants between buildings. MATSim will be run as a pre-process to simulate occupants' arrival and departure times from individual buildings throughout the city, accounting also for the influx and outflux of commuters across the city boundaries. Average travel speeds along each link for each trip will be used, in conjunction with the relevant vehicle performance data, to derive the associated energy use. Our occupant-agents will conserve the characteristics that influence their subsequent behaviours and associated energy implications while present within a given building.

Such comprehensive micro-simulation of building and transport energy use will enable detailed policy strategies to be tested, relating for example to: changes in land use to reduce transport demand; investment in public transport infrastructure to reduce private vehicular travel; financial subsidies to encourage investments in the renovation of buildings; and the substitution of private vehicles with more efficient alternatives, etc.

6.7 Case study: Westumfahrung, Zürich

Until 2009 the city of Zürich had no complete motorway bypass for long-distance through traffic. The new western bypass, Westumfahrung in German, is a 16km long combination of mostly bridges and tunnels, which now connects the northern bypass, the motorway in the direction of Bern/Basel, a new motorway towards Zug/Luzern/Gotthard with the motorway towards southeast Switzerland (Chur). Its opening was combined with major capacity reductions inside the city to safeguard for the local residents any gains from the relocation of the flows onto the new motorway against other traffic switching to the now available capacity. The canton of Zürich asked the IVT to employ MATSim to analyse the expected changes and in particular the localization of the winners and losers among the population following from the opening of the Westumfahrung (Balmer et al, 2009).

To this end, MATSim was implemented with the usual initial demand generation, random timing and duration modification and shortest-path modules for the steady state search. The traffic flow simulation allowed for traffic signals, incorporating a simplified description of their effects through the consideration of the effective green and red times. The 670,000 agents included in the iterations with their 2.2 million trips are those who travel by car through the area defined by a 35km radius around the centre of Zürich. We focussed on car travel here, as its change was the focus of the client and of any further policy. Despite being rather too sparse for this task, the network used was the national transport planning network (Vrtic et al, 2007), as this was the only one available at the time.

The study compared a number of scenarios, but we will focus here on the comparison between the situations without and with the western bypass. Plate 22 shows the evolution of the model without the bypass to steady state. After some rapid gains in travel time and utility score during the initial iterations, the convergence slows down to reach steady state after about 150 iterations. This slow convergence is due to the random mutation of the timings and durations. This can, however, be accelerated with the algorithms mentioned above, which find optimal durations and times.

The model was able to reproduce current traffic flow dynamics well overall. See Plate 23 for an example of one of the major city bridges, which shows that the dynamic pattern is well reproduced, but the level of flows shows deviations, in this case due to omissions in the modelling of the traffic lights.

While all the usual analyses are possible with the two sets of results, we specifically wanted to identify the winners and losers from among the agent population. Their locations are shown in Plate 24. Contrary to expectations, the winners and losers are widely scattered and intermingled over space. The removal of through traffic allows the residents of the city to participate in the gains by switching to an alternative route or by increasing their speed on their usual route, unless they used the now blocked inner western bypass (see for example the concentration of losers close to north end of Lake Zürich).

Table 6.7.1 describes the changes expected for the different groups of travellers. The through travellers gain most utility on average based on their substantial absolute reductions in travel time as well as in the timing of their activities. Across all residents the gain in utility is minor in spite of relatively large relative gains in travel times. The situation is better for those changing to the new bypass across all three measures above, whereas the residents along the old bypass gain only in terms of travel times. It is important to realize that MATSim searches for the steady state in terms of the schedules of the agents and is not limited to the travel elements of the schedule. The changes in timing and duration are not large, partly because the opening hours and the fixed activity sequences limit agents' flexibility.

This case study and other work undertaken elsewhere and since has shown that agent-based micro-simulation models, such as MATSim, are able to produce the results required for policy analysis in a consistent and reliable manner. However, the computational effort is still substantial and needs to be reduced before these models can start to replace or supplement the well established aggregate models for planning applications.

6.8 Summary and outlook

Transport modelling has been under development throughout the past 60 years. Starting from *ad hoc* approaches, the discipline is now solidly based on a

Table 6.7.1 Changes with the western bypass by agent category

	Without	With	Change (%)
Through traffic (about 58,000 persons)			
Average utility	64.84	69.31	6.90
Average travel time (min)	2:13:14	2:06:40	−4.93
Average travel distance (km)	189.77	189.40	−0.20
All Swiss car drivers (about 615,000 persons)			
Average utility	183.72	185.61	1.03
Average travel time (min)	16:22	14:23	−12.12
Average travel distance (km)	12.35	12.36	0.02
Car drivers changing from the inner to the new western bypass (about 16,000 persons)			
Average utility	158.26	165.08	4.31
Average travel time (min)	48:20	39:10	−18.97
Average travel distance (km)	45.61	46.69	2.38
Car drivers resident along the old inner bypass (about 2000 persons)			
Average utility	164.68	166.04	0.83
Average travel time (min)	21:54	18:57	−13.47
Average travel distance (km)	8.57	8.50	−0.87

Source: Balmer et al, 2009

micro-economic behavioural framework, which gives structure to the modelling and to expectations about the results. As all such frameworks, it grapples with well known inconsistencies between theoretical expectations and observed behaviour, which reflect the more complex and difficult to capture incentive and social structures in which individuals and groups of individuals act (see Simon, 1955; Kahneman and Tversky, 1979; Elster, 1989).

The emerging shift towards the modelling of activity schedules, which fully subsumes travel behaviour modelling, will further enrich our models and will allow for the inclusion of additional dimensions of policy interest (impacts of income inequalities; shifts in activity participation; budgeting for CO_2 constraints, etc.); likewise, the full acknowledgement of the interactions between long-term and short-term choices, for example coherent land-use and transport models will allow the field to provide better assessments of the welfare gains of infrastructure investment and regulatory changes, especially in the land use and environmental domain.

Both aggregate models and agent-based models are here to stay for some time. The advantage of aggregate models lie in their familiarity and in the widespread expertise of their use supported by active groups of both software developers and academic researchers. The basic logic of aggregate models is easy to explain to policy makers and members of the public alike, which makes their use for planning attractive. The commercial software packages implementing them also offer speed and ease of use. But aggregate models also suffer from systematic problems when applied to higher resolution networks and zones. The algorithms do not scale well when the required spatial, temporal or socio-demographic detail becomes finer. This is particularly true of the temporal dimension and the associated dynamic shifts of activity start and end times or, more particularly, for shifts in activity sequence. Here agent-based models come into their own, and their modular structure allows for the easy extension of their reach. Their algorithms also scale well and can be parallelized with ease.

At this point though, agent-based models are handicapped by a lack of familiarity, more complex model formulations and by a perception of larger data needs. The data needs are not larger than for aggregate models, but the modelling of the data is more complex due to the additional behavioural sensitivities, which the agent-based models allow for. The lack of familiarity will be overcome over time, as more agent-based models will be employed first to address issues that only they can address, and later when they become adopted even in cases where aggregate models would suffice.

In line with the objectives of this book, a further motivation for the future more widespread application of agent-based models relates to energy policy and the formulation and testing of energy planning proposals. As described earlier, a natural method for coupling detailed simulations of buildings and the activities accommodated within them and transport is via the exchange of occupants – from building to mode of transport and vice-versa. Such integrated simulations will be powerful resources to municipalities as they seek to improve the sustainability of their towns and cities.

A further example of this complementarity lies with the assessment of interactions among electricity networks, alternative energy sources and electric vehicles. Energy storage devices in the last of these are a potentially useful form of intermediate energy storage with which to resolve mismatches between energy demand and supply. But the optimal times for charging the electric vehicles' storage facility using excess power supply, or of discharging the accumulated energy during periods of undersupply, may conflict with the desired travel times. Integrated simulations can help with the formulation of differential pricing structures to minimize such conflicts.

Notes

1   A *stage* is the continuous movement with one mode or means of transport, for example walking, cycling, car driving, including any waiting times. A *trip* is the sequence of stages between two activities. A *journey* is the sequence of trips, which starts and ends at home. An activity is the meaningful interaction of the traveller with other persons or objects within the same environment. For further discussion of these and alternative definitions of the travel experience, see Axhausen (2008).
2   It is this stochastic error, which gives the SUE its name. The SUE is unique and computationally deterministic.
3   See for example Axhausen (2008) with regards to the integration of social network structures or alternative advances in the tradition of the activity-based approach (Jones et al, 1983).
4   See www.iatbr.com.
5   See www.matsim.org.

References

Akcelic, R. (1994) 'Estimation of green times and cycle time for vehicle-actuated signals', *Transportation Research Record*, vol 1457, pp63–72

Arentze, T. A. and Timmermans, H. J. P. (2008) 'Social networks, social interactions, and activity-travel behavior: A framework for microsimulation', *Environment and Planning B: Planning and Design*, vol 35, no 6, pp1012–1027

Arentze, T. A., Hofman, F., Mourik, H. and Timmermans, H. J. P. (2000) 'Albatross: A multi-agent rule-based model of activity pattern decisions', *Transportation Research Record*, vol 1706, pp136–144

Axhausen, K. W. (1989) Eine ereignisorientierte Simulation von Aktivitätenketten zur Parkstandswahl, *Schriftenreihe*, 40, Institut für Verkehrswesen, Universität (TH) Karlsruhe, Karlsruhe

Axhausen, K. W. (2008) 'Definition of movement and activity for transport modelling', in D. A. Hensher and K. J. Button (eds) *Handbook of Transport Modelling*, 2nd edition, Elsevier, Oxford, pp329–344

Balmer, M. (2007) 'Travel demand modeling for multi-agent transport simulations: Algorithms and systems', Dissertation, ETH Zürich, Zürich

Balmer, M., Horni, A., Meister, K., Charypar, D., Ciari, F. and Axhausen, K. W. (2009) *Wirkungen der Westumfahrung Zürich: Eine Analyse mit einer agentenbasierten Mikrosimulation, Schlussbericht*, Baudirektion Kanton Zürich, IVT, ETH Zürich, Zürich

Beckmann, M. J., McGuire, C. B. and Winston, C. (1956) *Studies in the Economics of Transportation*, Yale University Press, New Haven

Ben-Akiva, M. E. and Lerman, S. R. (1985) *Discrete Choice Analysis: Theory and Application to Travel Demand*, MIT Press, Cambridge

Bhat, C. R., Guo, J. Y., Srinivasan, S. and Sivakumar, A. (2004) 'A comprehensive econometric microsimulator for daily activity-travel patterns', *Transportation Research Record*, vol 1894, pp57–66

Bosserhoff, D. (2006) 'Verkehrsaufkommen durch Vorhaben der Bauleitplanungund Auswirkungen auf die Anbindung an das Straßennetz', in *Handbuch für Verkehrssicherheit und Verkehrstechnik*, Chapter 1.3, Hessische Straßen- und Verkehrsverwaltung, Wiesbaden

Bowman, J. L. and Ben-Akiva. M. E. (2001) 'Activity-based disaggregate travel demand model system with activity schedules', *Transportation Research Part A*, vol 35, no 1, pp1–28

Bowman, J. L., Bradley, M., Shiftan, Y., Lawton, T. K. and Ben-Akiva, M. E. (1999) 'Demonstration of an activity-based model for Portland', *World Transport Research*, vol 3, pp171–184

BPR (Bureau of Public Roads) (1950) *Highway Capacity Manual (1950)*, United States Government Printing Office, Washington DC

Bregman, L. M. (1967) 'The relaxation method of finding the common point of convex sets and its application to the solution of problems in convex programming', *U.S.S.R. Computational Mathematical Physics*, vol 7, no 3, pp200–217

Carpenter, S. and Jones, P. M. (eds) (1983) *Recent Advances in Travel Demand Analysis*, Gower, Aldershot

Carrasco, J. A. (2006) 'Social activity-travel behaviour: A personal networks approach', Department of Civil Engineering, University of Toronto, Toronto

CATS (Chicago Area Transportation Study) (1960) *Chicago Area Transportation Study*, Chicago Area Transportation Study, Chicago

Cetin, N. (2005) 'Large-scale parallel graph-based simulations', dissertation, ETH Zürich, Zürich

Charypar, D. (2008) 'Efficient algorithms for the microsimulation of travel behavior in very large scenarios', dissertation, ETH Zürich, Zürich

Charypar, D. and Nagel, K. (2005) 'Generating complete all-day activity plans with genetic algorithms', *Transportation*, vol 32, no 4, pp369–397

Charypar, D., Axhausen, K. W. and Nagel, K. (2007) 'An event-driven parallel queue-based microsimulation for large scale traffic scenarios', paper presented at the 11th World Conference of Transport Research, Berkeley, June

Ciari, F., Balmer, M. and Axhausen, K. W. (2008) 'A new mode choice model for a multi-agent transport simulation', paper presented at the *8th Swiss Transport Research Conference, Ascona*, October

Creighton, R. (1970) *Urban Transportation Planning*, University of Illinois Press, Champaign

Daganzo, C. F. and Y. Sheffi (1977) 'On stochastic models of traffic assignment', *Transportation Science*, vol 11, no 3, pp253–274

Daly, A., de Jong, G. and Pieters, M. (2005) 'The logsum as an evaluation measure: Review of the literature and new results', paper presented at the 45th Congress of the European Regional Science Association, Amsterdam, August

de Palma, A. and Picard, N. (2005) 'Route choice decision under travel time uncertainty', *Transportation Research A*, vol 39, no 4, pp295–324

Detroit Metropolitan Area Traffic Survey (DMATS) (1955) Lansing: State of Michigan Department of Transportation

Dijkstra, E. W. (1959) 'A note on two problems in connexion with graphs', *Numerische Mathematik*, vol 1, no 1, pp269–271

Domencich, T. A. and McFadden, D. L. (1975) *Urban Travel Demand: A Behavioural Analysis*, North Holland, Amsterdam

Downs, A. (1962) 'The law of peak-hour-expressway congestion', *Traffic Quarterly*, vol 16, no 3, pp393–409

Downs, A. (2004) 'Still Stuck in Traffic', *Brookings Institution*, Washington, DC

DUKES (Digest of UK Energy Statistics) (2009) *Digest of UK Energy Statistics 2009*, Department of Energy and Climate Change, London

Elster, J. (1989) *Nuts and Bolts for the Social Sciences*, Cambridge University Press, Cambridge

Feil, M., Balmer, M. and Axhausen, K. W. (2009) 'Generating comprehensive all-day schedules: Expanding activity-based travel demand modelling', paper presented at the European Transport Conference, Leeuwenhorst, October

Feil, M., Balmer, M. and Axhausen, K.W. (2010) 'New approaches to generating comprehensive all-day activity-travel schedules', paper presented at the 89th Annual Meeting of the Transportation Research Board, Washington, DC, January

Fellendorf, M., Haupt, T., Heidl, U. and Scherr, W. (1997) 'PTV Vision: Activity-based microsimulation model for travel demand forecasting', in D. F. Ettema and H. J. P. Timmermans (eds) *Activity-based Approaches to Travel Analysis*, Pergamon, Oxford, pp55–72

FGSV (Forschungsgesellschaft für Strassen und Verkehrswesen) (2001) *Handbuch für die Bemessung von Strassenverkehrsanlagen*, FGSV, Köln

FGSV (2008) *Richtlinien für die integrierte Netzgestaltung*, FGSV, Köln

Fienberg, S. E. (1970) 'An iterative procedure for estimation in contingency tables', *Annals of Mathematical Statistics*, vol 41, no 3, pp907–917

Fratar, T. J. (1954) 'Vehicular trip distribution by successive approximations', *Traffic Quarterly*, vol 1, no 1, pp53–65

Frei, A. and Axhausen, K. W. (2008) 'Modelling the frequency of contacts in a shrunken world', *Arbeitsberichte Verkehrs- und Raumplanung*, 532, IVT, ETH Zürich, Zürich

Fröhlich, P. (2008) 'Änderungen der Intensitäten im Arbeitspendelverkehr von 1970 bis 2000', dissertation, Department Bau, Umwelt und Geomatik, ETH, Zürich

Furness, K. P. (1965) 'Time function iteration', *Traffic Engineering and Control*, vol 7, no 7, pp458–460

Goulias, K. G. (ed) (2002) *Transport Systems Planning: Methods and Applications*, CRC Press, Boca Raton

Greenshields, B. D. (1935) 'A study in highway capacity', *Proceedings of the Highway Research Board*, vol 14, pp448–477

Gross, D., Shortle, J. F., Thompson, J. M. and Harris, C. M. (2008) *Fundamentals of Queuing Theory*, John Wiley and Sons, Hoboken

Hackney, J. K. (2009) 'Integration of social networks in a large-scale travel behaviour microsimulation', dissertation, ETH Zürich, Zürich

Helbing, D. (2001) 'Traffic and related self-driven many-particle systems', *Reviews of Modern Physics*, vol 73, no 4, pp1067–1141

Hensher, D. A. and Greene, W. H. (2003) 'The Mixed Logit model: The state of practice', *Transportation*, vol 30, no 2, pp133–176

Hensher, D. A. and Johnson, L. W. (1981) *Applied Discrete-Choice Modelling*, Croom Helm, London

Hensher, D. A., Rose, J. and Li, Z. (2009) 'Valuation of travel time reliability in an extended expected utility theory framework', paper presented at the 12th International Conference on Travel Behaviour Research, Jaipur, December

Hess, S., Erath, A. and Axhausen, K. W. (2008) 'Estimated value of savings in travel time in Switzerland: Analysis of pooled data', Transportation Research Record, 2082, pp43–55

Horni, A., Scott, D. M., Balmer, M. and Axhausen, K. W. (2009) 'Location choice modeling for shopping and leisure activities with MATSim: Combining micro-simulation and time geography', *Transportation Research Record*, vol 2135, pp87–95

Horni, A., Charypar, D. and Axhausen, K. W. (2011) 'Empirically approaching destination choice set formation', paper presented at the 90th Annual Meeting of the Transportation Research Board, Washington, DC, January

Hutchinson, B. G. (1974) *Principles of Urban Transport Systems Planning*, Scripta Book Company, Washington DC

IHT (1987) *Roads and Traffic in Urban Areas*, IHT, London

ITE (2008) *Trip Generation*, 8th edition, ITE, Washington DC

ITE (2009) *Traffic Engineering Handbook*, ITE, Washington DC

Joh, C. H. (2004) 'Measuring and predicting adaptation in multidimensional activity-travel patterns', *bouwstenen faculteit bouwkunde*, 79, dissertation, TU Eindhoven, Eindhoven

Jones, P. M. (ed) (1990) *Developments in Dynamic and Activity-Based Approaches to Travel Analysis*, Gower, Aldershot

Jones, P. M., Dix, M. C., Clarke, M. I. and Heggie, I. C. (1983) *Understanding Travel Behaviour*, Gower, Aldershot

Kahneman, D. and Tversky, A. (1979) 'Prospect theory: An analysis of decisions under risk', *Econometrica*, vol 47, no 2, pp263–291

Knight, F.H. (1924) 'Some fallacies in the interpretation of social costs', *The Quarterly Journal of Economics*, vol 38, no 4, pp582–606

Lee, D. B. (1975) 'Requiem for large-scale models', *ACM*, vol 6, no2–3, pp16–29

Lefebvre, N. and Balmer, M. (2007) 'Fast shortest path computation in time-dependent traffic networks', *Arbeitsbericht Verkehrs- und Raumplanung*, 439, IVT, ETH Zürich, Zürich

Leutzbach, W. (1988) *Introduction to the Theory of Traffic Flow*, Springer, Berlin

Löchl, M., Schönfelder, S., Schlich, R., Buhl, T., Widmer, P. and Axhausen, K. W. (2005) 'Stabilität des Verkehrsverhaltens', final report for SVI 2001/514, *Schriftenreihe*, 1120, Bundesamt für Strassen, UVEK, Bern

Lohse, D. (2000) 'Verkehrsnachfragemodellierung mit n-linearen Gleichungssystemen', *Stadt Region Land*, vol 69, pp27–44

Lohse, D., Bachner, G., Dugge, B. and Teichert, H. (1997) 'Ermittlung von Verkehrsströmen mit n-linearen Gleichungssystemen unter Beachtung von Nebenbedingungen einschließlich Parameterschätzung (Verkehrsnachfrage-modellierung: Erzeugung, Verteilung, Aufteilung)', *Schriftenreihe*, 5, Institutes für Verkehrsplanung und Straßenverkehr, TU Dresden, Dresden

Marshall, S. (2005) *Streets and Patterns*, Spon Press, London

Martin, B. V., Memmott, F. W. and Bone, A. J. (1961) *Principles and Techniques of Predicting Future Demand for Urban Area Transportation*, MIT Press, Cambridge

McFadden, D. L. (1974) 'Conditional logit analysis of qualitative choice analysis', in P. Zarembka (ed) *Frontiers in Econometrics*, Academic Press, New York, pp105–142

McFadden, D. L. (1981) 'Econometric models of probabilistic choice', in C. F. Manski and D. L. McFadden (eds) *Econometric Models of Probabilistic Choice in Structural Analysis of Discrete Data*, MIT Press, Cambridge, pp198–271

Meister, K., Frick, M. and Axhausen, K. W. (2005) 'A GA-based household scheduler', *Transportation*, vol 32, no 5, pp473–494

Meister, K., Balmer, M., Axhausen, K. W. and Nagel, K. (2006) 'planomat: A comprehensive scheduler for a large-scale multi-agent transportation simulation', paper presented at the 11th International Conference on Travel Behaviour Research, Kyoto, August

Meister, K., Rieser, M., Ciari, F., Horni, A., Balmer, M. and Axhausen, K. W. (2009) 'Anwendung eines agentenbasierten Modells der Verkehrsnachfrage auf die Schweiz', *Strassenverkehrstechnik*, vol 53, no 5, pp269–280

Nagel, K., Grether, D., Beuck, U., Chen, Y., Rieser, M. and Axhausen, K. W. (2008) 'Multi-agent transport simulations and economic evaluation', *Jahrbücher für Nationalökonomie und Statistik*, vol 228, no 2/3, pp183–194

Nash, J. (1951) 'Non-cooperative games', *Annals of Mathematics*, vol 54, no 2, pp286–295

Noland, R. B. and Polak, J. W. (2002) 'Travel time variability: A review of theoretical and empirical issues', *Transportation Reviews*, vol 22, no 1, pp39–54

Noland, R. B. and Small, K. A. (1995) 'Travel time uncertainty, departure time choice and the cost of morning commutes', *Transportation Research Record*, vol 1493, pp150–158

Ortuzar, J. de D. and Willumsen, L. G. (2001) *Modelling Transport*, Wiley, Chichester

Parker, D. C., Manson, S. M., Janssen, M. A., Hoffman, M. J. and Deadman, P. (2003) 'Multi-agent systems for the simulation of land-use and land-cover change: A review', *Annals of the Association of American Geographers*, vol 93, no 2, pp314–337

Patriksson, M. (1994) *The Traffic Assignment Problem: Models and Methods*, VSP, Utrecht

Peeta, S. and Ziliaskopoulos, A. K. (2001) 'Foundations of dynamic traffic assignment: The past, the present and the future', *Networks and Spatial Economics*, vol 1, no 3–4, pp233–265

Pendyala, R. M. (2004) 'Phased implementation of a multimodal activity-based travel demand modeling system in Florida: 2 – FAMOS users guide', Florida Department of Transportation, Tallahassee

Raney, B. and Nagel, K. (2006) 'An improved framework for large-scale multi-agent simulations of travel behavior', in P. Rietveld, B. Jourquin and K. Westin (eds) *Towards Better Performing European Transportation Systems*, Routledge, London, pp305–347

Recker, W. W., McNally M. G. and Root G. S. (1986a) A model of complex travel behavior: Part I – theoretical development, *Transportation Research A*, vol 20, no 4, pp307–318

Recker, W. W., McNally M. G. and Root G. S. (1986b) A model of complex travel behaviour: Part II – An operational model, *Transportation Research A*, vol 20, no 4, pp319–330

Rieser, M. (2010) *Adding Transit to an Agent-Based Transportation Simulation: Concepts and Implementation*, TU Berlin, Berlin

Rieser, M., Nagel, K., Beuck, U., Balmer, M. and Rümenapp, J. (2007) 'Agent-oriented coupling of activity-based demand generation with multi-agent traffic simulation', *Transportation Research Record*, vol 2021, pp10–17

Schnittger, S. and Zumkeller, D. (2004) 'Longitudinal microsimulation as a tool to merge transport planning and traffic engineering models: The MobiTopp model', paper presented at the European Transport Conference, Strasbourg, October

Schönfelder, S. and Axhausen, K. W. (2010) *Urban Rhythms and Travel Behaviour: Spatial and Temporal Phenomena of Daily Travel*, Ashgate, Farnham

Schüssler, N. and Axhausen, K. W. (2009a) 'Accounting for route overlap in urban and suburban route choice decisions derived from GPS observations', paper presented at the 12th International Conference on Travel Behaviour Research, Jaipur, December

Schüssler, N. and Axhausen, K. W. (2009b) 'Accounting for similarities in destination choice modelling: A concept', paper presented at the 9th Swiss Transport Research Conference, Ascona, October

Sheffi, Y. (1985) *Urban Transportation Networks: Equilibrium Analysis with Mathematical Programming Methods*, Prentice-Hall, Englewood Cliffs

Shiftan, Y. (1998) 'A practical approach to model trip chaining', *Transportation Research Record*, vol 1645, pp17–23

Simma, A. and Axhausen, K. W. (2003) 'Commitments and modal usage: An analysis of German and Dutch panels', *Transportation Research Record*, vol 1854, pp22–31

Simon, H. (1955) 'A behavior model of rational choice', *Quarterly Journal of Economics*, vol 69, no 1, pp99–118

Small, K. A. (1982) 'The scheduling of consumer activities: Work trips', *American and Economic Review*, vol 72, no 3, pp467–479

Train, K. E. (1986) *Qualitative Choice Analysis*, MIT Press, Cambridge

Train, K. E. (2003) *Discrete Choice Methods with Simulation*, Cambridge University Press, Cambridge

Vickrey, W. S. (1969) 'Congestion theory and transport investment', *American Economic Review*, vol 59, no 2, pp251–260

Vovsha, P., Petersen, E. and Donnelly, R. (2002) 'Microsimulation in travel demand modeling: Lessons learned from the New York best practice model', *Transportation Research Record*, vol 1805, pp68–77

Vovsha, P., Petersen, E. and Donnelly, R. (2003) 'Explicit modeling of joint travel by household members: Statistical evidence and applied approach', *Transportation Research Record*, vol 1831, pp1–10

Vrtic, M., Fröhlich, P., Schüssler, N., Axhausen, K. W., Dasen, S., Erne, S., Singer, B., Lohse, D. and Schiller, C. (2005) 'Erzeugung neuer Quell-/Zielmatrizen im Personenverkehr', report to the Bundesämter für Raumentwicklung, für Strassen und für Verkehr, IVT, Emch und Berger and TU Dresden, Zürich

Vrtic, M., Schüssler, N., Erath, A., Meister, K. and Axhausen, K. W. (2007) 'Tageszeitliche Fahrtenmatrizen im Personenverkehr an Werktagen im Jahr 2000', report to the Swiss Federal Office for Spatial Development, Swiss Federal Roads Authority and Swiss Federal Office for Transport, IVT, ETH Zürich, Zürich

Wardrop, J. G. (1952) 'Some theoretical aspects of road traffic research', *Proceedings of the Institute of Civil Engineers*, vol 1, no 2, pp325–378

Webster, F. V. (1958) 'Traffic signal settings', *Technical Paper*, 39, Road Research Laboratory, Crowthorne

Wegener, M. (2004) 'Overview of land-use transport models', in D. A. Hensher (ed) *Handbook of Transport Geography and Spatial System*, Elsevier, Oxford, pp127–146

Weis, C. and Axhausen, K. W. (2009) 'Induced travel demand: evidence from a pseudo panel data based structural equations model', *Research in Transport Economics*, vol 25, pp8–18

Wilson, A. G. (1970) *Entropy in Urban and Regional Modelling*, Pion, London

Wootton, H. J. and Pick, G. W. (1976) 'A model for trips generated by households', *Journal of Transport Economics and Policy*, vol 1, no 2, pp137–153

Xie, F. and Levinson, D. (2009) 'Modeling the growth of transportation networks: A comprehensive review', *Networks and Spatial Economics*, vol 9, no 3, pp291–307

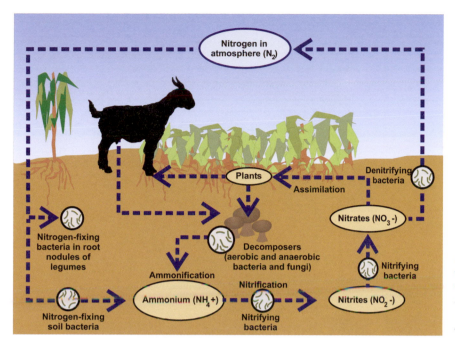

Plate 1 Circularity in resource flows: The relatively closed nitrogen cycle of a soil–plant system

Source: http://en.wikipedia.org/wiki/Nitrogen_cycle

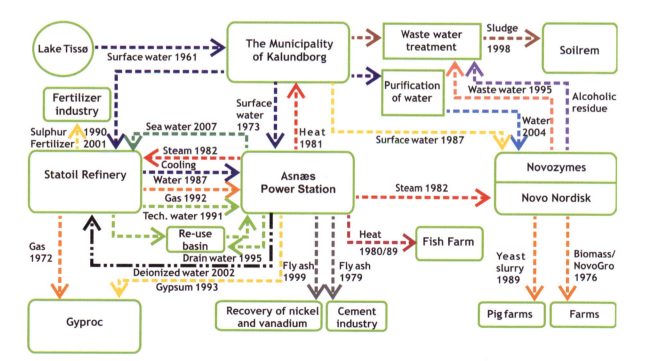

Plate 2 The industrial ecology of Kalundborg, Denmark

Source: re-created by LESO-PB from original provided by the Kalundborg Symbiosis Institute: www.symbiosis.dk.

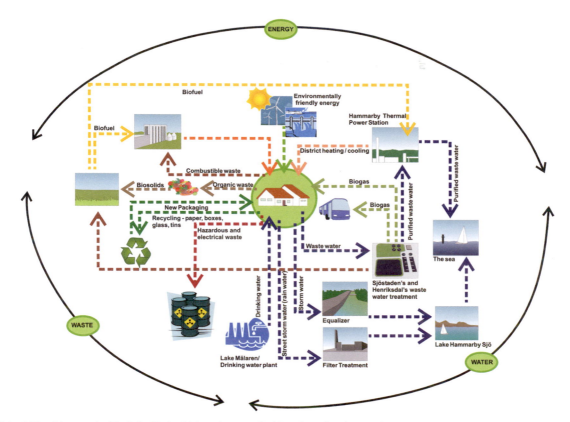

Plate 3 The 'Hammarby Model' of industrial ecology applied to urban development

Source: re-created by LESO-PB from original provided by Stockholm Municipality.

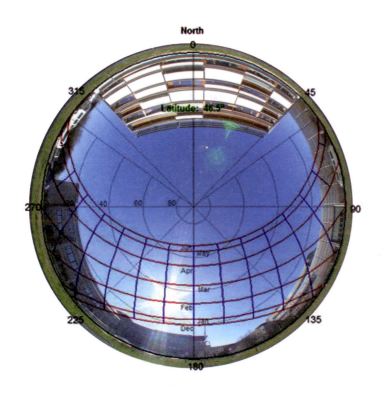

Plate 4 Sunpath diagram superimposed on a fish-eye view of an urban scene (i.e. a scene in spherical coordinates): a shading mask

Source: created by the LESO: Darren Robinson and Apiparn Borisuit.

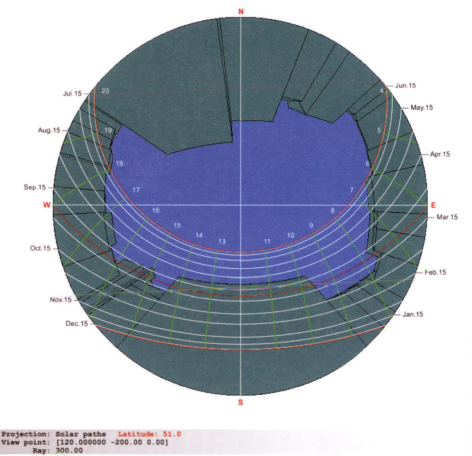

Projection: Solar paths   Latitude: 51.0
View point: [120.000000 -200.00 0.00]
         Ray: 300.00

Plate 5 Sunpath diagram superimposed on a 3D solid model rendered in spherical coordinates (Townscope)

Source: obtained from the site: http://www.townscope.com.

(a)   (b)

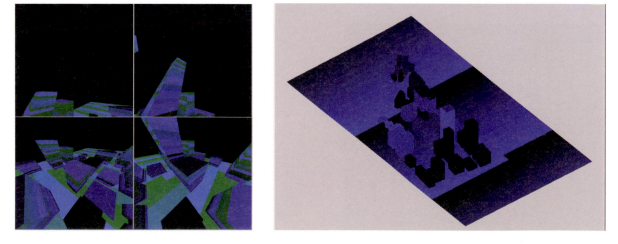

Plate 6 (a) Processing of rendered images to determine sky and obstruction view factors and (b) solar visibility

Source: Authors

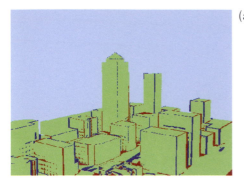

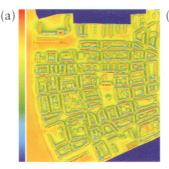

Plate 7 Annual shortwave irradiation (MWh.m⁻²) throughout a model of Canary Wharf in London, UK, with dark shaded areas corresponding to percentage differences exceeding 10 per cent in annual irradiation when using the simple surface splitting pre-process

Source: Authors

Plate 8 Falsecolour renderings of Matthäus, Basel: (a) unfiltered falsecoloured image of irradiation distribution for a parallel view from above using a scale extending from 0 to 1MWh/m²; and (b) filtered perspective view of a part of the Matthäus district – yellow pixels exceed 0.8kWh/m²

Source: Authors

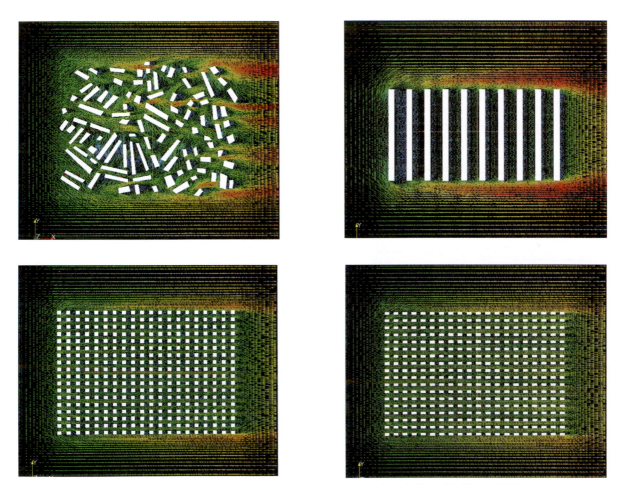

Plate 9 Velocity fields at 5.6m above the ground level for the four representations indicated in Figure 3.7.2.

Source: Authors

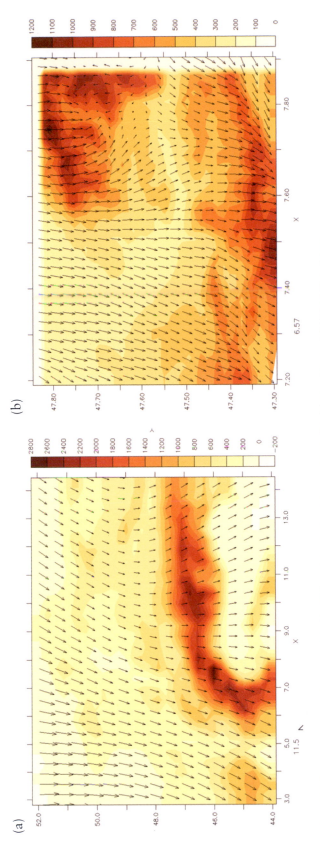

Plate 10 Interpolation of data from the global NCEP model onto the meso-scale model: (a) raw data and (b) interpolated data

Source: Authors

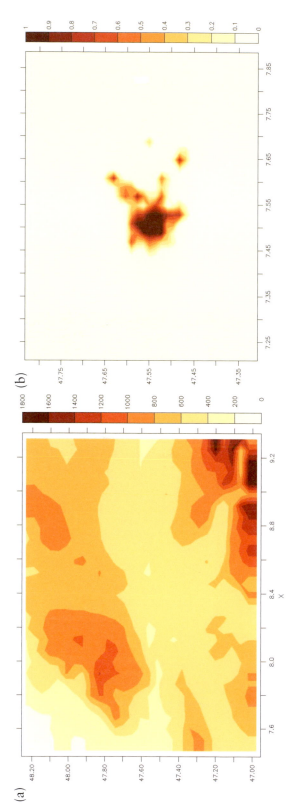

(a)

(b)

Plate 11 (a) Interpolated topography data and (b) land use data

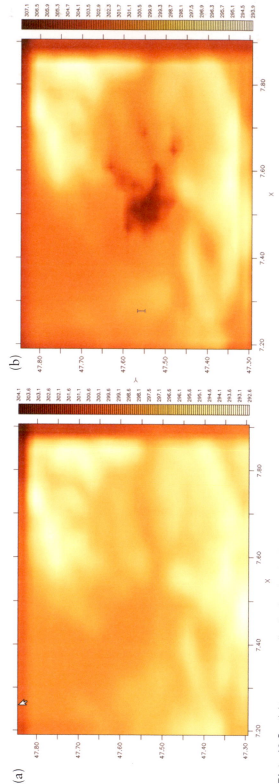

(a)

(b)

Plate 12 Spatial temperature distribution for the Basel region with (a) fully rural land cover and (b) using the correct land cover and urban canopy model parameters

Source: Authors

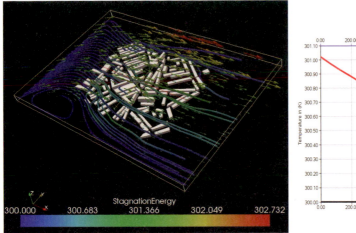
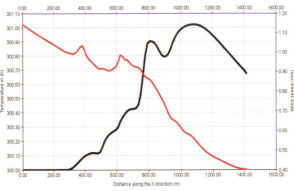

Plate 13 Results from micro-scale simulations with boundary conditions forced using the urban meso-scale model: streamlines and velocity vectors (left); temperature and velocity profiles along the x axis (the direction of flow) through the centre of the domain (right)

Source: Authors

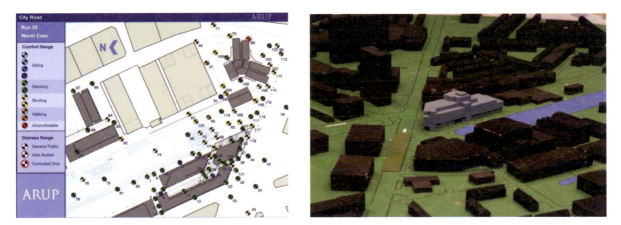

Plate 14 Pedestrian wind comfort assessment using wind tunnel measurements in conjunction with Lawson's criteria

Source: Arup (2004)

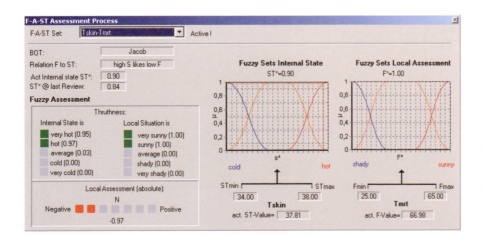

Plate 15 Evaluation system comparing the actual state of the agent (internal state ST) with the microclimate conditions offered (local assessment)

Source: Authors

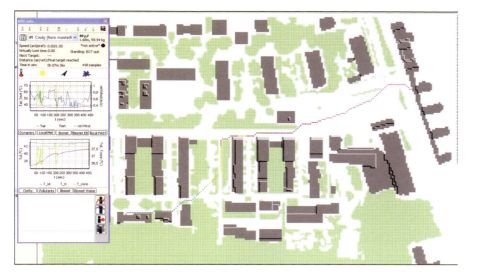

Plate 16 Route of the agent 'Cindy' through a model environment (the BOT walks from the left to the right)

Note: Colours in the trajectory correspond to skin temperature (blue=cold to purple=hot). The control window (left) shows time series plots of microclimate stimuli to which the agent was exposed (upper plot) and the corresponding human thermoregulatory system response (lower plot).

Source: Authors

(a)

DIVERSITY Map

Plate 17 (a) Environmental diversity mapping procedure; (b) preparation of annual diversity map and histogram – the percentage of open space within each category; and (c) of annual and seasonal diversity/desirability

Source: Ramos (2010)

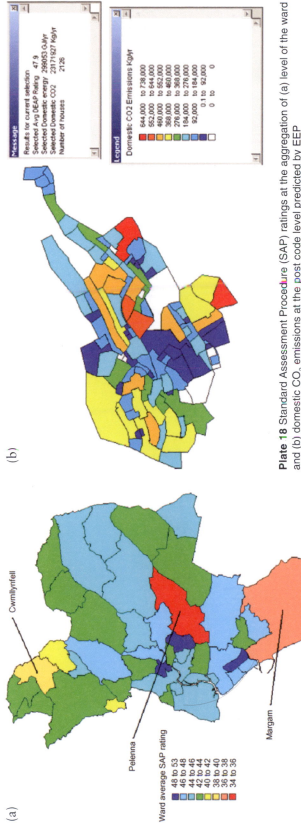

(a)

Cwmllynfell

Pelenna

Margam

Ward average SAP rating

48 to 53
46 to 48
44 to 46
42 to 44
40 to 42
38 to 40
36 to 38
34 to 36

(b)

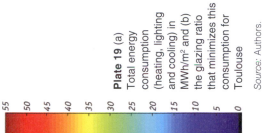

Message

Results for current selection
Selected Avg OEAP Rating   47.9
Selected Domestic energy   299053 GJ/yr
Selected Domestic CO2   23171927 Kg/yr
Number of houses   2126

Legend

Domestic CO2 Emissions Kg/yr

644,000 to 738,000
552,000 to 644,000
460,000 to 552,000
368,000 to 460,000
276,000 to 368,000
184,000 to 276,000
92,000   to 184,000
0.1 to   92,000
0 to   0

Plate 18 Standard Assessment Procedure (SAP) ratings at the aggregation of (a) level of the ward and (b) domestic CO_2 emissions at the post code level predicted by EEP

Source: Jones et al, 2007

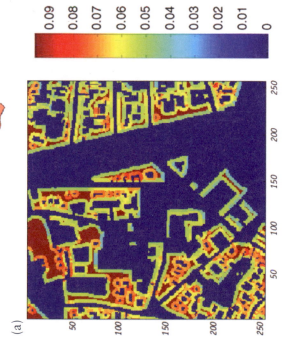

(a)

(b)

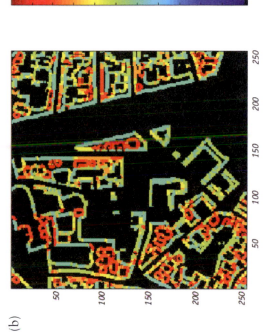

Plate 19 (a) Total energy consumption (heating, lighting and cooling) in MWh/m^2 and (b) the glazing ratio that minimizes this consumption for Toulouse

Source: Authors.

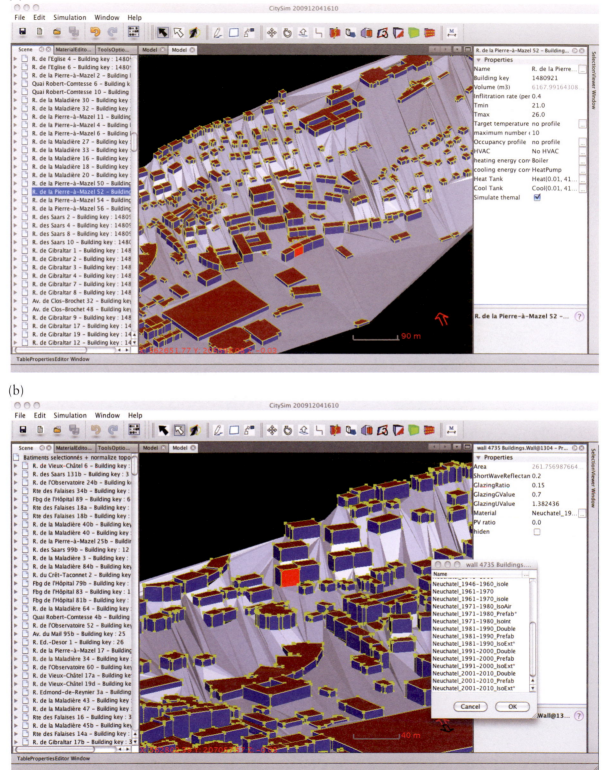

Plate 20 Model of a district of Neuchâtel, showing (a) building and (b) surface level attributes in CitySim

Source: Authors

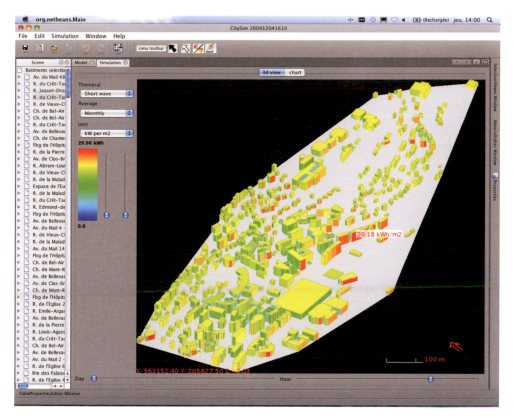

Plate 21 Falsecolour image of buildings' surfaces: The pixel value increases in proportion to the monthly total incident shortwave irradiation

Source: Authors

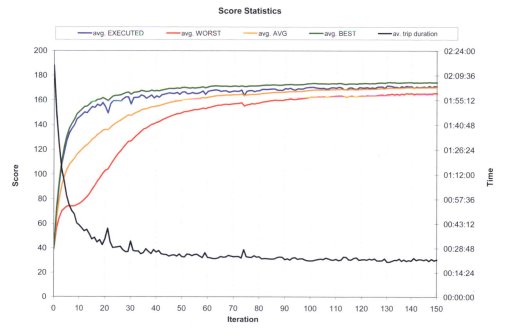

Plate 22 Westumfahrung: Evolution towards steady state (current situation)

Source: Balmer et al (2009)

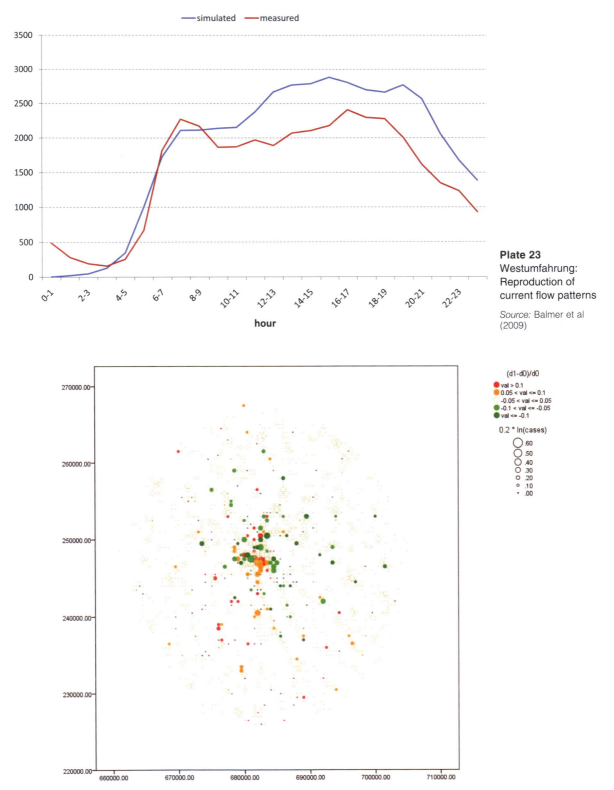

Plate 23
Westumfahrung:
Reproduction of
current flow patterns

Source: Balmer et al
(2009)

Plate 24 Westumfahrung: Number of winners (green) and losers (red) in terms of distance travelled after the opening of the new road

Source: Balmer et al (2009)

Basic scale		Enriched scale	
G	Favourable	G	Favourable
		G-	Favourable with some reserves
Y	Neutral	Y+	Neutral with positive elements
		Y	Neutral
		Y-	Neutral with negative elements
R	Unfavourable	R+	Unfavourable with some positive elements
		R	Unfavourable

Plate 25 Qualitative Hermione scale

Source: Authors

Favourable　　**Neutral**　　**Unfavourable**

| | G | Y | R | |
| 0 | 100 | 200 | 300 | 400 | 500 | 600 | 700 | 800 | 900 | 1000 (MJ/m².y) |

Plate 26 Definition of thresholds to qualify building energy consumption

Favourable　　**Neutral**　　**Unfavourable**　　**Dominating disadvantage**

| G | G- | Y+ | Y | Y- | R- | R | R* |
| 0 | 100 | 200 | 300 | 400 | 500 | 600 | 700 | 800 | 900 | 1000 (MJ/m².y) |

Plate 27 Definition of thresholds to qualify building energy consumption with finest qualitative attributes

Source: Authors

G	G	$G = 66\% \vee R=0 \wedge G^*$
	G⁻	$66\% > G = 50\% \vee R=0$

Y	Y⁺	$33\% < G < 50\% \vee R=0$
	Y	$(G < 33\% \vee R=0) \wedge (G = 66\% \vee R = 33\% \vee R^*=0)$
	Y⁻	$(R= 33\% \vee R^*=0) \wedge (G = 50\% \vee R= 50\% \vee R^*=0)$

R	R⁺	$(33\% < R = 50\% \vee R^*=0) \wedge (50\% < R \vee G = 33\% \vee R^*=0)$
	R	$50\% < R = 66\% \wedge R^* ? 0$

Plate 28 Hermione aggregation rules with 50% majority and 33% minority thresholds

Source: Authors

Plate 29 Evaluations from each of the 30 decision committee members for the site 'Parc de la Solitude'

Note: Each column represents the evaluation of a member of the decision committee (total of 30). The last column represents Hermione's aggregation of the 30 individual evaluations.

Source: Authors

Criteria	Site 1 Dorigny	Site 2 Pal'zieux g'art	Site 3 Hauteville	Site 4 La Prairie	Site 5 Les Andonces	Site 6 La Gare	Site 7 NaCl	Site 8 BCV Chauderon	Site 9 Halle CFF	Site 10 Parc de la Solitude	Site 11 Mus'e-Cit'
1. Conformity											
1.1 Accessibility											
1.2 Relationship with and attractiveness of the surroundings											
1.3 Quality of the site or of the buildings to rehabilitate											
2. Feasibility											
2.1 Procedures											
2.2 Acceptability and risks of opposition											
3. Society & culture											
3.1 Site and urbanism											
3.2 Community											
3.3 Identification to the project											
4. Economy											
4.1 Finances											
4.2 Economic environment											
4.3 Contributions from the local municipality to the project											
5. Environment											
5.1 Transport impacts											
5.2 Energy potential of the site											
5.3 Ground, landscape, nuisances											

Plate 30 Final synthetic result for the 11 candidate sites (columns) evaluated according to the 14 chosen criteria (rows)

Note: Arrows indicate the rejected sites.

Source: Authors

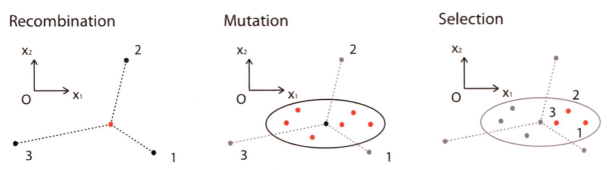

Plate 31 The three operators of the evolution for the CMA-ES, illustrated for an objective function in two dimensions: Three parents produce, by recombination and mutation, six children from which we select the new parents

Source: Authors

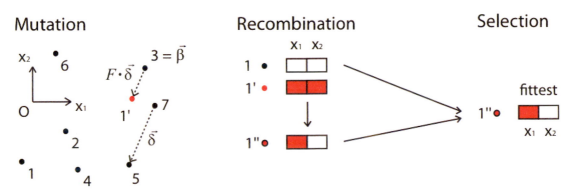

Plate 32 The three operators of the evolution for the HDE illustrated for an objective function in two dimensions

Note: For the first parent, a trial individual is created and recombined with the parent to produce a child. The fittest of the parent and child is selected.

Source: Authors

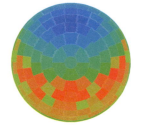

cumulative sky over a year
(hemispherical view)

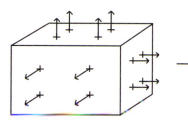

building surfaces decomposed into
sampling points with normal vector

RADIANCE →

annual irradiation I_i on n sampling
points, relating to a region of known
surface area A_i

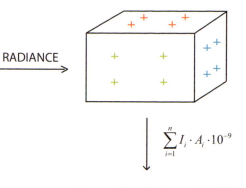

$$\sum_{i=1}^{n} I_i \cdot A_i \cdot 10^{-9}$$

total annual irradiation on building
(GWh)

Plate 33 Principle of
irradiation calculation
using RADIANCE

Source: Authors

| 1.1075e+06 | 830627 | 553752 | 276876 | 0 |

Plate 34 Optimal case for the Manhattan-style grid after 12,000 evaluations: The model with an irradiance map in Wh

Source: Authors

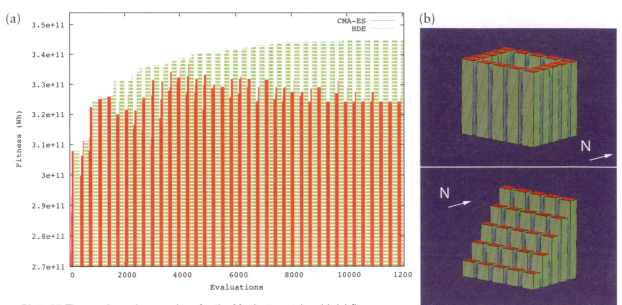

Plate 35 The results and comparison for the Manhattan-style grid: (a) fitness (solar energy potential) evolution for the Manhattan-style grid; (b) corona and stairs shapes

Source: Authors

Plate 36 Optimal case for the photovoltaic extension after 12,000 evaluations

Source: Authors

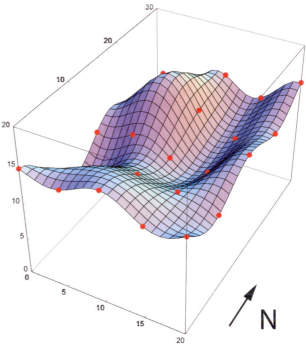

Plate 37 A roof represented by a 2D Fourier series

Source: Authors

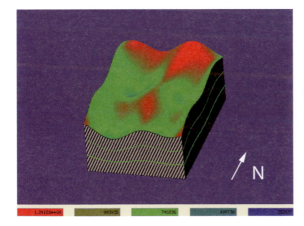

Plate 38 Result for small amplitudes after 12,000 evaluations: 3D view

Source: Authors

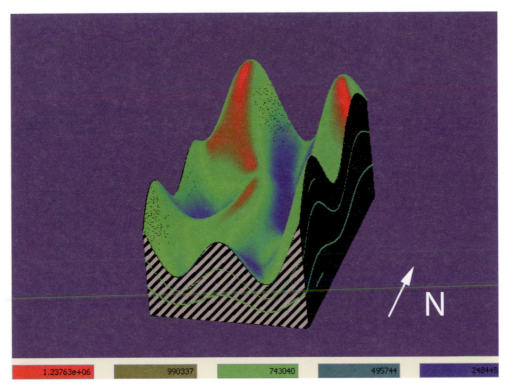

1.23763e+06	990337	743040	495744	248448

Plate 39 Result for medium amplitudes after 12,000 evaluations: 3D view

Source: Authors

1.24351e+06	958268	673031	387793	102556

Plate 40 Result for large amplitudes after 12,000 evaluations: 3D view

Source: Authors

Plate 41 The part of the Matthäus district used for the case study

Source: Authors

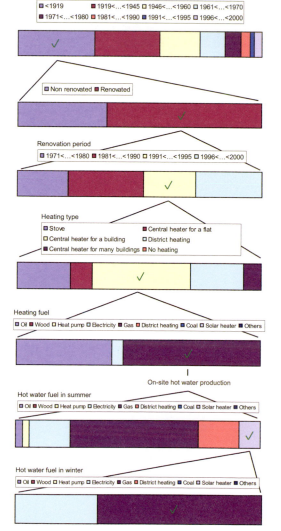

Construction period

| ■ <1919 | ■ 1919<...<1945 | □ 1946<...<1960 | □ 1961<...<1970 |
| ■ 1971<...<1980 | ■ 1981<...<1990 | ■ 1991<...<1995 | ■ 1996<...<2000 |

□ Non renovated ■ Renovated

Renovation period

| ■ 1971<...<1980 | ■ 1981<...<1990 | ■ 1991<...<1995 | □ 1996<...<2000 |

Heating type

■ Stove	■ Central heater for a flat
□ Central heater for a building	□ District heating
■ Central heater for many buildings	■ No heating

Heating fuel

□ Oil ■ Wood □ Heat pump □ Electricity ■ Gas ■ District heating ■ Coal □ Solar heater ■ Others

On-site hot water production

Hot water fuel in summer

□ Oil ■ Wood □ Heat pump □ Electricity ■ Gas ■ District heating ■ Coal □ Solar heater ■ Others

Hot water fuel in winter

□ Oil ■ Wood □ Heat pump □ Electricity ■ Gas ■ District heating ■ Coal □ Solar heater ■ Others

Plate 42 An example of the Monte-Carlo procedure of inferring missing data from a large sample

Source: Authors

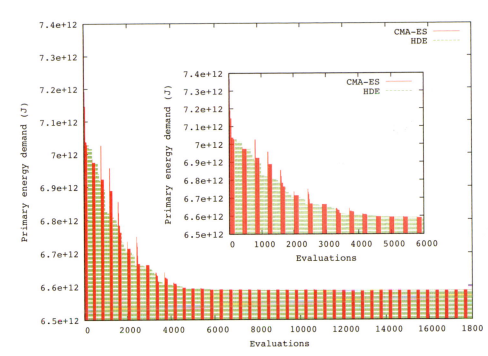

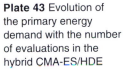

Plate 43 Evolution of the primary energy demand with the number of evaluations in the hybrid CMA-ES/HDE

Note: Inset is the same graph but focussing on the range (0–6000) evaluations.

Source: Authors

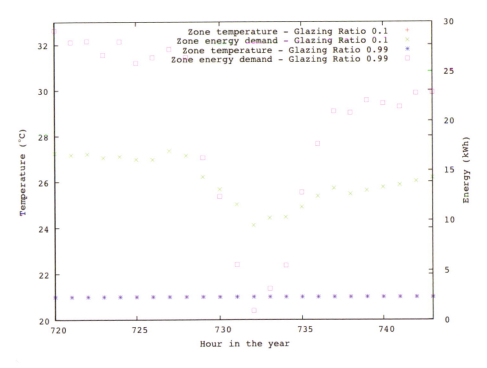

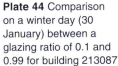

Plate 44 Comparison on a winter day (30 January) between a glazing ratio of 0.1 and 0.99 for building 213087

Source: Authors

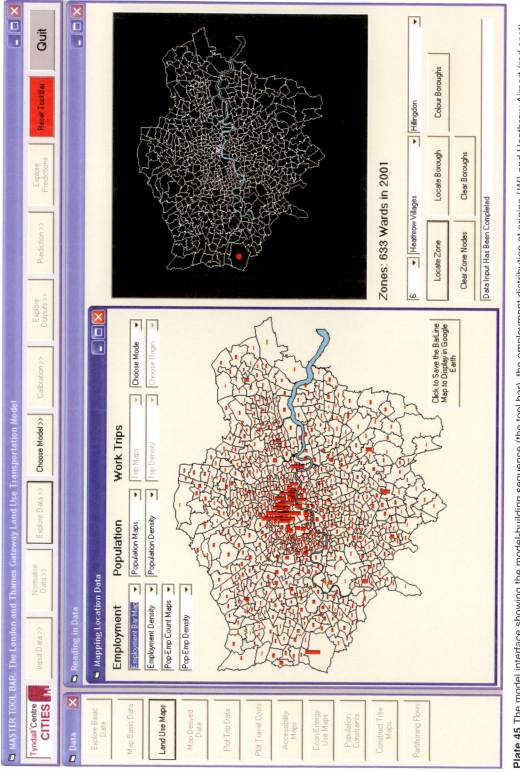

Plate 45 The model interface showing the model-building sequence (the tool bar), the employment distribution at origins $\{W_j\}$ and Heathrow Airport (red spot)

Source: Authors

(a)

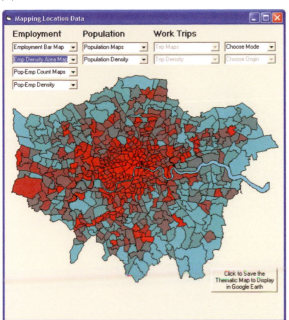

(b)

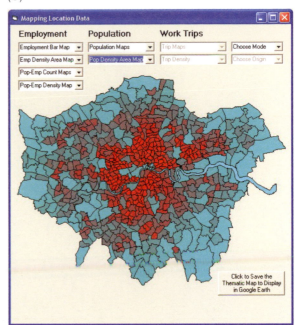

(c)

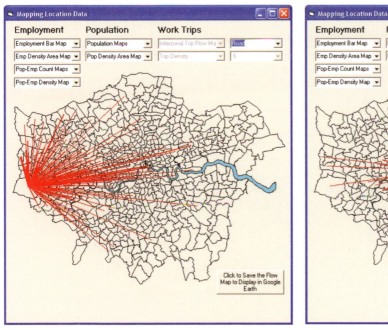

(d)

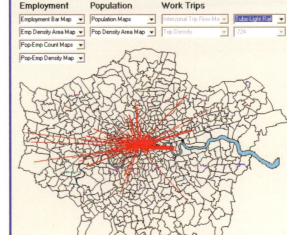

Plate 46 Snapshots of the model data illustrating the residential location process: (a) employment densities (origins), (b) population densities (destinations), (c) road trips from Heathrow $i = 6$, and (d) tube trips from St James, Westminster $i = 224$

Source: Authors

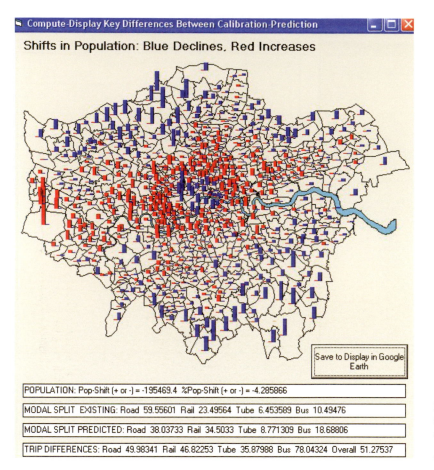

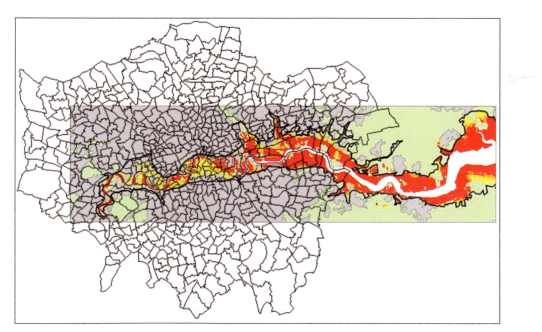

Plate 47 Change in population at residential locations due to a doubling of road transport costs

Source: Authors

Plate 48 Greater London and the inner Thames Gateway

Source: Authors

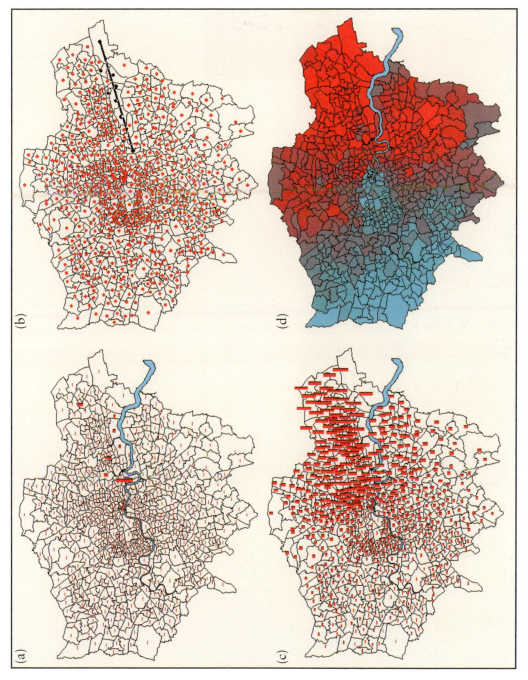

Plate 49 Generating a scenario that drives employment housing in east London and the Thames Gateway: (a) six selected inputs of employment based on existing centres; (b) location of a new heavy rail line to the east along the Thames (note that red spots are zone centroids and black spots are centroids on the fast rail line); (c) predicted distribution of population as percentage change; (d) absolute predicted distribution of population

Source: Authors

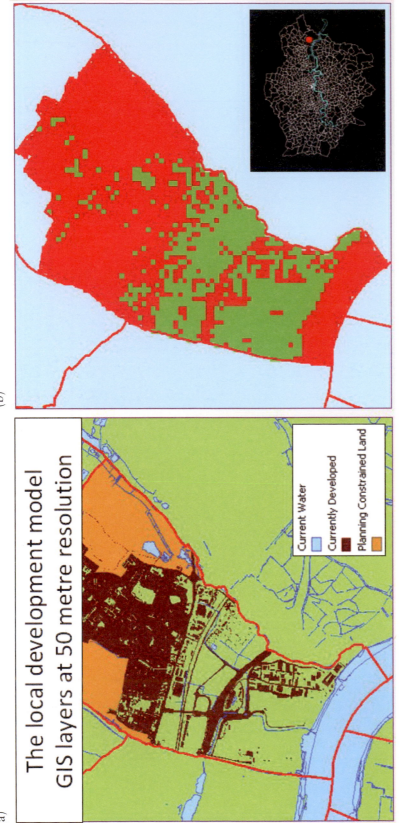

(a)

The local development model
GIS layers at 50 metre resolution

Current Water

Currently Developed

Planning Constrained Land

(b)

Plate 50 The urban development population site model pictured for the zone of south Hornchurch on the floodplain in east London

Source: Authors

Part III

Measures and Optimization of Sustainability

7

Measures of Urban Sustainability

Flourentzos Flourentzou

7.1 Introduction

Sustainability in the urban context is a notion that is both widely used and little understood; widely used because of the growing consensus that we need to improve the sustainability of our urban settlements, little understood because of the myriad diverse environmental, social and economic factors that influence it.

We open this chapter by first expanding on this quandary. We then go on to introduce the challenges facing us as we strive to make meaningful decisions on the basis of some holistic consideration of sustainability. This leads us to describe in detail a multi-criteria decision making methodology and the application of this methodology to a real project, based in the county of Vaud in Switzerland.

7.2 Labels and definitions[1]

As noted in the introduction to this book, it is estimated that over half of the global population is now living in urban settlements (UN, 2004), in which three quarters of global resources are consumed (Girardet, 1999). Energy derived from fossil fuels is key among these resources, so that urban settlements are responsible for the majority of greenhouse gas emissions. In order to improve both the security of energy supply and to curb the risks of climate change associated with fossil fuel combustion, there is increasing pressure on governments to achieve international consensus on reductions to greenhouse gas emissions. Within this landscape then, it is increasingly important that existing urban settlements are adapted and that proposed settlements are designed to minimize their net resource use. In short, urban settlements need to become more sustainable.

To this end we have in recent years witnessed a proliferation of urban development projects that attempt to demonstrate how we can achieve urban sustainability and that claim the label of *sustainable neighbourhood*, *sustainable district*, *sustainable town* or *sustainable city*, or simply a *sustainable development* or *settlement*. But what does this mean? To shed light on this deceptively complex question, let us first restrict ourselves to *environmental sustainability*.

In its purest sense an environmentally sustainable settlement, irrespective of its scale, would be an autarkic one. It would be a closed thermodynamic system, in which all consumed resources are provided for within its geographical boundaries. But this would not be viable in the long term. Due to irreversible internal processes, non-renewable resources (energy and matter) within the settlement would eventually be depleted. Furthermore, being starved of their photosynthetic driving force, solar energy, plants and the herbivorous animals that depend on them (and so on, up the food chain) would not survive; life would fade out (Filchakova et al, 2007). We thus need to allow for exchanges of renewable resources, especially solar energy, across our settlement boundaries: our system must be thermodynamically open. But this is fine. As mentioned in Chapter 1, ecologists have shown that nutrient cycles in complex ecosystems that import renewable resources (solar energy, wind, rain) and benefit from rich synergetic exchanges between species, such as forests, may be closed. Can this same status quo be achieved in anthropogenic ecosystems (urban settlements)?

Prior to the advent of chemically and mechanically assisted agriculture, we humans lived in a period when settlements' resource demands were largely satisfied by their immediate hinterland and non-renewable resources (for example tools) were efficiently recycled. Our settlements were fairly, but not completely, closed. We have since moved far from this state of near-equilibrium with our environment. Indeed we find ourselves in a period of globalization: an extreme case of an open system that relies on overexploitation of planetary resources (Marchettini et al, 2006). This regime may also be deemed to be inconsistent with physical laws, since it leads to the exhaustion of natural capacity: it is self-destructive. But perhaps our two extremes, autarky and globalization, define the boundaries of a liveability space in which we may be relatively sustainable at one extreme and unsustainable at the other. What remains then is to define a quantitative representation of these extremes as well as of the state of some real urban system that enables it to be placed somewhere between them. For the moment, this objective remains illusive.[2] This situation becomes more complex still if we consider less tangible socio-economic parameters (Figure 7.1.1). In this we need to consider a multitude of factors.

Figure 7.1.1 The three pillars of sustainability: social, economic and environmental and the overlaps between them

Note: An overlap between all three pillars is normally deemed to represent some notion of balanced sustainability.

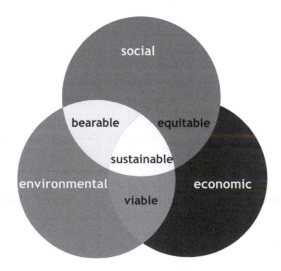

For example, whether the individuals and family units accommodated within our urban settlement have access to appropriate means of gainful employment and receive an equitable financial income; whether they have access to basic health, welfare and education amenities; whether they perceive there to be a strong sense of community within their neighbourhoods; whether they feel safe; whether they have adequate access to nature ..., to mention but a few.

To grapple with this complexity, to make sense of the myriad objective and subjective parameters influencing sustainability, requires the use of multi-criteria decision making tools, if we are indeed to choose the best course of action for a given urban settlement.[3]

7.3 Multi-criteria decision making for urban sustainability

7.3.1 Background

The purpose of computer modelling for sustainable urban design is to inform stakeholders so that they make well-informed decisions, knowing what the likely consequences of their decisions will be. But decision making is a complex cognitive construction process, involving fact perception and human preferences. These preferences depend on how reality is perceived by decision makers, which in turn may be influenced by simulation; enabling decision makers to better understand the current state or the potential future state of the system under investigation. Thus, simulation enlarges the decision maker's perception. According to constructivist cognitive theory (Flourentzou, 2001), this modification depends on the quality of interaction between subjects' cognitive structures (the decision makers' minds) and the perceived environment.

Now, myriad criteria intervene in the decision making process and they are often non-commensurable. This complicates our perception and thereby our analysis of the system under investigation, which in turn renders decisions difficult to justify and to communicate and complicates negotiations of stakeholders' conflicting interests.

Repeated failures of otherwise grand projects, technically excellent but misunderstood by the populace, suggest that modelling rigour and precision is not enough in itself to ensure that the most appropriate decisions are made. Rather, modelling will leverage sustainable action if, and only if, decision makers assimilate and appropriate simulation results into their system of values.

But it is tempting to try to internalize the decision making process within a computer model. Indeed, this is necessary if we are to use computer algorithms to search our available parameter space for a globally optimum combination of parameter values for a particular problem. In this case, decision theory tries to encapsulate human preference and associated responses in an algorithm, to emulate human decisions or behaviours. This is normally achieved by deriving a utility function (Schärlig, 1990) – an aggregate measure of the utility, positive or negative, that we humans ascribe to the factors that influence our perception.

The simplest utility function is a weighted mean of multiple performance criteria, each evaluated using a common homogeneous scale. A variation of this modelling approach is the credit point system, in which a sum of credits represents the overall system performance instead of the weighted mean. The criteria weights or credit points represent stakeholders' preferences in the system model.

But stakeholders tend to have difficulties in ascribing mathematical values, for use in a utility function, to their subjective interpretations or preferences. For example Flourentzou (2001) showed that independently of education level, people are not able to place correctly on a linear decimal scale a series of seven weights, volumes or densities. This indicates that cognitive transformation from a quality to a quantity introduces bias into model inputs. The well-known principle, 'garbage in – garbage out', may be correctly transposed to 'bias in – bias out', so reducing decision model credibility. A global performance expressed in a single figure is thus a manifestation of each individual input bias. Indeed, mathematical operations on these inputs may even magnify this source of bias on the final result.

Much criticism has been levelled at utility function bias (Roy, 1985, 1992, 1999; Schärlig, 1990; Meystre et al, 1994), but most disconcerting is the application of utility functions to (arbitrarily) compare objects that are ultimately incomparable in the decision makers mind.

7.3.2 Utility functions

In the environmental sciences, a range of aggregate indicators of system environmental performance are employed. Some methods choose a single indicator, supposing that this indicator has a dominant impact over other possible indicators or that other indicators are linearly related to it. The Swiss building performance label Minergie for example chooses weighted primary energy as its key performance indicator (KPI), whereas the French carbon accounting method (or *bilan carbone*) considers CO_2 emissions. Lifecycle assessment (LCA) methods, by contrast, attempt to exhaustively integrate all key forms of pollution. They use utility functions that weight both objective quantities, such as pollution, and incommensurable impacts using a single homogeneous scale. For example, the ecological scarcity method calculates UBP (Umweltbelastungspunkte) points, whereas Impact 2002 calculates mid and end points, aggregating to 14 indicators (mid points such as aquatic ecotoxicity or global warming) or to four more synthetic indicators (end points such as human health or resources) and the ecological footprint expresses everything in terms of m^2 of used landscape.

By way of illustration of the differences between these diverse methods, consider the example of four heat production systems applied to a villa that has a heating power demand of 10–15kW:

1   Ground source heat pump (GSHP).
2   Condensing modulating gas boiler.
3   Wood pellet furnace.
4   Condensing oil boiler.

Let us also assume that these systems are representative of current good practice (the coefficient of performance (COP) for the heat pump is 3.5–3.9, the overall condensing gas boiler efficiency is 0.95 and wood furnace efficiency is 0.85).

If we take as our single indicator of system environmental performance the primary energy use to produce 1MJ of heat, including the equipment, then according to the EcoInvent database,[4] the wood pellet furnace option is preferred, far and away above the others – 1MJ of heat produced by GSHP (based on the Swiss electricity generating mix) entails more than twice the primary energy use relative to that of the wood furnace (Figure 7.3.1); fossil fuels four times.

However, wood furnaces emit more oxides of nitrogen (NO_x) and small particulates having a diameter of less than 10μm. To account for this, the Minergie label corrects its primary energy weighting coefficient to 0.8 for wood furnaces, as compared to 1 for condensing fossil fuel boilers, and 0.57 for geothermic heat pumps. This now changes the preferred option.

In France, a recent political emphasis on CO_2 reductions has led to the development of the carbon accounting method. If we now plot the equivalent kg of CO_2 emissions of the same heat production systems, the order of preference once again changes. Wood furnaces and GSHPs have similar impacts (five to six times less than fossil fuels). Even direct electric heating would be less polluting than fossil fuel combustion in France, where 78 per cent of electricity is produced by nuclear power stations (Figure 7.3.2).

In both cases, the decision criteria are not exhaustive. When considering primary energy, air pollution and nuclear waste are not explicitly considered; the latter is also not considered by equivalent CO_2 emissions. Indeed, how many kg of CO_2 would be equivalent to a kg of high degree radioactive waste?

Complete LCA methods aim to account for all, or almost all, forms of pollution of the air, water and soil compartments of the geosphere as well as for natural resource depletion. Each method uses a form of pollution function (a type of utility function). Each individual pollution impact is assigned a number of points, with some factors grouped to give an intermediate aggregate

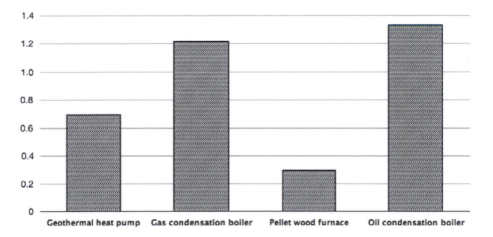

Figure 7.3.1 Units (MJ) of non-renewable energy used per unit of heat produced

Source: Author

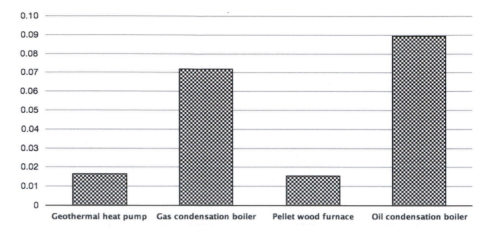

Figure 7.3.2 Grams of emitted CO_2 equivalent per MJ of heat produced

Source: Author

for a particular domain of pollution. These points (or weights) express governmental or societal preferences/perceived importance with respect to a particular type of elementary pollution. For example, the ecological scarcity method (Jolliet et al, 2010) has based its weighting on Swiss Confederation objectives, whereas Impact 2002+ (Jolliet et al, 2010) tries to integrate social aspects, with human health being one of its five aggregation categories. By way of example, 1GWh of electricity produced in France leads to 17 Impact 2002+ points of pollution concerning human health, of which six are for human toxicity, three for ionizing radiation and eight are for respiratory effects. Human health points represent 16 per cent of the total. Alternatively, the ecological footprint focuses on footprints for land occupation, CO_2 emissions and nuclear waste, expressing an equivalence between these three forms of footprint to calculate a global footprint: the area of the earth that is required either to supply the resources used in a sustainable way or to absorb/offset pollutants.

Each method aims to support decision makers in choosing the most ecologically responsible option from among a set of alternatives. Let us once again compare our four heat production systems (Figure 7.3.3).

The first information the decision maker processes is likely to be the global result. We can see in Figure 7.3.3 that for all methods the oil boiler is consistently the most polluting; particularly so in respect of its ecological footprint. Our earlier example of a Minergie-standard villa uses around 38kWh/m² per year, or 137MJ/m². Using an oil boiler would thus require 33m² of land in total (137MJ/m² × ~0.25m²/MJ), per m² of occupied space, to offset the corresponding emissions. In the case of a pellet furnace, a GSHP and a gas boiler this cost is reduced to 15m², 19m² and 24m², respectively.

Impact 2002+ suggests that in addition to the environmental footprint, human health impacts are important. So, although the pellet furnace has a low impact on the earth, it has a high impact on human health; scoring 7.8 Impact 2002+ milli-points more per MJ per year than the GSHP. But this result, which

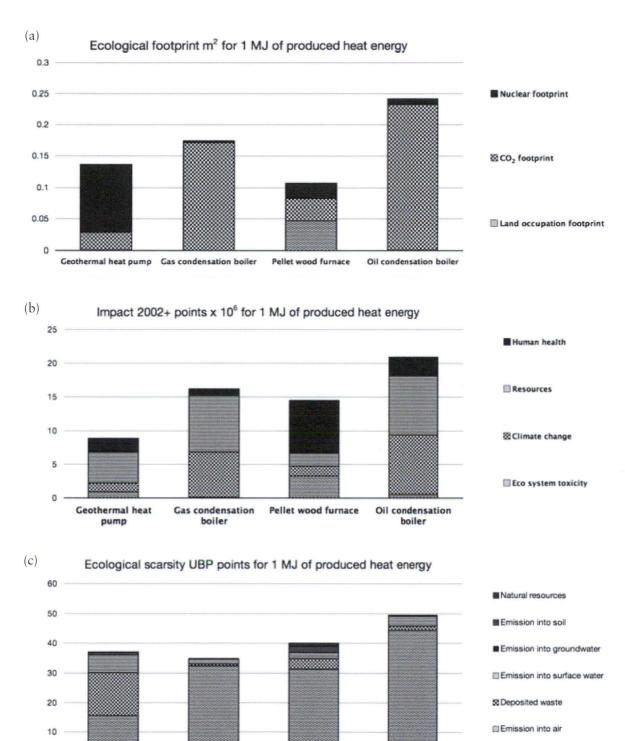

Figure 7.3.3 Three alternative LCA evaluations of four heat production systems: (a) ecological footprint, (b) Impact 2002+ and (c) ecological scarcity

is in principle more comprehensive, is less easy to interpret than the more tangible ecological footprint, which has greater communication power.

The ecological scarcity method associates 50UBP/MJ for oil boilers and between 30 and 40 for the other systems. Local combustion-based systems entail higher air emissions, whereas the GSHP leads to more deposited waste (nuclear).

In summary, based on aggregated results, the pellet furnace is preferred when basing one's analyses on primary energy, CO_2 emissions or the ecological footprint. But by re-weighting primary energy, as with the Swiss Minergie standard, the heat pump is preferred; as it is with the Impact 2002+ method. But the ecological scarcity method suggests the use of gas boilers in marginal preference to heat pumps or pellet furnaces.

Thus, the conclusions are not consistent between the methods used, based on the evaluation criteria and the relative weights employed, even when these methods use the same input database (EcoInvent).[5] If decision makers trust the model criteria and weights and delegate their decision authority to the aggregation model, the final decision will depend on the choice of that model. Impact 2002+ will give a different result to either that of the environmental footprint or ecological scarcity models.

To help deal with this, criteria weighting should be transparent and unacceptable compensation should be made unacceptable by the model. Pictet and Bollinger (2003) analysed in detail a range of utility function modelling problems suggesting ways of avoiding significant errors. Nevertheless, users of utility function methods should be aware of possible hidden bias and try to read between the lines and explain non-aggregated results.

Thus far we have been dealing with subjectively weighted objective variables. But in sustainable urban design we also need to take into account subjective socio-economic factors that are not easily quantified in the form of a utility function (see Section 7.2). For this, some form of aggregation algorithm is required, to sort, rank and select the preferred candidate from among comparable options based on multiple criteria.

7.3.3 Multi-criteria decision making: Comparison methods

Advances in multi-criteria decision making tools were pioneered by an inter-disciplinary community of experts from mathematics, operational research, natural sciences, environmental sciences, sociology and cognitive sciences, called the European constructivist decision aid group. The work of this group led to three families of methods:

1   *The Electre/Promethé family*: these methods sort, rank or select from a set of candidates by comparing them two by two and establishing an outranking relation (A is strongly preferred to B, A is slightly preferred to B, there is no preference for either A or B, etc). Analysis of over-ranking relation graphs establishes a global preference. These methods may declare two actions incomparable if there is not enough evidence to declare a global over-ranking relation from individual criteria comparisons.

2 *Knowledge-based decision support:* these apply multi-criteria rules informed by past experience. Application of rough set theory by Roman Slowinski (1992) gave promising results in cases where there exists a database of past decisions.

3 *The Macbeth interactive and constructivist method*: this is an approach designed for building a cardinal numerical scale, measuring the attractiveness of the elements of a set *X*, throughout a learning process supported by visual interactive software. More specifically, Macbeth offers two outcomes for each question. It then tests the consistency of the answers, offers suggestions to bypass inconsistent situations and provides the analyst with the means adequate for aiding the decision maker to enter into the domain of cardinal measurement (Bana e Costa and Vansnick, 1995). This avoids the pitfall of traditional approaches for cardinal value measurement, which require the decision maker to answer very difficult judgemental questions and do not offer any practical way to verify the reliability of the obtained preference information.

Returning once again to our four heating systems, to make our choice using the Electre method, we should define the comparison criteria, give a relative weight for each of them and compare two by two all possible pairs of actions. To decide if a heat pump is globally preferred to a gas boiler, according to one of our LCA methods, we should define preference, indifference and veto thresholds and compare the two systems criterion by criterion, rather than simply by comparing aggregate points. According to the ecological footprint method we should compare the two systems according to land occupation, CO_2 and nuclear footprints. In our case, GSHP is preferred for land occupation, while the wood furnace is preferred for nuclear and CO_2 is rather indifferent. But depending on the veto threshold for the nuclear footprint, the two systems could be declared incomparable.

So these multi-criteria approaches are less compensative than utility functions. But even though their authors claim a constructive decision making process, decision makers should still formulate their preferences in the form of criteria, weights and criteria evaluations in a way that can be correctly interpreted by the model. Thus, the decision maker delegates the ability to perform a global judgement or preference to a mathematical model. This can create resistance among stakeholders. As noted earlier, experience shows that they perceive a loss of control when delegating their authority to a black box. But with the help of a trusted expert as an intermediary between model and stakeholder, these methods can be a good alternative to a simple weighted mean. At the very least they do not pretend to know more than the decision maker does or to compare objects that are incomparable in his or her mind. They do not attempt to compensate a very bad score by a series of small advantages.

The process of assembling the criteria used by these approaches is also important, as this leads stakeholders to interact with the criteria space. In this way, when an action is declared incomparable by the decision system, the stakeholder can offer insight as to why this might be the case or informatively contradict this result.

7.3.4 Qualitative constructivist multi-criteria analysis

In an attempt to overcome some of the above difficulties, a new multi-criteria decision making approach was developed at the LESO-PB at EPFL. Instead of attempting to model stakeholder preferences and then to substitute their judgement, the effort is focused on structuring the problem so that the decision maker directly interacts with his or her problem. In this an effort is also made to reduce the complexity of the task to a level where substantial information is not lost, but at which the decision maker may aggregate in his or her mind the various influencing factors. Otherwise, simple aggregation rules may be used but the decision maker has the possibility to validate or otherwise any algorithmic aggregation. The basic method is called Hermione (Flourentzou et al, 2003) but a series of other multi-criteria environmental methods (Appendix A7.1) use it to structure their evaluations.

7.4 Hermione: Principles

As noted earlier, the qualitative multi-criteria aggregation method Hermione (Flourentzou et al, 2003) works on the basis of rules and aggregates users' evaluations into a synthesis. Below we explain the principles of this method and the stages involved in its application before demonstrating in Section 7.5 its application to a site selection scenario.

7.4.1 Defining a family of criteria

By structuring the consequences of a decision to be taken as an exhaustive family of criteria reflecting previously defined stakes, we create a systematic framework for an evaluation, considering all key factors influencing our choices.

The consequences are grouped in so-called macro-criteria (or topic) families containing several criteria and subcriteria. Their hierarchical structure may cover two or three levels.

Certain methods based on Hermione (see Appendix A7.1) include predefined criteria sets and a detailed three-level structure. Their macro-criteria usually correspond to predefined principal stakes.

The criteria families supplied by these methods can be used in three ways:

1   Validate and use without modification.
2   Apply light changes by ignoring the evaluation of a number of subcriteria or by adding others, without changing the balance or the spirit of the structure.
3   Reorganize in depth or simplify or add important stakes to the project. The list of criteria can be simplified through a reduction of the number of hierarchical levels to two or even one.

If the criteria structure is not suitable because the specific stakes of a project differ considerably from those of the general case covered by a method, a criteria family needs to be defined from scratch. In this case, it is up to the user to judge how many hierarchical levels are needed to coherently model consequences. Since the structuring of a family is work intensive, the user may want to limit the criteria families to one or two hierarchical levels. If a new criteria structure is defined or if the one predefined by the applied method is considerably modified, the consistency of the new structure must be verified for compliance with the following requirements:

- *Exhaustivity* – all stakes must be represented. No important aspect of a decision is to be forgotten or ignored under the pretext that it is difficult to evaluate in an objective manner.
- *Non-redundancy* – none of the aspects should be taken into account twice through two criteria expressed in different ways. For example, if we define a criterion 'energy use' for the selection of an oil fired boiler, we must not define an additional criterion 'CO_2 emissions' as the two criteria are used to evaluate similar aspects of system performance. Equally, the criterion 'number of restaurants in the vicinity' might be redundant if 'proximity to city centre' is considered in the choice of a site.
- *Importance equilibrium* – the Hermione method recommends that criteria weights not be quantified. Instead, criteria of comparable importance are placed in the same branch of the hierarchical tree. However, the following conditions apply:
  - Criteria must be sufficiently important. Test: if a scenario presents an 'unfavourable' evaluation for one criterion, it cannot be globally 'favourable' at the macro-criterion level, even if all other criteria are 'favourable'. Otherwise the criterion is not sufficiently important to have criterion status and we need to change its place in the hierarchical structure, either by transforming it into a subcriterion of another criterion or by regrouping it with other criteria of little significance to create a new one.
  - A criterion should not be overly important. Test: if a scenario presents an 'unfavourable' evaluation for one criterion, the global judgement at the macro-criterion level must not be 'unfavourable' if all other criteria are 'favourable'. Otherwise the criterion has too much weight and must be subdivided into less important criteria.

The importance equilibrium test is fundamental for the correct use of the method. The definition of criteria as described above leads decision makers to think carefully about the issue before they decide on a scenario.

The subcriteria must also be balanced, but if this condition is not completely respected, the impact of the imbalance is limited to one criterion and is less important for the global sorting.

7.4.2 Evaluation of scenarios or of a multi-criteria diagnosis

Any evaluation requires a scale. Hermione's capacity to deal equally with both qualitative and quantitative aspects, in a rich and simple way, is due to the scale it uses. Three basic ranks expressing the qualities favourable, neutral and unfavourable are represented by the colours green, yellow and red (Plate 25). Two more ranks labelled 'vetoes' are represented by red and green accompanied by a star (veto characteristics are described later).

To moderate judgements, Hermione offers a scale enriched with secondary attributes. The sub-attribute '+' is used to assign a particular advantage and the sub-attribute '−' to express a minor reserve. What is essential is that the qualitative difference between 'favourable' and 'unfavourable' is respected, with ranks in between that can be qualified as neither favourable nor unfavourable.

The user evaluates every subcriterion on the given base scale, or the enriched scale if she or he chooses to make more subtle judgements. If a family of criteria with hierarchical levels has been defined, the lowest hierarchical level is evaluated. The pluses and minuses are not counted in the aggregation rules.

In qualitative evaluations, the qualities are attributed on the basis of arguments explained by a text, a photograph or both. Behind every colour there is a quality and the evaluator must be able to justify the judgement in a convincing way. A quantitative evaluation makes sense if a minimum of two thresholds can be defined, one indicating the limits of favourableness and one indicating the limits of unfavourableness.

Plate 26 illustrates how the energy use of a building constructed before 1990 can be normalized. The value of 230MJ/m² corresponds approximately to the threshold values of the corresponding standard of the Swiss Society of Architects and Engineers (SIA 380/1) and the value of 690MJ/m² is situated at the threshold between the F and G classes of the European 2007 Energy Label (SIA 2031).

If a scale with secondary attributes + and − or a veto is preferred, thresholds can be defined for this purpose (Plate 27). The thresholds must not be arbitrary but have a physical significance and a sense. It is better to adopt the existing principal thresholds than to define arbitrary thresholds. A threshold for the pluses and minuses of ± 10 per cent corresponds to a reasonable confidence level for calculations. The significance of green in such a case would mean that the value is too close to the threshold value (within the confidence value limits of the calculation).

There are cases where users will find it hard to define thresholds. For instance, what would be the thresholds defining the acceptability, conditional acceptability or unacceptability of infrastructure investment costs? To define such threshold values, reference values must be studied so that a stance with regard to a given amount can be taken. A value without a favourability judgement is of no use and should not be considered in the evaluation.

It is important that the spirit of the scale is respected. When a scenario is evaluated as 'red', it is unfavourable with regard to a reference but not necessarily worse than another. As noted above, we can use + and − to distinguish scenarios among themselves, but we cannot declare a scenario to be unfavourable just to distinguish it from another. In Hermione, the colours have *an absolute and not a relative sense*. Thus there needs to be a fixed external reference for the favourable or unfavourable evaluation of a performance.

In qualitative evaluations there are also references for an evaluation to be declared unfavourable or favourable. For example, a judgement can be 'red' if 'the risks of exceeding the deadlines are judged unacceptable' or 'green' if 'there are no procedures that are likely to lead to delays', and so on.

7.4.3 Synthesis and aggregation

The evaluations of subcriteria are synthesized into macro-criteria evaluations (Figure 7.4.1). If the user wishes to do so, he or she can also aggregate the evaluations of these macro-criteria into a global evaluation, but this is not generally recommended as the information becomes too diluted. The more levels of aggregation that exist, the more evaluations tend to resemble one another, except in clearly favourable or unfavourable scenarios.

Hermione's aggregation rules are based on the concept of conditional majority. An element is favourable if the majority of the sub-elements at the lower hierarchical level are favourable, without there being any unfavourable element. The degree of concordance to form a majority and the degree of tolerated discordance by a minority are parameters that can be changed. Generally speaking, 50 per cent is considered sufficient to form a majority and 33 per cent is considered as the upper limit of negative evaluations before an evaluation is considered to be globally negative. If we apply these threshold limits Hermione's rules may be formulated as follows:

- Result 'green': an absolute majority of green without the presence of red gives green (positive scenarios) (Plate 28). The presence of a positive veto also gives green, independent of the evaluation of the other elements.
- Result 'yellow': a majority of yellow without the presence of red gives yellow (average scenarios). Yellow is also attributed to scenarios that have many positive qualities (green) but a few serious problems (red), which is expressed by an absolute majority of green greater than or equal to 66 per cent and a red minority of lower than or equal to 33 per cent. The positive credit (yellow +) is attributed to scenarios without any red evaluations and 33 per cent or more green evaluations. The reserve (yellow −) is indicated when the red proportion is lower than 33 per cent and there is not a majority of green

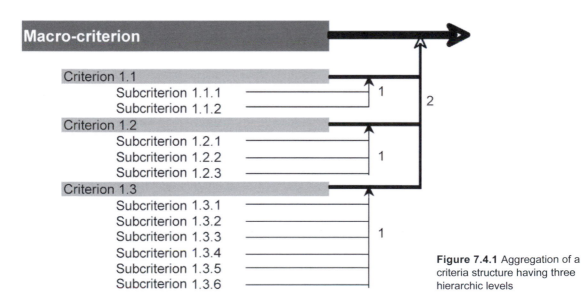

Figure 7.4.1 Aggregation of a criteria structure having three hierarchic levels

points or when there is a majority though not an absolute majority of green evaluations and less than 50 per cent red evaluations.

- Result 'red': when red evaluations exceed 33 per cent or there is a red veto, the global result is red. The positive credit (red +) is indicated when there are more than 33 per cent of green evaluations.
- Incoherent result: the presence of a positive veto as well as a negative veto is incoherent; the user must choose one over the other.

The Hermione aggregation rules allow for a differentiation of scenarios and the elimination of those that are clearly insufficient. Often the method sheds light on a situation by eliminating one or several clearly insufficient scenarios. Sometimes, after elimination of clearly insufficient scenarios, there remain a few scenarios that have both advantages and disadvantages. But these advantages and disadvantages are clearly exposed so that the decision maker can choose a compromise, thereby accepting some disadvantages, or can look for an additional scenario that eliminates or mitigates unpleasant consequences.

7.5 Hermione: Application to select a site for Lausanne's fine art museum

The local government of the county of Vaud in Switzerland wished to establish a new fine art museum. But in 2008 a referendum led to the cancellation of the county's proposal to locate such a museum in Lausanne, next to Leman Lake. An inquiry revealed that this was mainly due to a negative perception of both the location and of the proposed building shape. Indeed opponents during the referendum argued that the lakeside would be spoiled and that the building would negatively impact on local public transport.

Unperturbed, the local government decided to continue with the project; but they wished to ensure that their new site would meet with local peoples' aspirations while satisfying their own ambitions. To help in this quest, the Department for Infrastructure and Culture decided on the following strategy:

- Organize a public call for site proposals. Any citizen, association or municipality could propose a site for the fine art museum, according to a set of criteria and predefined technical specifications. This was part of the county's aim to guarantee a *democratic and transparent* process.
- Set up a largely representative committee (33 people) to analyse the propositions and submit a recommendation to the local government. In this decision committee there were artists, representatives of the main regions of the county, environmental activists, representatives of the affected public services (urban planning, culture, sites and monuments, infrastructure, mobility), and social and business personalities from throughout the county. In this they hoped to achieve *representative participation* of the key interest groups in the decision making process.
- Use a multi-criteria analysis method to evaluate the sites. A decision support committee comprised of architects, urban planners, environment analysts and art managers provided expert knowledge to the decision committee. They used the Albatros method (Appendix A7.1) to structure

the evaluation process. This was to guarantee, through structured analysis, a *rigorous, informed and comprehensive* decision making process.

Within the decision committee there was initially a high degree of suspicion regarding the local government's intentions and the role of the multi-criteria decision making method in the process. But this suspicion was quickly alleviated through transparency, the invitation of members of the decision committee to attend expert sessions or discussions and an appreciation that the method would not decide for them, but would rather help them to reach their decisions in a consensual way, by collecting and structuring information. In this way the committee was motivated to actively participate in the decision making process.

7.5.1 Decision stakes

The first meeting of the decision committee was dedicated to discussing the factors that might influence decisions. This global discussion was important to understand the stakeholders' objectives and to develop a common understanding of the project in hand. The results from this discussion are summarized in the box below.

The list of objectives communicates group intentions and common interests

The aim of this project was to establish a cultural project of major importance for the county of Vaud in Switzerland within the current government legislature. For this the key objectives were as follows:

- The site must accommodate multiple complementary activities. It should reinforce the aura and identity of the museum, and promote its integration with local cultural networks.
- The number of museum visitors should be significantly increased due to the capacity of the site and the ability of the new museum to attract its target visitors.
- Immediately available, the site should not present major procedural risks or unexpected works that may jeopardize its completion; it should also have the potential to be developed further.
- The project should not only be harmoniously integrated with its local natural or built environment, it should also have a structuring effect on future adjacent developments and be easily accessible by public transport.
- It should evoke interest and sympathy among the inhabitants of the county, irrespective of their generation or background, so that they can identify positively with their new county art museum.
- Transparency in investment and adequate running costs must be combined with concrete financial support from the host city. Potential economic risks linked to the creation of a new art museum need to be evaluated.
- Ground and resources are to be used rationally, avoiding negative impacts on landscape and the natural environment.

Particularly interesting was that everybody in the committee agreed upon these project objectives according to which the winning entry should be selected. True, some members found them very general with many possible interpretations, but the purpose here was simply to agree upon a kind of compass: to have a rough but exhaustive formulation of project objectives. These objectives were translated into more specific families of criteria in the next stage of the decision making process (Table 7.5.1). Four workshops with the interested members of the committee and the concerned experts then led to the formulation of an exhaustive list of criteria, prior to publication of the call for site propositions.

7.5.2 Decision criteria

As noted earlier, certain of these criteria were qualitative while others were quantitative. As can be seen from Table 7.5.2 for example, the criterion *urban dynamics* (3.1) is purely qualitative and should be evaluated by an urban designer, while the impact of transport (5.1) may be evaluated quantitatively by a transport engineer.

Table 7.5.1 Criteria families

1. Conformity
1.1 Accessibility
1.2 Relationship with and attractiveness of the surroundings
1.3 Quality of the site or of the buildings to rehabilitate
2. Feasibility
2.1 Procedures
2.2 Acceptability and risks of opposition
3. Society
3.1 Site and urbanism
3.2 Collectivity
3.3 Identification of the project
4. Economy
4.1 Finances
4.2 Economic environment
4.3 Contributions from the local municipality to the project
5. Environment
5.1 Transport impacts
5.2 Energetic potential of the site
5.3 Ground, landscape, nuisances

Note: 14 criteria were defined, of which nine addressed the sustainable development domains society, economy and environment, and five tackled compliance with the project brief and feasibility.

Table 7.5.2 Definition of decision criteria

3.1	Site and urbanism	5.1	Transport impacts
	The installation of a new public infrastructure of primary importance gives the site a positive image. It structures urban development as it promotes cultural, commercial, economic as well as social activities and positively transforms town planning. The establishment of a museum triggers a development dynamism that favours the installation of new activities linked to culture.		The impact of transport is extremely important for an infrastructure project whose foremost objective is to attract a maximum number of visitors. It is comparable to that of an administrative building of the same size. The cantonal planning directives stipulate that travelling by public transport and non-motorized means of transport (by bicycle, on foot) must be increased. This criterion outlines the conditions for the site of the museum to meet the defined objectives.
3.1.1.	**Contribution to urban dynamics**	5.1.1.	**Use of public transport**
	Evaluate the integration in the existing urban fabric, the coherence with planning directives for the given zone and the project's contribution to a high quality urban development. Consider the project scale coherence when evaluating the urban development capacity of the site.		The use of public transport depends on different factors linked to the possibility of using a car (number of parking spaces) and to public transport itself. Evaluate the adequacy of public transport services in terms of travelling time, service intervals, number of changes and waiting time at each intersection. Evaluate the complementarity of different means of transport, which influences the choice of locomotion of staff and visitors.
3.1.2.	**Contribution to urban dynamics**		
	Evaluate project integration in the existing regional dynamism and coherence with the masterplan for the region.		
3.1.3.	**Finding solutions for existing activities**	5.1.2.	**Use of non-motorized means of transport**
	Study the consequences of relocating current activities from the site or the buildings.		Examine the possibility of promoting non-motorized means of transport (bicycle, walking). For this purpose, take into account the proximity of urban zones and a railway station (considered as an almost inevitable changing place) as well as the quality of the public area to be travelled through.
3.1.4.	**Adequacy with regard to vocation and structure**		
	Land or building use for a new museum might compromise the establishment of a more appropriate activity (from an economic, social, cultural, commercial or lodging point of view). Favour sites for which the proposed activity best meets the requirement 'adequate activity for adequate place'. Evaluate the adequation between proposed activity and site vocation and structure.	5.1.3.	**Motorized means of transport**
3.1.5.	**Promotion of patrimony**		Measure the centeredness of the site with regard to the concerned population pool, an essential parameter for the determination of the mean number of kilometres covered for a given motorized means of transport. The position of the site also influences the impact of transport necessary for the operation of the museum (supplies, delivery, partners).
	Determine if the renovation, reassignment or construction of a new building increases the value of the patrimony (an old building, an existing structure, a site) or if the programme has a negative effect.		

Note: Criterion 3.1 is purely qualitative while criterion 5.1 is quantitative.

7.5.3 Evaluation

Now, a total of 11 sites were proposed. Of these six sites were located in the capital Lausanne of which three were proposed by the municipality and three by independent citizens. Two sites were proposed by municipalities of smaller towns such as Morges and Yverdon and a further three sites were in small communes far away from the centre. In each case, the municipality owners presented a dossier of predefined format and prepared a poster of their site. They also presented their respective sites in a public meeting.

All members of the decision committee and the expert decision support group visited the 11 proposed sites. After a brief presentation of their site the owners, and their chosen representatives (from local political, artistic or architectural society) were asked many questions to better understand the qualities and disadvantages in each case.

In parallel with these presentations, the expert group analysed each site according to their standard criteria and presented to the decision committee an exhaustive report based on these findings. A criterion evaluation was presented as a table of 12 cells. The first cell contained the criterion definition and the following 11 contained the written evaluations of each site. Table 7.5.3 presents an example of two cells relating to criterion 5.1. Thus, the whole expert evaluation was summarized in 14 tables, one per criterion.

Each member of the decision committee independently studied the 14 tables of the written evaluation report. Based on these written evaluations and the judgements that they had developed from their site visits and the corresponding presentations, they then performed their own evaluations of each site using the Hermione scale. By way of example Plate 29 presents the evaluations from each of the 30 decision committee members for the site 'Parc de la Solitude'. In this case, Hermione's aggregation rules were adapted to aggregate not the dispersed individual criteria evaluations but rather the dispersed committee members' evaluations. Thus, the last column of Plate 29 shows the aggregated evaluation representing the group's general opinion.

As noted above, each member of the decision committee independently evaluated each site proposal. As a second phase they were asked to interact with one another to agree upon a proposition that was supported by the majority. Initially each member was invited to revise or otherwise his or her evaluation knowing how their peers voted, but without knowing the aggregate result. This led to a degree of harmonization of evaluations that subsequently assisted with the acceptance of the aggregate results, once these were disclosed (summarized in Plate 30). Indeed, the members decided that the results were sufficiently clear that there was no need for further criteria aggregation. Those sites having more than one red evaluation were rejected, following from discussions with the decision committee members, so that only four sites remained for further analysis.

Following from these analyses, the trade-offs were clear for the final choice. The site in the fourth column in Plate 30 was an average candidate without any

Table 7.5.3 Example evaluations of two sites according to criterion 5.1: Transport impacts

Site A	Site B
Public transport is expected to be used very little. Proximity of motorway, convenient car parks and a ratio of travel time using public transport to travel time by car of around 1.7 all favour car usage. The possibility to combine different activities in the region using non-motorized forms of transport.	The following favours the use of public transport: its proximity, direct link and visibility from the railway station, its central position without direct access to the motorway, the limited availability of car parks, the ratio of the time spent in public transport versus the time spent in a car of around 1.1.
The site is non-central, with a mean distance covered by visitors travelling by car of 50km. Predominant use of individual means of transport increases the impact of car travelling.	The remoteness of the next large agglomeration limits the use of non-motorized forms of transport to the inhabitants of the town in which the museum is located.
	The site is reasonably central with a mean covered distance per car of between 30 and 40km, but the wide use of public transport limits the impact of car travelling.

major disadvantages but also without any major advantages. It was thus rejected. The three remaining sites presented many advantages and either a single or several small disadvantages. If we consider the criteria classifications without appreciating the qualitative sense that they represent, we might consider that 'La Gare' (site 6) is the best, because it presents only favourable evaluations. However, favourable and unfavourable are large notions. Their sense is sufficiently rich to make a first classification but too poor to make a final choice between two or three sites. A favourable evaluation could represent an extraordinary quality, or simply an adequate satisfaction of needs.

But following from the Hermione multi-criteria analysis, a shortlist of three from the 11 possible sites was prepared and the relative strengths and weaknesses of the remaining candidates were clear.

A. Musée Cité – site 11

This proposition emanated from the citizens of Lausanne. It is an original idea, proposing a superstructure over the entrance to an underground car park at Rippone Place in Lausanne. According to the evaluation report, the new built volume redefines spatially the place's dimensions, giving it a new urban coherence. The new organization of the place solves a number of ongoing problems, impossible to resolve otherwise, and creates synergies with other cultural activities in the square, inserting the new museum into the city's cultural network (Figure 7.5.1).

The evaluation committee noted in particular the following:

- Advantages: situated in a dense cultural network, contribution to a convincing urban renewal of the square; possibility of constructing a low energy building, without any planning or ownership conflicts.
- Uncertainties: high risk of opposition by activist groups; difficulties relating to the reorganization of access to the underground parking.
- Problems: limited scope for extension if the need arises.

Figure 7.5.1 Site 11: Musée Cité

Source: Author

B. The CFF locomotive hall – site 9

The municipality of Lausanne and the Swiss train company (CFF) proposed that a disused hall, previously used for the maintenance of locomotives, be reallocated to a cultural use. The evaluation report noted that this site of eminent historical interest reveals romantic charms that contemporary sensitivities appreciate when rediscovering industrial sectors of the town. The report also highlights the challenge of rendering this hidden site visible to the public realm, and of protecting works of art in a location in close proximity to heavy goods transportation, likewise the knock-on implications of reorganizing the remainder of this railway site (Figure 7.5.2).

The synthetic remarks from the evaluation highlighted the following:

- Advantages: extraordinary accessibility; contribution to urban dynamism; reuse of an already allocated polluted site; strong support from the train company and the city authorities; land immediately available.
- Uncertainties: the capacity of the building's load-bearing structure; precautions related to the prevention of major accidents due to heavy rail traffic.
- Problems: heavy and expensive refurbishment with considerable constraints; a site that is spatially hidden with little pedestrian visibility.

The third option was seen as a good alternative, in case the local government wanted to reinforce the development of cultural activities outside of its administrative centre.

C. Yverdon-les-Bains – La Gare – site 6

The second largest town in the county, Yverdon-les-Bains (25,000 inhabitants) proposed a site near its railway station, at the juxtaposition between the old

Figure 7.5.2 Site 9: CFF locomotive hall

Source: Author

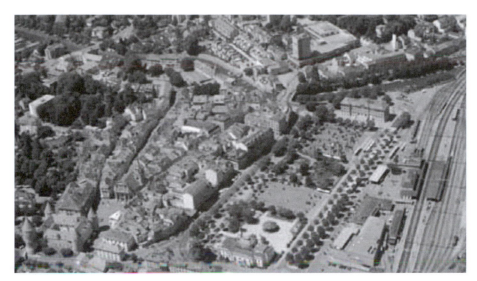

Figure 7.5.3 Site 6: Yverdon-les-Bains train station

Source: Author

and new parts of town near Lake Neuchâtel. The evaluation group reported that although this site received consistently favourable evaluations, no dominating advantages (strong green) were noted by the 30 evaluators. This indicates that the location is acceptable but not excellent. The group noted that the dislocation of the major cultural institution of the county outside its cultural centre would be a major political act of territorial policy. The group did not wish to take this political responsibility and for this reason it proposed that this site would be the best alternative only if the local government wished to support this political decision (Figure 7.5.3).

The following were identified:

- Advantages: excellent accessibility; land immediately available; good acceptance by local authorities and citizens alike; contribution to a coherent urban development of the city.
- Uncertainties: possibility for future extension; high risks related to rail traffic proximity.

7.5.4 The decision

The local government decided that the second proposition (the CFF locomotive hall, site 9) offered the greatest potential to satisfy the strategic objectives of the project: to develop a cultural project of major importance and to reinforce the county's image with respect to the arts. It was also considered that this scheme had the added value of transforming a disused industrial site, in partnership with the rail company, and that the scheme would ultimately attract the largest number of visitors; in part because of its location at a major national and international rail intersection, which also coincides with a city that hosts a diverse range of complementary cultural activities. Furthermore, it was considered that the site could be rendered highly visible to the public and that the renovated museum could be very effectively integrated with the existing urban fabric; indeed that it would contribute towards a new urban dynamic.

The local government did not reveal why it preferred the locomotive hall site over the other two. Reading between the lines, we may interpret the statements 'this choice will deliver the desired new museum' and '[this project benefits from a] well-established partnership between the owner of the land, the city and the state', to be in contrast with the risks of the first proposition. Although an original idea to restructure one of the city's major (malfunctioning) squares, this ambitious project needed the consensus and partnership of a larger group of actors; whereas the museum project is limited in duration to a time schedule of just four years. Furthermore, the appreciation of the local government of the central and well-designed location of the winning entry is also in contrast with the third proposition (Yverdon-les-Bains).

In short, the chosen solution was the best solution for the museum, whereas the other candidates offered strong associated advantages: site 11 for the renovation as a malfunctioning square and site 6 for the further development of an important secondary town. But these sites presented either an added risk or a cost premium for the museum.

7.5.5 Discussion

This example is an effective illustration of what we mean by 'multi-criteria decision support': the formulation by consensus of exhaustive criteria, the preparation of aggregation rules and the application of these criteria and aggregation rules to synthesize the effectiveness (or otherwise) of competing solutions to a given problem, to inform the final decision.

A decision normally results from rational reasoning; explaining and justifying a preference. It is constructed during the decision process as a result of interactions between the decision makers' minds, their past experiences and their environment. When the 11 candidate sites were presented, the local government had an initial perception of them. But it mandated the evaluation committee to thoroughly investigate them and present a recommendation. Each member of the evaluation committee also had an initial perception of each of the sites; perhaps even an established preference. This preference was founded on a partial knowledge of the sites and a partial understanding of their strengths and weaknesses, depending on the members' background. A member of the committee with an artistic background might understand differently a site compared to an environmentalist or an urban historian. Interaction between the group members helped them to construct a new more complete individual perception.

Thus, and in line with constructivist theory (Flourentzou, 2001), the initial perceptions of the individual group members were reconstituted and reconstructed. This took place in several iterations. First, the process of formulating the decision criteria structure changed the whole decision landscape; each member learned that the final decision should take into account a broader range of issues than can be addressed by their competence alone. Thus, preference reconstruction was different following from this iteration. Even if the preferred site was unchanged, this preference was founded on different rationale.

A further reconstitution and reconstruction took place when the committee visited each of the sites; yet another during informal discussions while travelling between the sites; yet another when the site stakeholders presented their cases and responded to questions; another upon reading experts' evaluation reports; another when they became acquainted with one another's evaluations (Plate 29) and so on. Thus, constructivist decision support helped to provide the necessary interactions, to enlarge the information spectrum and cover the key issues that might have a bearing on the decision making process – to make these decisions more rational, systematic and intelligible.

It seems unlikely that this process, which led to the preference of site B over sites A and C, could be substituted, with equivalent rigour and impartiality, with a single number (utility function) with which to compare the three sites. Indeed the absence of such a systematic consensual decision making process led to the rejection, following from a public referendum, of the local government's previously preferred solution.

7.6 Conclusions

We opened this chapter by challenging some of the popular perceptions and the language that is used in connection with urban sustainability; suggesting that sustainability in the urban context is a term that is somewhat misunderstood and overused. But this is in part symptomatic of the bewildering complexity of the subject, of the diverse range of factors that influence environmental, social and economic sustainability. In recognition of this complexity we suggest, at least for the immediate future, that multi-criteria decision support is an effective means for grappling with this complexity, that this can support the formulation by consensus of exhaustive criteria, the preparation of aggregation rules and the application of these criteria and aggregation rules to synthesize the effectiveness (or otherwise) of competing solutions to a given problem, so informing the final decision. Indeed, the effectiveness of this methodology has been demonstrated with respect to a project to choose the most appropriate location for a new fine art museum.

But the methodology outlined in this chapter is not directly amenable for use by computational optimization algorithms, which require a problem to be reduced to some numerical measure(s) of fitness. In this there may be little risk of arriving at false conclusions where the parameters being evaluated are essentially objective in nature; for example relating to urban energy use and associated emissions. But for more holistic measures of sustainability, considerably more work is required, perhaps based upon some kind of heuristic method for ranking potential solutions. This though would require some care to avoid introducing unacceptable bias into the evaluation and ranking process.

Appendix A7.1: Decision making tools based on Hermione

The Albatros method uses Hermione to find a site for public infrastructure according to sustainable criteria development (Merz et al, 2001).

Albatros D (for diagnosis) is an extension of Albatros for urban sustainability diagnosis (Desthieux et al, 2008).

'Boussole Vaudoise du Développement Durable' (Vaud sustainable development compass) uses Hermione to evaluate public policies and projects in administration decisions (www.boussole21.ch).

Smeo is an evaluation and decision support system for buildings' sustainability (www.smeo.ch).

Investimmo is a decision support system for sustainable investment in building stock management.

EstiaVia is a decision support method for the evaluation of sustainable logistics in transport (of goods).

All of these methods support decision makers to structure decision criteria, define qualitative evaluation scales and evaluate individual or aggregated criteria and sort actions as being favourable, uncertain or unfavourable.

Notes

1   Written by Darren Robinson.
2   In the meantime, we are encouraged to content ourselves with somewhat vague statements, such as the standard definition for sustainable development, which is development that 'meets the needs of the present without compromising the ability of future generations to meet their own needs'. But what do we mean by development? Do we understand this to mean *growth* or do we rather take this to mean *improvement*?
3   This also implies a degree of consensus as to which parameters should be considered when evaluating an urban settlement's sustainability.
4   www.ecoinvent.ch.
5   Despite the criticisms that may be levelled at utility function biases, this generic approach is convenient, useful and thus extensively used. Even if these methods are not always consensual, the oil boiler is always less preferred and the wood furnace is a greater source of local pollution. We might thus choose a heat pump for a town centre and a wood furnace in a rural setting where particles may be readily dispersed.

References

Bana e Costa, C. A. and Vansnick, J. C. (1995) 'General overview of the MACBETH approach', in P. M. Pardalos, Y. Siskos and C. Zopounidis (eds) *Advances in Multicriteria Analysis*, Kluwer Academic Publishers, pp93–100

Desthieux, G., Flourentzou, F. and Merz, C. (2008) 'Albatros D: Méthode de diagnostic urbain participatif : Application dans le cadre de l'aménagement de la Place du Marché de Vevey en Suisse', *Proc. OPDE*, Quebec, available at www.opde.crad.ulaval.ca/2008/documents/communications/Desthieux.pdf, last accessed 17 December 2010

Filchakova, N., Robinson, D. and Scartezzini, J.-L. (2007) 'Quo vadis thermodynamics and the city: a critical review of applications of thermodynamic methods to urban systems', *Int. J. Ecodynamics*, vol 2, no 4, pp222–230

Flourentzou, F. (2001) 'Constructivisme Piagetien dans l'Aide à la Décision. Contribution au Développement Durable en Architecture', PhD thesis No 2418, EPFL, Lausanne

Flourentzou, F., Greuter, G. and Roulet, C.-A. (2003), *'Hermione, une nouvelle méthode d'agrégation qualitative basée sur des règles', Proc. 58èmes journées du groupe de Travail Européen Aide Multicritère à la Décision, Moscow*, 9–11 October

Girardet, H. (1999) *Creating Sustainable Cities*, Schumacher Briefing 2, Green Books, Dartington, UK

Jolliet, O., Saadé, M. and Crettaz, P. (2010) *Analyse du cycle de vie*, Presses polytechniques et unversitaires romandes, Lausanne

Marchettini, N., Pulselli, F. M. and Tiezzi, E. (2006) 'Entropy and the city', *WIT Transactions on Ecology and Environment*, vol 93, pp263–272

Maystre, L. Y., Pictet, J. and Simos, J. (1994) *Méthodes multicritère Electre*, Presses polytechniques et unversitaires romandes, Lausanne

Merz, C., Gay, J.-B. and Flourentzou, F. (2001) 'Evaluation globale des besoins des choix initiaux', note interne, projet DD A1, LESO-PB, EPFL, Lausanne

Pictet, J. and Bollinger, D. (2003) *Adjuger un marché au mieux-disant – Analyse multicritère, pratique et droit des marchés publics*, Presses polytechniques et universitaires romandes, Lausanne

Roy, B. (1985) *Méthodologie multicritère d'aide à la décision*, Economica, Paris

Roy, B. (1992) Science de la décision ou science de l'aide à la décision?, *Revue internationale de la systémique*, Vol 6 No 5, Paris, 1992

Roy, B. (1999) Decision-aiding Today: What Should We Expect?, *Multiple Criteria Decision Making – Advances in MCDM Models, Algorithms, Theory and Applications*. T. G. et. al. Dordrecht, Kluwer: 1–35

Schärlig, A. (1990) *Décider sur plusieurs critères: Panorama de l'aide à la décision multicritère*, PPUR, Lausanne

Slowinski, R. (1992) (ed) *Intelligent Decision Support, Handbook of Application and Advances of the Rough Sets Theory*, Kluwer Academic publishers, Dordrecht

UN (2004) *World Urbanization Prospects: The 2003 Revision*, Department of Economic and Social Affairs/Population Division, UN, New York

8

Optimization of Urban Sustainability

Jérôme Kämpf and Darren Robinson

8.1 Introduction

The parameter space is infinitely large in which an optimal configuration of the variables that influence the sustainability of a new urban development is found, given that several of these variables may be continuous. In the case of the refurbishment of an existing development, the number of variables may be considerably reduced, constrained and perhaps only discrete. Our parameter space is thus much smaller but remains nevertheless too large to be effectively explored by manual trial and error or simple parametric studies within reasonable time constraints. It is appropriate then to use computational methods to efficiently explore this parameter space in the search for the most promising or optimal solutions.

Candidate methods include direct, indirect and heuristic search. Direct methods search for the optimal configuration in a random (for example Monte Carlo simulation) or in an algorithmic (for example Hooke-Jeeves) way that is not based on derivatives of the function being evaluated. Although more reliable than manual trial and error, random methods are relatively inefficient and algorithmic methods may become trapped in the region of a local optima. Indirect methods use mathematical techniques to identify an optimum in the parameter space, for example, by moving in a direction of steep gradient (steepest descent) where the solution should lie, but as with direct algorithmic methods, this optimum may also be a local and not a global one. Improved efficiency is thus contrasted by uncertainty. Heuristic methods, however, adapt, using stochastic operators, according to what they have learned about a given system. Such methods are relatively robust and efficient and can be applied to a wide variety of problems.

Following from a review of applications of heuristic optimization algorithms both generally and in the context of building simulation (Kämpf, 2009), the class of evolutionary optimization algorithms was selected for the basis of optimizing urban sustainability. In this chapter we describe the nature of the general optimization problem that we wish to resolve before presenting a new hybrid algorithm that has been developed and tested with the express purpose of optimizing urban sustainability. We go on to describe applications of this algorithm that, for the present time, are limited to optimizing buildings' energy performance. In this two types of application are described. The first addresses the optimization of urban geometry for the utilization of available solar radiation, while the second considers a considerably broader range of variables in optimizing buildings' primary energy use, using CitySim as the basis for energy simulation.

8.2 The optimization problem

In all generality, optimization algorithms search for a minimum[1] of a function f that depends on n independent decision variables. In formal terms, we are looking for the infimum and the corresponding set of variables that minimizes the function, as in [8.2.1]:

$$\inf\left\{f(\bar{x})\middle|\bar{x} \in M \subseteq \mathbb{R}^n\right\} \hspace{3cm} [8.2.1]$$

where $n \in \mathbb{N}$ is the dimension of the problem; $f : M \to \mathbb{R}$ is the objective function; $M = \left\{\bar{x} \in \mathbb{R}^n \middle| g_j(\bar{x}) \geq 0, \forall j \in \{1,...,m\}\right\}, M \neq 0$ is the feasible region; and $m \in \mathbb{N}$ is the number of constraints.

The set of inequality constraints $g_j : \mathbb{R}^n \to \mathbb{R}, \quad \forall j \in \{1,...,m\}$ includes a special case of constraints due to the domain boundaries $l_i \leq x_i \leq h_i$, where $l_i, h_i \in \mathbb{R}$ and $i = 1..n$. The symbol l_i refers to the lower bound and h_i to the upper or higher bound of the domain.

The function f has been found to be non-linear, multi-modal, discontinuous and hence non-differentiable in the simulation-based optimization of buildings' energy performance. In contrast with indirect search algorithms, which rely on the function's derivatives, heuristic methods do not require smoothness of the objective function, but instead use probabilistic operators to search for an improvement in this function. They are thus better adapted to this type of problem. We are mindful, however, that one cannot guarantee that the global optimum will be found with a finite number of simulations. But heuristic algorithms are able to find a good solution in a computationally tractable way.

8.3 A new hybrid evolutionary algorithm

Evolutionary algorithms (EAs) are a family of optimization methods based upon the principles of Darwinian natural selection (Mitchell, 1998; Goldberg, 1992; Fogel, 2006). They are population-based heuristic algorithms, where each individual represents a potential solution of the function to optimize. A population of μ individuals is randomly chosen as a starting point. This first, and each subsequent generation, then passes through three evolutionary operators: recombination between individuals, random mutation of their alleles and selection of the fittest. One iteration of the strategy is a step from a population P^n to P^{n+1}, where n is the generation number, and can be written as:

$$P^{n+1} := opt_{EA}(P^n) \qquad\qquad [8.3.1]$$

The optimization of P^n is defined by the operators *sel* (selection), *mut* (mutation) and *rec* (recombination) in the following way:

$$opt_{EA} := sel \circ (mut \circ rec)^\lambda, \qquad\qquad [8.3.2]$$

where λ corresponds to the number of new individuals (children).

According to the type of EA, a phase of adaptation of the parameters or migration of individuals might follow from their selection. The termination criterion for each iteration is met when the maximum number of function evaluations is reached. Since this is roughly proportional to the total computing time, we are able to define an (approximate) upper limit of time required for the optimization process, provided of course that we know in advance how long it takes to evaluate the function of interest. When reached, the algorithm exits and returns the individual that has performed best up to that point. The objective function value for a potential solution is often referred to as the fitness of an individual.

The first evolutionary algorithms, proposed in the mid-1960s, were the genetic algorithms (GAs) of John Holland (Holland, 1975) from the University of Michigan, the evolutionary programming (EP) of Lawrence Fogel (Fogel et al, 1966) from the University of California in San Diego and independently the evolution strategies (ESs) of Ingo Rechenberg (Rechenberg, 1973) from the Technical University of Berlin. Their work introduced a wide class of optimization methods for difficult problems where little is known about the underlying search space. John Koza (Koza, 1992), with the introduction of genetic programming (GP) at the beginning of the 1990s, further enriched the class of EAs.

ESs were first developed by Rechenberg (1973) and Schwefel (1995) and have evolved into the cumulative step path adaptation evolution strategy (CSA-ES) algorithm (Beyer and Schwefel, 2002; Dirk and MacLeod, 2006) and the covariance matrix adaptation evolution strategy (CMA-ES) algorithm (Hansen and Ostermeier, 2001; Hansen and Kern, 2004). The variables of the function to optimize are coded using a floating point representation and are associated in phenotypes with standard deviations for mutation purposes. The CMA-ES has been used to solve a wide range of optimization problems (Hansen and Kern, 2004) and is regarded as one of the best algorithms for real value coded variables. However, Hansen and Kern (2004) conclude that CMA-ES is outperformed by the differential evolution (DE) algorithm in situations where the function to optimize is additively separable. The DE algorithm was developed by Storn and Price in 1996 (Storn and Price, 1996) and has proven to be another good candidate for real value optimization problems. DE, which is based on stochastic search, is very simple to implement and relies only on variables with a floating point representation. However, one of its drawbacks is the need for a large population to overcome local optima. To address this shortfall, Chang et al (2007) have developed a hybrid differential evolution (HDE) algorithm to allow for the use of a smaller population. For all kinds of DE, the results are very sensitive to the algorithm control parameters (Nobakhti and Wang, 2008), so that these parameters must be carefully chosen.

Reiterating the conclusion of Hansen and Kern (2004): 'Only if the function is additively separable, Differential Evolution strongly outperforms the CMA-ES'. We therefore considered that a hybrid CMA-ES/HDE algorithm might combine the advantages of the two optimization methods, since in real life applications we tend to face optimization problems where the dependence of the function on its variable is unknown. This then might be a good compromise in terms of robustness and convergence speed, as it should perform well on both additively and non-additively separable functions.

In urban energy use minimization problems, buildings that are distant from one another and are not served by the same finite capacity energy network in a simulated scene, have weak or inexistent interactions. Therefore, with respect to their variables, the objective function is essentially additively separable. But this is not necessarily the case for adjacent buildings, for which the objective function is rather non-additively separable. This reinforces the development of a hybrid optimizer that may face both additively and non-additively separable problems.

8.3.1 Covariance matrix adaptation evolution strategy

A detailed description of this algorithm can be found in Hansen and Ostermeier (2001) and Hansen and Kern (2004). Each individual in the population $P = \{\vec{a_1}, \vec{a_2}, ., \vec{a_\mu}\}$ referred to by an index $k = 1..\mu$ has a phenotype $\vec{a_k} = (\vec{x_k}, \vec{z_k})$ with $\vec{x_k}, \vec{z_k} \in \mathbb{R}^n$, where $\vec{x_k}$ is the standard ES parameter vector and $\vec{z_k}$ is the associated standard deviation vector. ESs are known to be phenotypic algorithms as they operate directly on the parameters of the system itself, unlike GAs that operate at the genotypic level and need a coding/decoding step to obtain the phenotype. Each element of the phenotype is known as an allele. Three matrices are needed for the algorithm: the covariance matrix $C \in \mathbb{R}^{n \times n}$, the eigenvector matrix of C named $C \in \mathbb{R}^{n \times n}$ and the diagonal matrix of the square rooted eigenvalues of C, named $C \in \mathbb{R}^{n \times n}$. The μ individuals of the initial population are randomly defined ($\vec{x_k}$ are randomly chosen within the domain boundaries of f and $\vec{z_k}$ are set to the null vector). Matrix B is set to the identity matrix and the diagonal matrix D is set to represent the domain boundaries $D_{ii} = h_i - l_i, \forall i = 1..n$. C is calculated as the product of BD and its transpose: $BD \cdot (BD)^t$. Plate 31 shows graphically the operators of recombination, mutation and selection for a function of two parameters (x_1, x_2). The functioning of these operators is described in the following sections.

Recombination

Using the global weighted intermediate recombination method in conjunction with a sorted population (the best individual is number 1, the worst is μ), λ identical children are created with a phenotype:

$$(\vec{x_b})_i = \sum_{k=1}^{\mu} \omega_k \cdot (\vec{x_k})_i, \forall i = 1..n \qquad [8.3.3]$$

$$(\vec{z_b})_i = 0, \forall i = 1..n \qquad [8.3.4]$$

in which the individual index h goes from $(\mu+1)$ to $(\mu+\lambda)$ and ω_k are the weights of the recombination, which are themselves parameters of the algorithm. In this study we take $\omega_k = \dfrac{\log(\mu+1)-\log(k)}{\sum\limits_{l=1}^{\mu}(log(\mu+1)-log(l))}$ from Hansen and Ostermeier (2001), which gives more weight to the best individuals of the population.

Mutation

The main mechanism of the mutation operator is changing the allele values by adding random noise drawn from a normal distribution. The randomness from the normal distribution is stored in the individual phenotype and used in the adaptation phase. The mutation acts on each of the λ children with a modification of their phenotype in the following order:

$$(\vec{z_h})_i \leftarrow N_i^h(0,1), \forall i = 1..n$$

$$(\vec{x_h})_i \leftarrow (\vec{x_h})_i + \sigma_F \cdot \sum_{k=1}^{n} B_{ik} \cdot D_{kk} \cdot (\vec{z_h})_k, \forall i = 1..n \tag{8.3.5}$$

where $N_i^h(0,1)$ is a random number drawn from a normal distribution sampled anew for each element i of each individual $h = (\mu+1)..(\mu+\lambda)$ and the symbol $\leftarrow$ means that $(\vec{z_h})_i$ and $(\vec{x_h})_i$ will take the values on their RHS. The global step size $\sigma_F \in \mathbb{R}_+$ is a (problem-dependent) parameter of the algorithm.

A mutated individual may happen to be outside the box constraints, if this is the case, it is put back inside the domain by taking:

$$(\vec{x_h})_i \leftarrow \min\left((\vec{x_h})_i, h_i\right) \tag{8.3.6}$$

$$(\vec{x_h})_i \leftarrow \max\left((\vec{x_h})_i, l_i\right) \tag{8.3.7}$$

In order to provide random numbers that follow a normal distribution, we use the Ziggurat method (Marsaglia and Tsang, 2000).

Selection

Elitist selection is used to retain the μ best individuals of the λ children.

Adaptation

Three parameters of the algorithm are adapted in this phase. These are the global step size σ_F, the orthogonal matrix B and the diagonal matrix D. More precisely, the covariance matrix C, used for the determination of B and D, is adapted. The global step size $\sigma_F \in \mathbb{R}_+$ is adapted using a 'conjugate' evolution path $\vec{s} \in \mathbb{R}^n$, in the following order:

$$\vec{s} \leftarrow (1-c_s)\vec{s} + \sqrt{\mu_{eff} \cdot c_s(2-c_s)} \cdot B \cdot \sum_{k=1}^{\mu} \omega_k \vec{z}_k,$$

[8.3.8]

$$\sigma_F \leftarrow \sigma_F \cdot exp\left(\left(\frac{s}{\chi_n}-1\right) \cdot \frac{c_s}{d_s}\right),$$

where $\quad \overline{\chi_n} = \sqrt{n}(1-1/4n+1/21n^2)$, $\quad c_s = \dfrac{\mu_{eff}+2}{n+\mu_{eff}+3}$, $\quad d_s = 1+2 \cdot max$

$\left(0, \sqrt{\dfrac{\mu_{eff}-1}{n+1}}-1\right)+c_s$, $\mu_{eff} = 1/\sum_{k=1}^{\mu} \omega_k^2$ and s is the vector norm of $\vec{s}$. The initial

conjugate evolution path is $\vec{s} = \vec{0}$.

The covariance matrix $C \in \mathbb{R}^{n \times n}$ is adapted using the evolution path $\vec{c} \in \mathfrak{R}^n$ in the following way:

$$\vec{c} \leftarrow (1-c_c)\vec{c} + H_s \cdot \sqrt{\mu_{eff} \cdot c_c(2-c_c)} \cdot BD \cdot \sum_{k=1}^{\mu} \omega_k \vec{z}_k$$

[8.3.9]

$$C \leftarrow (1-c_{cov})C + c_{cov} \cdot \frac{1}{\mu_{eff}} \cdot \vec{c} \cdot \vec{c}^t + c_{cov} \cdot \left(1-\frac{1}{\mu_{eff}}\right) \cdot \sum_{k=1}^{\mu} (BD \cdot \vec{z}_k)(BD \cdot \vec{z}_k)^t$$

where $c_{cov} = \dfrac{1}{\mu_{eff}} \cdot \dfrac{2}{\left(n+\sqrt{2}\right)^2} + \left(1-\dfrac{1}{\mu_{eff}}\right) \cdot min\left(1, \dfrac{2\mu_{eff}-1}{(n+2)^2+\mu_{eff}}\right)$, $c_c = \dfrac{4}{n+4}$ and

$H_s = 1$ if $\dfrac{s}{\sqrt{1-(1-c_s)^{2(g+1)}}} < \left(1.5+\dfrac{1}{n-0.5}\right)\overline{\chi_n}$ or 0 otherwise (the symbol g

corresponds to the generation number). The initial evolution path is $\vec{c} = \vec{0}$.

Once adapted, the orthogonal matrix B and diagonal matrix D are obtained through principal component analysis of C (i.e. $C = BD^2B^t$).

8.3.2 The HDE algorithm

Following Storn and Price (1996), Feoktistov (2006) and Chang et al (2007), the individuals are coded with real value representations. The population $P = \{\vec{a}_1, \vec{a}_2, .., \vec{a}_{NP}\}$ is composed of NP individuals and their phenotype is given by $\vec{a}_k = (\vec{x}_k), \vec{x}_k \in \mathbb{R}^n$ where $\vec{x}_k$ is the parameter vector for individual $k = 1..NP$. The initial population is randomly distributed in the domain of the function to optimize. Plate 32 shows graphically the operators of mutation, recombination and selection for a function of two parameters (x_1, x_2). The functioning of the operators is described in the following.

Recombination and mutation

For each candidate member of the parent population $k = 1..NP$ a trial individual $\vec{w}_k \in \mathbb{R}^n$ is generated thus:

$$\overrightarrow{\omega}_k = \overrightarrow{\beta}_k + F \cdot \overrightarrow{\delta}_k,$$

[8.3.10]

where F is the differentiation constant (which controls the amplification of the differentiation), $\vec{\beta}_k$ is the base vector and $\vec{\delta}_k$ is the differentiation vector.

The differentiation strategy used in our study is *Rand3* (Feoktistov, 2006) where $\vec{\delta}_k = \vec{\xi}_1 - \vec{\xi}_2$ and $\vec{\beta}_k = \vec{\xi}_3$. $\{\vec{\xi}_1, \vec{\xi}_2, \vec{\xi}_3\}_k$ are randomly chosen individuals in the population sampled anew for each $k = 1..NP$.

A crossover is then carried out between the trial and the corresponding candidate:

$$\overrightarrow{(\omega_k)}_i \leftarrow \begin{cases} \overrightarrow{(\omega_k)}_i, & if\ (rand_i(0,1) \geq C_r\ or\ R = i) \\ \overrightarrow{(a_k)}_i, & otherwise \end{cases} \qquad [8.3.11]$$

where C_r is the crossover probability, R is a randomly selected allele number defined before the crossover (this forces at least one allele to change) and $rand_i(0,1)$ is a random number between zero and one sampled anew for each allele i.

But the trial individual may happen to be outside of the box constraints. In this case, it is returned randomly inside the domain by taking:

$$\overrightarrow{(\omega_b)}_i \leftarrow rand_i(l_i, h_i), \qquad [8.3.12]$$

where $rand_i(l_i, h_i)$ is a randomly chosen number within the upper h_i and lower l_i boundaries of allele i.

The resulting trial individuals are contained in a set of NP individuals for the selection phase.

Selection

The best individual between the candidate in the parent population and the corresponding trial is kept.

Migration

In order to reduce the population size and avoid stagnation in the region of a local optimum, Chang et al (2007) proposed a migration technique. When the diversity ρ of the population is too small (i.e. $\rho < \varepsilon_1$), all individuals are modified according to the rule:

$$\overrightarrow{(x_k)}_i \leftarrow \begin{cases} \overrightarrow{(x_k)}_i + \rho_1 \cdot (L_i - \overrightarrow{(x_b)}_i), & if\ \rho_2 < \dfrac{\overrightarrow{(x_k)}_i - L_i}{H_i - L_i} \\ \overrightarrow{(x_k)}_i + \rho_1 \cdot (H_i - \overrightarrow{(x_b)}_i), & otherwise \end{cases} \qquad [8.3.13]$$

where $i = 1..n$, $\vec{x}_b$ is the best individual of the actual population and ρ_1, ρ_2 are two random numbers chosen between 0 and 1 and sampled anew for each element of each individual.

The diversity ρ is defined as follows:

$$\rho = \sum_{k=1}^{\mu} \sum_{i=1}^{n} \frac{\chi_{ki}}{n \cdot (\mu - 1)} \qquad [8.3.14]$$

where:

$$\chi_{ki} = \begin{cases} 1 & if \left| \dfrac{(\bar{x}_k)_i - (\bar{x}_b)_i}{(\bar{x}_b)_i} \right| > \varepsilon_2 \quad and \quad \left| (\bar{x}_k)_i - (\bar{x}_b)_i \right| > (\bar{\varepsilon}_3)_i \\ \\ 0 & otherwise \end{cases}$$ [8.3.15]

with $\varepsilon_2 \in \mathbb{R}_+$ and $\bar{\varepsilon}_3 \in \mathbb{R}_+^n$, which are respectively the relative precision and the absolute precision vectors for the problem solved. We have introduced the parameter $\bar{\varepsilon}_3$, which was not originally included in the HDE, to take into account the desired number of decimal places in these variables.

8.3.3 The hybrid algorithm (CMA-ES/HDE)

Figure 8.3.1 depicts the proposed hybrid algorithm in schematic form. The HDE and CMA-ES operate in series. We distinguish two populations: popHDE and popCMA-ES that are associated with the HDE and the CMA-ES. We start

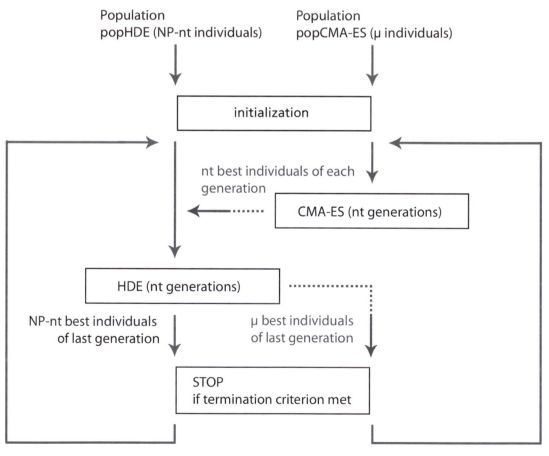

Figure 8.3.1 The hybrid algorithm – a coupling of CMA-ES and HDE

Note: Two distinct populations popHDE and popCMA-ES go through evolution process (solid lines) exchanging individuals (dashed lines).

with the CMA-ES, using a random population for *nt* steps (or generations). This then feeds the best *nt* individuals at each step to the population of HDE and the missing (*NP* – *nt*) individuals in popHDE are randomly generated. We then continue with the HDE for *nt* generations. We retain from the last generation of HDE the *μ* and (*NP* – *nt*) best individuals. If the termination criterion is met, the algorithm is stopped; otherwise it loops and switches over to the CMA-ES. For the following applications, we have chosen to run each algorithm for *nt* = ten generations.

This hybrid CMA-ES/HDE algorithm has been found to consistently locate the global optimum of the standard Ackley and Rastrigin benchmark functions (Kämpf and Robinson, 2009). It also outperforms, in terms of robustness, a hybrid of the Particle Swarm Optimization and Hooke-Jeeves (PSO/HJ) algorithms when applied to real-world problems (Kämpf et al, 2010).

Constraint handling and applications

Constraint handling

The feasible domain *M* is generally written in the form:

$$M = \left\{ \vec{x} \in \mathbb{R} \mid g_j(\vec{x}) \leq 0, \forall j \in \{1,...,m\} \right\} \qquad [8.3.16]$$

where $g_j : \mathbb{R}^n \rightarrow \mathbb{R}, \forall j \in \{1,...,m\}$ are *m* constraint functions of the parameters $\vec{x}$. For computational reasons we want to avoid evaluating potential solutions that do not satisfy the constraints. To this end we have redefined the objective function:

$$\hat{f}(\vec{x}) = \begin{cases} f(\vec{x}) & \vec{x} \in M, \\ +\infty & \text{otherwise,} \end{cases} \qquad [8.3.17]$$

and implemented the 'Modification of the Selection Operation' proposed by Feoktistov (2006). This redefines the 'is better than' operator, by taking into account a pure Pareto dominance defined in a constraint function space. This operator is defined as follows: $\vec{x_1}$ is better than $\vec{x_2}$ if and only if $\Phi \vee \Psi$, where:

$$\Phi = \left(\forall k \in \{1,.,m\} : g_k(\vec{x_1}) \leq 0 \wedge g_k(\vec{x_2}) \leq 0 \right) \wedge \left(f(\vec{x_1}) < f(\vec{x_2}) \right),$$

$$\Psi = \left(\exists k \in \{1,.,m\} : g_k(\vec{x_1}) > 0 \right) \wedge \left(\forall k \in \{1,.,m\} : \max(g_k(\vec{x_1}),0) \leq \max(g_k(\vec{x_2}),0) \right). \qquad [8.3.18]$$

The important thing to consider here is that this method of handling constraints allows individuals violating the constraints to survive in the first generations of the algorithms. In this way they participate in the recombination process, so bringing diversity and allowing the borders of the constrained parameter space to be approached. The application of this comparison operator within the CMA-ES and HDE is explained below.

In CMA-ES, the mutation phase is repeated on an individual as long as it remains outside of the constrained space, but for a maximum of ten times. The comparison operator described above is applied to the population of children for sorting, prior to the elitist selection of the new generation's parents.

In HDE, in the selection phase, the comparison operator is used to compare the candidate with the trial (in that order). If the candidate is better than the trial, the candidate is kept; otherwise the trial is kept. This ensures that when both individuals satisfy the constraints and the objective functions are equal, the trial is preferred, bringing diversity to the population and preventing stagnation. Moreover, when both individuals do not satisfy the constraints, the candidate individual is kept only if it dominates over all constraints at the same time, allowing the trial to be selected in most cases, for the same diversity reasons.

Benchmark function

The following benchmark function has 13 variables and 9 linear constraints, it was designed to test different constraint handling methods (Michalewicz and Schoenauer, 1996):

$$f(\bar{x}) = 5x_1 + 5x_2 + 5x_3 + 5x_4 - 5\sum_{i=1}^{4} x_i^2 - \sum_{i=5}^{13} x_i + 15, \qquad [8.3.19]$$

subject to the following constraints:

$$2x_1 + 2x_2 + x_{10} + x_{11} \leq 10, \quad -8x_1 + x_{10} \leq 0, \quad -2x_4 - x_5 + x_{10} \leq 0,$$

$$2x_1 + 2x_3 + x_{10} + x_{11} \leq 10, \quad -8x_2 + x_{11} \leq 0, \quad -2x_6 - x_7 + x_{11} \leq 0,$$

$$2x_1 + 2x_3 + +x_{11} + x_{12} \leq 10, \quad -8x_3 + x_{12} \leq 0, \quad -2x_8 - x_9 + x_{12} \leq 0.$$

Its domain is $0 \leq x_i \leq 1$, for all $i = 1..9$ and $i = 13$ with an absolute precision $\bar{\varepsilon}_{3i} = 0.01$ and $0 \leq x_i \leq 100$ for $i = 10, 11, 12$ with $\bar{\varepsilon}_{3i} = 0.1$. The function is quadratic with a global minimum at $f(1,1,1,1,1,1,1,1,1,3,3,3,1) = 0$.

The topology of the feasible region and the characteristic of the objective function are quite significant measures of the difficulty of problems according to Michalewicz and Schoenauer (1996). In this benchmark function even though the objective function is only quadratic, the topology of the nine linear constraints makes it very difficult to resolve unless the algorithm has access to the objective function value outside of the constrained domain.

Results

In a total of 100 simulations, 39 runs converged to the global minimum (considered by a fitness of under 0.2) within 4207±1328 evaluations, using a limit of 10,000 evaluations. This performance is relatively poor compared to other methods that do evaluate the objective function outside of the constrained domain (Runarsson and Yao, 2000), but the choice of our constraint handling method, which does not necessitate an objective function evaluation, was made for computational cost and robustness reasons. Due to its recombination and mutation operators, the CMA-ES/HDE tends to explore the interior of the domain boundaries, making it difficult to approach the boundaries where the global minimum is found. However, thanks to the constraint handling procedure within the mutation phase of the CMA-ES algorithm, we observe that the border of the domain can sometimes be approached and the global minimum successfully identified. This result is rather encouraging, as in real world applications the global minimum does not generally lie exactly at the domain boundaries, making the problem less difficult to resolve for the CMA-ES/HDE.

8.4 Solar irradiation maximization with constraints

In recent studies Cheng et al (2006) and Montavon (2010) have used simulations of annual solar irradiation incident on built surfaces to identify, by trial and error, an optimal configuration of urban design variables. But the region of the available parameter space that is explored in this way is infinitesimal and thus unlikely to locate a global optimum or indeed to suggest with confidence what form this optimum might take. In this first application of the hybrid CMA-ES/HDE algorithm we attempt to resolve this issue, to identify global optima for some arbitrarily chosen building and urban geometry optimization problems.

8.4.1 Solar irradiation potential determination

In order to predict as precisely as possible the irradiation on building envelopes, we use the ray tracing program RADIANCE (Larson and Shakespeare, 1998). In a similar fashion to PPF (Compagnon, 2004), we define grid points and normal vectors on each surface of our building envelopes. Such information may be used by the program *r-trace* to calculate the incident irradiance (W/m²) given a sky radiance distribution and sun position and radiance. However, to compute the irradiation (Wh/m^2) as opposed to irradiance (W/m^2), we define a cumulative sky, as in Robinson and Stone (2004), for the period of interest (see Chapter 2). The product of this irradiation (Wh/m^2) and the surface area covered by the grid point (m^2), for the whole set of grid points, gives the total irradiation received by a building (Wh). This irradiation calculation is summarized in Plate 33.

Each measuring point corresponds to a subsurface on which the irradiation is supposed to be uniform. The distribution of the grid points on the building surfaces should be reasonably uniform and their number should be adapted to the precision we desire in the prediction of total irradiation. We therefore devised a method to decompose the building's surfaces into four smaller surfaces that can in turn also be subdivided. Figure 8.4.1 shows the procedure

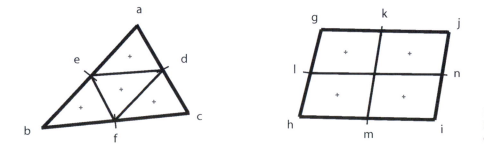

Figure 8.4.1 The building's surface decomposition

for triangular and quadrilateral decomposition, depending on whether the original surface is triangular or quadrilateral.

The criterion to stop this subdivision is a maximum allowable surface area. Due to the potentially large number of sampling points, it is desirable to find a compromise between accuracy and computing time. To this end, a sensitivity analysis was carried out to determine both the maximum allowed surface area and the RADIANCE simulation parameters.

8.4.2 A Manhattan-style grid

In this application a hypothetical city comprised of cuboidal shapes was created with the objective of maximizing the annual irradiation incident on all buildings. The initial configuration is shown in Figure 8.4.2.

Each of the 25 buildings may have their height varied, so that there are in total 25 parameters, which describe the number of floors (a maximum of 123) in each building:

$$\left\{\vec{x} \in \mathbb{R}^{25} \middle| x_i \in [0,123], i = 1..25\right\} \qquad [8.4.1]$$

These parameters are rounded to the nearest integer before the evaluation and the floors are each considered to be 3m high. Simulating all possibilities would require 124^{25} evaluations of the solar potential, which is not feasible. To reduce the cost of the evaluation process to a reasonable minimum, reflected radiation is ignored.

The constrained parameter space is defined by the total built volume remaining within 10 per cent of half of the maximum ($25 \cdot 40 \cdot 60 \cdot 123 \cdot 3/2 \pm 10\% \text{m}^3$). Expressed mathematically this constraint gives:

$$\underbrace{v(\vec{x}) - v(\vec{x}_{max}) \cdot 50\% \cdot 110\%}_{g_1(\vec{x})} \leq 0, \qquad [8.4.2]$$

(a)   (b)

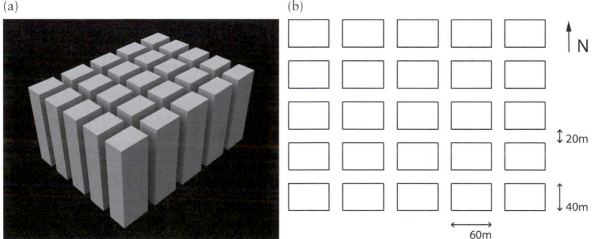

Figure 8.4.2 (a) A RADIANCE generated image of the Manhattan style grid and (b) a schematic view from top

$$\underbrace{-v(\vec{x}) + v(\vec{x}_{max}) \cdot 50\% \cdot 90\%}_{g_2(\vec{x})} \leq 0, \qquad\qquad [8.4.3]$$

where $\vec{x}_{max} = (123,...,123)$ and $v(\vec{x})$ is the volume corresponding to parameters in $\vec{x}$. We thus have two linear constraints, giving a range of possible volumes.

Results

A candidate solution, presented in Plate 34 and Figure 8.4.3, was found after some 12,000 evaluations.

Buildings at the northern edge of this grid are all at maximum height, whereas buildings at the east and particularly south and west edges are irregular, with some at or approaching the maximum height and some considerably lower. This arrangement provides solar access for the lower interior buildings and (more particularly) for the southern façades of the buildings at the northern edge.

Plate 35a shows the evolution of the fitness (annual solar irradiation) of the candidates along with the evaluations made in the evolutionary algorithm. The CMA-ES part of the algorithm provides a steep rise in fitness at the beginning of the simulation, while the HDE part goes deeper in fine-tuning the solution.

In Table 8.4.1, we can see the improvement gained with our optimization algorithm relative to two subjectively chosen variants – the corona and stair shaped layouts shown in Plate 35b, both of which satisfy the constraints mentioned earlier. Relative to the corona shape, the optimized shape (which would not necessarily be arrived at by intuition) yields an 8 per cent improvement for a similar built volume; whereas relative to the stairs layout the

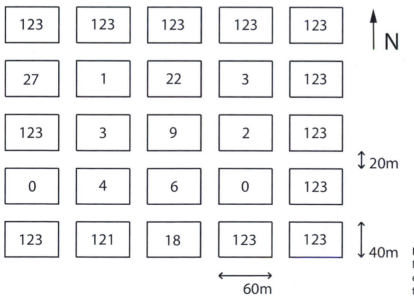

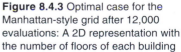

Figure 8.4.3 Optimal case for the Manhattan-style grid after 12,000 evaluations: A 2D representation with the number of floors of each building

Table 8.4.1 Irradiance values comparison for the optimized case, the corona and stairs cases

Parameters	Irradiation (GWh)	Volume (-10^7 m³)
Stairs shape (floors are multiple of 22, see Plate 35	282.2 (82%)	1.188
Corona shape (border buildings with 105 floors, internal buildings with one floor)	319.5 (93%)	1.216
Optimal shape after 12,000 evaluations	344.9 (100%)	1.217

improvement is 22 per cent. This is interesting because conventional site planning guidance suggests that buildings should be progressively stepped-up towards the north of a site to maximize solar access (Littlefair et al, 2000).

8.4.3 An extension of a mansion to integrate photovoltaic cells

An extension of a mansion was planned as part of an architectural studio design project, for which it was intended to install photovoltaic panels on the newly created building surfaces. In this the objective was to orient and tilt the roof surfaces so that they would receive the maximum available irradiation throughout the year. The scene is shown in Figure 8.4.4, in which the extension is decomposed into triangles on the schematic plan. For computational reasons, reflected radiation is once again neglected.

Each of the 31 triangle vertices may take a height of between 3 and 6m:

$$\left\{ \vec{x} \in \mathbb{R}^{31} \middle| x_i \in [3,6], i = 1..31 \right\} \qquad [8.4.4]$$

A key constraint is that the roof must maintain a convex shape, as observed from above. In other words, the height of each internal point must be greater

(a)   (b)

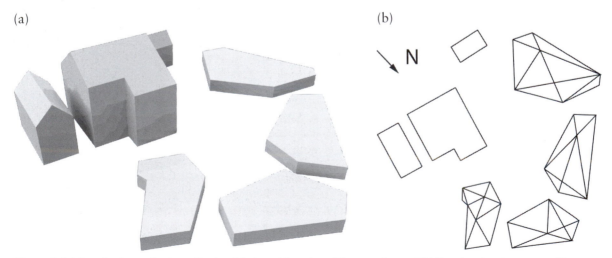

Figure 8.4.4 A projection and schematic plan (a) viewed from top of the mansion and (b) its extension decomposed in triangles on the 2D schematic plan

than or equal to that of the external point(s) to which it is connected. In total then we have 32 constraints.

Results

For this case, a candidate solution, shown in Plate 36 and Figure 8.4.5, was found after 12,000 evaluations. Compared to flat roofs at heights of 3m and 6m, the improvement is about 10 per cent in annual irradiation (see Table 8.4.2). With an annual irradiation of 1.234GWh and an average photovoltaic efficiency of 10 per cent, the gain is equivalent to 11.6MWh of electrical energy, which is non-negligible. Roof-integrated photovoltaics would appear to be viable in this case.

8.4.4 2D Fourier series generation of roof geometry

In this hypothetical application, we use a 2D Fourier series to describe the geometry of a roof as a continuous function with relatively few terms; the

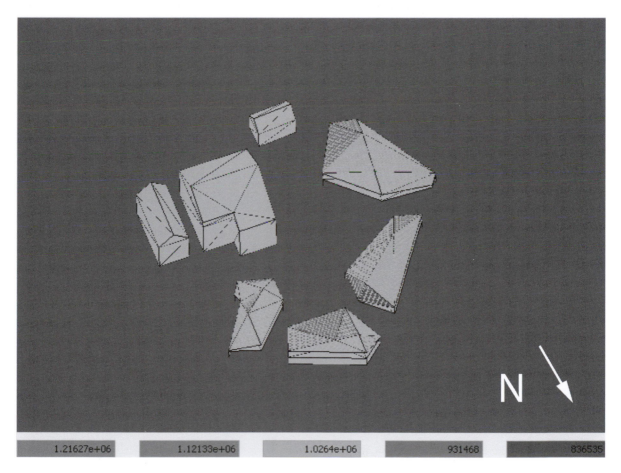

| 1.21627e+06 | 1.12133e+06 | 1.0264e+06 | 931468 | 836535 |

Figure 8.4.5 Optimal case for the photovoltaic extension after 12,000 evaluations

Table 8.4.2 Irradiation values comparison for the optimized case and flat roofs

Parameters	Irradiation (GWh)
Minimal values $h_i = 3\ m, i = 1..31$	1.118 (91%)
Maximum values $h_i = 6\ m, i = 1..31$	1.131 (92%)
Optimal shape after 12,000 evaluations	1.234 (100%)

objective here being to test the use of the EA as a generator of visually interesting shapes, as a stimulus for architectural and urban design. Once again we seek to maximize the utilization of annual solar irradiation, this time on both the roof and the vertical façades. Plate 37 and Figure 8.4.6 show an example of a roof shape described by a 2D Fourier series.

For this application, the 2D Fourier series is expressed in terms of sines and cosines with N and M impairs:

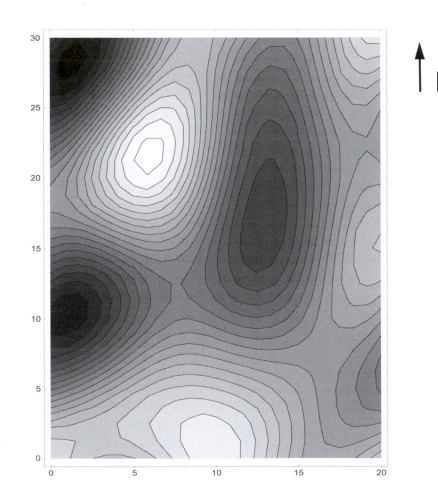

Figure 8.4.6 A roof represented by a contour plot representing the height

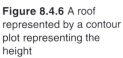

$$h(x,y) = \sum_{k=-\frac{N-1}{2}}^{\frac{N-1}{2}} \sum_{l=-\frac{M-1}{2}}^{\frac{M-1}{2}} C_{kl} \cdot e^{\left(2\pi i k \frac{x}{L_x \frac{N}{N-1}} + 2\pi i l \frac{y}{L_y \frac{M}{M-1}}\right)}$$

$$= \sum_{k=-\frac{N-1}{2}}^{\frac{N-1}{2}} \sum_{l=0}^{\frac{M-1}{2}} A_{kl} \cdot \cos\left(2\pi k \frac{x}{L_x \frac{N}{N-1}} + 2\pi l \frac{y}{L_y \frac{M}{M-1}}\right) \qquad [8.4.5]$$

$$+ B_{kl} \cdot \sin\left(2\pi k \frac{x}{L_x \frac{N}{N-1}} + 2\pi l \frac{y}{L_y \frac{M}{M-1}}\right),$$

where $h : \mathbb{R}^2 \to \mathbb{R}$ gives the height as a function of the position (x,y) in the plane, $x \in [0, L_x], y \in [0, L_y]$, L_x and L_y delimit the domain of interest in x and y, $C_{kl} \in \mathbb{R}$ are coefficients of elements in the Fourier basis and $A_{kl}, B_{kl} \in \mathbb{R}$ are the amplitudes of the sines and cosines.

By definition, the function $h(x,y)$ is periodic in x and y. The period is $T_x = L_x \frac{N}{N-1}$ and $T_y = L_y \frac{M}{M-1}$ respectively for x and y. Multiplication by the factors $\frac{N}{N-1}$ and $\frac{M}{M-1}$ is introduced in order to avoid repetition in the domain of interest $x \in [0, L_x]$ and $y \in [0, L_y]$.

By considering the Fourier series in [8.4.5] as a backward discrete Fourier transform we have a continuous function that can pass through a grid of $N \cdot M$ regularly spaced points in the domain of interest. Such points are shown in Figure 8.4.6 and Plate 37, with the corresponding backward Fourier transform superimposed (for $N = M = 5$). It can be shown that the coefficients A_{kl} for $l = 0$ are symmetric with k, so that $A_{k0} = A_{-k0}$. Likewise the coefficients B_{kl} for $l = 0$ are antisymmetric with k, i.e. $B_{k0} = -B_{-k0}$. Therefore to describe a surface that goes through $N \cdot M$ points, we need $N \cdot (M-1)/2 + (N-1)/2 + 1$ amplitudes for A_{kl} and $N \cdot (M-1)/2 + (N-1)/2$ for B_{kl}, which also gives $N \cdot M$ amplitudes. This observation allows us to use directly the amplitudes of the sines and cosines as parameters in the optimization process.[2]

For our numerical application, the domain boundaries were chosen to be $L_x = 20\text{m}$, $L_y = 30\text{m}$ and $N = M = 5$, giving just 25 parameters. The amplitude A_{00} is the base amplitude, which is a constant value throughout the domain. It was chosen to vary between 0 and 10m. The other amplitudes are limited between a lower and an upper limit; in total three cases are tested:

1) $A_{kl}, B_{kl} \in [-\frac{1}{2}, \frac{1}{2}]$ but $A_{00} \in [0,10]$

2) $A_{kl}, B_{kl} \in [-1,1]$ but $A_{00} \in [0,10]$

3) $A_{kl}, B_{kl} \in [-2,2]$ but $A_{00} \in [0,10]$

A minimal cut value was chosen in the height of the surface at 0m, so that when the surface goes below the ground (placed at 0m), it is not taken into account in the irradiation calculation. Further constraints dictate that the volume contained by the roof surface must remain within 10 per cent of 80 per cent of the maximum allowed volume, which is defined by a parallelepiped of 10m by 20m by 30m (i.e. $10m \cdot L_x \cdot L_y$). In mathematical form these constraints are similar to those of the first application ([8.4.2] and [8.4.3]).

Results

The results, after 12,000 evaluations, are shown in Figures 8.4.7, 8.4.8 and 8.4.9, and Plates 38, 39 and 40.

We observe that the volumes for the optimal cases are close to the maximum allowed value of 5280m³ (see Table 8.4.3), suggesting that the volume that intercepts rays should be as large as possible. It is also noteworthy that in each case depressions are created in the volume about its centre and there is a tendency to maximise the peaks to the north end of the building. There seems to be an attempt, with this continuous trigonometric function, to emulate the staggered arrangement of the example from Section 8.4.2, which maximizes solar access to south facing collecting surfaces. Note that, as with that example, incident irradiation on façades is also taken into account.

The dimensions L_x = 20m times L_y = 30m are arbitrary and the calculation in RADIANCE is scale free, so that the resultant forms are equally applicable to proportionally smaller or larger buildings.

8.5 Optimization of urban energy performance

The optimization of urban geometry for the utilization of solar radiation, while interesting and useful, considers only a small subset of the potentially available parameters that influence urban energy performance. The potential of this optimization is therefore somewhat limited. Indeed, by only considering the availability of solar irradiation and not the implications of this energy for buildings' energy balances, one may even arrive at false conclusions: the objective function is too restrictive. Of more value then is to consider not only the potential supply of energy, but the actual (predicted) supply and its coupling with its predicted demand and indeed storage. This considerably increases the

Table 8.4.3 Optimal irradiation after 12,000 evaluations for roof forms defined by a Fourier series compared to that of a flat roof enclosing a similar volume

Parameters	Irradiation (GWh)	Volume (m³)
Flat roof ($A_{kl}, B_{kl} = 0$ except $A_{00} = 8.8$)	1.1292 (68%)	5280
Small amplitudes ($A_{kl}, B_{kl} \in [-\frac{1}{2}, \frac{1}{2}]$ except $A_{00} \in [0,10]$) (Figure 8.4.7)	1.2728 (76%)	5234
Medium amplitudes ($A_{kl}, B_{kl} \in [-1,1]$ except $A_{00} \in [0,10]$) (Figure 8.4.8)	1.4075 (84%)	5222
Large amplitudes ($A_{kl}, B_{kl} \in [-2,2]$ except $A_{00} \in [0,10]$) (Figure 8.4.9)	1.6685 (100%)	5131

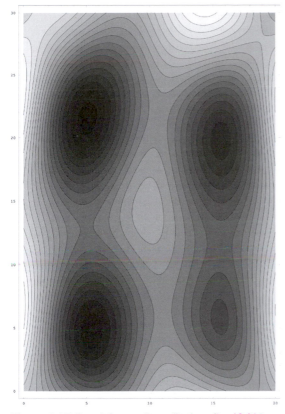

Figure 8.4.7 Result for small amplitudes after 12,000 evaluations: contour plot

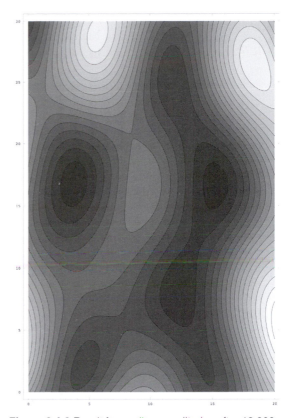

Figure 8.4.8 Result for medium amplitudes after 12,000 evaluations: greyscale contour plot representing height

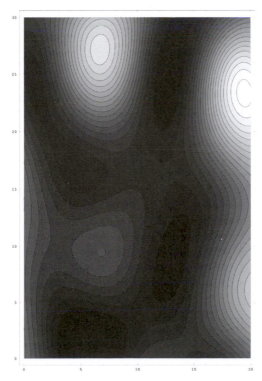

Figure 8.4.9 Result for large amplitudes after 12,000 evaluations: contour plot

potential to improve upon the energy performance of an urban development but also the robustness of the conclusions reached. To this end then, we have coupled CitySim with the hybrid CMA-ES/HDE algorithm.

8.5.1 Coupling CitySim with the hybrid CMA-ES/HDE (CitySim-EA)

The approach to coupling the hybrid CMA-ES/HDE algorithm and CitySim is shown schematically in Figure 8.5.1 below. The first step is to create an XML template of the simulated scene, in which each parameter of the study is replaced by a special character combination. The template XML is then used by the CitySim solver in the evaluation phase to determine the potential solution's energy performance.

Now the CitySim solver, as described in Chapter 5, contains both deterministic and stochastic models – the latter for the simulation of occupants' presence and behaviour. But the use of stochastic models, essentially adding random noise to our objective function, means that the location of our global optimum will change from one simulation to another. It is desirable then to replace these stochastic processes with deterministic representations. This we have done for the models of occupants' presence, use of windows and use of blinds.

For blinds a simplified model has been implemented in which the unshaded fraction is a function of the irradiance incident on the façade. After Wienold (2007), the automatic cut-off with fixed height strategy is represented as follows: the blinds are lowered completely if the façade irradiance exceeds 150W/m^2, and are retracted if this falls below 50W/m^2. This strategy we implement using a logit function, in which the unshaded blind fraction f_u is given as follows:

$$f_u = \frac{1}{1 + e^{\lambda(I_f - 100)}},$$

[8.5.1]

where I_f is the façade irradiance (W/m^2) and λ the logit scale factor, taken as 0.2. This function allows for a smooth transition between the open and closed states of the blinds.

In addition to occupants' presence and blind control described above, a deterministic window opening strategy was taken from Beausoleil-Morrison

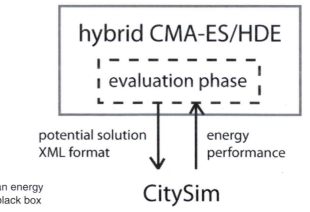

Figure 8.5.1 Optimization of urban energy performance using CitySim as a black box

(2009), in which the windows are open if $T_a > T_{min} + 1°C$ and $T_a - T_{ext} + 1°C$, where T_a is the internal air temperature (°C), T_{ext} is the outside air temperature (°C) and T_{min} is the minimum allowed air temperature (°C) for the heating calculation. When the windows are open, a ventilation rate n_{vent} (h^{-1}) is considered between the outside air node and the inside air node of CitySim's thermal model. The ventilation rate is approximated using the following logit function (Haldi and Robinson, 2009):

$$n_{vent} = n_{vent,max} \cdot \frac{\exp(1.459 + 0.1448 \cdot T_{ext} - 0.1814 \cdot T_a)}{1 + \exp(1.459 + 0.1448 \cdot T_{ext} - 0.1814 \cdot T_a)}, \qquad [8.5.2]$$

with $n_{vent,max}$ the maximum ventilation rate (h^{-1}), considered as an average over the simulation time step of one hour, taken to be $n_{vent,max} = 2h^{-1}$.

8.5.2 Case study: The district of Matthäus in Basel

For this first application of the coupling between CitySim and the hybrid EA we have selected a part of the district of Matthäus in Basel (Switzerland). This choice was motivated by the fact that a 3D geometric model of the whole district was available to us; likewise a subset of the national census data for the year 2000 and the results from a recent visual field survey of the district. From the 2000 census we have the construction year, the last renovation date, the heating fuel used and the number of inhabitants for each building. From the district visual survey we have observations of the glazing ratio and the state of the façades backed up by photographs from which we are able to make informed judgements regarding the composition of the envelope. Indeed with the help of these observations and the advice of renovation specialists (EPIQR Rénovation, Lausanne) we have linked the construction year/renovation date and the physical properties of the walls, roofs and windows needed by CitySim to simulate the buildings' thermal performance. Finally, we have access to meteorological data measured at a weather station in Basel, which is available as part of the software Meteonorm.

For computational reasons we decided to use only a part of the Matthäus district: a block located between Matthäusstrasse, Müllheimerstrasse, Klybeckstrasse and Feldbergstrasse (Plate 41).

This block consists of 26 individual buildings, which date from between the beginning of the 19th century to the 1970s, with some buildings having been renovated between the 1970s and the 1990s. The buildings have central heating systems but are not equipped with air-conditioning. The chosen part of the district is subdivided administratively by the city authorities into three zones as shown in Figure 8.5.2.

The Schutzzone is a historical part of the city that is protected, so that we are not allowed to change the walls, the roofs or the fire walls. The Schonzone is less restrictive: only the external appearance of the building should not be modified. The remaining Zone 5a is not historical and may be modified under the approbation of the authorities.

Data extrapolation

With the geometric information available to us, we are able to create an XML description file that will be used by the solver of CitySim, which is then completed

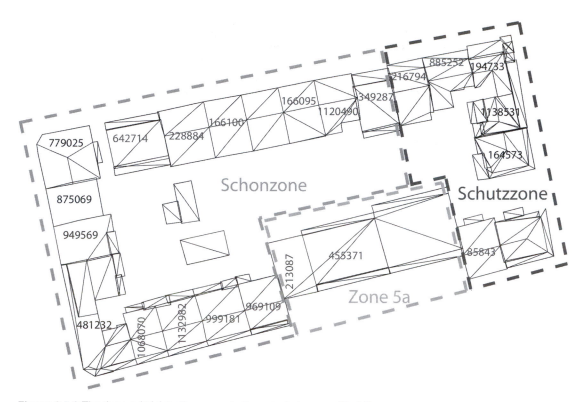

Figure 8.5.2 The three administrative zones in the selected group of buildings

by the physical properties of each building. Each building in the census and visual survey has a unique identification number that allowed us to link the street address and the building characteristics. In Figure 8.5.2 we have superimposed the identification number on each of the buildings in our case study site.

Unfortunately, our dataset was not complete for all buildings within our case study site; indeed we had nothing more than the 3D information for four buildings out of the 26. Although this is helpful for the estimation of the envelope characteristics, there are many other attributes for which it is of no use whatsoever. To address this we have developed a procedure to infer the missing attributes from the data available to us for other buildings, provided of course that their number is statistically significant. In Matthäus, the census and the visual field survey data are available for a sample in excess of 1000 buildings. Using this data we derive a probability of occurrence of each value that a given variable may take and from this define a cumulative distribution function (CDF). We then draw a random number and, from the CDF, we determine which value of our variable this corresponds to. Plate 42 shows an example of the procedure for the data available from the CENSUS 2000 dataset.

Further assumptions

As noted above, for this optimization study we wish to represent the presence of our inhabitants, the number of which is given by the 2000 census, in a deterministic way. After Jones (2001) we assume that, when present, each occupant emits 90W of sensible heat. For these residential buildings we furthermore assume that occupants are present outside of standard working hours, so that on weekdays, people are at home until 7am, from 12am to 1pm and from 6pm in the evening; on Saturdays, people are at home until 10am, from 12am to 2pm, and from 5 pm in the afternoon; on Sundays, people are at home until 10am, from 12am to 2pm, and from 4pm in the afternoon.

The heating set-point is assumed to be 21°C for all buildings. Initial CitySim simulations of this block of buildings revealed that the use of blinds and window openings reduces cooling energy demand to a negligible value, compared with heating demands. Therefore, cooling loads are neglected in the objective function.

8.5.3 Minimization of primary energy demand

Parameterization

We have refined the subdivision of the three administrative zones in Matthäus (see Figure 8.5.2) to take into account the last renovation date. To simplify our analysis, but also to take into account realistic changes to glazing, the windows may remain as they are or be replaced by double glazed low emissivity (U-value of 1.1 W/(m^{2}K)) or triple glazed low emissivity units (U-value of 0.5 W/(m^{2}K)). The energy conversion systems can be: (1) a natural gas condensing boiler ($\eta_{th} = 0.96$), (2) an air heat pump ($\eta_{tech} = 0.35$, $T_{target} = 35°C$), (3) a cogeneration natural gas engine ($\eta_{th} = 0.72$, $\eta_{el} = 0.27$) or (4) a combined cogeneration natural gas engine with an air heat pump ($\eta_{th} = 0.72$, $\eta_{el} = 0.27$, $\eta_{tech} = 0.35$, $T_{target} = 35°C$). We also consider a maximum allowable insulation thickness of 20cm. In total then, we have 41 discrete and continuous parameters (see Table 8.5.1).

The parameters that belong to an ensemble of discrete values, such as the windows' U-value and energy conversion system, were coded using natural numbers starting from 0, but these are shown in a more human readable format in Table 8.5.1. For these discrete parameters, the absolute precisions (ε_3) were chosen to be 1. For the insulation thickness they were set to be 1cm, for the glazing ratio to 0.01 and for the photovoltaic panels to 1 per cent of the roof area.

Constraints

To add realism to this (albeit hypothetical) scenario we use as a constraint the maximum total purchase price p_{invest} that can be invested in our renovations, for which each individual renovation intervention is associated with an approximate price. Therefore, we can write:

$$g_1(\vec{x}) = p_{insulation} \cdot \sum_{i \in \{1,4,7,10,13,16,19,32,37\}} x_i \cdot A_{wall,i}$$

$$+ \sum_{i=\{2,5,8,11,14,17,20,22,24,26,28,30,33,38\}} p_{window}(x_i) \cdot A_{window,i}$$

$$+ \sum_{i=\{3,6,9,12,15,18,21,23,25,27,29,31,35,40\}} p_{system}(x_i)$$

$$+ \sum_{i=\{36,41\}} p_{pv} \cdot x_i \cdot A_{roof,i} - p_{invest} \leq 0, \qquad [8.5.3]$$

Table 8.5.1 The 41 (discrete[a] and continuous) parameters for the group of buildings in Matthäus

Group	Parameter description	Symbol and domain
Schonzone built <1919	Walls internal insulation (cm)	$x_1 \in [0, 20]$
– non-renovated (2 buildings)	Windows U-value $(W/(m^2K))$	$x_2 \in \{0.5, 1.1, 6.0\}$
	Energy conversion system[b]	$x_3 \in \{1, 2, 3, 4\}$
Schonzone built <1919	Walls internal insulation (cm)	$x_4 \in [0, 20]$
– renovated 1971 to 1980 (1 building)	Windows U-value $(W/(m^2K))$	$x_5 \in \{0.5, 1.1, 2.8\}$
	Energy conversion system[b]	$x_6 \in \{1, 2, 3, 4\}$
Schonzone built <1919	Walls internal insulation (cm)	$x_7 \in [0, 20]$
– renovated 1981 to 1990 (3 buildings)	Windows U-value $(W/(m^2K))$	$x_8 \in \{0.5, 1.1, 2.8\}$
	Energy conversion system[b]	$x_9 \in \{1, 2, 3, 4\}$
Schonzone built <1919	Walls internal insulation (cm)	$x_{10} \in [0, 20]$
– renovated 1991 to 1995 (6 buildings)	Windows U-value $(W/(m^2K))$	$x_{11} \in \{0.5, 1.1, 2.0\}$
	Energy conversion system[b]	$x_{12} \in \{1, 2, 3, 4\}$
Schonzone built <1919	Walls internal insulation (cm)	$x_{13} \in [0, 20]$
– renovated 1996 to 2000 (2 buildings)	Windows U-value $(W/(m^2K))$	$x_{14} \in \{0.5, 1.1, 1.5\}$
	Energy conversion system[b]	$x_{15} \in \{1, 2, 3, 4\}$
Schonzone built 1946 to 1960	Walls internal insulation (cm)	$x_{16} \in [0, 20]$
– renovated 1981 to 1990 (1 building)	Windows U-value $(W/(m^2K))$	$x_{17} \in \{0.5, 1.1, 2.8\}$
	Energy conversion system [b]	$x_{18} \in \{1, 2, 3, 4\}$
Schonzone built 1961 to 1970	Walls internal insulation (cm)	$x_{19} \in [0, 20]$
– non-renovated (1 building)	Windows U-value $(W/(m^2K))$	$x_{20} \in \{0.5, 1.1, 5.5\}$
	Energy conversion system[b]	$x_{21} \in \{1, 2, 3, 4\}$
Schutzzone built <1919	Windows U-value $(W/(m^2K))$	$x_{22} \in \{0.5, 1.1, 6.0\}$
– non-renovated (1 building)	Energy conversion system[b]	$x_{23} \in \{1, 2, 3, 4\}$
Schutzzone built <1919	Windows U-value $(W/(m^2K))$	$x_{24} \in \{0.5, 1.1, 2.8\}$
– renovated 1971 to 1980 (1 building)	Energy conversion system [b]	$x_{25} \in \{1, 2, 3, 4\}$

Table 8.5.1 The 41 (discrete[a] and continuous) parameters for the group of buildings in Matthäus (*Cont'd*)

Group	Parameter description	Symbol and domain
Schutzzone built <1919	Windows U-value ($W/(m^2K)$)	$x_{26} \in \{0.5, 1.1, 2.8\}$
– renovated 1981 to 1990 (3 buildings)	Energy conversion system [b]	$x_{27} \in \{1, 2, 3, 4\}$
Schutzzone built <1919	Windows U-value ($W/(m^2K)$)	$x_{28} \in \{0.5, 1.1, 2.0\}$
– renovated 1991 to 1995 (1 building)	Energy conversion system [b]	$x_{29} \in \{1, 2, 3, 4\}$
Schutzzone built <1919	Windows U-value ($W/(m^2K)$)	$x_{30} \in \{0.5, 1.1, 1.5\}$
– renovated 1996 to 2000 (1 building)	Energy conversion system [b]	$x_{31} \in \{1, 2, 3, 4\}$
Zone 5a built 1961 to 1970	Walls external insulation (cm)	$x_{32} \in [0, 20]$
– non-renovated (2 buildings)	Windows U-value ($W/(m^2K)$)	$x_{33} \in \{0.5, 1.1, 5.5\}$
	Glazing ratio	$x_{34} \in [0.1, 1]$
	Energy conversion system [b]	$x_{35} \in \{1, 2, 3, 4\}$
	Photovoltaic panels (% roof area)	$x_{36} \in [0, 100]$
Zone 5a built 1971 to 1980	Walls external insulation (cm)	$x_{37} \in [0, 20]$
– non-renovated (1 building)	Windows U-value ($W/(m^2K)$)	$x_{38} \in \{0.5, 1.1, 2.8\}$
	Glazing ratio	$x_{39} \in [0.1, 1]$
	Energy conversion system [b]	$x_{40} \in \{1, 2, 3, 4\}$
	Photovoltaic panels (% roof area)	$x_{41} \in [0, 100]$

Note: [a] The discrete parameters are handled internally by the CMA-ES/HDE using real-values between $[0, n-1]$, where *n* is the number of discrete choices, and are rounded to the lower integer value. [b] 1=boiler, 2=heat pump, 3=cogeneration, 4=cogeneration + heat pump.

where $p_{insulation}$ is the price of the insulation per m³, $A_{wall,i}$ is the total wall area of the considered building(s) in m², $p_{window}(x_i)$ is a function that returns the investment for windows, $A_{window,i}$ is the total window area of the considered building(s) in m², $p_{system}(x_i)$ is a function that returns the investment for the energy conversion system, p_{pv} is a function that returns the price of the corresponding photovoltaic panels per m² and $A_{window,i}$ is the total roof area of the considered building(s) in m².

For the present application, approximate values in Swiss francs (CHF) for the investments were obtained by contacting the suppliers (private companies). Note that our purpose here is simply to test the principle of a financially constrained optimization of an urban renovation strategy, rather than on the absolute precision of the predictions upon which this is based. For this we simply estimate the material and equipment purchase prices; we have not obtained price estimates for their installation, which may be specific to each building.

The estimated price of façade insulation is:

$$p_{insulation} = 150 \; CHF \, / \, m^3 \qquad\qquad [8.5.4]$$

For windows this price is:

$$p_{window}(x_i) = \begin{cases} 600 \; CHF \, / \, m^2 & if \; x_i = 0.5 \\ 450 \; CHF \, / \, m^2 & if \; x_i = 1.1 \\ 0 \; CHF \, / \, m^2 & otherwise \end{cases} \qquad\qquad [8.5.5]$$

For energy conversion systems we use a price of:

$$p_{system}(x_i) = \begin{cases} 4500 \; CHF & if \; x_i = 1 \\ 18000 \; CHF & if \; x_i = 2 \\ 31000 \; CHF & if \; x_i = 3 \\ 49000 \; CHF & if \; x_i = 4 \end{cases} \qquad\qquad [8.5.6]$$

For photovoltaic panels we use a price of:

$$p_{pv}(x_i) = 1700 \; CHF \, / \, m^2 \qquad\qquad [8.5.7]$$

The minimum investment for refurbishment corresponds to the installation of a condensing boiler in every house, which costs CHF63,000. The maximum investment for refurbishment (the most expensive technology and insulation) costs CHF4,198,000 in total, which involves CHF136,000 for insulation, CHF2,328,000 for the replacement of windows, CHF686,000 for cogeneration with a heat pump and CHF1,049,000 for photovoltaic panels. Within this range we have set a total investment limit of CHF2 million.

Objective function

The objective function in this optimization is the sum of the annual primary energy used for the group of simulated buildings, which is minimized. The calculation takes into account the efficiencies in energy transformation:

$$f(\bar{x}) = Q_{gas}(\bar{x}) \, / \, \eta_{gas} + E_{el}(\bar{x}) \, / \, \eta_{el}, \qquad\qquad [8.5.8]$$

where $\bar{x}$ are the parameters, Q_{gas} is the on-site energy use (J) in gas form, η_{gas} is the energy conversion efficiency for gas production and transport, E_{el} is the on-site electricity use (positive) or production (negative) in J and η_{el} is the energy conversion efficiency for electricity production and transport. The energy conversion efficiencies are the inverse of the source energy factors, which are defined as the ratio of the primary energy use to use the on-site energy. For these we use values of 2.057 for electricity and 1.007 for gas, using a calculation method taken from EPA (2007) and data for Switzerland (SFOE, 2007). As noted above, and in Table 8.5.1, we consider in this study four possible energy conversion systems: boiler, heat pump, cogeneration system and cogeneration system combined with a heat pump. The combined efficiencies for these systems, assuming an average source temperature of 15°C (by way of indication) for the heat pump, are 0.95, 2.63, 1.27 and 2.16 respectively.

Results

A plateau was found in the objective function after around 5,000 evaluations, as shown in Plate 43. The best configuration found for the buildings used about 6.587TJ of primary energy per year (or 1823MWh/year and an average of 70MWh/year/building).

The CMA-ES and HDE have both contributed to the improvement of the objective function. Indeed in Plate 43 we see that both algorithms (indicated by different colours) bring an improvement to the objective function, suggesting that the hybrid CMA-ES/HDE is well adapted to this particular type of urban modelling problem, where the objective function is a mixture of additively separable and non-additively separable components.

Table 8.5.2 shows the parameters resulting from this optimization.

It is encouraging that our optimizer consistently chooses the energy conversion system with the highest combined conversion efficiency (the heat pump). The optimizer also suggests that photovoltaic panels should cover 100 per cent of the roof area and that the thickness of insulation should be maximized (to 20cm). However, the replacement of all windows, which is a large investment (twice the price of photovoltaics) was not systematically proposed by the optimizer. Instead, only a proportion of windows were replaced according to our total investment threshold (the actual total cost was predicted to be CHF1,983,000, which is very close to the maximum amount allowed by the constraint).

Finally, the glazing ratio in the last two groups of buildings was chosen to be the smallest possible (0.1). To understand this, we have simulated a building (identified by number 213087) for a typical winter day for the imposed cases of a glazing ratio of 0.1 and the extreme of 0.99; assuming all windows to be replaced by triple glazing. With this changed in the group of buildings, the investment was of CHF2.191 million and the total primary energy consumption grew to 6.686TJ (+1.5 per cent) (Plate 44).

The increased solar gains during the day for the larger windows, which do reduce daytime heating demands, do not compensate for the excess thermal losses through these windows during the night. Here we reached a limit in the models currently implemented in CitySim at the time of this study: in particular there is no daylighting model, so that photo-responsive control of artificial lighting was not considered, which may change this trend. The modelling of mechanical cooling in this scenario. These restrictions in CitySim no longer apply.

Table 8.5.2 Results of the 41 parameters for the group of buildings in Matthäus

Group	Parameter description	Value
Schonzone built <1919	Walls internal insulation (cm)	$x_1 = 20$
– non-renovated (2 buildings)	Windows U-value $(W/(m^2K))$	$x_2 = 0.5$
	Energy conversion system[a]	$x_3 = 2$
Schonzone built <1919	Walls internal insulation (cm)	$x_4 = 20$
– renovated 1971 to 1980 (1 building)	Windows U-value $(W/(m^2K))$	$x_5 = 2.8$
	Energy conversion system[a]	$x_6 = 2$
Schonzone built <1919	Walls internal insulation (cm)	$x_7 = 20$
– renovated 1981 to 1990 (3 buildings)	Windows U-value $(W/(m^2K))$	$x_8 = 1.1$
	Energy conversion system[a]	$x_9 = 2$
Schonzone built <1919	Walls internal insulation (cm)	$x_{10} = 20$
– renovated 1991 to 1995 (6 buildings)	Windows U-value $(W/(m^2K))$	$x_{11} = 2.0$
	Energy conversion system[a]	$x_{12} = 2$
Schonzone built <1919	Walls internal insulation (cm)	$x_{13} = 20$
– renovated 1996 to 2000 (2 buildings)	Windows U-value $(W/(m^2K))$	$x_{14} = 1.5$
	Energy conversion system[a]	$x_{15} = 2$
Schonzone built 1946 to 1960	Walls internal insulation (cm)	$x_{16} = 20$
– renovated 1981 to 1990 (1 building)	Windows U-value $(W/(m^2K))$	$x_{17} = 0.5$
	Energy conversion system[a]	$x_{18} = 2$
Schonzone built 1961 to 1970	Walls internal insulation (cm)	$x_{19} = 20$
– non-renovated (1 building)	Windows U-value $(W/(m^2K))$	$x_{20} = 5.5$
	Energy conversion system[a]	$x_{21} = 6.0$
Schutzzone built <1919	Windows U-value $(W/(m^2K))$	$x_{22} = 6.0$
– non-renovated (1 building)	Energy conversion system[a]	$x_{23} = 2$
Schutzzone built <1919	Windows U-value $(W/(m^2K))$	$x_{24} = 0.5$
– renovated 1971 to 1980 (1 building)	Energy conversion system[a]	$x_{25} = 2$
Schutzzone built <1919	Windows U-value $(W/(m^2K))$	$x_{26} = 2.8$
– renovated 1981 to 1990 (3 buildings)	Energy conversion system[a]	$x_{27} = 2$
Schutzzone built <1919	Windows U-value $(W/(m^2K))$	$x_{28} = 0.5$
– renovated 1991 to 1995 (1 building)	Energy conversion system[a]	$x_{29} = 2$
Schutzzone built <1919	Windows U-value $(W/(m^2K))$	$x_{30} = 0.5$
– renovated 1996 to 2000 (1 building)	Energy conversion system[a]	$x_{31} = 2$
Zone 5a built 1961 to 1970	Walls external insulation (cm)	$x_{32} = 20$

Table 8.5.2 Results of the 41 parameters for the group of buildings in Matthäus (*Cont'd*)

Group	Parameter description	Value
– non-renovated (2 buildings)	Windows U-value ($W/(m^2K)$)	$x_{33} = 5.5$
	Glazing ratio	$x_{34} = 0.1$
	Energy conversion system[a]	$x_{35} = 2$
	Photovoltaic panels (% roof area)	$x_{36} = 100$
Zone 5a built 1971 to 1980	Walls external insulation (cm)	$x_{37} = 20$
– non-renovated (1 building)	Windows U-value ($W/(m^2K)$)	$x_{38} = 0.5$
	Glazing ratio	$x_{39} = 0.1$
	Energy conversion system[a]	$x_{40} = 2$
	Photovoltaic panels (% roof area)	$x_{41} = 100$

Note: [a] 1=boiler, 2=heat pump, 3=cogeneration, 4=cogeneration + heat pump. The suggested energy conversion system for all buildings is the heat pump, due to the combination of its efficiency and the corresponding source energy ratio.

8.6 Conclusion

The methodology developed in this chapter for optimizing urban energy performance is very general; it has the advantages of handling analytical constraints and parallelizing the function evaluations. It is also true that with some adaptation, any optimizer (such as the hybrid PSO/HJ algorithm of GenOpt) could be used in place of our hybrid CMA-ES/HDE. But our hybrid algorithm has proven to be *particularly* robust in identifying global optima with respect to highly multi-modal functions. We have applied the new hybrid CMA-ES/HDE to two types of constrained problem: the optimization of building and urban form for the utilization of available solar radiation; and the optimization of the physical characteristics of buildings to minimize primary energy use.

From the solar optimization applications we have found that:

- the new algorithm consistently converges to a good solution while taking constraints into account;
- the solar energy available for utilisation may be increased by up to 20 per cent (with respect to an initial subjectively chosen form);
- the forms of these solutions tend to be highly non-intuitive (and correspondingly unlikely to be arrived at by subjective selection).

Concerning the last point, it is hoped that computational tools of this nature might provide a useful source of inspiration to architects and urban designers, from which to derive a solution to a given design problem.

We have also shown that urban energy fluxes, as modelled by CitySim, can be optimized. In this, the objective was to minimize the primary energy use of a part of a city, taking as parameters possible refurbishment options. Constraints arising from local regulations were also considered; likewise those due to limits in the capital available for investment. The optimizer successfully identified a trade-off between the investment (set *a priori*) and the primary energy use of the group of buildings.

It would be interesting in the future to test the sensitivity of predictions to variations in the parameters resulting from the optimization. Analysing not only the best candidate found by the optimizer but also those in its vicinity may also provide useful insights into the robustness of the region in the available parameter space in which our candidate solution is found. By robust we mean that the objective function (for example primary energy use) should not be excessively sensitive to modest changes in the parameter values.

Another interesting application of the hybrid CMA-ES/HDE would be in the calibration of CitySim parameters using measured data. In this the objective function to minimize would be the difference between measured and predicted energy use. Another useful application would be in the optimization of strategies for the control of energy demand, storage and supply and their interactions with system dimensions. Finally, the CMA-ES/HDE should see its comparison operator improved for multi-objective optimization and be fitted with a ranking algorithm.

Notes

1   A maximization may also be performed by reversing the sign of the objective function.
2   Note that an alternative could have been to work with the $N \cdot M$ grid-point heights, and to smoothen the roof with a backward Fourier transform in order to produce a continuous and differentiable function.

References

Beausoleil-Morrison, I. (2009) 'On predicting the magnitude and temporal variation of cooling loads in detached residential buildings', in *Proceedings of the 11th International Building Performance Simulation Association Conference*, IBPSA: Glasgow, pp300–307, available at www.ibpsa.org/m_papers.asp, last accessed 17 December 2010

Beyer, H.-G. and Schwefel, H.-P. (2002) 'Evolution strategies: A comprehensive introduction', *Natural Computing*, vol 1, pp3–52

Chang, C. F., Wong, J. J., Chiou, J. P. and Su, C. T. (2007) 'Robust searching hybrid differential evolution method for optimal reactive power planning in large-scale distribution systems', *Electric Power Systems Research*, vol 77, no 5–6, pp430–437

Cheng, V., Steemers, K., Montavon, M. and Compagnon, R. (2006) 'Urban form, density and solar potential', in *PLEA 2006 Proceedings*, Passive and Low Energy Architecture, Geneva, available at www.arct.cam.ac.uk/PLEA/home.aspx, last accessed 17 December 2010

Compagnon, R. (2004) 'Solar and daylight availability in the urban fabric', *Energy & Buildings*, vol 36, no 4, pp321–328

Dirk, V. A. and MacLeod A. (2006) 'Hierarchically organised evolution strategies on the parabolic ridge', in *GECCO'06 Proceedings*, Proceedings of the 8th annual conference on genetic and evolutionary computation, Seattle, pp437–444

EPA (Environment Protection Agency) (2007) 'Energy star performance ratings methodology for incorporating source energy use', Technical report, US Environment Protection Agency, Washington DC

Feoktistov, V. (2006) *Differential Evolution: In Search of Solutions*, Springer, Heidelberg

Fogel, D. B. (2006) *Evolutionary Computation: Toward a New Philosophy of Machine Intelligence*, Wiley, New York

Fogel, L. J., Owens, A. J. and Walsh, M. J. (1996) *Artificial Intelligence through Simulated Evolution*, John Wiley and Sons, New York

Goldberg, D. E. (1992) *Genetic Algorithms in Search, Optimization and Machine Learning*, Addison-Wesley, Reading, MA

Haldi, F. and Robinson, D. (2009) 'Interactions with window openings by office occupants', *Building and Environment*, vol 44, no 12, pp 2378–2395

Hansen, N. and Kern, S. (2004) 'Evaluating the CMA evolution strategy on multimodal test functions', in *Parallel Problem Solving from Nature*, Springer-Verlag, Heidelberg, Proceedings of the 8th international conference on parallel problem solving from nature, Birmingham, UK, pp282–291

Hansen, N. and Ostermeier, A. (2001) 'Completely derandomized self-adaptation in evolution strategies', *Evolutionary Computation*, vol 9, no 2, pp159–195

Holland, J. H. (1975) *Adaptation in Natural and Artificial Systems*, University of Michigan Press, Ann Arbor, Michigan

Jones, W. P. (2001) *Air Conditioning Engineering*, 5th edition, Butterworth-Heinemann, Oxford

Kämpf, J. H. and Robinson. D. (2009) 'A hybrid CMA-ES and HDE optimization algorithm with application to solar energy potential', *Applied Soft Computing*, vol 9, pp738–745

Kämpf, J. H., Wetter, M. and Robinson. D. (2010) 'A comparison of global optimization algorithms with standard benchmark functions and real-world applications using EnergyPlus', *Journal of Building Performance Simulation*, vol 3, no 2, pp103–120

Koza, J. R. (1992) *Genetic Programming*, MIT Press, Cambridge, MA

Larson, G. W. and Shakespeare, R. (1998) *Rendering with Radiance: The Art and Science of Lighting Visualization*, Morgan-Kaufmann, San Francisco, CA

Littlefair, P. J., Santamouris, M., Alvarez, S., Dupagne, A., Hall, D., Teller, J., Coronel, J. F. and Papanikolaou, N. (2000) *Environmental Site Layout Planning: Solar Access, Microclimate and Passive Cooling in Urban Areas*, Construction Research Communications Ltd, Peterborough

Marsaglia, G. and Tsang, W. W. (2000) 'The Ziggurat method for generating random variables', *Journal of Statistical Software*, vol 5, no 8, pp1–7

Michalewicz, Z. and Schoenauer, M. (1996) 'Evolutionary algorithms for constrained parameter optimization problems', *Evolutionary Computation*, vol 4, no 1, pp1–32

Mitchell, M. (1998) *An Introduction to Genetic Algorithms*, MIT Press, Cambridge, MA

Montavon, M. (2010) 'Optimization of urban form by the evaluation of the solar potential', unpublished PhD thesis, no 4657, EPFL, Lausanne

Nobakhti, A. and Wang, H. (2008) 'A simple self-adaptive Differential Evolution algorithm with application on the ALSTOM gasifier', *Applied Soft Computing Journal*, vol 8, no 1, pp350–370

Rechenberg, R. (1973) *Evolutionsstrategie: Optimierung technischer Systeme nach Principen der biologischen Evolution*, Fromman-Holzboog Verlag, Stuttgart

Robinson, R. and Stone, A. (2004) 'Irradiation modelling made simple: The cumulative sky approach and its applications', in *Plea 2004 Proceedings*, Passive and Low Energy Architecture, Eindhoven, available at www.arct.cam.ac.uk/PLEA/home.aspx, last accessed 17 December 2010

Runarsson, T. and Yao, X. (2000) 'Stochastic ranking for constrained evolutionary optimization', *IEEE Transactions on Evolutionary Computation*, vol 4, pp284–294

Schwefel, H.-P. (1995) *Evolution and Optimum Seeking*, Wiley-Interscience, New York, USA

SFOE (Swiss Federal Office of Energy) (2007) 'Statistique globale suisse de l' 'energie', Technical report, SFOE, Bern

Storn, R. and Price, K., (1996) 'Minimizing the real functions of the ICEC'96 contest by differential evolution', in *Proceedings of the IEEE Conference on Evolutionary Computation*, Institute of Electrical and Electronics Engineers, Piscataway, USA pp842–844

Wienold, J. (2007) 'Dynamic simulation of blind control strategies for visual comfort and energy balance analysis', in *Proceedings of the 10th International Building Performance Simulation Association Conference*, Beijing, pp1197–1204, available at www.ibpsa.org/m_papers.asp, last accessed 17 December 2010

Part IV

An Eye to the Future

9
Dynamics of Land-Use Change and Growth

Mike Batty

9.1 Introduction

There are many ways of representing cities that range from focussing on tangible physical form such as their buildings, infrastructures and terrain to more abstract conceptions that consider cities in terms of the spatial distribution of their populations and socio-economic attributes. Generic issues such as energy use and flow, climate change and social equity cut across these representations, offering different ways of understanding their impact that are reflected in different scientific styles and different methods of forecasting. In this chapter, we examine the implications for energy flow and change with respect to how people travel, from work to home primarily, which leads directly to questions about the form of cities in terms of energy costs that different morphologies incur. We begin with a review of the different elements of this representation and then illustrate a typical model of residential location that offers a generic template for many kinds of interactions that involve flows of people and uses of energy in their transport. We develop this model for four different modes of transport in the Greater London region and illustrate its operation with respect to the impact of a doubling of the cost of travel. This enables us to focus on population and mode shifts that occur as energy costs change. We then show how this model is nested within a wider framework of integrated assessment that contains models that change in scale from the regional to the site specific. We finally illustrate how our own model is used within this framework to assess the impact of sea level rise and flooding in the Greater London region as part of the debate about longer-term climate change.

9.2 Energy flows and human activities in cities

Throughout this book, the focus has been on how energy is processed in buildings and cities and the perspectives taken so far have largely concerned the actual flows of energy that keep the physical fabric of the city in functioning form. The use of energy has also been linked to the flows of materials having a long residence time (buildings and infrastructure) and only indirectly have these flows been explored in terms of human decision making. In this chapter, we change course a little, by thinking of energy in cities as being generated by people making decisions about where to travel and how to locate, transferring the focus onto theories and models that associate decisions about the use of energy to decisions about how far to travel, what mode of transport to use, and what kind of activity to develop or engage in with respect to the multitude of locations that are linked with different land uses and buildings in the city. One of the greatest challenges in developing integrated and effective perspectives on urban sustainability in which energy is a central issue, is linking material flows directly associated with the physical fabric of the city with decisions regarding how people react spatially in terms of living and working in cities. Populations do not function directly with energy use in mind, but rather indirectly insofar as the decisions and costs involving life choices reflect the use and transformation of energy. In this chapter, we seek to map out how such populations act and interact with respect to spatial locations in ways that have immediate implications for the use of energy in terms of the way resources are used.

There are many ways in which we can define the physical and socio-economic form of cities, and to explore the way energy might enter the analysis directly, we immediately need to review these possibilities. There are at least four patterns of flow that involve energy: first materials flows that routinely and often automatically drive production and maintenance processes in which building and transport are maintained, new products are produced and waste is dispersed; second, commodity flows that involve physical movements of goods, typically freight that drives production and the ultimate consumption of goods; third, population flows that involve individuals engaging in production and consumption that are typically manifest in journeys to work, school, shopping and so forth; and finally, information flows that run in parallel to all of these physical flows, again sustaining and motivating production and consumption. This last set of flows is growing rapidly as substitutes but also as complements to physical flows and these run alongside the first three flow systems identified.

All energy flows that involve the development, restructuring and maintenance of cities are driven by human decision making, even if some of these flow processes appear to operate naturally and spontaneously. Right down to decisions to site and install utility lines, these processes depend on the demand and supply for activities by human populations and as we climb these hierarchies from physical to social, and from energy to information, human decision making becomes more central to our methods of explanation and control. Energy has been the standard measure of flows that are physical in that they involve the movement of material and people but in the rapid transition from industrial to post-industrial society, the focus is beginning to change from flows based on energy to information. In fact, despite the interest in underpinning human systems through energy analysis, there is to date no well worked out theory that relates the structure of materials flows to population flows. Odum's (2007) notions, for example, about energetics that generalize thermodynamics to ecological systems and urban populations have never embraced theories of human action. In economics, the focus has been almost exclusively on metrics such as money with only lip service paid to more physical quantities that in turn are driven by monetary considerations, apart from a number of approaches that have sought to theorize directly the economics of materials flows and energy markets. When it comes to information flows, the emergence of a digital world that is now upon us has barely been absorbed in terms of its implications for traditional sources of energy and indeed, for the traditional monetary system.

In this chapter, our focus is at the level of human populations in cities, emphasizing how individuals and groups locate and interact in space with respect to the energy demands that they generate and the energy needs that are associated with spatial interactions. The way we represent the urban system is grounded in the location of populations. For these purposes, we do not describe the system in terms of buildings, transport or utility infrastructures, nor as aggregates of these into different land uses, but as more abstract entities based on locational units, often administratively organized. These units are used to define aggregates of population between which flows of people on transport systems represent the glue that binds these together in realizing the scale and agglomeration economies that define cities in the first instance. In terms of the temporal scales over which we study energy, we examine processes in cities that are operated routinely during the working day over which most work, industrial production and shopping activities take place. We also look at longer-term processes that lead to changes in the location of activities. In this sense, our models are generalized to various timescales relating both to the delivery of energy resources as well as to changes in their provision over longer time periods.

In this chapter, we first develop various templates for describing and classifying these activities and this enables us to examine flows and movements that consume resources and generate various costs, a large proportion of which are associated with the use of energy. We then develop typical models of spatial flow or interaction that bind various activities and their land uses together, and cast these in analogy to thermodynamic interactions in which energy and its use is central. We sketch a land-use transportation model for Greater London and then embed this into a framework for integrated assessment of key issues involving urban change over the next 50 years, specifically changes associated with climate change and rising sea levels and as well as dramatic shifts in the cost of using fossil fuels. Finally, we examine a case study for Greater London in which transport costs associated with travel by car are doubled and then examine the impacts of such changes on interaction and location, in the manner of typical 'before' and 'after' analysis that dominates the use of these tools for urban forecasting.

9.3 A template for spatial energy and interaction accounting

There are many ways of organizing the physical elements, infrastructures and populations that define cities. Before we introduce the key components of energy that underpin urban land-use and transportation structures, we attempt a rudimentary classification based on the four kinds of flow that we have already defined with respect to systems for production and consumption. In Table 9.3.1, we array these two sectors against the four flow patterns and within each cell of the table, specify the key flows that define movements associated with production and consumption with respect to materials, commodities, population and information. Flows of materials that involve energy in the production and consumption sectors involve the way populations are sustained through the provision of utilities, while in the production sector itself, such flows define the very processes that are used to produce goods for consumption. Demand for and supply of these materials are generated by populations acting for purposes of survival and economic gain and to explain these flows, links to the various economic and social processes that drive the economy of the city are required.

In terms of the ways in which production and consumption generate products, either as intermediate inputs to other processes or as products that are part of what is often called 'final demand' (by consumers), these generate flows of commodities that in themselves use energy in their transit. At the next level, populations provide the labour for production and the demand for consumption as these generate flows to work and flows to purchase products and services, all of which use energy with respect to movement. The distinction between consumption and production is less distinct in these terms, for populations both work in producing and also consume an array of products that they produce, not only in retailing, commercial services, manufacturing and agricultural industries but also in health, education and in social activities that broadly constitute leisure. Moreover, the patterns of production and consumption that define these flows often overlay one another but in essence it is the movements to enable these processes to take place that is a dominant focus of interest from the perspective of cities.

The last sector that generates flows is somewhat different in that such flows relate to ways in which information is used in production and consumption. Information complements all three previous sets of flows in that it is used to support movements of all kinds with respect to how such flows are accomplished. Increasing amounts of information are used in the digital domain, some to substitute for face-to-face contacts, thereby reducing some movements in

Table 9.3.1 Types of flow associated with production and consumption

Flows Activity	Materials	Commodities	People	Information
Production	All sectors	Inter-industry linkages, exports, imports	Journeys to work, school, health and related commercial sectors	Working from home, online learning, inter-industry flows
Consumption	All sectors	Retailing, commercial services	Journeys to retail, commercial, health, leisure	Leisure, entertainment, health, financial services

volume and frequency. But in general information flows are quite unlike flows of energy and to date there is no clear way of translating such information into energy equivalents, despite the intriguing possibility that all energy is in fact information (Tribus and McIrvine, 1971).

Demand and supply for the resources that drive production and consumption provide another perspective on this mix of energy flows. It is too simplistic to associate demand with consumption and supply with production for this ignores demand and supply that is internal to production and consumption, internal to the industrial and related sectors, and to the consumption sector associated with population. Moreover, in cities these sectors are more associated with human activities that reveal themselves in land uses in different locations. Accordingly, to cut through the maze of possible classifications, we conceive of cities as being composed of distinct land-use activities that we define broadly as industrial (and possibly agricultural), retailing, commercial services, health, education, related social/welfare services and leisure services (which include social activities). These are all classes of production and to complete the structure, we identify residential land use that is composed of housing and related services as constituting the activity focus of all populations when they are not engaging in production in any of the previous categories. In the context of the city, demand for the products and services produced by these sectors is driven by the population, largely associated with locations where populations reside (although demand is also generated from places where the population works), while supplies are generated from the places where people work, except for internal services that the population provides for itself, usually in residential locations. The products and services that generate significant flows of energy are those that are formally produced and supplied to places where they are consumed. We thus classify activities that have distinct locations and generate spatial demand and supply involving energy flows in Table 9.3.2.

Table 9.3.2 Traffic flows between urban activities that use energy resources

Activity	W	R	S	C	H	E	L
W	Intermediate production	Journey to work	Work to shop	Work to commerce	Work to health	Work to education	Work to leisure
R		Internal services	Journey to shop	Journey to commerce	Journey to health care	Journey to school	Journey to leisure
S			Internal retailing	Retail to commerce	Retail to health	Retail to school	Retail to leisure
C				Internal commerce	Commerce to health	Commerce to school	Commerce to leisure
H					Internal health flows	Health to commerce	Health to leisure
E						Internal education	Education to leisure
L							Internal leisure

Table 9.3.2 is a matrix of linkages between these seven distinct sectors – Work (*W*), Residential (*R*), Shopping (*S*), Commercial (*C*), Health (*H*), Education (*E*) and Leisure (*L*). All of these are defined by specific land uses and associated activities, all of which comprise different patterns of demand and supply which manifest themselves through movement patterns that link these activities together with respect to the provision of labour and capital that drives production and consumption. How these sectors are configured relative to one another defines urban spatial structure as well as the transportation patterns that sustain these structures at any point in time. These structures change as patterns of demand and supply change, as populations grow and decline and as migration into and out of cities changes this balance. These changes are determined by the interaction of demand and supply through various markets. It could be argued that what we require for a comprehensive theory of how energy enters this picture is a fully fledged urban theory that enables us to see how cities develop in terms of the way energy is used as urban spatial structure changes in time. In fact, most theories that we have are extremely partial in that energy is not to the fore in any of them. Urban theories that have been developed usually focus on specific sectors and markets such as housing to the exclusion of many others, using micro-economic theories of how individuals locate in cities. These are quite different in style and type from explanations of production that depend on macro-economic structures or on location theories of individual firms that do not scale to entire urban structures.

Here we take a much more pragmatic view of how cities are explained with respect to the flow of energy by literally formulating models of how the various sectors in Table 9.3.2 are articulated as sets of flows between different land uses and activities. In terms of Table 9.3.1, we focus on the population column (shown in grey), and in terms of Table 9.3.2, we demonstrate such flows for the work, residential and shopping sectors (which constitute some of the most significant flows). We leave the other sectors aside on the assumption that similar models can be set up to explain how the flows associated with these sectors complete this picture of urban structure. The sectors that we focus on in Table 9.3.2 are also shown in grey. In one sense, Table 9.3.2 implies that each of the flow categories is equally significant but this is not the case. For example the sectors relating work to residence and residence to retailing account for about 49 per cent of all passenger movements – trips – in urban areas. Journeys to school/education and health have grown in importance over the last decade, as indeed has leisure and in Table 9.3.3 we show the breakdown of passenger trips across all categories for the UK, noting that over 95 per cent of the population live in urban areas. The sectors we focus on here are also coloured in grey.

Let us first represent generic flows between two typical sectors that, to fix ideas, might be work and residence as illustrated by the journey to work. If we call the origin location of the flow zone i and the destination location zone j, then we can write the flow volume as F_{ij} that is measured in terms of the volume of individuals, in this example, moving from work to home or vice versa. There are many measures associated with this flow, particularly the cost of making each trip, which we can define as c_{ij} and which clearly encapsulates the resources that are associated with the energy ε_{ij} used in such movement.

Table 9.3.3 Proportion of trip flows by type

Trip category	Total volume (trips/capita/year)	Percentage
Commuting/business	187	18.811
Education	105	10.551
Shopping	198	19.959
Other escort/health	96	9.671
Personal business	103	10.348
Leisure	260	26.221
Other	44	4.439

Source: NTS (2009) *www.dft.gov.uk/pgr/statistics/datatablespublications/modal*

This notation is enough to indicate the total costs C and total energies E associated with all these flows, which can be obtained by simply counting the costs and the energies involved over all possible interactions between the origin and destination zones. These are defined as:

$$C = \sum_i \sum_j F_{ij} c_{ij}, \quad E = \sum_i \sum_j F_{ij} \varepsilon_{ij} \quad and \quad F = \sum_i \sum_j F_{ij}$$
$$\bar{C} = \sum_i \sum_j F_{ij} c_{ij} \Big/ F \quad and \quad \bar{E} = \sum_i \sum_j F_{ij} \varepsilon_{ij} \Big/ F$$

[9.3.1]

where F is the total flow in the system, and $\bar{C}$ and $\bar{E}$ are the respective (average) costs of travel and energy use per journey. We assume that there are n origin zones {i} and the same n destination zones {j} and that all summations are with respect to this range from 1, 2, ..., n. In these terms, it is quite easy to see how the pattern of costs and energy used in these movements can change the total resources involved. The essence of building good models of the city system that pick up these potential changes is based on explaining the volume and patterns of flow between the various sectors. For example, placing constraints on where people might live through control of housing can have an important impact on the pattern of travel and thence the costs and energies involved. Equally, if the cost of energy changes then good models will redistribute the pattern and volume of flows to take account of the relative opportunities for substituting between, say, different modes of travel and/or of changing the location of work or residences or any of the other land-use activities that define the system of interest.

These sorts of accounts are rather different from those used in mainstream energy accounting such as those associated with material balances, as they are largely constituted from an economic viewpoint. They are also static in conception, or at least only dynamic in so far as the flows pertain to those that maintain the structure of the city at a point in time (in equilibrium) rather than indicating how activities in the city might grow and change. We need to complete this accounting by defining flows and the cost and energy measures that are associated with origin and destination places, i and j. Then if we sum F_{ji} over i to define flows destined for each j and over j to define flows destined for each i, then we derive these as:

$$F_j = \sum_i F_{ij}, \quad F_i = \sum_j F_{ij} \tag{9.3.2}$$

The total costs and total energies associated with travelling from i or travelling to j and the average cost and energy use are defined in analogy to the accounts shown in [9.3.1] as:

$$\left. \begin{array}{l} C_j = \sum_i F_{ij} c_{ij}, \quad C_i = \sum_j F_{ij} c_{ij}, \quad E_j = \sum_i F_{ij} \varepsilon_{ij}, \quad E_i = \sum_j F_{ij} \varepsilon_{ij}, \\[2mm] \bar{C}_j = \sum_i F_{ij} c_{ij} \Big/ F_j = C_j / F_j, \quad \bar{C}_i = \sum_j F_{ij} c_{ij} \Big/ F_i = C_i / F_i, \\[2mm] \bar{E}_j = \sum_i F_{ij} \varepsilon_{ij} \Big/ F_j = E_j / F_j, \quad \bar{E}_i = \sum_j F_{ij} \varepsilon_{ij} \Big/ F_i = E_i / F_i \end{array} \right\} \tag{9.3.3}$$

It might be supposed that models exist that consistently link all the sectors that we have defined in Table 9.3.2 together, but these are rare. Some do exist (see Iacono et al, 2008) but most models tend to focus on one or two sectors, for the great difficulty is integrating all these sectors consistently in a way that traces appropriate cause and effect relations. So many activities in cities are determined by multiple causes that vary in time, are difficult to observe, and are hard to embody in structures that balance demand and supply in an appropriate form, that partial models of the urban system are the norm. Moreover, when we focus on the production sector, models to explain how industries relate to one another through chains of intermediate demand and supply are usually developed using rather different model structures from those we develop here. These models tend to be macro-economic structures such as input–output models that are often non-spatial and operate at a scale above our spatial representation of the city by small area zones that we articulate here. In fact, many of these models relate to traditions more associated with regional and national economic forecasting and in this sense they lie beyond the scope of the ideas that are the focus of this book. Nevertheless in taking an integrated view to energy assessment in cities, these more macro scales still need to be considered, as we note again later in this chapter.

9.4 Modelling residential and retail interaction and location

There is a very well worked out theory of location and interaction in which flows of populations and related economic volumes are understood in analogy to the way particles are distributed in a physical system using statistical thermodynamics. In essence, it is possible to distribute populations to locations by finding the most probable distribution with respect to the total cost of location, which in turn can be assumed to be the cost or total resource or indeed total energy available to make that pattern of locations possible. It is easy to guess that if the total (economic and social) cost of location in one specific location were zero, and the cost everywhere else was greater than zero, then only one location would be selected; we might say that only one location was possible and the probability of locating there would be unity, all others being zero. At the opposite extreme, if all the costs of location were the same and were finite, then no one location would have any advantage over any other, and thus every location would be equally probable and population would thus locate evenly over the available space. It is easy to see that in these cases, much more energy/cost would be locally incurred where all locations were occupied than in the case where only one would be occupied.

We can generalize this argument further to a situation where we are not directly simulating where populations locate but where they interact; in short, we want to find the most probable distribution of trips between origins and destinations that use a certain cost or quantity of energy. Again imagine that a trip maker located at each origin i incurs an infinite cost if they were to make a trip to any destination other than to the origin where they are already located. Then the most probable distribution would be where no one travelled and the travel cost was at a minimum. However, if the travel costs were all the same wherever a person were to travel to, then individuals would travel with equal probability from every origin to every destination, assuming the origins were constrained. In this case, the cost or energy used would be at a maximum. If we were then to add up the travel that is generated in this way using the accounting in [9.3.1] and [9.3.3], then we would find that the location patterns would differ markedly between the minimum and maximum energy cases, suggesting that different patterns of costs and energy use determine very different configurations of city form.

We now need to be crystal clear about the way we are defining costs and energies in this model. We assume that transport costs vary directly with energy costs, notwithstanding that there are other costs to be borne such as the cost of time (which might even incur different energy costs), and physical costs of engaging in the trip such as parking. Different modes of transport of course will incur different energy costs and this will be a central issue in the models that we apply below. The key issue in the costs or energies incurred is not the costs or the energies associated with what it costs to travel between origins and destinations (which are a disaggregation of the costs of location as we see in [9.3.3]), but the flow volumes that are generated. If flow volumes are zero, then the cost of travel is zero for no one travels and this is independent of the actual cost. Indeed, if the cost of travel is infinity everywhere other than a trip from the origin to the same origin location, then everyone stays in the same place and no one travels. Hence the travel cost and energy costs are zero. If the cost of travel is the same everywhere, then people engage in the same amount of travel independent of their origin or destination and the amount of cost incurred is at a maximum. The actual unit of travel or energy cost in this argument is not relevant, for it is the distribution of costs that are important as these are what determine the flow volumes.

In short, in systems where costs are extremely large, less people will travel and thus the costs incurred and energy used will be at a minimum. The extreme case is where everyone lives and works in the same place. This is the ultimate compact city. At the other extreme, people are indifferent to travel and in such a case every origin and destination has the same amount of travel, the costs are uniform and the energy used at each location is the same. This represents a situation where every location is occupied by the same volume and energy costs are at a maximum. This is the case where the city is uniformly developed and in principle, dependent upon the total cost and volumes involved, the city can spread out 'indefinitely', the ultimate case of urban sprawl.

To generate the appropriate models where the dominant constraint is on total interaction cost that could, among others, be interpreted as a constraint on total energy used, we maximize a probability function that gives the greatest number of ways in which individual trips can be associated with a specific pattern of interactions that meet this constraint. In essence, the pattern of trips generated is one that has the greatest number of ways in which individual trips that define micro-states can be assigned to the macro pattern. In one sense, this process of generating the most probable distribution is based on the assumption that we do not know the actual allocation of specific individuals to origins and destination and, as we are never likely to know this, then the resulting distribution that is the most probable is the distribution that is associated with the greatest number of micro-states. This process is akin to finding the most probable distribution in a statistical system where there is a constraint on the total energy. It is in fact the process of maximizing entropy (which in turn is a measure of uncertainty or information) subject to the energy constraint and it has an intimate relation to the way a system is configured in a thermodynamic equilibrium. We do not probe further into the meaning of the process in this context, but suffice it to say that the process is well suited to simulating very large systems where individuals respond to constraints on energy and where there are more and more interactions between particles – individuals – when the particles respond to higher temperatures (or higher energy costs) (Atkins, 1994). The method was first popularised for urban and regional systems by Wilson (1970) but its specific uses in thinking about actual energies and entropies in city systems is more recent (Wilson, 2009; Morphet, 2010).

Although the constraint on energy or travel cost is key to the distributions generated, there are other constraints that the spatial distribution must meet and this pertains to the degree of generality and often the available data that the model needs to take into account. Here we assume that as well as a constraint on cost, there is a constraint on the origin of activity; that is, we wish to derive a model that meets a constraint on the amount of travel generated at an origin in analogy to the accounting constraints above. We develop the model for the journey to work where we now write these two constraints as:

$$\sum_j T_{ij} = W_i \quad and \quad \sum_i \sum_j T_{ij} c_{ij}^T = C^T \qquad [9.4.1]$$

We define T_{ij} as the number of individuals working in location i and living in residential location j and W_i are the number of jobs generated at i. The most probable distribution of trips can be derived using a standard method that gives:

$$T_{ij} = W_i \frac{\exp(-\beta c_{ij}^T)}{\sum_j \exp(-\beta c_{ij}^T)}, \quad and \quad P_j = \sum_i T_{ij} \qquad [9.4.2]$$

where β is a parameter that ensures that the cost constraint in [9.4.1] is met. The summation over origins gives the predicted activity – the population P_j at each destination, and this activity is not constrained by the model.

This model form is a variant of the Boltzmann-Gibbs distribution that mirrors the standard allocation of energies in a closed thermodynamic system with fixed cost C^T (or energy). It is easy to show that $\beta \sim 1/C^T$ where C^T varies in proportion to the temperature (cost) of the system. This implies that when $\beta \to 0$, then the distribution of trips becomes uniform for each origin (within the constraints imposed by the origins), and thus temperature tends to infinity and the system reaches maximum entropy. It is easy to see that when this occurs, the model in [9.4.2] simplifies to:

$$T_{ij} = \frac{W_i}{n}, \quad and \quad P_j = \sum_i \frac{W_i}{n} = \frac{W}{n}, \; \forall j \qquad [9.4.3]$$

where W is the total employment in the system that is equally allocated to all zones. This is the equivalent of a system that is completely spread out in uniform fashion. The opposite system where everybody resides in the places j where they work is achieved when the temperature tends to zero, that is, when $\beta \to \infty$ and the entropy is at a minimum. If the intrazonal cost $c_{ii} < c_{ij}, \; \forall i \neq j$, then this implies that no one travels in the system except to the zone in which they work and the model simplifies to:

$$T_{ii} = W_i, \quad T_{ij} = 0, \; \forall i \neq j, \quad and \quad P_j = \left\{ \begin{array}{l} W_i, \; \forall i = j \\ 0, \; \forall i \neq j \end{array} \right. \qquad [9.4.4]$$

Note that if all the activity were located in a single zone then everybody would reside in the same zone. If there were no constraints on origins, then the distribution of origin activity would mirror the distribution of residential activity when $\beta \to 0$ and where $\beta \to \infty$, the patterns of interaction, origin activity and destination activity would be entirely uniform, that is $T_{ij} = W/n^2$, $P_j = W/n^2$ and $W_i = W/n^2$.

We could say a great deal more about the implications of probability maximizing (or entropy maximizing as it is often called) and the various interpretations of this application of statistical thermodynamics to city systems (Wilson, 2009). Suffice it to say, however, that our main concern is the fact that as we vary the constraint on cost (or energy) by changing the distributions of costs c_{ij}^T (or energies ε_{ij}^T) or indeed the total, there are fundamental implications for the pattern of interactions (trips T_{ij}) as well as for the location of predicted activities (populations P_j). To extend the residential model to retailing, we can couple the population distribution P_j to retail services provision by considering the spatial demand for retail services S_k defined in locations or centres k using a similar formulation to that specified in [9.4.1] and [9.4.2]. The retail location model which predicts flows S_{ik} is subject to constraints on demand conserved at population origins and to a constraint on total travel cost:

$$\sum_k S_{jk} = P_j \quad and \quad \sum_k \sum_j S_{jk} c_{jk}^S = C^S \tag{9.4.5}$$

where P_j is related to the demand for services at j. The most probable distribution of trips is derived as:

$$S_{jk} = P_j \frac{\exp(-\lambda c_{jk}^S)}{\sum_k \exp(-\lambda c_{jk}^S)}, \quad and \quad S_k = \sum_j S_{jk} \tag{9.4.6}$$

where λ is the parameter that is related to the subsystem cost C^s and temperature. Now one can generate a chain of such interaction models with linkages from populations to other sectors, the first such model being demonstrated by Lowry (1964). In principle all sectors can be linked in this way, as Table 9.3.2 implies, although it is essential to ensure consistency in the specification of these flows and to ensure that the order to solving any coupled equation systems results in a unique and stable solution. This is as much a matter of model design as it is of the substantive representation of the urban system, and to date there have been few if any urban models that have been developed in this way (but see Batty, 1986; de la Barra, 1989; Simmonds, 1999; Echenique, 2004). In the model that we demonstrate here, although the extended system is being developed, we simply concentrate on the residential location model in [9.4.1] and [9.4.2].

9.5 A residential location model for Greater London

The model we have developed is part of a wider process of integrated assessment to evaluate the impact of rising sea levels on the London region and we sketch this process in the next section (Dawson et al, 2009). Here, however, we begin with an outline of the model and some results of its calibration before using it to assess the impact of changes in transport costs on travel, thus illustrating how models of this kind can be used to explore changes in energy use and mitigation with respect to transport usage and the residential location of a population. The model extends the design we have introduced by disaggregating travel costs into four modes of transport that we define by the index m where $m = 1$ is road-related journeys to work, mainly by car, $m = 2$ is heavy rail, $m = 3$ is tube and light rail, and $m = 4$ is public bus. We now define trips as $T_{ij}(m)$, costs as $c_{ij}(m)$ omitting the superscript T, total costs as $C(m)$ and average costs as $\bar{C}(m)$. We have not as yet disaggregated employment W_i or population P_j and we do not constrain the modal split to meet predetermined totals, for the model simulates the competition between modes that is essential if we are to gauge the impact of changes in travel cost/energies. In essence, this is a travel demand model but there are no supply considerations.

The model does not reallocate trips that it predicts to the transport system, so capacity is not an issue with respect to prediction. This is partly because we are interested in very long-term adjustments in the system but also more pragmatically because the four travel networks used to determine costs are not yet embedded within the model structure itself. In this sense any predictions that result assume a first response to changes in travel costs (or any other independent variables such as levels of employment). This first response would clearly be moderated once capacity is taken account of and the chain of adaptation that accompanies such change invoked.

The model is driven visually on the desktop through the standard process of data exploration, model calibration and prediction (Batty, 1992). Conditional predictions of the 'what if' variety are established either 'on-the-fly' with the user developing specific proposals within the desk top visual environment or externally by users and stakeholders who provide the model with the relevant data pertaining to scenarios. A feature of the model is that at every stage the user has a wide array of map, 3D software (such as Google Earth) and visual analytics that can be immediately accessed in real time to explore the model's data, calibrations or predictions. In Plate 45 we show the typical interface where the origin activity (employment) is graphed and a key location (Heathrow Airport) is identified for reference purposes. In Plate 46 we show employment density, population density and the pattern of work trips by road $T_{6j}(1), j = 1, 2, ..., 633$ *zones* from Heathrow to all other zones and from St James in Westminster by tube/light rail $T_{224j}(3)$, $j = 1, 2, ..., 633$ *zones* to give some sense of the richness of the model. The observed percentage split of trip makers between the road, rail, tube and bus modes is 39, 12, 33, 16. Note that we do not model in this version the walk-cycle mode that we know constitutes some 19 per cent of all trips in Greater London but we simply assume that this proportion of walking and cycling trips are allocated to the intrazonal links within the zone itself. In a more elaborate version of the model, this mode is represented explicitly. In the context of energy and climate change, this is perhaps the mode that might change the most in the mid-term future as people switch to more sustainable and less costly forms of transport and as the city is further adapted to the pedestrian and the cyclist.

The model has been calibrated to data assembled for the period 2001–2005 by determining parameter values $\beta(m)$, $m = 1, 2, 3, 4$ through solving the maximum likelihood (maximum entropy) equations implicit in the disaggregated modal split model represented in [9.4.1] and [9.4.2]. The fit of the model is reasonable, though not as good as it might be with more considered measurement of transport costs and capacities, but about 59 per cent of the variance in overall trip distribution is explained with slightly less explanation (55 per cent) for the location of population. We have not constrained the model to meet constraints on modal split but we are confident that the differences that might be generated using the model predictively with respect to changing modes would be in the right direction. Of course in models of this kind, the pattern of equilibrium that is predicted is that which is implicit in the existing spatial structure, almost in an unconstrained manner. In a sense, as Lowry (1964) argued so cogently, it is the pattern that might result if the city were to be built according to the observed patterns of transport costs and observed configuration of employment at the base date, rather than an attempt to explain how the city evolved to the cross-section that we observe. In short, the model produces, in Lowry's (1964) terms, an 'instant metropolis'.

What we are able to do with this model is to construct scenarios on-the-fly that involve major and systematic changes in the key input variables, namely the employment origins $\{W_i\}$ and the travel costs $\{c_{ij}(m), m = 1, 2, 3, 4\}$. In fact, to build a scenario that involves individually tweaking each location or interaction pair is far too laborious but the program has been modified to enable users to change the overall balance of transport costs, to add major new sources of employment, and to add in key transport links between centroids that are then used to update the shortest paths in the cost matrices. To illustrate this and to impress the sorts of change that might be occasioned with big switches in energy costs, what we have done is to assume that the relative cost of road transport is doubled, in short that $c_{ij}^{new}(1) = 2c_{ij}(1)$, $\forall ij$ leaving the three other modal cost matrices unchanged. In fact, because road transport cost is made up of a suitably weighted combination of fuel costs ε_{ij}, value of time v_{ij} and costs such as parking ρ_j less any benefit ascribed to the comfort of travelling by car b_{ij} as, for example, in $c_{ij}(1) = \varepsilon_{ij} + v_{ij} + \rho_j - b_{ij}$, then it is clear that if all this rise were attributable to fuel costs, then this would probably involve increasing fuel costs by over 200 per cent of the previous cost. We can of course build scenarios that are much more elaborate than these in which network changes as well as differential changes in transport costs are considered. If capacity is added to the model, which would involve completing the travel demand model cycle by adding an assignment (to network) stage and reiterating until equilibrium, highly realistic futures might be generated. In fact some of the larger land-use transport models under construction such as ILUTE (see Hunt et al, 2005) enable such testing to take place.

Here we simply run the model with the system-wide change and then evaluate the results in terms of shifting modal split, differences in total cost of travel (hence energy used) and differences in the allocation of residential population caused by such a change. We would expect there to be considerable shifts from road to other modes of transport, although London is so complex with respect to competition between modes that it is hard to know which modes car travellers would switch to as the cost of travel by rail and tube is considerably higher anyway. We would also expect the population to shift inwards – for the city to compact – as car users tend to dominate the suburbs rather than the inner city where the provision of alternative modes of transport are much better and where parking, congestion and the costs of these are much greater. In fact, the easiest changes to visualize are in the population. In Plate 47 we therefore show the changes in population with respect to whether each destination grows (red bars) or declines (blue bars). What is surprising is that the absolute shift that we can measure as $\phi = \Sigma_j \left| P_j - P_j^{pred} \right| / 2$ is quite small in comparison with total population. That is, $\zeta = \phi / \Sigma P_j = 0.04$, which indicates that very little population actually shifts. Note that the overall shift is zero, in that changing travel costs simply lead to a redistribution of populations rather than to migration across the city boundaries, that is $\Sigma_j (P_j - P_j^{pred}) = 0$ (Batty et al, 1974). To put this in perspective, we now need to examine shifts in modes.

There is a massive shift out of car/road use to other forms of transport, particularly rail and bus. Some 36 per cent of car users shift, while rail grows by 46 per cent, tube by 36 per cent and bus by a staggering 78 per cent. To an extent, big shifts in modal split that are encompassed within a city where there is very little adjustment of activity located at residential destinations are a consequence of the fact that there are many more degrees of freedom with respect to the extent to which trip makers can switch between modes without changing their residential locations. In one sense, this is intrinsic to the way we can treat these types of system in analogy to statistical thermodynamics, for the very model that we are generating is based on the notion that there are many different allocations at the micro-level that produce the same pattern at the macro. These changes illustrate that we need to keep these impacts in perspective. It is extremely unlikely that the capacity exists in the transport system to enable anything like the scale of these changes to be put in place. Possibly the greatest changes could take place with respect to bus and then rail (which in fact show the greatest percentage increases) but the tube is at capacity. We have not examined other transport flows that incur energy costs such as those that relate to industry. In short, the internal flows in Table 9.3.2 generate considerable demands for transport, and capacity, particularly in the road system released by shifts of workers to other modes, could easily be mopped up by these demands. This is what largely happened in central London when congestion charging was introduced in 2003 – a 30 per cent fall in vehicles that first occurred has eventually disappeared as traffic has built back to 2003 levels not through growth in commuting by car, but through growth in buses and delivery vehicles. 'What if' scenarios of the kind sketched out here are a first step in a dialogue concerning changes in energy and sustainability, as embodied in the wider context of other tools such as those developed for planning support systems (Batty, 2008).

Table 9.5.1 shows the specific changes in total trips, total and average costs and related variables for the 'before' and 'after' situations. Total trips in the system are constant (apart from some rounding errors associated with very small trip volumes) but the distribution changes between the 'before' and 'after' situations in that trips made by car are attracted to other modes. This is reflected in the total and average costs of travel. What happens is that the total costs drop even more massively than total trips by car while increasing proportionately for the other modes. Although the average travel cost by road falls steeply, other average costs hardly change at all and this suggests that the switch from car to other modes is from longer trips – with the distribution across each of these other modes reflecting the existing composition of those modes in terms of origins and destinations. In Table 9.5.1 we have also included measures of the entropy of the system. This measure is really one of spread or variation, with car more spread out than rail, which in turn is followed by bus and then tube. This definitely confirms our perceptions of the way the infrastructure systems are configured in London. After the change, these patterns still recur with the exception of rail, which becomes more spread than car; or rather the pattern of car/road usage tends to compact a little, something that is again consistent with all the other results from this prediction.

Table 9.5.1 Changes in trip volumes and costs before and after the doubling of road transport costs

	Road	Rail	Tube	Bus	All modes
Total trips before	2,715,867	1,071,446	294,295	478,581	4,560,189
Total trips after	1,734,279	1,573,148	399,920	852,066	4,559,413
Total costs before[1]	105,107,000	83,652,340	17,567,680	7024,457	213,351,477
Total costs after	41,145,340	123,942,500	23,931,430	11,899,650	200,918,920
Average costs before[1]	38.701	78.074	59.694	14.678	46.781
Average costs after	23.725	78.786	59.841	13.966	44.058
Modal split before	0.596	0.235	0.065	0.105	0.596
Modal split after	0.380	0.345	0.088	0.187	0.380
Modal parameter	0.043	0.045	0.062	0.161	na
Entropies before	11.781	10.605	9.616	9.987	11.582
Entropies after	11.025	11.151	10.002	10.229	11.252

Note: [1] Total and average costs are measured in minutes of travel time; all specific costs have been converted into a standardized unit of travel time and thus average costs can be determined by dividing total costs by total trips.

9.6 A wider framework for integrated assessment

The model we have developed is part of a wider process of integrated assessment to evaluate the impact of climate change on London and the Thames Gateway, the corridor running east of the City to the River Thames Estuary. The significant risk over the next 100 years is flooding and if sea levels rise by 2m by 2100, as forecast by UKCIP (2009), then urban infrastructure of all kinds located in the floodplain will be badly damaged on a scale that is much greater than the floods of 1953, which led to heavy loss of life. The Thames Barrage that was developed in the 1970s–1980s to guard against extreme events, such as the surge tides that led to the 1953 floods, will no longer be fit for purpose by 2025 at the current rate of sea level rise. The key problem is that the Thames Gateway was identified, as recently as 2000, as the general area for locating London's future population growth; the east is relatively deprived and requires substantial investment in jobs and housing if it is to raise prosperity and cater for the local population in more effective ways than at present. These policies were put in place long before climate change was on the current agenda and in this sense these policies betray the direct contradictions in London planning that need to be resolved. The floodplain and the wider Gateway are shown in Plate 48. It is clear that the model we have already described is relevant to predicting populations in the Greater London area that overlaps this region and falls within the Gateway. Wards that form the zones of the land-use transportation model are overlaid with the Environment Agency[1] flood map showing the flood plan with areas with high vulnerability (red) and lesser vulnerability (yellow).

The model was originally developed as part of a process of integrated assessment devised as a framework to handle informed policy making with respect to climate change in large cities. It was developed under the auspices of the Tyndall Centre for Climate Change Cities project (Hall et al, 2009), which involved building a framework for coupling different models together across scales and sectors from socio-economic to physical. The framework is designed to explore how the effects of flooding might be best assessed with respect to informed predictions about the medium- and long-term futures involving the distribution of employment, population and related land-use types and activities in large cities. These models begin at the national–regional level in the form of economic and demographic models that predict total employment by sector and population by age and sex at the regional level – in this case at the Greater London level. The economic models are based on input–output models developed by Barker et al (2008), while the demographic model is only being developed for the current variant of the model and is based on micro-simulation (Wu et al, 2008). Employment estimates are then factored down to the small area level – in this case wards that constitute the zoning system of the land-use transportation model – using a technique based on factoring that is trend-based but modified by key policy initiatives in the city that we know will change the forecast distribution. The demographic totals are used as inputs to ensure the total populations generated meet the trend forecasts that embody a whole series of factors pertaining to demographic forecasting that involve birth, death, migration and fertility rates as well as social and related welfare policies.

Once the model makes predictions of the kind we have already seen for the populations of small areas, these are taken in turn as control totals and redistributed to a much finer spatial scale that takes account of local factors of a more physical nature. This stage of the model is reminiscent of a cellular automata development model, in which physical data controls development based on constraints, neighbourhood factors and local accessibility measures. The model, written within GIS by Ford and Barr (2009), leads directly to the engineering models that predict flood events and flood plain invasion under different climate change scenarios. The way these models are coupled is shown in Figure 9.6.1, which is notable through its absence of feedback loops. Of course there are many such loops. The fact we leave them out from the block diagram is simply to reduce the confusion that such loops can imply but we need to remind readers that over long periods of time such as 50 to 100 years, these kinds of equilibrium forecast are not meant to account for the massive adaptation

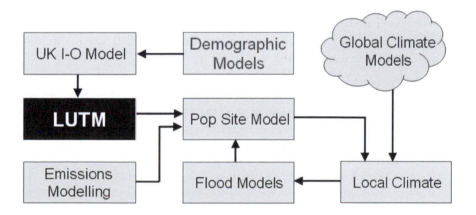

Figure 9.6.1 A framework for the integrated assessment of climate change in Greater London and the Thames Gateway

Source: Author

and mitigation strategies that will surely be involved in moving to these end points under these various scenarios. In short, the aim of this framework is to suggest how stakeholders might think about climate change and begin to explore different policies that would then be tested in iterative dialogue between model builders, model users and the wider political constituency.

To further illustrate the use of the land-use transportation model, we have implemented a crude form of East London development policy, which has tended to be the main focus of London plans during the last 20 years (of which the Olympics Games 2012 site will be the most obvious legacy). We doubled the size of employment at each of seven key employment hubs in the east, of which the most significant is at Canary Wharf, London's second central business district (CBD). We have also implemented a new high speed rail line from Canary Wharf eastwards to Canning Town, Beckton, the river area of Barking and Dagenham, South Hornchurch and Rainham, which reduces travel cost on this line by 30 per cent (mainly due to reductions in travel time). In fact we have not tested these two alternatives separately. Therefore, we have not yet determined if the high speed line leads to growth in locations nearer or further away from the large additions of employment at Canary Wharf. Nevertheless, this is the kind of 'what if' scenario that can easily be tested using judicious combinations of the various changes that are proposed.

The results of our scenario are shown in Plate 49. The spread of population is considerably wider than the location of the changes in employment at a very small number of hubs and the location of the high speed heavy rail line along the Thames corridor. The biggest predicted changes in absolute populations are in the eastern corridor as expected, but what is surprising is the spread to the south of the river into southeast London and even into north London. We have not been able to validate any of these kinds of scenarios in developing the model for we do not have any data on before and after studies at a large scale, but it is possible that in future development of the model we may be able to use the data from the introduction of the congestion charge in 2003 to initiate such validation. What we can be confident about is that it is clear that the centre acts as a strong barrier to any of this employment moving farther west (of the centre) even though Canary Wharf has good travel links to inner west London. The mapped population in Plate 49d also shows how local pockets of accessibility show up in the eventual distribution of population. It is quite clear from this prediction that those zones closest to the river and liable to flooding receive considerable amounts of new population. To assess the flood risk, the next stage of the model is invoked and this involves moving to a finer scale, $50m^2$, where the data used is mainly physical in form.

We will not take this example any further other than to illustrate how the analysis proceeds to the population site level using Ford and Barr's (2009) urban development model. In Plate 50 we show the zone of South Hornchurch that is on the north bank of the river. Plate 50 plots the pattern of urban development (in its configuration in Plate 50a) and shows this as developed or constrained land (red) in Plate 50b. These sorts of constraints are included in many pixel layers in the GIS, which is used to represent and store these layers. The logic of this stage in modelling is to consider two related functions: first, to see if the development levels predicted make physical sense, and second, to assess if this development is subject to any flood risk. At this stage, there is a crucial feedback loop, for if the capacities examined are not sufficient to enable these predictions to be accepted and analysed further, then the model system must be reiterated with changed residential attractors that reflect the constraints invoked at this stage. This is not yet implemented in the model but it would require a feedback loop from the population site model to the land-use transportation model in Figure 9.6.1. The model contains various physical layers shown in Plate 50a that act as local accessibility of places as well as physical constraints on development. In Plate 50b, we show areas not affected by any constraints in green.

9.7 Next steps and future research

We have explored in some detail the way in which energy flows between different land uses with respect to transportation impact on the distribution of employment and population in large cities. We can take this further in many ways, for example by extending our models to deal with many more sectors and their constituent flows as well as by translating flows of people into commodity and material flows at the physical level and information flows at the ethereal. As we have argued, these translations are not well worked out and there are no comprehensive and convincing models and theories that cement all these energy flows together to give a coherent picture of the functions of cities in terms of their spatial structure and dynamics. In this book, many different perspectives on urban energy are presented and by now it must be clear to readers that there is an enormous challenge ahead of us if we are to fashion an integrated view of energy in urban systems. To an extent, such theoretical advances are a prelude to a better understanding of cities' functioning.

We have not developed a series of indicators of sustainability for this was not our purpose, but it must be evident to all who have absorbed this message that our quest is to explore how energy is used in cities in more efficient and effective ways. In fact there are many developments of sustainability indicators that spin off from urban models, several of which involve accessibility and density as well as measures involving physical constraints such as those that are embodied in the urban development model that is one of the ultimate stages in the integrated assessment sketched in the previous section. Measures of accessibility and density are computed in our London model as a matter of course and changes in these measures, occasioned by the sorts of scenarios that we have developed, are routine. The full array of measures in models such as these is quite well worked out, as for example in the MEPLAN, TRANUS and IRPUD land-use transportation models that comprise part of the PROPOLIS planning support system (Lautso et al, 2004), where a range of indicators is generated from model outputs that enable users to examine city systems with respect to their sustainability. In this, physical measures such as emissions and related pollutants are linked to travel volumes and modes while measures of density and configuration that relate to local accessibility can be derived. In fact, in PROPOLIS the same kind of coupling of models that we have used in the Tyndall project is invoked between the land-use transportation models and the urban development model, referred to there as the RASTER model. It is interesting to note that in developing indicators that link the socio-economic to the physical, it is necessary to deal with more than one spatial scale.

These links between different scales and perspectives concerning the ways in which energy is important to building form, urban spatial structure and the cement that links the city together through flows from materials to people to information, need to be understood in a much more integrated manner. The chapters in this book all provide examples of these differences at different scales and from different perspectives but there is an urgent need to consistently link the socio-economic to the physical in ways that relate different types of data traditionally not considered together. Flows of material that are generated as utilities servicing people living and working in buildings need to be linked to decisions about how the energy used in such flows relates to use of energy at different locations and how these can be factored into the sorts of decisions that individuals make with respect to the demand and purchase of such energies as part of their household and firm decision making. This in turn needs to be linked to decisions about how buildings are located and supplied and then to how individuals and developers engage in markets that enable supplies of buildings to meet demands for their use and occupation. Nothing short of fully fledged energy accounting at the level of the individual is implied in this research programme for developing more consistent models.

This will require a massive disaggregation of social and economic activities to the point where populations begin to be matched against individual physical elements such as buildings and transport vehicles. This in and of itself will require us to move to much more microscopic methods of simulation. We are proposing to extend the chain of models in integrated assessment to include micro-simulation of demographic processes at the levels of individuals and households but so far no one has developed a consistent means of disaggregating all elements of the models in the coupled framework down to the physical level where such resource flows become explicit. There are models of such flows that exist for buildings and other infrastructures (see Robinson et al, 2007) but these have not yet been linked to more aggregate approaches and the interface between the physical and socio-economic activity levels is not well worked out. This is as much because of limits on data as of the difficulties inherent in being able to pass seamlessly from social populations to physical resources. Only now for the first time are researchers beginning to develop ways of partitioning and disaggregating populations that are collected at street addresses to physical properties in the quest to couple micro-simulations of land-use transport interactions with resource flows. They are only at the very beginning of this long-term challenge that will require that some fundamental data management problems be resolved. As we noted early in this chapter, there is also an urgent demand for theory that reconciles resource flows with population flows and this makes the challenges noted here even more severe. The modelling strategies described in this chapter are but a preliminary foray into meeting this grand challenge.

Acknowledgements

Steve Evans (CASA, UCL) helped with the data and was instrumental in building the interface between the input–output predictions and the land-use transportation model. Stuart Barr and Ali Ford (University of Newcastle-upon-Tyne) developed the transportation network analysis and the urban development model at the site specific level. Plate 50 is partly based on their work.

Note

1   http://maps.environment-agency.gov.uk/

References

Atkins, P. W. (1994) *The 2nd Law: Energy, Chaos, and Form*, W. H. Freeman and Company, New York

Barker, T., Foxon, T. and Scrieciu, S. (2008) 'Achieving the G8 50% target: Modelling induced and accelerated technological change using the macro-econometric model E3MG', *Climate Policy*, vol 8, S30–45

Batty, M. (1986) 'Technical issues in urban model development: A review of linear and non-linear model structures', in B. G. Hutchinson and M. Batty (eds) *Advances in Urban Systems Modelling*, North Holland Publishing Company, Amsterdam, pp133–162

Batty, M. (1992) 'Urban modeling in computer-graphic and geographic information system environments', *Environment and Planning B*, vol 19, pp663–685

Batty, M. (2008) 'Planning support systems: Progress, predictions, and speculations on the shape of things to come', in R. K. Brail (ed) *Planning Support Systems for Cities and Regions*, Lincoln Institute of Land Policy, Cambridge, MA, pp3–30

Batty, M., Hall, P. G. and Starkie, D. N. M. (1974) 'The impact of fares-free public transport upon urban land use and activity patterns', *Transportation Research Forum*, vol 15, pp347–353

Dawson, R., Hall, J., Barr, S., Batty, M., Bristow, A., Carney, S., Dagoumas, A., Evans, S., Ford, A., Harwatt, H., Kohler, J., Tight, M., Walsh, C. and Zanni, A. (2009) 'A blueprint for the integrated assessment of climate change in cities', in K. Tang (ed) *Green Citynomics: The Urban War Against Climate Change*, Greenleaf Publishing, Chippenham, pp32–51

de la Barra, T. (1989) *Integrated Transport and Land Use Modeling: Decision Chains and Hierarchies*, Cambridge University Press, Cambridge

Echenique, M. H. (2004) 'Econometric models of land use and transportation', in D. A. Hensher, K. J. Button, K. E. Haynes and P. R. Stopher (eds) *Handbook of Transport Geography and Spatial Systems*, Pergamon, Amsterdam, pp185–202

Ford, A. and Barr, S. (2009) 'Accessibility analysis by generalised cost in a GIS framework, *Proceedings of GISRUK 17*, Durham, 1–3 April

Hall, J. W., Dawson, R. J., Walsh, C. L., Barker, T., Barr, S. L., Batty, M., Bristow, A. L., Burton, A., Carney, S., Dagoumas, A., Evans, S., Ford, A. C., Glenis, V., Goodess, C. G., Harpham, C., Harwatt, H., Kilsby, C., Köhler, J., Jones, P., Manning, L., McCarthy, M., Sanderson, M., Tight, M. R., Timms, P. M. and Zanni, A. M. (2009) *Engineering Cities: How Can Cities Grow Whilst Reducing Emissions and Vulnerability?*, Department of Civil and Geomatic Engineering, Newcastle University, Newcastle-upon-Tyne

Hunt, J. D., Miller, E. J. and Kriger, D. S. (2005) 'Current operational urban land-use-transport modelling frameworks: A review', *Transport Reviews*, vol 25, pp329–376

Iacono, I., Levinson, D. and El-Geneidy, A. (2008) 'Models of transportation and land use change: A guide to the territory', *Journal of Planning Literature*, vol 22, pp323–340

Lautso, K., Spiekermann, K., Wegener, M., Sheppard, I., Steadman, P., Martino, A., Domingo, R. and Gayda, S. (2004) *PROPOLIS Planning and Research of Policies for Land Use and Transport for Increasing Urban Sustainability*, Contract No: EVK4-1999-00005, Final Report, European Commission, Fifth Framework Programme, Energy, Environment and Sustainable Development, www1.wspgroup.fi/lt/propolis/

Lowry, I. S. (1964) *A Model of Metropolis*, Memorandum RM-4035-RC, The Rand Corporation, Santa Monica, CA

Morphet, R. (2010) *Thermodynamic Potentials and Phase Change for Transport Systems*, Working Paper 155, Centre for Advanced Spatial Analysis, UCL, London, www.casa.ucl.ac.uk/publications/workingPaperDetail.asp?ID=154

Odum, H. T. (2007) *Environment, Power, and Society for the Twenty-First Century: The Hierarchy of Energy*, Columbia University Press, New York

Robinson, D., Campbell, N., Gaiser, W., Kabel, K., Le-Mouele, A., Morel, N., Page, J., Stankovic, S. and Stone, A. (2007) 'SUNtool – a new modelling paradigm for simulating and optimising urban sustainability', *Solar Energy*, vol 81, no 9, pp1196–1211

Simmonds, D. C. (1999) 'The design of the DELTA land-use modelling package', *Environment and Planning B*, vol 26, pp665–684

Tribus, M. and McIrvine, E. C. (1971) 'Energy and information', *Scientific American*, vol 225, pp179–188

UKCIP (United Kingdom Climate Impacts Programme) (2009) *Rising to the Challenge: The Impacts of Climate Change in the South East*, UK Climate Impacts Programme, Oxford University Centre for the Environment: Oxford, www.ukcip.org.uk/images/stories/Pub_pdfs/se_sum.pdf

Wilson, A. G. (1970) *Entropy in Urban and Regional Modelling*, Pion Press, London

Wilson, A. G. (2009) 'The "thermodynamics" of the city: Evolution and complexity science in urban modelling', in A. Reggiani and P. Nijkamp (eds) *Complexity and Spatial Networks*, Springer, Berlin, pp11–31

Wu, B., Birkin, M. and Rees, P. (2008) 'A spatial microsimulation model with student agents', *Computers Environment and Urban Systems*, vol 32, pp440–453

10
Conclusions

Darren Robinson

As outlined in the introduction to this book, urban settlements are becoming both more numerous and more densely populated and this trend is set to continue: cities will be responsible for an increasing share of global resource consumption and the corresponding implications for global climate change; potentially with feedback, so reinforcing urban resource consumption. But although it seems inevitable that the urban *share* of global resource consumption will increase, cities can in principle be transformed to process the resources they consume more efficiently; the *magnitude* of urban and thus global resource consumption can be reduced. We do not have to accept the inevitability that finite resources will continue to be depleted, that manmade climate change will increase in its intensity. Cities can reduce their demands for applied resources and manage more efficiently the resources that they do consume. But to understand how this might be best achieved and whether we are, both locally and globally, on track to achieve targets for reduced resource consumption and associated pollutant emissions, we need computer models.

This is the basic premise of this book. These models should, in the future, enable us to simulate the dynamic processes that drive demands for changes in land and building use, the activities accommodated by these buildings, the transport of goods and services between buildings and of course the demands for resources that are necessary to sustain cities' inhabitants, buildings and transport systems and the feedback with the urban and indeed global climate. The purpose of this book has been to present the current status quo, to describe the nature of the challenge that lies ahead of us as we strive to make cities more sustainable and how we might go about using and developing models to help in tackling that challenge.

To this end we close this book by reflecting on the different themes that we have addressed so far (climate and comfort, metabolism, measuring and optimizing sustainability and land-use transport dynamics) and speculating as to how these themes should further develop and ultimately be integrated to provide for the comprehensive computer modelling capability that we believe city development stakeholders will need in the future.

10.1 Climate and comfort

The modelling of radiation exchange in the urban context is relatively well resolved; at least, under the assumption that urban surfaces are predominantly diffusely reflecting (Lambertian). There is, however, considerable scope for efficiency improvements by solving repetitive, but separate, processes in parallel. One obvious example relates to the computation of view factor information for the matrices of the simplified radiosity algorithm described in Chapter 2. Such code parallelization, in conjunction with efficient methods for storing matrices, will make possible the modelling of radiation exchange within entire towns and cities in a computationally tractable way. This may be useful in itself to understand the potential for converting solar energy into useful heat and/or electricity.

More challenging is the modelling of the urban climate, which we understand to mean the computation of temperature, pressure and velocity fields. Considerable progress has been made in recent years, in that we now seem to have a robust methodology for the nesting of multiple models each addressing different scales, from the global to the micro (Chapter 3). But this remains a very demanding problem, both computationally and in terms of the derivation of the parameters required by the kind of urban canopy models that are embedded within meso-scale atmospheric flow models. This 'equivalent geometry problem' is currently an essentially manual process. A simplified 3D model is built, this is then parsed to a solver for computation of drag and irradiation absorption and an equivalent geometry is deduced by trial and error. Thus we cannot be sure of locating a global optimum to this problem, even if drag and irradiation are in themselves a sufficient measure of fitness in this context. In fact we can almost be sure of *not* locating this optimum. For this we would require some form of optimization algorithm, but this comes at a significant computational cost. But again, different members of a population may be tested on different processors, or different elements of the objective function for a single member may be computed on different processors. Nevertheless, this is but a pre-process for the meso-scale simulations. If we are to simulate the climate of the city for an entire year, further progress must also be made to identify the appropriate spatio-temporal discretization to be applied to this problem, as well as the appropriate subset of physical models. These meso-scale solvers will also need to be effectively parallelized. The challenge is compounded if we also seek to nest a micro-scale domain within a cell of a meso-scale grid to accurately model the local microclimate, accounting for the set of superscale influences. Whereas meso-scale simulations are in themselves sufficient for models of urban metabolism, we require micro-scale simulations if we are to predict the comfort of pedestrians in a convincing way. Fortunately, however, the errors in neglecting feedback from a micro-scale domain to a meso-scale domain may not be significant so that meso-scale simulations may be performed as a pre-process and perhaps also be made publicly available via an internet server.

So radiation modelling is relatively straightforward whereas urban climate modelling is far from straightforward, but it is a research domain that is increasingly well understood and that is being intensively explored by physical and computer scientists. This is in part evidenced by the growing activity of the International Association for Urban Climate.[1]

In contrast, research is at a relatively embryonic stage with respect to our ability to predict the comfort of pedestrians. Several field survey campaigns have been conducted with a view to developing empirical models, but these have failed to consider pedestrians' recent thermal history (activity and the conditions in which this activity took place), which is essential given the transient nature of human thermoregulation. Earlier attempts at using numerical models involved either using stationary models or simplified dynamic models but again with the recent thermal history being ignored. Bruse has recently pioneered the coupling of pedestrians' movement with simplified models of both the microclimate experienced by these agent pedestrians and their thermoregulation (see Chapter 4). But further empirical work is required to calibrate the simplified rules upon which pedestrians' movements are based and possibly also the mapping between thermal sensation and comfort, which may not necessarily be the same indoors as that experienced outdoors. Models of pedestrians' adaptation of activity and clothing levels might also usefully be considered in the future. But the greatest challenge will be to couple models of the range of environmental comfort domains with each other: visual, aural and olfactory; accounting for possible feedback between them and for pedestrians' sociological wellbeing. These diverse measures of comfort and wellbeing should then be integrated in a coherent way. Resolving this challenge, if indeed it is possible, will involve some considerable coordinated effort in the years to come.

10.2 Urban metabolism

As mentioned repeatedly in this book, cities consume resources predominantly to support the conditioning of buildings, the activities that take place within them and the transport of goods and people between them. Buildings and transport systems dominate urban metabolism. And yet building physicists have only relatively recently turned their attention to the modelling of building-related resource flows at the urban scale (Chapter 5). Thus far, two strategies have been employed: identify representative typologies of buildings, model these and extrapolate to the number of instances of each type to build up a picture of the entire building stock; model each individual building explicitly in its immediate spatial context. The former approach is attractive since both data needs and computational overheads are rationalized, but the latter micro-simulation approach has some significant advantages. This approach provides a basis for accounting for: occlusions to sources of solar radiation and of reflections from these occlusions; local urban climate; connections with district energy centres; and couplings with modes of passenger and goods transport. It also means that scenarios can be tested for improving the performance of specific buildings. This is interesting because such models may be used as an ongoing resource by municipalities to manage their own stock and service infrastructure as well as to analyse private sector new build or renovation projects. But as we increase the scale of these micro-simulation models, so we must confront the data and computational challenges posed. We need standardization in the geo-referencing of buildings by providers of diverse data (cadastral, census, energy use, occupant revenue etc.). We need efficient ways for providing data not currently routinely archived (façade glazing ratio, constructional composition, integrated solar energy conversion systems etc.). We need a standard data model – call this an *urban information model* – for the representation of the above entities within databases and the diverse urban modelling software to ensure the databases and the effective management and reuse of acquired data that may be coupled to them. In common with urban climate models, we also need to make the best possible use of multi-core processors by performing computations in parallel. There is also a need to extend the scope of physical models. CitySim for example should include a more complete representation of occupants' activities and related behaviours, in particular with respect to electrical and water appliances; a water modelling capability needs to be integrated; and further attributes should also be associated with materials and systems, in particular their cost and embodied energy content. There is also a need for abstract representations of resource intensive (industrial) processes accommodated within buildings to test the impact of potential synergetic exchanges and a utility to examine the sensitivity of results to input uncertainties for the range of models. Also exciting would be the modelling of appliances that are aware of one another, their function and the status of the local supply and storage network – so that demand, storage and supply can be dynamically optimized, in the form of a smart grid.

In contrast with building models, transport models (Chapter 6) are relatively well developed, as there has been a demand for disaggregate models to respond to specific transport planning questions for the past half a century or more. We are, however, currently witnessing a paradigm shift from models based on transitions from zones of origin to zones of destination (origin–destination matrix models) to explicit micro-simulations of individual vehicular journeys throughout physically defined networks, albeit represented or resolved in abstracted form. This opens the door to detailed simulations of the consumption of resources due to travel, not only of time but also of monetary and energetic cost and associated emissions. This may in the future prove to be a deciding factor in the transition from the use of simplified zonal models to comprehensive micro-simulation models, accounting for the range of modes of transport of both people and of goods and indeed transitions between these modes. This in itself will require considerably more work, particularly in respect of the transport of goods, of mixed mode passenger transport and of leisure transport beyond cities' boundaries. A related challenge is the development of discrete choice models of investment in new more efficient personal vehicles and the ways in which financial incentives can motivate these choices; likewise with respect to alternative modes of transport, in particular the substitution of personal with public modes of transport, which may involve multiple stages and modes. In principle, similar models could also be deployed to predict the probability with which buildings' owners would invest in their renovation or indeed the acquisition of more efficient appliances.

There seems thus to be a common tendency to develop micro-simulation models of buildings and transport systems.

10.3 Measuring and optimizing sustainability

In Chapter 7 we posed the seemingly innocent question: how do we measure urban sustainability and is it theoretically possible for modern urban settlements to be sustainable? At present it is not possible to answer the latter question, since we do not as yet have consensus as to how to respond to the former. But it seems clear, given the myriad factors which contribute to urban (un)sustainability, that some form of relatively pragmatic multi-criteria decision making mechanism is required. In Chapter 7 we present one such solution. But this approach requires (necessarily subjective) manual intervention: it is not readily amenable to reduction to some form of computer algorithm. A considerable challenge for the future is to fully define what we mean by sustainability – we do not as yet even have a consensus with respect to environmental sustainability – and to develop some robust, pragmatic basis for evaluating sustainability in algorithmic form. This is necessary if we are to exploit computer processing power to its full potential.

On this note, we presented in Chapter 8 a new hybrid evolutionary algorithm and described its application to optimize built forms for their potential utilization of solar energy and the renovation strategies of a block of buildings given primary energy as the objective function and total cost as a constraint. But these applications merely demonstrate the *potential* use of evolutionary algorithms to optimize urban sustainability rather then a definitive application to do so. For this we need both a more complete objective function (a more complete measure of sustainability in all of its complexity) *and* a more complete physical urban model that provides the necessary inputs to this objective function.

Concerning the latter point, we speculate below how the research community might respond to provide for a complete model of the factors influencing the dynamics of urban sustainability.

10.4 The future: Towards fully coupled models

The first three parts of this book are dedicated to modelling the urban climate and the comfort of pedestrians within this climate, to the modelling of urban metabolism, in particular the energy demands of buildings and transport systems, and to optimizing this metabolism given some measure of fitness (sustainability). There remains a considerable amount of work to do before we will have fully developed models within these different domains, but the problems to be resolved are relatively well understood as is the pathway to resolving them; with the exception of defining some unified measure of sustainability or of pedestrians' comfort. Nevertheless, research to resolve these outstanding issues may be regarded as being short to medium term.

We opened this fourth part of the book (Chapter 9) by exploring the relationship between transport costs (and thus energy demands) and land use and how these may be modelled in a simplified (zonal) way. We also demonstrated the use of one such model to understand the impacts of changes in transport costs on chosen modes of transport (and by analogy the relative environmental consequences) as well as increased employment intensity and public transport capacity on residential locations and trips between residential and work locations.

This kind of simplified model is undoubtedly valuable, but the real future challenge, indeed where the fun really begins, lies with the further development and coupling of models to really deepen our understanding of how cities function and how this functioning may be positively influenced so that cities emergently develop along a more sustainable trajectory.

Concerning buildings' energy demands, our understanding of radiation exchange processes in the urban context and how to compute them efficiently is already well advanced; so that appropriate models have already been tested and

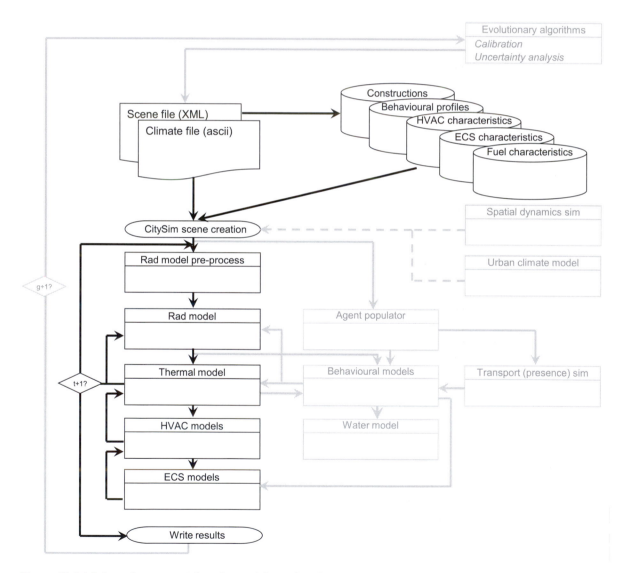

Figure 10.4.1 Schematic representation of potential couplings between the range of models, placing the resource flow model at the core

integrated with CitySim. This is not currently the case with respect to urban climate modelling (see above), but in the relatively near term we can expect that urban climate models will be available for annual simulations of the urban meso-climate (Figure 10.4.1). Such simulation results could then be made available as a pre-process for urban scale modelling of buildings' energy demands.

Also in the near term we are likely to see the first results from experiments to couple building and transport micro-simulation programs through the exchange of people-agents (Chapter 7). To achieve this coupling, a population of agents will need to be generated and these agents assigned characteristics relating to their travel plans (home, workplace and leisure activities) as well as socio-demographics (age, gender, income level etc.) and environmental preferences (temperature, illuminance etc.). The former characteristics will influence the simulation of agents' travel, while the latter will influence their ownership of appliances (for those living within the city), their indoor activities and their actions to adapt their personal (clothing and activity) and environmental (building envelope and HVAC system) attributes to maintain their comfort. Regarding this point, we may also envisage a more general transport model, in which the movement of pedestrians is explicitly simulated between buildings and/or other modes of transport, these agents being immersed within a simulated microclimate using a multi-scale model of the type discussed above.

Such an agent-based model also opens up the future possibility for simulating a broad range of socio-economic mechanisms and their variations with time, as mentioned in Chapter 9. One can envisage a future platform in which our people-agents form unions with one another, procreate, purchase or rent a home, furnish this home, renovate this home, purchase a motor vehicle or invest in public transport season tickets, and so on. At a hierarchical level above, firms could employ individuals to improve their productivity, exchange goods and services with other firms as well as individual consumers both within and beyond the city and to locate to different premises. Meanwhile the building model would simulate the resource demands of the buildings and activities accommodated within them as well as potential synergetic exchanges between them, while the transport model would simulate the exchanges of passengers and goods between buildings. At a further level of abstraction, some representation of the processes of governance, of economic market fluctuations and of climatic trends could perturb our firms' and individuals' behaviours, whether via some form of predictive model or by users' interventions. One could also conceive of the use of evolutionary algorithms to identify the range of external factors that are most likely to lead our city to develop along a relatively sustainable trajectory, or indeed to which our city's evolution is highly sensitive. In the same vein, and certainly more realistic, one could apply such algorithms to identify the most sustainable (given some appropriate combined measure) combinations of physical variables from which our city should be composed for a given snapshot in time, and to which its performance is most sensitive. This may also assist with the targeting of model and data collection efforts to reduce predictive uncertainties in sensitive regions of our parameter space.

But these future tasks would be incredibly computationally demanding. Fortunately Moore's law, that the number of transistors integrated into central processing units (CPUs) increases every two years, seems to continue to hold true. But as noted above, to capitalize on this, programs need to be parallelized to benefit from multi-core CPUs; many of which may in principle be combined. Nevertheless, achieving a tractable representation of the above computational tasks, even in the medium to long term, will require some form of compromise between resolution and available computing resource. Another significant challenge is the acquisition and management of data to calibrate these models (and to maintain them) so that they achieve a reasonable degree of realism.

Perhaps most exciting in this somewhat speculative programme for future research in urban modelling is the acute need for closely conducted interdisciplinary research; for the coordinated input from geographers, economists, social scientists, statisticians, computer scientists, physicists etc. But should researchers succeed in this quest, our future city planners would have an incredibly powerful resource at their disposal with which to guide our cities towards a more sustainable future for all.

Note

1   www.urban-climate.org.

Index